A MATERIAL HISTORY OF THE BIBLE, ENGLAND 1200–1553

A British Academy Monograph

British Academy Monographs showcase work arising from:

British Academy Postdoctoral Fellowships
British Academy Newton International Fellowships

A Material History
of the Bible,
England 1200–1553

Eyal Poleg

Published for THE BRITISH ACADEMY
by OXFORD UNIVERSITY PRESS

Oxford University Press, Great Clarendon Street, Oxford OX2 6DP

First edition published in 2020
Paperback edition 2020

British Library Cataloguing in Publication Data
Data available

Library of Congress Cataloging in Publication Data
Data available

Typeset by Servis Filmsetting Ltd, Stockport, Cheshire
Printed in Great Britain by TJ International Ltd, Padstow

ISBN 978-0-19-726696-0

To Riki and Michael Poleg, with much love *in tempore pestilentiae*

Contents

Abbreviations

BL   London, the British Library

Bodl.   Oxford, the Bodleian Library

CUL   Cambridge, Cambridge University Library

DMH   *Historical catalogue of printed editions of the English Bible, 1525–1961. Revised and expanded from the edition of T. H. Darlow and H. F. Moule, 1903*, ed. A. S. Herbert (London: British and Foreign Bible Society, 1968)

LMB   Late Medieval Bible

PL   *Patrologiae cursus completus, series Latina*, 217 text vols, gen. ed. Jacques-Paul Migne (Paris, 1844–55)

STC   *A short-title catalogue of books printed in England, Scotland, and Ireland, and of English books printed abroad, 1475–1640. Compiled by A. W. Pollard and G. R. Redgrave*, ed. W. A. Jackson, F. S. Ferguson and Katharine F. Pantzer, 2nd edn, 3 vols (London: The Bibliographical Society, 1976–91)

Figures

Preface

This is a different book from the one I set out writing a decade ago. What was to be a detailed bibliographical survey has veered in unexpected directions. Examining scores of Bibles in manuscript and in print has led me to reassess the nature of change and tradition, to explore vernacular liturgies and to immerse myself in the religious and political turmoil at the end of Henry VIII's reign. Across 350 years, the late medieval and early modern Bible has become a mirror for technological innovation and religious reform. Those producing these Bibles, and those reading them, have all left their mark on the pages of the books, marks which became the basis for my analysis.

This book touches lightly on the text of the Bible. Biblical translations and the study of the Bible are likewise explored only as auxiliary evidence. Rather, I have mined Bibles for evidence of creation and use, unfolding how religion and technology have shaped Sacred Scripture. The production and sale of Bibles was a commercial enterprise that gave a physical form to a sacred text. It was made as the combined undertaking of reformers and craftsmen alike. This, in turn, dictated discrete means of exploring their message, leading generations of readers in their active engagement with the text and unfolding of its meaning.

Two interrelated prisms are deployed in this exploration of the Bible: religion and materiality. Church reformers have been the driving force behind new translations of the Bible, and have innovated in biblical layout and tools. Bibles were read by priests and devout laymen and women, who used their books for prayer, study and preaching. These Bibles, however, were also the result of prolonged processes of production, and the objects of technological innovations. Scribes, stationers and printers have all used their tools to inscribe sacred texts on parchment or paper.

The book's chronological sequence reveals the transformations that Bibles underwent in the later Middle Ages and early modernity. The material evidence enables us to move away from clear teleologies, revealing the complex and multifaceted nature of religious and technological change. It has necessitated deploying diverse methodologies and questions. Those needed for the examination of Wycliffite Bibles of *c.*1400 differ from those necessary for the study of the modest Latin Bible printed in England in 1535, although both analyses assist in breaking down dichotomies of orthodoxy and heterodoxy, tradition and reform. Moving chronologically, each chapter explores a distinct type of Bible and its period, from the innovative Latin Bibles of the early thirteenth century to the proliferation of printed Bibles in the short reign of Edward VI, two periods remote from one another, yet, as shown in the conclusion, surprisingly similar.

Acknowledgements

It has been a long journey, in which I have benefitted from the advice of friends and colleagues. Nicolas Bell, Julia Boffey, Jim Bolton, Marjorie Burghart, Paul Cavill, Rita Copeland, Raffaele Danna, Lucie Doležalová, Ayelet Even Ezra, Ceri Law, Diane Reilly, Paul Saenger, Lesley Smith and Elizabeth Solopova have all offered advice and generously shared their expertise. Chiara Ruzzier and Alex Devine have shared their dissertations and immense knowledge of the Late Medieval Bible. I greatly benefitted from discussions about liturgy in our newly created seminar at the Institute of Historical Research, and especially from the insights of Eleanor Giraud, Helen Gittos and John Harper. The European perspective was kept alive through discussions with Wim François, Suzan Folkerts, Sabrina Corbellini and August den Hollander. Peter Stallybrass's kind invitation enabled me to present initial discoveries at the Material Texts seminar in the University of Pennsylvania. Graham Davis gave his time and expertise to devise the digital analysis, which made possible vital research underpinning the conclusions of Chapter 3. Sarah Reakes, Hugh Massam and Gareth Stedman Jones have provided ways out of an impasse.

When writing a book on books one becomes indebted to librarians and curators. I wish to thank the staff at the manuscript and rare books reading rooms of the British Library, the National Library of Scotland, Edinburgh University Library, the Bodleian Library and the Fitzwilliam Museum. Librarians at Cambridge Colleges have provided access to manuscripts at Magdalene, Gonville and Caius, Christ's, Emmanuel, Jesus and Sidney Sussex. Kathryn McKee, sub-Librarian of St John's College, Cambridge, has countered even the most obscure requests with a smile. At Lambeth Palace Library Rachel Cosgrave and Giles Mandelbrote assisted Prof Davis and myself in digitally removing layers from Berthelet's 1535 Bible. Delphine Mercuzot offered much needed assistance at the BnF. This book is produced with the generous assistance of a grant from the Isobel Thornley's Bequest to the University of London.

Three institutions have supported this book. A British Academy postdoctoral fellowship (PDF/2008/601) provided the opportunity to conduct initial research, while a sabbatical leave from Queen Mary University of London gave me the time necessary to finalise research and write this book. My greatest institutional debt is to Cambridge University Library. It has become my academic home for the year of writing the book. Without the kind, patient and generous help of its staff, it would have been a much lesser book. They provided books and advice, even when these involved spreading all eleven of Edward VI's Bibles on long tables or conjuring industrial scales to weigh books. I wish to thank the staff of the University Library, and especially James Freeman, Curator of Medieval Manuscripts, Onesimus Ngundu, Librarian of the Bible Society, and above all, Suzanne Paul, Keeper of Rare Books and Early Manuscripts. The University Library also hosted a series of public lectures on the Material History of the Bible in England, 1200–1600, which provided a unique opportunity to present the book's five chapters to wider audiences. Respondents to each paper—Tessa Webber, James Freeman, Scott Mandelbrote, Theodor Dunkelgrün and Alex Walsham—helped shape the book and avoid errors. I also thank Scott Mandelbrote, the reader for the British Academy, for many useful comments and suggestions.

Special thanks are due for colleagues who have given their time to read and comment on parts of the book: Laura Light's knowledge and friendship have helped shape Chapter 1; Michael Kuczynski and Matti Peikola (Chapter 2); Alec Ryrie and James Carley (Chapter 3); Richard Rex and Lucy Wooding (Chapter 4). Orietta da Rold has been an ideal sabbatical companion, and a great interlocutor in shaping both our books. An indefatigable Miri Rubin, the ever-ideal reader, has read and commented on the entire book. Lastly, Ian Green, the book's academic advisor, has read draft versions of each chapter. His immense knowledge of early modern print has been second only to his generosity.

Early in the production of the book the British Academy agreed to widen its outreach and dissemination. Sammie Cunningham and Matt Russell have done a stellar job in commenting on the approachability of the book for undergraduate students, while at the British Academy Geetha Nair and James Rivington were willing to experiment with layouts and pricing. Błażej Mikuła and Anna Johnson assisted in creative imaging, while Elizabeth Stone and Bhaskar Raman saw the manuscript through production. Last but not least, I want to thank, time and again, Stav for her help and patience, and Ionathan and Daniel, for taking me out of my books.

Conventions

Biblical Quotations

When not replicating specific manuscripts or early printed books, biblical quotations follow the Clementine Vulgate (for the Latin) and the Douai-Rheims with Challoner's revisions (for the English). Psalm numbers differ slightly between the Vulgate and reformed Bibles, the latter mirroring the Hebrew Psalm-numbering. In this book both systems are presented in the following format: Vulgate/Hebrew.

Transcription and Translation

As a rule, English translations are supplied in the body of the text, while the original is provided in the notes, unless the vocal or graphic qualities of the original text are central to the argument. When transcribing texts from manuscripts and early printed books abbreviations have been expanded silently; editorial insertions are in [square brackets] and suggested corrections are in {curly brackets}; Middle and early modern English quotations have been modernised throughout, except when in titles.

Measurements

Centimetres and grams are used for measurements throughout the book. Unless otherwise stated, measurements of manuscripts and early printed books are based on the size and width of the pages themselves, rather than the binding boards. When supplied, weight should be seen as an approximation, rather than an absolute value, as it includes the weight of the (most commonly later) binding.

Psalm Terminology

- Superscriptions: short verses preceding the Psalms in the Hebrew Bible, linking individual Psalms to biblical events or Temple worship.
- Incipits: the first few words of the Psalm itself (following the superscription) in Latin, often used to identify individual Psalms throughout the Middle Ages and early modernity.
- Tituli: short allegorical interpretations of the Psalms, based on the works of Church Fathers or medieval exegetes.

Glossary

Anthropomorphic	Displaying God with human characteristics.
Book of Hours	One of the most popular books of the later Middle Ages. It facilitated daily devotions of laywomen and men, mirroring the use of breviaries (see below) by the religious.
Breviary	A book containing readings and chants for the celebration of Divine Office (see below).
Canticles	Hymns taken from the Old and New Testament, which are commonly chanted during liturgical services.
Divine Office	The day-long cycle of worship practised by monks and nuns, as well as friars and canons. During Office the entire Psalter was chanted in weekly or bi-weekly cycles.
(in) Duodecimo	A smaller book size, in which each sheet of paper would make twelve leaves. This size is typical of pocket books.
Epistles (liturgical reading)	Biblical lessons read during Mass (alongside the Gospel reading, see below). These readings are commonly taken from books of the New Testament other than the Gospels, but could be from the Old Testament as well.
Eusebian Canons	A system for navigating the Four Gospels created in Late Antiquity. The main goal of this complex division system (often noted in the margins of the biblical text and in separate Canon Tables) was to identify parallel sections across the Gospels.
Exegesis	Study of the Bible with the aim of harmonising Bible and theology.
Feria	A weekday (in liturgical time).
(in) Folio	A larger book size, in which each sheet of paper would make two leaves. This size is typical of large lectern books.
Gloss	Commentary on a key text (typically the Bible). In glossed manuscripts these commentaries are provided

	either between the lines (interlinear) or in the margins (marginal).
Gospels (liturgical reading)	Biblical lessons read during Mass (alongside the Epistles reading, see above). These readings are taken from the Four Canonical Gospels, which were seen as the epitome of the Christian message.
Homily	A form of preaching. In this more traditional form preachers read and explicated the entire pericope.
Lectern	A stand which supports the reading of a book. These were often used for liturgical books or Bibles in churches.
Lectio continua	*lit.* continuous reading. The custom of reading the Bible (nearly) in its entirety, practised by monastic communities in the Middle Ages, and introduced to parish churches with the Book of Common Prayer.
Lectionary	A book containing the readings of the Gospels and Epistles, mandated for liturgical services in parish churches.
Liturgy	Structured worship, commonly performed in churches. It includes a complex cycle of biblical readings.
Manicule	Pointing hands. A common way for medieval and early modern readers (and printers in early modernity) to note places of interest in their books.
Mendicants (Orders or Friars)	*lit.* beggars. Members of several religious orders, which were formed in the thirteenth century, and adopted Apostolic poverty and an emphasis on preaching. The Franciscans, Dominicans and Augustinians all formed part of the mendicant orders.
Missal	A book containing readings and chants for the celebration of the Mass.
(in) Octavo	A smaller book size, in which each sheet of paper would make eight leaves. This size is typical of smaller books.
Pericopes	Biblical lessons read in the course of the liturgy. These short narrative units followed a complex cycle of readings.
Psalter	A book of Psalms, commonly used within Church liturgy.
(in) Quarto	A medium book size, in which each sheet of paper would make four leaves. This size is typical of portable study books.

Responsory	Liturgical chant which often followed readings with a series of versicles and responses.
Rubricator	In medieval manuscripts and early printed books, a scribe responsible for providing rubrics, or red explanatory sections and titles.
Sarum Use	The liturgy of Salisbury, which became the dominant form of worship in late medieval England.
Tetragrammaton	The Hebrew sacred name of God, commonly transcribed as YHWH. Used by Church reformers as a substitute to anthropomorphic (see above) depictions of God.
Vademecum	*lit.* go with me. A portable book.
Vulgate	The most common translation of the entire Bible into Latin, used in the Middle Ages. It was made primarily by St Jerome at the end of the fourth century and was seen as divinely inspired by the medieval Church.

Introduction:
Towards a Material History of the Bible

This book traces the creation of Bibles and evidence for their use over three and a half centuries. Spanning the later Middle Ages and early modernity, this survey of biblical manuscripts and prints over an extended period of time directs our attention to little-explored moments in the history of the Bible, and locates biblical manuscripts and prints within the long history of English religion and society. Through the materiality of the Bible we can re-assess the impact of religious reform and technological innovation. Rather than a clear story of change and growth, it moves us away from common narratives and teleology and into a more turbid realm of uncertainties and protracted trans-formation. This reveals continuities and uncertainties, as well as unexpected fault lines and the merging of linguistic and devotional spheres in the history of English books and religion.

In this investigation Bibles emerge as complex objects, which were copied and printed, taken on the road or placed upon lecterns, studied and even van-dalised. Exploring the materiality of Bibles, one is easily overwhelmed by the multiple layers of information encoded in each book, the traces of explicit or casual acts that have shaped it. Numerous decisions were made by the origi-nal production teams, often nearly invisible to modern scholars. Stationers, patrons or printers determined the type and quality of paper or parchment used, as well as the ink and pigments used for decoration; scribes employed specific scripts, and printers fonts, to make the words which were then shaped into columns, divided into units and identified by running titles and rubrics; the size of pages, the width of the volume and the weight of books likewise determined the ways in which these Bibles could be used.

The books we currently have are not the same objects that left the sta-tioner's or the printer's shop. Medieval and early modern books underwent transformations that stretched across centuries. Readers commented on the text, writing in margins, on empty pages and between lines. They crossed out and inscribed, actively engaging with the text, at times entering into a con-troversy with the book's editors and translators. Appreciating the materiality of books transforms the way we see them. At first they appear deceptively dormant, resting on library shelves, desks or lecterns. Their study, however, reveals volatile objects in a constant state of flux, objects which reflect changing environments, individual beliefs and attitudes towards the past, all made by generations of readers.

Sacred books are a prime example for the study of books and their materiality. Belief in the divine truth underpinning the biblical text did not inhibit creators and users from actively engaging with the material artefact. Frequently at the epicentre of religious turmoil, sacred books distil religious attitudes and changing times, and seem to have served as a magnet for controversies and reforms; pious and heretic alike have left a mark on their pages. These books were often the first to manifest religious transformations and were the object of controversy, adoration and destruction. Bibles emerge as weathervanes for the turmoil of English religious history. This book examines Bibles which were created and used during a period that saw major religious reforms and the transformations of English Church and monarchy. And their pages still attest to the producers and readers who lived through, and reacted to, these events.

The study of the Bible's materiality examines both the history of religion and of the book. And both religion and book underwent major transformations in the period under investigation. From the rise of the mass-produced Latin single-volume Bibles *c.*1200 to the end of the reign of Edward VI in 1553, this was a time of technological transformations and religious confrontations, primarily the introduction of moveable-type print and the Reformation. Seeing the printing press as an agent of change, or highlighting the break ushered in by the Reformation, lends itself to narratives of rise and progress. Such views were put forward by medieval and early modern reformers wishing to highlight the novelty of their works. Living through these events, chroniclers, priests and theologians often presented a binary view of time, of gender, language and religiosity. Thus, for example, early modern reformers had contrasted a Latin and restrictive medieval past with the vernacular and widely accessible Bibles of their present. The material evidence, however, tells a story which differs somewhat from the narrative of Church polemicists. In accordance with modern historiography, it reveals an uncertain course of change and moves us away from dichotomies and teleologies, from polarised views and reading history backwards.

This book looks beyond one of the most obvious facets of every Bible—its text. Works on the early modern Bible have habitually explored its language and text. This is evident in the publications coinciding with the 500th anniversary of the King James Version, or in the 2015 special issue of *Renaissance Studies*, dedicated to the Psalms and the English Reformation. The recent

Oxford Handbook of the Bible in England, c.1530–1700, has no section on the Bible as a book, and only one-tenth of its chapters (primarily those written by Green, Gribben, Molekamp and Willie) engage with print and materiality.[1] A similar emphasis can be discerned in the study of the Wycliffite Bible. A current major research project on the Wycliffite Bible aims at laying the grounds for a new edition of its text. Nevertheless, an early publication from this project, as well as the study by Mary Dove, have significant sections on its manuscript culture.[2]

The emphasis on text and translation has furthered our understanding of the English Bible and helped trace the evolution of political discourse, regional dialects and the integration of reformed vocabulary into the biblical text. It has nevertheless shaped the field in specific ways. The study of text and translation directs our attention to discrete translation campaigns and the distinctive texts they produced. It also highlights the role of translators and editors in shaping the English Bible. These prominent reformers have been explored as the epitome of the English Bible. Thus, the biographies of John Wyclif, William Tyndale and Miles Coverdale have all been intertwined with the history of the English Bible: J. F. Mozley's 1953 book is named *Coverdale and His Bibles*, while the chapters of Gerald Hammond's 1982 *The Making of the English Bible* follow discrete translation campaigns, starting with 'In the Beginning: William Tyndale'.[3] A similar structure underpins David Daniell's magisterial book on the English Bible, which is dedicated to Tyndale, the subject of his earlier biography.[4]

The history of the English Bible merges with that of the English Reformation. Early reformers engaged in translation campaigns and placed a great emphasis on lay access to Scripture.[5] Already in the sixteenth century

1   Gordon Campbell, *Bible: the story of the King James Version, 1611–2011* (Oxford: Oxford University Press, 2010); Harold Bloom, *The shadow of a great rock: a literary appreciation of the King James Bible* (New Haven, CT: Yale University Press, 2011); David Crystal, *Begat: the King James Bible and the English language* (Oxford: Oxford University Press, 2010); Naomi Tadmor, *The social universe of the English Bible: scripture, society and culture in early modern England* (Cambridge: Cambridge University Press, 2010); David S. Katz, *God's last words: reading the English Bible from the Reformation to fundamentalism* (New Haven, CT: Yale University Press, 2004); Kevin Killeen, Helen Smith and Rachel Willie (eds), *The Oxford handbook of the Bible in England, c. 1530–1700* (Oxford: Oxford University Press, 2015).

2   Mary Dove, *The first English Bible: the text and context of the Wycliffite versions*, Cambridge studies in medieval literature 66 (Cambridge: Cambridge University Press, 2007); Elizabeth Solopova (ed.), *The Wycliffite Bible: origin, history and interpretation*, Medieval and Renaissance authors and texts 16 (Leiden: Brill, 2016).

3   James Frederic Mozley, *Coverdale and his Bibles* (London: Lutterworth Press, 1953); Gerald Hammond, *The making of the English Bible* (Manchester: Carcanet New Press, 1982).

4   David Daniell, *The Bible in English: its history and influence* (New Haven, CT: Yale University Press, 2003).

5   A re-assessment of Reformers' attitude to Scriptures, viewing the term 'Sola Scriptura' ('By Bible alone') as a nineteenth-century creation, is Henk van den Belt, 'Sola scriptura: an inadequate slogan for the authority of scripture', *Calvin Theological Journal* 51:2 (2016), 204–26.

this was woven into a grand narrative of reform and struggle, in which biblical translations were a key battleground between Latin and English, between clerical oppression and unmediated lay access to Scripture.[6] This influenced reformers' view of the past. John Wyclif (†1384) was seen as the Shining Star of the Reformation, and the Bible affiliated with him as an emblem of proto-reform. Modern histories of the English Bible often continue the narrative of the rise of the English Bible as a central facet of the English Reformation, and of the Reformation as the moving force behind the creation and dissemination of Bibles.

Histories of the English Bible, from the sixteenth century to the present day, have often adopted a triumphalist tone. Faced with adversity, such as the condemnation of Wyclif or the martyrdom of Tyndale, translators and editors moved clearly and resolutely towards placing the English Bible in the plough-boy's hands, as Tyndale had hoped to do.[7] The link between Bible and Reform cannot be denied. Nevertheless, its omnipresence in research has created a teleology often at odds with the material evidence. By looking at the books produced and read in late medieval and early modern England we see that the course of change was far from unwavering or unidirectional. The biblical text was indeed translated and edited by scholars bent on reforming Church and realm. Yet biblical books were produced by artisans, traders and administrators, whose interests extended from religious piety, through commercial viability and technical capabilities, to political and financial gains. These books were then taken up by readers who were not always sure how to read them, and often did not adhere to the intentions of reformers, priests or monarchs in this matter.

A grand narrative of progress has often underpinned views of the English Reformation, as well as of technology (specifically print). Both have been recently challenged by scholars who have placed these transformations in context, to demonstrate the gradual nature of both technological and religious change.[8] Against such narratives of progress and of teleology, I have often

---

6   This is most evident in the narrative presented by John Fox, whose sixteenth-century *Book of Martyrs* (or *Acts and Monuments*) became a template for Reformation history. Text: John Foxe, *Actes & monuments of these latter and perillous dayes [...]* (London: John Day, 1563), available online at https://www.johnfoxe.org. Analysis: Elizabeth Evenden and Thomas S. Freeman, *Religion and the book in early modern England: the making of Foxe's 'Book of Martyrs'*, Cambridge studies in early modern British history (Cambridge: Cambridge University Press, 2011).

7   As in Foxe's depiction of Tyndale's rejection of the papacy, which leads him on a project to instil biblical knowledge in every ploughboy: Foxe, *Actes & monuments of these latter and perillous dayes [...]*, p. 570, available online at https://www.johnfoxe.org/index.php?realm=text&gototype=&edition=1563&pageid=570, accessed 12 February 2019. For analysis and comparison between editions see Jan J. Martin, 'William Tyndale, John Foxe, and the '"Boy That Driveth the Plough"', *Religious Educator* 17:2 (2016), 86–105.

8   For new approaches to Reformation history, with additional bibliography, see Peter Marshall, '(Re) defining the English Reformation', *Journal of British Studies* 48:3 (2009), 564–86; Diarmaid MacCulloch, 'Changing historical perspectives on the English Reformation: the last fifty years', in *The Church on its*

found myself fondly employing the term 'underwhelming' while exploring the material evidence. In a history of triumph and change, books lacking innovative features, books that do not accord with reformed theology, or whose technique is deficient, would evidence neglect and decline. For me, on the other hand, these moments unfold the cracks in the grand narratives, the places where scribes, stationers or printers worked to their best capacities, but were still limited in their grasp of change or their technologies. Rather than the achievements, these are the moments which are often the most revealing in the history of the Bible; the places where we can see the complex and uncertain course of change.

A material history leads one to examine specific, and often lacking, types of evidence. The study of textual traditions is supported by a relative abundance of evidence, especially for the early modern period. Scholars of biblical texts and translations are able to compare translations, with their work aided by modern editions and reprints, as well as by the recent proliferation of digital resources. Bibles contain prologues and dedications explicitly reflecting on translation practices and devotional merit. Wyclif, Tyndale and Coverdale were all prolific writers whose works enable the reconstruction of their intellectual biographies. This is hardly the case for a material history of the Bible. Little external evidence has survived (if it ever existed) on the production and use of Bibles throughout the period under investigation. Unfortunately for us, craftsmen and readers rarely had posterity in mind (from a book-history perspective, that is) when engaging with the Bible. Without the devotional graphomania or the detailed accounts of tradesmen of later generations, explicit evidence is sparse and erratic.

The production of Bibles has left scant explicit evidence. In the period under investigation, Bibles were produced as a collaborative enterprise, encompassing a range of craftsmen: parchmeners, scribes, rubricators, illuminators and stationers, for the earlier period; type-casters, typesetters, printers,

---

past: papers read at the 2011 summer meeting and the 2012 winter meeting of the Ecclesiastical History Society, ed. Peter D. Clarke and Charlotte Methuen, Studies in church history 49 (Woodbridge: Published for The Ecclesiastical History Society by The Boydell Press, 2013), pp. 282–302; Rosemary O'Day, *The debate on the English Reformation*, 2nd edn, Issues in historiography (Manchester: Manchester University Press, 2014). For recent analysis of the boundaries between manuscripts and printed books, with additional bibliography, see Julia Boffey, 'From manuscript to print: continuity and change', in *A companion to the early printed book in Britain, 1476–1558*, ed. Susan Powell and Vincent Gillespie (Woodbridge: Boydell & Brewer, 2014), pp. 13–26; Eva Nyström, 'Codicological crossover: the merging of manuscript and print', *Studia Neophilologica* 86:sup1 (2014), 112–33; Michael Johnston and Michael Van Dussen (eds), *The medieval manuscript book: cultural approaches*, Cambridge studies in medieval literature 94 (Cambridge: Cambridge University Press, 2015). A useful critical study of the historiography of the Reformation paradigm, concentrating on the Bible and its books, is Andrew Gow, 'Challenging the Protestant Paradigm: Bible reading in lay and urban contexts of the later Middle Ages', in *Scripture and pluralism: reading the Bible in the religiously plural worlds of the Middle Ages and Renaissance*, ed. Thomas J. Heffernan and Thomas E. Burman, Studies in the history of Christian traditions 123 (Leiden: Brill, 2005), pp. 161–91.

correctors, factors and others for the later period. Their professionalisation is evident in their invisibility, the creation of a seamlessly produced artefact.[9] Communications within the production team therefore left little trace. In the professional *scriptoria* of the later Middle Ages these are revealed on the rare occasions when illuminators had neglected their job, failing to fill spaces left by scribes, or to scrape out the rough marks left in the margins of a manuscript, where instructions on their tasks were inscribed. In the print era, production teams were sometimes split geographically, necessitating written correspondence between the different actors, and thus offering rare insights into their motivations and anxieties. Such instances of survival, however, are the exception rather than the rule, and more often than not the books themselves are all that we have.

Unfolding how Bibles were used relies on methodologies commonly employed by book historians, and especially those engaging with sacred books. The works of Sherman and Duffy for the early modern era, or of Rudy and the team led by Sabrina Corbellini in the study of 'Holy Writ and Lay Readers' for the later Middle Ages, have developed means of mining readers' annotations and active engagement with the book, revealing them to be treasure troves for the study of devotion and reading practices.[10] Evidence of readership tends to be sporadic and is often hard to date and localise. Bibles from the period under consideration rarely contain the names of lay readers who were not affiliated with academic study. Readers' engagement with the text is often limited to signalling out a place of interest, commonly by a marginal pointing hand (a *manicule*) or 'note' (*nota* in Latin), or to noting a few words which would make sense primarily to the readers themselves. Extracting information from such annotations requires a certain degree of detective work. This difficulty is often exacerbated by erasures of annotations and readers' marks. Such vandalism further complicates the task of the historian. It could, however, be analysed on its own terms. Readers who defaced, scraped, brushed with paint or pasted over with paper were in fact actively engaging with the book, entering into a dialogue with previous editors and readers. Their obliterations reveal an

---

9   This is part of the wider phenomenon of the invisibility of efficient mediation, which I touched upon in Eyal Poleg, *Approaching the Bible in medieval England*, Manchester medieval studies (Manchester: Manchester University Press, 2013), p. 209.

10   Eamon Duffy, *Marking the hours: English people and their prayers 1240–1570* (New Haven, CT: Yale University Press, 2006); William H. Sherman, *Used books: marking readers in Renaissance England*, Material texts (Philadelphia: University of Pennsylvania Press, 2008); Kathryn Rudy, 'Kissing images, unfurling rolls, measuring wounds, sewing badges and carrying talismans: considering some Harley manuscripts through the physical rituals they reveal', *Electronic British Library Journal* (2011), 1–56 (Article 5); Kathryn M. Rudy, *Piety in pieces: how medieval readers customized their manuscripts* (Cambridge: Open Book Publishers, 2016); Sabrina Corbellini *et al.*, 'Challenging the paradigms: Holy Writ and lay readers in late medieval Europe', *Church History & Religious Culture* 93:2 (2013), 171–88.

affinity or an animosity towards annotations, illuminations and the theology of past generations.

Invaluable for the current investigation is a methodology rarely employed in the history of the Bible: the exploration of little-studied subsequent copies, reprints and editions.[11] Historians of the English Bible have often scrutinised its first editions.[12] From the earliest manuscripts of the Wycliffite Bible to the first edition of the King James Version, these books have received most scholarly attention and are treasured in libraries and auction houses alike. Yet here too, putting the objects centre stage transforms our perspective. These first editions are but a fraction of surviving Bibles, outnumbered by a proliferation of subsequent editions, copies and reprints. More importantly, subsequent editions and reprints were not copied blindly from an original text. Changes and modifications are a treasure trove of information regarding the production and use of Bibles. Time and again, the gap between first and subsequent editions and reprints demonstrates how religious ideals met commercial concerns or popular expectations; in the process innovations were omitted, reform-minded statements subdued and language rearranged for greater clarity. This transition is indicative of a major force in the history of the Bible: commerce. Stationers and printers sought to capitalise on the creativity of reformers by mass-producing books for growing audiences. They modified books to make theology more palatable to wider audiences, and often retraced some of the most reformed or innovative features of their models.

The new methodology has dictated the sample used in this study of the English Bible. For the early modern period, I have surveyed all major and minor reprints of single-volume Bibles in England and/or in English between 1535 and 1553.[13] For Bibles with few surviving copies (such as Berthelet's 1535 Latin Bible), I aimed at surveying all copies. For others, I have sampled primarily the copies in Cambridge University Library and the Bible Society, two of the most comprehensive collections of early printed English Bibles. This was supported by the study of records for compilation, as well as early modern devotional books and theological treatises. The situation is inevitably more complex for the study of the medieval evidence. Manuscripts do not

---

11   Such a methodology has been employed, to great value, in the analysis of Foxe's *Books of Martyrs*: Evenden and Freeman, *Religion and the book*.

12   This is most evident in the study of the early modern Bible, where 'first' editions are more discernible, and subsequent editions are overlooked in the vast majority of studies. The exception is works heavily embedded within book studies, such as Peter W. M. Blayney, *The Stationers' Company and the printers of London 1501–1557* (Cambridge: Cambridge University Press, 2013); Ian Green, *Print and Protestantism in early modern England* (Oxford: Oxford University Press, 2000); Femke Molekamp, 'Using a collection to discover reading practices: the British Library Geneva Bibles and a history of their early modern readers', *The Electronic British Library Journal* (2006): article 10.

13   In this I employed DMH (alongside the STC) as a guide.

adhere to specific print-runs, and without title pages, printers' devices and colophons, ascertaining date and provenance is much more complex. For the Latin evidence I have surveyed all post-1200 single-volume Bibles with medieval English or uncertain provenance in the collections of the British Library, Lambeth Palace Library, Edinburgh University Library, the National Library of Scotland and Cambridge University Library. This has assisted in revealing a smaller group of primarily mendicant Bibles, which is explored in Chapter 1 and presented in Appendix 1. For the Wycliffite Bible, I have surveyed manuscripts in Cambridge University Library and Cambridge Colleges. Assisted by the studies of Dove and Kennedy, as well as the recent catalogue of Solopova, I targeted specific manuscripts in London and Oxford libraries containing liturgical traces or variants in the layout of the Psalter.[14]

The Bible was one of the most popular books throughout the period under investigation and survives nowadays in hundreds of late medieval manuscripts; thousands of early modern printed Bibles attest to dozens of editions and reprints. The sheer quantity of books complicates their analysis and prevents the possibility of compiling an exhaustive study. Many works single out a specific type of book or period as a means of delving deeper into the book and religious cultures.[15] For the current study, however, the ability to look over an extended period is essential. Breaking the historiographical boundaries separating the later Middle Ages from early modernity enables the re-contextualisation of religious and technological transformations, such as the rise of moveable-type print, vernacular literature and religious reforms. It also enables us to follow long-term changes, and better identify trends and dead ends in the history of the English Bible.

This book explores *c.*350 years in the history of the Bible. It starts with the rise of the first mass-produced Bibles at the beginning of the thirteenth century. This was a time when single-volume Bibles became the norm for biblical books. These Bibles were subjected, on the whole, to uniform layout and textual divisions, which became the standard for centuries. It then follows key moments in the history of the Bible in England, through the proliferation of the Wycliffite Bible—the first translation of the entire Bible into English at the end of the fourteenth century—and two very different Bibles at the end of Henry VIII's reign. The book ends at the close of

---

14   Dove, *The first English Bible*; Kathleen E. Kennedy, *The courtly and commercial art of the Wycliffite Bible*, Medieval church studies 35 (Turnhout: Brepols, 2014); Elizabeth Solopova, *Manuscripts of the Wycliffite Bible in the Bodleian and Oxford College libraries*, Exeter medieval texts and studies (Liverpool: Liverpool University Press, 2016).

15   Such as Eyal Poleg and Laura Light (eds), *Form and function in the Late Medieval Bible*, The written word: the manuscript world 27:4 (Leiden: Brill, 2013); Solopova, *The Wycliffite Bible: origin, history and interpretation*; S. L. Greenslade, *The Coverdale Bible, 1535* (Folkestone: Wm. Dawson & Sons, 1975).

Edward VI's reign, just as a period of intense creativity in print and reform stopped abruptly with the accession of Mary. Prior to the spiralling number of editions and reprints ushered in by the unprecedented popularity of the Geneva Bible, the period under consideration enables us to identify key actors, transformations and lost gambles. It leads us to appreciate some of the little-explored moments in the history of the English Bible: an experimental group of Late Medieval Bibles used by members of the mendicant orders, or the first (Latin) Bible printed in England, both nearly invisible for scholars of Bible and religion alike. The Bibles of the reign of Edward VI (the topic of Chapter 5) have been of little interest to historians of the English Bible. In my initial plan, the period's Bibles were to be discussed in a paragraph; their survey, however, has revealed their importance to the history of the Bible in England, and soon they occupied a chapter in their own right. The material perspective also enables us to shed new light on some better-known Bibles, such as the Wycliffite Bible or Henry VIII's Great Bible. Commonly seen as landmarks of reform, their materiality reveals both orthodoxy and hesitation, an uncertain course of religious and technological change.

As much as its temporal scope, the geographical range of this book needs clear delineation. The history of the Bible in the later Middle Ages and early modernity is inevitably a pan-European phenomenon, and throughout the period under consideration England cannot be separated from the Continent. Innovative biblical manuscripts developed simultaneously on both sides of the Channel in the early thirteenth century, and scholars nowadays still struggle to tell apart those copied in northern France from those made in south-east England. At the time, friars and university students, prime audiences for these manuscripts, were highly mobile, not confined in their persons nor in their books to a single location. The Wycliffite Bible was part of a much wider phenomenon, a proliferation of vernacular Bibles across Europe in the fourteenth and fifteenth centuries, which is manifested in the vibrant book cultures of Germany, the Low Countries, France and Italy, as well as key translation campaigns in Central Europe. Throughout the period under consideration the book trade was likewise pan-European. Manuscript books were imported into England, with production centres in the Low Countries specialising in catering for an English clientele. This dependency grew with the rise of moveable-type printing, as the English book market relied heavily on Continental printers. The first Bible printed in England emulated Continental books, and even the most national English Bible, the Great Bible of Henry VIII, began its life in Paris, relocating to England only after a crackdown by the French authorities.

For the current study English is not a language nor a secluded island. It is a manifestation of a much wider phenomenon. The emphasis on England, however, enables us to identify trends and transformations in the evolution of Bibles and their use. Some aspects explored in the book (such as the miniaturisation of Bibles in the thirteenth and sixteenth centuries, or the mendicant experimentation with the liturgy) were shared across regional boundaries. Other patterns, such as the value of subsequent editions or the role of female religious in vernacular piety, could likewise be seen elsewhere. But this is not a quasi-random choice aimed at facilitating a manageable corpus for investigation. The English example stands out in both its technology and its religion, the two underlying themes of this book. The peculiarities of the English manuscript and print trade, with its dependency on the Continent, had a great impact on the materiality of Bibles. The hesitant production of Bibles in England, especially in the sixteenth century, sheds important light on English society and religion, as explored in Chapters 3, 4 and 5. Similarly, the English Church moved in a distinct direction. The 1407/9 Constitutions of Archbishop Arundel, aimed at regulating the reading of vernacular Scripture, introduced an unease with vernacular theology, setting it on a path apart from its Continental counterparts. This difference was exacerbated with the break from Rome and subsequent attempts at consolidating a nationwide religious culture, first under Henry VIII, and even more so under Edward VI. The history of the English Bible is therefore a unique local phenomenon that cannot—and should not—be separated from its wider counterparts.

What is the Bible? It is an elusive term, which could be seen as a book, a text or a concept. For the current investigation, however, a clear focus is paramount, as is the need to delineate a manageable corpus. Here, too, I am guided by the material evidence. Sacred texts proliferated in the period under investigation, so considering all books containing parts of Scripture would inevitably bring into our orbit most surviving books. Widely used liturgical manuscripts, Books of Hours, sermon collections and devotional literature all drew heavily on biblical texts and stories. To achieve coherency and feasibility this book explores single-volume Bibles, as well as projects aimed at producing a full Bible (such as the Wycliffite Bible, whose earliest manuscripts are single-volume Bibles, although most surviving copies comprise the New Testament, or Berthelet's 1535 part-Bible, whose preface alludes to a companion volume). This necessarily omits some of the most popular books of late medieval and early modern England: independent Psalters, Books of Hours, New Testaments and liturgical lectionaries. Further omitted are landmarks of the English Bible such as the Anglo-Norman Apocalypses, and even the ground-breaking works of William Tyndale, who published individual biblical books.

The investigation of single-volume Bibles enables a like-for-like comparison across the period, tracing the evolution and deployment of cross-biblical aids and layout. It also supports the identification and isolation of specific ele-ments within the Bible. Biblical books differ considerably from one another in their text, style and language, which impacted upon the way they were presented and read. Within Bibles, the Psalms were typically inscribed in a way unlike any other biblical text. The Psalms were chanted day and night by the clergy, a practice imitated by devout laywomen and men. This shaped biblical mnemonics, influencing the way that biblical book was known and depicted in manuscripts and prints.[16] Against the background of more 'stand-ard' biblical books, such variations of layout and design are both significant and revealing. During the period different biblical books were subjected to an inner-biblical hierarchy. The New Testament was seen as the apogee of Scripture. It was, alongside the Psalms, the backbone of the liturgy, and influ-enced the materiality of many Wycliffite Bibles. Such a hierarchy is captured well by the author of the fifteenth-century *Myroure of oure Ladye* (discussed in Chapter 2) arguing that '[l]ike as holy scripture passes all of other scripture. And as the gospel of saint John passes all other parts of holy scripture.'[17]

Within these textual, spatial and temporal parameters, I have made other choices to facilitate a manageable corpus and to support a coherent narrative. I have focused on Bibles which were created for the English market, either in England or abroad, as these aimed to shape or reflect English faith and society. This has led me to avoid (except as auxiliary evidence in the study of other Bibles) the important group of Continental fifteenth- and sixteenth-century Latin Bibles, which were used in England but were made for a pan-European clientele. Similarly, I have not addressed the unique group of French Bibles (such as the *Bibles historiale* or the *Bible du XIIIᵉ siècle*), which were owned and read by the English nobility, but rarely extended beyond that group. The proliferation of Bibles in the 1530s has necessitated further choices. I have concentrated on books whose production was linked to Henry VIII, either through the Bible printed in 1535 by the King's Printer, or Henry's Great Bible, which was produced under the supervision of Thomas Cromwell, Henry's Chief Minister. Two biblical editions from the 1530s—the Matthew Bible of 1537 and the Taverner Bible of 1539, the first seeking to capitalise on the dissemination of Bibles in parish churches, and the latter another lost gamble made by Thomas Berthelet, the King's Printer—have not

---

16   A fuller exploration of the layout of the Psalms across a longer period is Eyal Poleg, 'Memory, per-formance and change: the Psalms' layout in late medieval and early modern Bibles', in *From scrolls to scroll-ing: Sacred texts, materiality, and dynamic media cultures in Judaism, Christianity, and Islam*, ed. Brad Anderson (Berlin: de Gruyter, 2020), pp. 119–51

17   *The myroure of Oure Ladye: containing a devotional treatise on divine service, with a translation of the offices used by the Sisters of the Brigittine Monastery of Sion, at Isleworth, during the fifteenth and sixteenth centuries*, ed. John Henry Blunt, Early English Text Society ES 19 (London: Trubner for the Early English Text Society, 1873), p. 102.

received their own chapters, and are discussed only in passing. Coverdale's Bible, which has attracted considerable scholarly attention as the first printed single-volume Bible in English, is examined primarily with a view to contextualise its Latin contemporary, which has attracted nearly none.

This book moves chronologically from 1200 to 1553, addressing key moments in the history of the English Bible over three and a half centuries. Its opening chapter explores the Late Medieval Bible (LMB), the mass-produced single-volume Bible which is often linked to the nascent universities and the mendicant orders. Rather than delineating a smaller group of Bibles based on textual criteria (often referred to as 'Paris Bible') or on size ('pocket' or 'portable Bible'), I have employed criteria which delineate a much wider group of single-volume Bibles which adhere to a uniform layout and the 'modern' chapter division.[18] In scholarly analyses the LMB is seen as a force for innovation, a transformative moment in the history of the Bible and in the evolution of the pre-modern book.[19] The wider grouping of LMBs in Chapter 1 offers a more balanced picture, addressing both its transformational and traditional elements. It explores these Bibles against the background of the Glossed Bible, which, in the words of Lesley Smith, 'in some sense, has become the Bible' in the previous century.[20] The thirteenth century saw the introduction and proliferation of the modern chapter division, which has been used in Bibles ever since. Medieval exegetes and preachers made use of the new chapter division, as well as of other innovative features of the LMB's layout. Through the prism of appearance and use we can delineate a small group of mostly mendicant Bibles, whose layout and addenda reveal a concerted attempt at revolutionising the liturgy. The creators and users of these Bibles experimented with biblical mnemonics, embedding new means of navigating the Bible into liturgical chants, one of the most conservative forms of biblical mediation. This, however, was not to be. The vast majority of LMBs remained more traditional in separating chant from the new retrieval system. The chapter ends by suggesting how, in the course of the fourteenth and fifteenth centuries, the LMB spread beyond its original audiences, with manuscripts appearing in parish churches and its layout adopted in books for lay and less scholarly readers.

18   For the rationale of delineating the Late Medieval Bible as a coherent group of Bibles see Eyal Poleg and Laura Light, 'Introduction', in *Form and function in the Late Medieval Bible*, ed. Eyal Poleg and Laura Light, The written word: the manuscript world 27:4 (Leiden: Brill, 2013), pp. 1–7.

19   Christopher de Hamel, *The book: a history of the Bible* (London: Phaidon, 2001); Alexander L. Devine, 'A portable feast: The production and use of the thirteenth-century portable Bible 1200–1500' (Ph.D., University of Pennsylvania, 2016). This has been an underlying rationale for the 2013 edited volume on the LMB and is explicated in its introduction: Poleg and Light, 'Introduction'.

20   Lesley Smith, *The Glossa ordinaria: the making of a medieval Bible commentary*, Commentaria 3 (Leiden: Brill, 2009), p. 1.

A prime example for the reception of the LMB is the Wycliffite Bible. This Middle English Bible originated in the heterodox circle of the followers of the Oxford theologian John Wyclif. Soon, however, Wycliffite Bibles were produced commercially, aimed at a wider, and often more orthodox, readership. The move away from its heterodox roots is evident in the transformation of book and layout, as in the modification of the table of lections—the most common addendum to the Wycliffite Bible. That table, and the Wycliffite Bible as a whole, suggests cohabitation of English and Latin in the liturgy performed in nunneries, chapels or for lay brothers. It directs our attention to the poorly documented and little-explored liturgy practised outside monastic centres and cathedrals. The move between English and Latin is most evident in the Book of Psalms, which became a site of competing mnemonics. There, reform and common knowledge influenced discrete means of presenting the biblical text, attesting to tensions and transitions in the creation and reception of vernacular Bibles.

Then followed a long silence. As explored at the start of Chapter 3, the century between the heyday of the Wycliffite Bible and the first printed single-volume Bibles of the 1530s saw no new Bible produced in England, following both the unease of the English Church with vernacular theology, as well as the state of English printing and its reliance on the Continent. An in-depth examination of the first Bible printed in England unearths a modest book, a Latin part-Bible which is deliberately archaic in its text, layout and addenda. Its origins reveal dependency on Continental models, modified to create a book carefully placed between tradition and reform. Printed by the King's Printer, it attempted, and initially secured, royal patronage. However, this was quickly withdrawn, leaving the book in political limbo. Reflecting the state of English printing, its materiality was significantly inferior to its clandestine contemporary, the English reformed Bible compiled by Miles Coverdale on the Continent. The analysis of readers' marks and annotations in Berthelet's Bible sheds additional light on the hesitant course of reform during Henry VIII's reign. As priests, scholars, children and crooks left their marks on the Bible, they bore witness to uncertainties and changes in the history of the early modern Bible.

The Great Bible of Henry VIII is often seen as a landmark in the history of the English Bible, a national monument of statehood and reform. Chapter 4 views this Bible from a different perspective, unfolding the controversies and hesitations linked to its inception and reception. Correspondence between the production team in Paris and England reveals the innate tension between empowering and controlling lay readership. As people moved in and out of Henry's grace, the Bible changed shape to reflect a delicate political and religious environment, its title page revealing, for example, Thomas Cromwell's fall from grace, or an unknown portrait of Jane Seymour. The Great Bible revolutionised the landscape of biblical books in England in a way often unnoticed by scholars. It was the first parish Bible in England, which every church in the realm was ordered to acquire. A closer look reveals that its use was incompatible with a liturgy which was still traditional, rendering it a useless book and setting its materiality on a collision course with Church customs. The result attracted the wrath of Church reformers and conservatives alike, causing Henry VIII to retract his hesitant acceptance of the Bible, and to curb lay readership of it in 1543, a mere four years after the introduction of the Bible.

Henry's death was to change all this. Chapter 5 explores the short minority reign of Edward VI (1547–53), a pivotal moment which has rarely been explored in histories of the English Bible. With reformed clergy and nobility at the helm, printers were given unprecedented freedom in the production of the Bible. The result was transformative. Eleven different Bibles were printed during his reign, innovating text, appearance, size and addenda. English liturgy likewise underwent a transformation with the introduction of the Book of Common Prayer, which created a unified and simplified national liturgy. The Bible was at the heart of this reform, which created a complex cycle for the reading of Scripture (almost) in its entirety. In order to facilitate this intricate task, chapter divisions, whose introduction we considered in Chapter 1, were deployed in new ways. The link between Bible and liturgy gradually shaped the layout of Edwardian Bibles, with its last Bible evidencing the reign's achievements, as well as its abrupt end. The conclusion of the book explores the wider history of the Bible in England, revealing a gradual move of Bibles from elite clerical audiences, through nunneries and chapels, and into each parish church and lay hands in the sixteenth century. It also addresses the rate of change, one of the major impacts of the introduction of moveable-type printing.

1

The Late Medieval Bible: Beyond Innovation

Introduction

Accounts of the first three decades of the thirteenth century easily lend themselves to a vocabulary of innovation and transformation. The nascent universities grew side by side with the professionalisation of the medieval book trade; novel forms of preaching and exegesis coincided with a renewed emphasis on pastoral care and the dissemination of theology; the new orders of friars—itinerant poor religious dedicated to preaching to the laity—embraced the use of ever-smaller books, written in minute scripts on extremely thin parchment. At the epicentre of all those transformations stood a new type of Bible. It was the first mass-produced, single-volume Bible, which adhered to a strikingly uniform layout. It survives in hundreds of manuscripts in collections all around the globe. Emerging from the centres of learning in Paris, southern England and northern Italy around 1230, these Bibles spread rapidly across Europe. Within fifty years, Latin Bibles from Bohemia to Spain and from Denmark to Italy adhered to a uniform layout that remained the standard for over two centuries. Modern scholars find it challenging to differentiate between books written in Oxford and Paris; those written in 1250 or in 1400 are remarkably similar in design. Their impact extended far beyond the world of Latin scholarship, as their layout was emulated in vernacular Bibles in French, Italian, German or English, and served as a template for the first printed Bibles over two centuries later. In a process that spanned centuries, these single-volume, small and easily navigable codices transformed biblical knowledge and access to it.

When one handles such a Bible it is hard not to be overwhelmed by the technological feats that enabled its creation. Many volumes are small. Measuring less than 20 cm in length, they are no larger than a modern pocket Bible. Their gothic script is typically clear and easily legible (although reading such minute script quickly becomes a challenge, especially without a

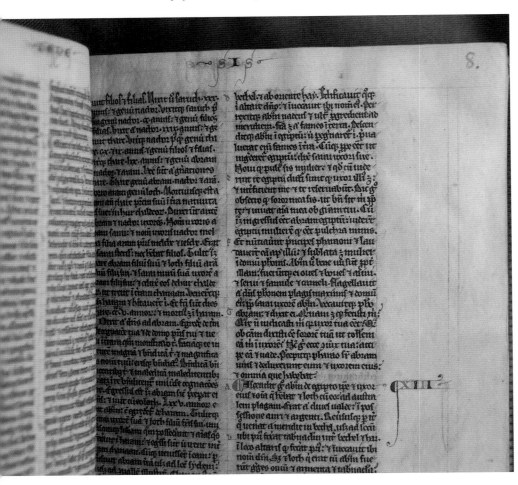

Figure 1.1 The minute and highly uniform layout of a Late Medieval Bible. These mass-produced Bibles were the product of professional teams of scribes, illuminators and stationers, often working in university towns. Victoria and Albert Museum, Reid MS 21, fol. 8rb (detail).

magnifying glass). Their distinct layout (see Figure 1.1), written in two textual columns with red and blue running titles, capital letters and chapter numbers, was replicated across space and time. The parchment used is so fine that it resembles tissue paper in thinness, while being more robust and enduring.

Modern historians have emphasised the Bible's innovative qualities and viewed the time of its creation as a transformative moment in the history of the Bible.[1] Scholars have often linked these Bibles to the nascent mendicant orders, as well as to innovations in preaching and exegesis. Other, more tra-

---

1   A more comprehensive discussion is Eyal Poleg and Laura Light (eds), *Form and function in the Late Medieval Bible*, The written word: the manuscript world 27:4 (Leiden: Brill, 2013) with bibliography on pp. 1–4. To this should be added two important dissertations: Alexander Devine, 'A portable feast: the production and use of the thirteenth-century portable Bible 1200–1500' (Ph.D., University of Pennsylvania, 2016) and Chiara Ruzzier, 'Entre Université et Ordres mendiants: la miniaturisation de la Bible au XIIIe siècle' (Ph.D., Université Paris 1 Panthéon-Sorbonne, 2010).

ditional, facets have commonly been sidelined. Thus, for example, the use of these Bibles in prayer—a more conservative form of biblical mediation—does not fit easily within the paradigm of innovation and novelty, and hence was first explored only in 2013.[2] The emphasis on innovation and origins is reflected in the terminology associated with this class of Bibles. It is often called the 'University' or 'Paris' Bible, attesting to its origins at the University of Paris and the stationers affiliated with it. While some scholars employ this term to address all Latin Bibles of the thirteenth and fourteenth centuries, Laura Light has employed it to delineate a smaller group of Bibles based on layout and specific textual criteria.[3] Other scholars have chosen to highlight its size, naming it 'Pocket' or 'Portable' Bible, alluding to one of its most innovative features. I will break away from this nomenclature to embrace a name that is simultaneously vaguer and more accurate—the Late Medieval Bible (LMB). This name brings together the vast number of Latin Bibles written after 1230—small and large alike—which were presented in a highly uniform layout; these Bibles were divided into uniform chapter divisions and were typically single-volume Bibles affixed with a biblical glossary (the *Interpretations of Hebrew Name*). Delineating this group of Bibles supports a more nuanced view of the production and use of Latin Bibles in the later Middle Ages, one that accepts its innovation while at the same time explores its more traditional facets. Beyond the innovation paradigm, we can appreciate the ways in which it took time for new technologies to be accepted and to influence biblical reading and knowledge. These transitions are most evident in the interplay between biblical study, preaching and the liturgy, which stands at the heart of this chapter.

Size Matters

The differences between the LMB and its twelfth-century predecessors are evident without opening a single book. On the shelves of libraries, the LMB is often dwarfed by the large Romanesque Bibles of the twelfth century, as it is by early medieval Bibles. Until *c*.1200, Bibles had traditionally been large and cumbersome, commonly divided into multiple volumes. By the mid-thirteenth century this was no longer the case. Some Bibles were large and lavish, but this was a matter of choice rather than of necessity. Many were small or even minute, and a great number of Bibles fall into the category of

---

2   Laura Light, 'Thirteenth-century pandects and the liturgy', in *Form and Function in the Late Medieval Bible*, ed. Eyal Poleg and Laura Light (Leiden: Brill, 2013), pp. 185–215.

3   Laura Light, 'The thirteenth century and the Paris Bible', in *The new Cambridge history of the Bible: from 600 to 1450*, ed. Richard Marsden and E. Ann Matter (Cambridge: Cambridge University Press, 2013), pp. 380–91.

pocket books, whose height is 20 cm or less, and whose weight can be as low as 360 g.[4]

The technologies that enabled the creation of ever-smaller Bibles are evident upon opening any such specimen. New methods of parchment-making enabled parchmeners to refine skins to a previously unknown thinness (0.03–0.28 mm). Spuriously referred to as 'Uterine Vellum', it enabled the creation of compact volumes comprising hundreds of leaves.[5] The script used in these Bibles was developed in the previous century for the creation of glossed Bibles. It is a scribal feat of minuteness and accuracy. A typical, and by far not the smallest, example is a Bible produced in mid-thirteenth-century England (see Figure 1.1). Its scribe wrote the text in four and a half lines per centimetre, with a script which equals typeset Times New Roman, point 7.5, line space 0.75 of a modern word processor. Such an achievement could not be matched by early printers. Gutenberg's celebrated 42-line Bible was a lectern Bible, more like a twelfth-century Bible in size, and the first octavo Bibles printed in England during Edward VI's reign were large and bulky compared with the LMB.[6]

Size can be misleading. Nearly all surviving LMBs have been rebound several times since their compilation. We cannot take for granted that the size of medieval manuscripts nowadays is identical to their original dimensions. On the contrary, manuscripts have often been trimmed by modern binders, leaving pen-work or running titles truncated. Traces of this can be seen in Figure 1.1, where the upward projections of the title initials have been truncated. A few surviving manuscripts (see Figure 1.2) have extremely large margins, indicating that minuteness was important for producers and clients of the LMB, but not paramount.

The size of Bibles had a direct impact on ownership and reading practices. Smaller manuscripts required less parchment—an expensive commodity—and hence could be significantly cheaper than their large counterparts (although the works of scribes and illuminators, as well as the materials they could employ, had a considerable effect on book prices).[7] It also created a new type of book, which facilitated different reading practices. Margaret Aston

---

4   The best codicological analysis of the LMB is Ruzzier, 'Entre Université et Ordres mendiants'; summarised in Chiara Ruzzier, 'The miniaturisation of Bible manuscripts in the thirteenth century: a comparative study', in *Form and function in the Late Medieval Bible*, ed. Eyal Poleg and Laura Light (Leiden: Brill, 2013), pp. 105–25. The weight is based on BL Add. MS 5,160 (a minute volume whose margins, nevertheless, were truncated by a modern binder).

5   Sarah Fiddyment *et al.*, 'Animal origin of 13th-century uterine vellum revealed using noninvasive peptide fingerprinting', *Proceedings of the National Academy of Sciences*, 112:49 (2015), 15066–71.

6   Chapter 5, 'Size Matters (2)'

7   The most extensive study of production and sale prices of LMBs is Devine, 'A portable feast', ch. 4: '"The economics of use": the early professional book trade and the costs and prices of 13th-century portable Bibles', pp. 292–396. The difficulty in ascertaining book prices is explicated on pp. 304–5.

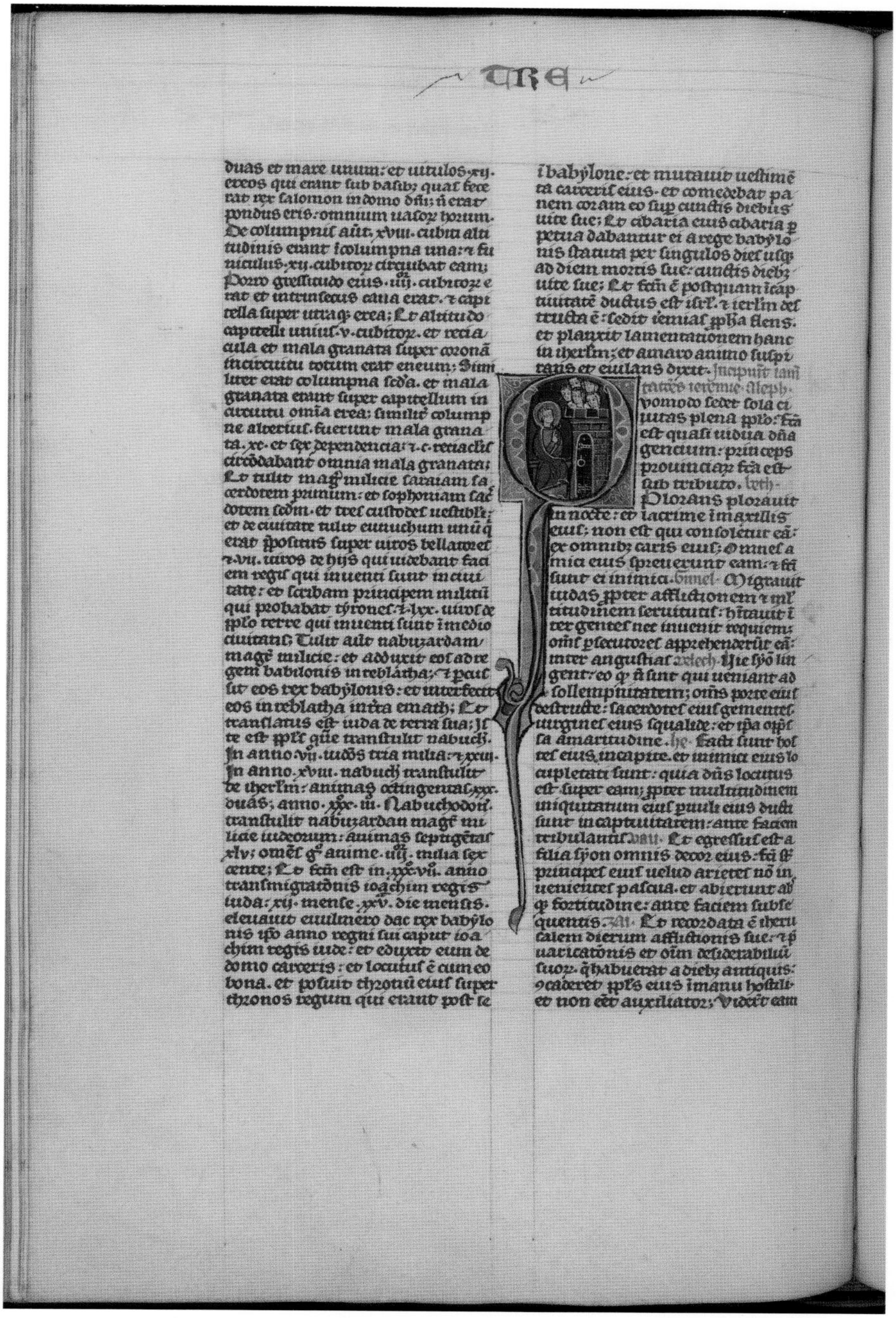

Figure 1.2 Wide empty margins in a Late Medieval Bible. These suggest that the stationers' goal was not to simply produce the smallest possible Bible. Edinburgh University Library MS 2, fol. 299v. Edinburgh University Library Special Collections.

had divided early modern devotional books into 'lectern' and 'lap' books, in a division that impacts audience and patterns of use.[8] This accords with the evidence for the LMB. Large and expensive volumes typically resided in libraries of wealthy establishments, be they monasteries, cathedrals or colleges. Smaller Bibles, on the other hand, were purchased and owned by a wider range of patrons, with evidence for the rise of personal ownership of these smaller Bibles, primarily by the upper echelons of Church and society.[9] The Mendicants, whose innovativeness merged with practical needs emanating from their education, preaching mission, and their transient life and oath of poverty, embraced the concept of *vademecum* Bibles for study, preaching and the performance of the liturgy. Their experimentation with biblical mnemonics is preserved in a small group of Bibles, explored in the following section, 'Praying the Late Medieval Bible'.

The revolution of the LMB is hidden in plain sight to the modern reader. As argued by Laura Light, '[t]he emphasis on the new portable Bible has to some extent overshadowed the equally important fact of the adoption of the pandect as the predominate format'.[10] This was the first time that the Bible became a single-volume book. While such books did exist previously, they were the exception.[11] Now, they became the norm.[12] We are so used to this

---

8   Margaret Aston, 'Lap books and lectern books: the revelatory book in the Reformation', in *The Church and the book: papers read at the 2000 summer meeting and the 2001 winter meeting of the Ecclesiastical History Society*, ed. R. N. Swanson, Studies in Church history 38 (Woodbridge: Boydell for the Ecclesiastical History Society, 2004), pp. 163–89; discussed on pp. 138–9.

9   The most substantial work on ownership of LMBs is two unpublished dissertations: Josephine Case Schnurman, 'Studies in the medieval book trade from the late twelfth to the middle of the fourteenth century with special reference to the copying of the Bible' (B.Litt., St Hilda's College, Oxford, 1960) and Devine, 'A portable feast'.

10   Laura Light, 'Non-biblical texts in thirteenth-century Bibles', in *Medieval manuscripts, their makers and users: a special issue of Viator in honor of Richard and Mary Rouse*, ed. Christopher Baswell (Turnhout: Brepols, 2011), pp. 169–83 at 170. This article is also the best survey of addenda to the LMB.

11   Such as the Theodulf Bibles in the Carolingian period, or the mammoth Anglo-Saxon Bible which is the Codex Amiatinus. For a survey of early single-volume Bibles (with additional bibliography) see Devine, 'A portable feast', pp. 26–44.

12   This becomes evident through surveys of Latin Bibles, omitting glossed Bibles and Psalters (two different categories of books), in manuscript catalogues. There, the supremacy of part-Bibles before 1200 and the overwhelming majority of single-volume Bibles after 1200 is clearly evident. This can be seen across different libraries and types of catalogues. Thus, for example, the survey of dated and datable manuscripts in the British Library (Andrew G. Watson, *Catalogue of dated and datable manuscripts, c.700–1600 in the Department of Manuscripts, the British Library* (London: British Library, 1979)) enumerates twelve part-Bibles prior to 1200, with only one possible single-volume Bible (single leaves in BL Add. MSS 37,777 and 45,025), whereas after 1200 there are six single-volume Bibles and a sole part-Bible (Add. MS 16,410, was probably once a full Bible; see Robert Branner, *Manuscript painting in Paris during the reign of Saint Louis: a study of styles*, California studies in the history of art 18 (Berkeley: University of California Press, 1977), p. 114). The Catalogue of illuminated manuscripts in Cambridge University Library (P. N. R. Zutshi, Paul Binski and Stella Panayotova, *Western illuminated manuscripts: a catalogue of the collection in Cambridge University Library* (Cambridge: Cambridge University Press, 2011)) likewise reveals two part-Bibles prior to 1200 and thirty-two single-volume Bibles after 1200. These two catalogues enumerate English and Continental books alike. Similar results for English medieval libraries appear in Richard Sharpe and James

nowadays that it is hard to envision the impact of such a transformation, the creation of compact tomes comprising more than 700,000 words. We can see not only the rise of cross-biblical aids, such as glossaries or concordances, but also the ideal of the self-encompassing book, which contains the entirety of the biblical text and the addenda needed for its interpretation, the lock and the key, to borrow from the imagery associated with biblical glossaries.[13] A direct line could therefore be traced from the LMB to the self-sufficient portable Bibles of the late sixteenth century. The rise of the single-volume Bible also began a slow process of transformation, subjecting all biblical components to the same layout and the mnemonics, thus ushering in a new way of approaching the biblical text. The materiality of the new Bibles had another impact on the ways they were read. Even in well-lit reading rooms nowadays, their minute script inhibits lengthy readings. Readers of these Bibles embraced forms of fragmented reading, which was eased by their innovative layout.

A single-volume Bible introduces its own problems. The Bible is a long and cumbersome miscellany, one that does not easily lend itself to cover-to-cover reading. The innovative layout of the LMB ushered in a reading strategy which eased navigation and promoted browsing at the expense of continuous reading. The layout of the page, written in two narrow textual columns, supports such fragmented reading. This visual cue to the vertical aesthetics of Gothic architecture also befitted easy identification of specific components.[14] A single textual block favours continuous reading. Dual columns, on the other hand, facilitate quicker retrieval of individual sections. The space between columns was open for marks and annotations by scribes and readers, identifying and directing readers to elements of interest. This was accompanied by a new retrieval system. The LMB was the child of the scholastic book, with its preference for complex compilations and divisions.[15] An array of titles and divisions transformed the Bible into a

---

Willoughby, 'MGLB3 (Medieval Libraries of Great Britain)', http://mlgb3.bodleian.ox.ac.uk, accessed 29 November 2019, where there are around ninety-six single-volume Bibles post-1200, and only a handful of single-volume Bibles earlier (such as the twelfth-century Cambridge, Trinity College MS B.5.1).

13   Eyal Poleg, 'The Interpretations of Hebrew Names in theory and practice', in *Form and function in the Late Medieval Bible*, ed. Eyal Poleg and Laura Light (Leiden: Brill, 2013), pp. 217–36 at 226–7.

14   Rosanna Miriello, 'La Bibbia portabile de origine italiana del xiii secolo: Brevi considerazioni e alcuni esempi', in *La Bibbia del xiii secolo. Storia del testo, storia dell'esegesi: Convegno della Società Internazionale per lo studio del Medioevo Latino (SISMEL) Firenze, 1–2 Giugno 2001*, ed. Giuseppe Cremascoli and Francesco Santi, Millennio medievale 49 (Florence: SISMEL, 2004), pp. 47–77 at 56–7; Albert Derolez, *The palaeography of Gothic manuscript books: from the twelfth to the early sixteenth century* (Cambridge: Cambridge University Press, 2003), pp. 34–9.

15   See Richard H. Rouse and Mary A. Rouse, 'Statim invenire: schools, preachers, and new attitudes to the page', in *Renaissance and renewal in the twelfth century*, ed. Robert L. Benson, Giles Constable and Carol D. Lanham (Oxford: Oxford University Press, 1982; reprint, ch. 6 in *Authentic witnesses: approaches to medieval texts and manuscripts* (Notre Dame, IN: University of Notre Dame Press, 1991), pp. 191–219), pp. 201–25, and p. 36.

useful reference book and eased navigation, as can be seen in Figure 1.1. A carefully prepared page, with intricate ruling lines, established the place of each textual column, and left space for titles and divisions. At the top of the page a running title in alternating blue and red initials identifies the biblical book, often spanning an entire opening (in Figure 1.1 this is broken into GENE | SIS).

One of the most enduring and influential features of the LMB is its chapter division.[16] Until the end of the twelfth century, Bibles adhered to various, and differing, systems of chapters, sometimes numbered, sometimes not. These were often accompanied by summaries, known as *capitula*, *breves* or *tituli*. These divisions varied greatly in length and appearance, and served as both division (within the text) and summary (preceding the biblical book with a list of titles for each section).[17] Within the LMB, a uniform and numerical system was embraced by scribes, stationers and readers, to become one of its longest-lasting legacies. The 'modern' chapter division, which is still employed in Bibles nowadays, has often been accredited to Stephen Langton, master at the University of Paris and later Archbishop of Canterbury (†1228). Paul Saenger, however, has argued convincingly for a twelfth-century appearance of chapter division in a few English manuscripts, predating their dissemination by Langton.[18] The new chapter division innovated biblical reading. Liturgical divisions and some earlier *capitula* were identified by their first few words, known as incipit. These were often narrative units, befitting a textual identification. Chapter divisions, on the other hand, were purely numerical and introduced unprecedented ease and uniformity into locating biblical components. The chapter division not only facilitated navigation, but also provided

16   The most substantial study of chapter divisions is still Otto Schmid, *Über verschiedene eintheilungen der Heiligen Schrift insbesondere über die Capitel-eintheilung Stephan Langtons im XIII Jahrhunderte* (Graz: Leuschner & Lubensky, 1892). The recent series of *Pericope: Scripture as Written and Read in Antiquity* (Leiden: Brill, 2000–) provides insights into the creation and use of textual divisions in the Bible. A connection between chapter divisions and lectures at the University of Paris was made by Beryl Smalley, *The study of the Bible in the Middle Ages*, 3rd edn (Oxford: Blackwell, 1983), pp. 222–4.

17   Similar divisions, often unnumbered, existed in Hebrew Bibles. These were often noted by either an empty space or a blank line. The liturgical portions of the Pentateuch (*Parashot*), identified by their incipits, are still employed nowadays. The Jewish Bible as a whole, however, proved equally receptive to the introduction of the LMB's chapter divisions. For a summary see David Stern, *The Jewish Bible: a material history* (Seattle: University of Washington Press), pp. 25–6, 145; Paul Saenger, 'Jewish liturgical divisions of the Torah and the English chapter division of the Vulgate attributed to Stephen Langton', in *Pesher Nahum: texts and studies in Jewish history and literature from Antiquity through the Middle Ages, presented to Norman (Nahum) Golb*, ed. J. L. Kraemer and M. G. Wechsler (Chicago: The Oriental Institute of the University of Chicago, 2012), pp. 187–202.

18   Paul Saenger, 'The British Isles and the origin of the modern mode of biblical citation', *Syntagma* 1 (2005), 77–123; followed by Paul Saenger and Laura Bruck, 'The Anglo-Hebraic origins of the modern chapter division of the Latin Bible', in *La fractura historiográfica: Las investigaciones de Edad Media y Renacimiento desde el tercer milenio*, ed. Javier San José Lera (Salamanca: Universidad de Salamanca, 2008), pp. 177–202.

subtle means of understanding the biblical text. Thus, for example, by dividing the story of Creation into the first three chapters of Genesis, some ambiguity arising from its parallel narratives was resolved, separating the creation of the world from that of Adam and Eve. It would be a mistake, however, to think of chapter divisions as units of narrative. Biblical sections read during liturgical services (known as pericopes, see pp. 19, 21–2 were shorter than chapters and often comprised a single story, as did some earlier divisions. Chapter divisions, on the other hand, established segments of roughly equal length,[19] which did not simply follow a narrative rationale. This led to the joining of seemingly distinct units. So, for example, 1 Regum chapter 14 contains not only the story of the battle of Jonathan, son of Saul, and its aftermath, but also a short description of the House of Saul; Matthew chapter 21 presents the account of Christ's Entry to Jerusalem, followed by casting the moneylenders out of the Temple, Cursing the Fig Tree, and the Parables of the Two Sons and of the Wicked Tenants.

A key reason for the success of the chapter division becomes evident in comparison with an earlier retrieval system. The *Eusebian Canons* were a biblical navigation system developed in Late Antiquity to facilitate a comparison between the Four Gospels. Each Gospel was divided into numerical divisions, which were shorter (and inevitably more accurate) than the later chapter divisions. These divisions, called canons, were noted in the margins of each episode, alongside references to parallel episodes in other Gospels. At the beginning of the Gospel Book, a comprehensive list of all canons across the Four Gospels was presented, often in the form of decorated arches (see an example from a lavish late Anglo-Saxon Gospel Book, Figure 1.3). This precise and sophisticated system facilitated the complex task of comparing the parallel narratives of the Four Gospels.[20] However, as argued by Bruno Reudenbach, already in the early Middle Ages this device, which relied on extremely accurate copying to facilitate comparison, had fallen into disuse. It was still copied in Gospel Books, at times with elaborate iconography, but served a primarily symbolic function.[21] Chapter divisions, on the other hand,

---

19   Chapter divisions could still vary in length. In the Book of Genesis, for example, the longest chapter is 1,205 words (Ch. 24) and the shortest is a mere 276 (Ch. 16). These, however, are the exception, and the majority of chapters are between 350 and 600 words. A general uniformity is evident across the Bible with an average of 458.93 words and a median of 430 words. The analysis of chapter length is based on statistics drawn from 'The Clementine Text Project', http://vulsearch.sourceforge.net, accessed 12 June 2019. I thank Marjorie Burghart for her assistance in this analysis.

20   A comprehensive study of the Eusebian Canons in Late Antiquity and the early Middle Ages is Matthew R. Crawford, *The Eusebian Canon Tables: ordering textual knowledge in Late Antiquity*, Oxford early Christian studies (Oxford: Oxford University Press, 2019).

21   Bruno Reudenbach, 'Books for liturgical reading? Remarks on structure and function of early medieval Gospel Books', in *Clothing Sacred Scriptures: book art and book religion in Christian, Islamic, and Jewish Cultures*, ed. David Ganz and Barbara Schellewald, Manuscripta Biblica 2 (Berlin: De Gruyter, 2019), pp. 261–72.

Figure 1.3 Lavish
Canon Tables in
an Anglo-Saxon
Gospel Book.
This complex
finding aid was
more decorative
than practical in
many medieval
manuscripts.
Cambridge, Trinity
College MS
B.10.4, fol. 9r. By
permission of the
Master and Fellows
of Trinity College
Cambridge.

could withstand less ardent copying. More importantly, unlike the Eusebian
Canons, the modern chapter division was not created with a single goal in
mind. Rather, this was a more versatile tool, which could be bent to suit a
variety of uses by individual readers.

The success of this system is attested in thousands of late medieval manuscripts, as well as in its great longevity. Chapter divisions appear in Latin
and vernacular Bibles and were applied in concordances, exegetical works

and model sermons. They were introduced to earlier manuscripts of the Latin Bible, bringing them up to date, or integrated into Hebrew Bibles, thus facilitating their study alongside a Vulgate, or in the course of religious disputations.[22] This success story should be qualified somewhat, in favour of a more gradual and hesitant acceptance and dissemination of chapter division. Paul Saenger's careful study of minor variations within chapter division unfolds regional discrepancies, which took centuries to be ironed out. In France, Italy or England, LMBs still differed from one another in the exact location where chapters started or ended. As evident in explorations of Psalms' mnemonics throughout this study, not all parts of the Bible were equally suited to such change, nor did all ways in which the Bible was mediated befit the new form of retrieval and identification. In the study of the material history of the Bible, the reception of the new chapter division serves as a useful litmus test in assessing the alternation between reform and tradition.

Chapters are still large textual units. On average more than 450 words long, the identification of specific components within each chapter could still be somewhat slow. Numbered verse division became a feature of Bibles only in the sixteenth century. In some LMBs verses were indicated by a touch of red at their first letter, easing readers' way through the biblical text, but offering little help in retrieval of specific components. Before moveable-type print, noting a number for each and every verse would have been an extremely cumbersome and costly enterprise, so a less labour-intensive—and inevitably less efficient—system evolved. It was employed by the Dominican friars and is often accredited to Hugh of St Cher (†1263). The original system was complex and virtual, requiring no marks on the page, but relying on well-trained professionals to identify specific elements within biblical chapters. Biblical references found in Dominican concordances or preachers' handbooks provided alongside the chapter reference a letter between 'A' and 'G'. This can be seen in Figure 1.4, a fourteenth-century sermon collection, in which the *thema* is identified on the second line as 'Apo. ٦. c.' that is Revelation chapter 2 (in a medieval rendering of the Arabic numeral) part c, which is Rv 2:10b. The reader was expected to divide the chapter into seven equal-length parts in his mind (or into four sections for a short chapter), and then identify the relevant section. This system saved the labour of scribes and rubricators. It was a versatile but blunt instrument that relied on skilful readers, who could mentally sub-divide each chapter. As a non-specific tool,

---

22   For earlier Latin Bibles see Richard Gameson, 'Durham's Paris Bible and the use of communal Bibles in a Benedictine Cathedral Priory in the later Middle Ages', in *Form and function in the Late Medieval Bible*, ed. Eyal Poleg and Laura Light (Leiden: Brill, 2013), pp. 67–104. For Hebrew Bibles see Eyal Poleg, 'Inanimate conversion', *Material Religion* 14:4 (2019), 485–99.

Figure 1.4
Innovative
graphical features,
typical of scholastic
books, in the layout
of a fourteenth-
century sermon
collection.
Cambridge, Trinity
College MS
B.2.5 fol. 1r. By
permission of the
Master and Fellows
of Trinity College
Cambridge.

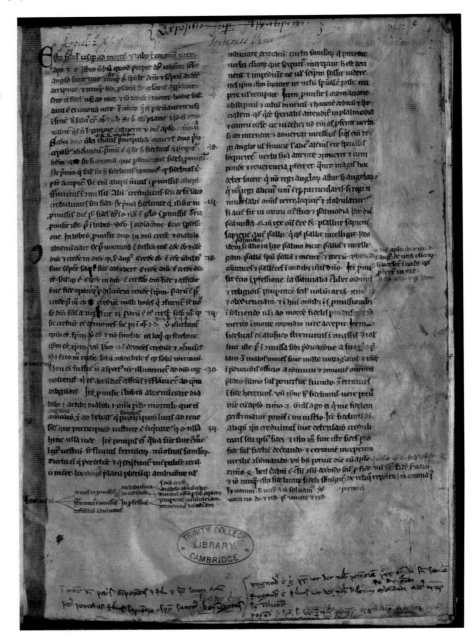

sub-divisions varied from one reader to another; and even this division broke
the text into paragraphs of around seventy-five words, rather than individual
verses. To help mitigate some of these problems, in a few LMBs these divisions were noted down by scribes, readers or rubricators. This custom grew
in popularity in the fifteenth and sixteenth centuries as more and more Bibles

were employed outside monasteries and universities by a greater variety of readers, and as printers employed this system in their presentation of the biblical text.[23]

But this is jumping ahead. The layout of the thirteenth-century Bible is indicative of its intended audience. The schools and universities were its prime home, and it was often produced by stationers affiliated with these institutions. Its appearance likewise was aimed at the trained professionals—students, biblical exegetes or preachers—who employed these books alongside concordances or preachers' aids. The chapter division, and even more so the virtual sub-division, was not created for the novice, and its efficient use relied on previous knowledge and expertise. Nearly two hundred years after the introduction of this system, the scribes and stationers of the Wycliffite Bible, anticipating new types of users, took care to explicate it to their readers.[24]

From *Glossa ordinaria* to Late Medieval Bible: The Triumph of Plain

The move from the Eusebian Canons to the 'modern' chapter divisions is a move from a more complex and specific system to a simpler and more general one. A similar transition could also be seen in the rise of the LMB against the background of its immediate predecessor—the twelfth-century glossed Bible, with its distinctive group of *Glossa ordinaria* manuscripts adhering to stricter textual criteria.[25] Glossed books combined biblical text and commentary. They were a feat of the twelfth-century schools, a visual manifestation of their exegetical innovativeness. Lesley Smith, in her exploration of the *Glossa ordinaria*, has convincingly stated that '[t]he Gloss, in some sense, had become the Bible'.[26] By the mid-thirteenth century, however, this was no longer the case. As Smith has shown, manuscripts of the *Glossa ordinaria* were compiled in the thirteenth century, possibly even in greater numbers than ever before. Yet the un-glossed LMB dominated the book market, with its innovative manner of engaging with the biblical text. The transition from the *Glossa ordinaria* to the LMB had a very practical rationale. When put side by

---

23   This inaccurate system varied in early modern Bibles, as can be seen in Chapter 3, p. 96.
24   Chapter 2, 'Table of Lections and New Modes of Reading'.
25   A more book-history perspective on glossed Bibles and the *Glossa ordinaria* is Christopher De Hamel, *Glossed books of the Bible and the origins of the Paris booktrade* (Woodbridge: D. S. Brewer, 1984). The sudy of biblical exegesis has been taken up by Lesley Smith, *The Glossa ordinaria: the making of a medieval Bible commentary*, Commentaria 3 (Leiden: Brill, 2009).
26   Smith, *Glossa ordinaria*, 1.

side, it is impossible to ignore one major difference: The single-volume LMB is dwarfed by the *Glossa ordinaria*. Commonly written in twenty-one large volumes, the *Glossa ordinaria* was the outcome of an immense investment in scribal time and parchment, which subsequently increased its cost significantly. Practicalities, however, are only part of the story. The transition from the *Glossa ordinaria* to the LMB also reveals changing notions of the Bible and its use around 1200.

Glossed Bibles were a scribal triumph whose intricate layouts grew in sophistication in the course of the twelfth century. These manuscripts were carefully designed to link the biblical text, often in a central textual column, with the commentaries of Church Fathers and early medieval exegetes in two flanking columns (see Figure 1.5). Complex *mise-en-page* and scribal marks enabled readers to link discrete biblical components with the appropriate section of commentary, while differentiating between individual commentators. The biblical text was written in large letters in a central textual block, while commentaries were written either between its lines (for shorter notes) or in the marginal space surrounding it. Such a complex use of space is a visual manifestation of the scholastic love of plurality. The twelfth-century dictum of 'diverse, not adverse' ('diversa sunt, non adversa') distils how school masters accommodated seemingly contradictory opinions into a single narrative.[27] This is reflected in the appearance of glossed Bibles, which focused the mind of readers on the complexity of the biblical text and the multiplicity of its interpretations. The plurality of the scholastic method—the harmonisation of different voices and the active exegetical engagement that infused doctrine into the biblical text—were all part of the appearance of the gloss. It facilitated the constant interplay between gloss and Bible. This necessitated a fragmentation of the biblical text, which left its mark on the LMB. The basic biblical unit of the gloss was short texts, which were demarcated and commented upon. This was an early stage in the move away from the biblical narrative, and into a more fragmented view of the Bible, which sees it as a web of interlinked textual units. This fragmentation is evident in the way the layout of the gloss evolved over time, as scribes and stationers gradually moved away from a single central biblical column and into short textual blocks surrounded by commentary.

Glosses vary considerably in length. The need to link glosses of varying sizes to discrete biblical components stretched the skills of scribes and stationers to their limits. The creativity manifested in the production of the

---

27   Catherine Brown, *Contrary things: exegesis, dialectic, and the poetics of didacticism*, Figurae (Stanford, CA: Stanford University Press, 1998), ch. 1: 'Diversa sed non adversa: the poetics of exegesis', pp. 15–35.

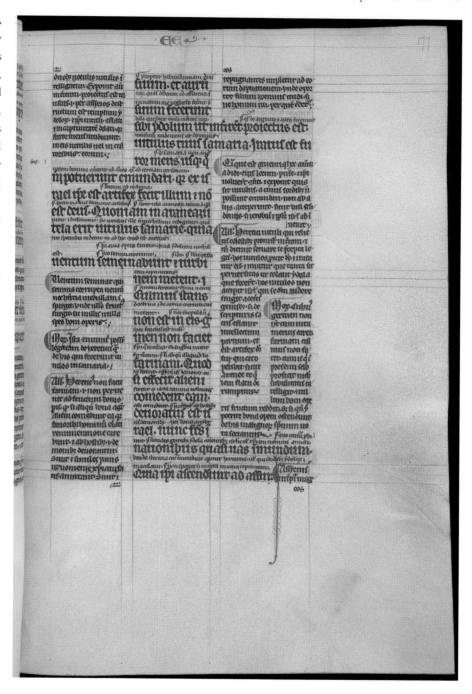

Figure 1.5 A thirteenth-century glossed Bible. This complex layout, linking Bible and interpretation, stretched the skills of scribes and stationers to their limits. CUL MS Ii.2.6 fol. 177r. Reproduced by kind permission of the Syndics of Cambridge University Library.

Glossa ordinaria, however, cannot mask a rigidity that had made it cumbersome and curbed its usefulness. The layout of glossed Bibles had clear limitations. Accommodating glosses into small interlinear or marginal spaces had led scribes to truncate original works and avoid writing words in full. This highly abbreviated style made the notes less comprehensible even for some educated readers. The glosses themselves preserved a moment frozen in the history of exegesis. The works of Church Fathers and Carolingian exegetes, which were the backbone of the *Glossa ordinaria*, were supplemented by later glossators, who commented upon the *Glossa ordinaria*, but whose works were not embedded into it. Reading the gloss thus required a challenging three-dimensional navigation of highly complex texts: linking biblical text, commentaries and commentaries upon those commentaries. Various textual and design solutions were employed,[28] but none was able to fully mitigate the difficulties linked to the rigidity of the gloss.

The growing complexity of the *Glossa ordinaria* limited its audience and usability. It led Lesley Smith to wonder whether the *Glossa ordinaria* became something akin to a medieval coffee-table book.[29] The elaborate structure of the *Glossa ordinaria* was designed to facilitate biblical study and was less useful for accommodating other uses. No one wrote or commissioned the *Glossa ordinaria* out of interest in the biblical text alone. The Bible stood in the background, a frame for the array of exegetical works surrounding it and permeating its central text. The biblical text became the grounds for building exegetical edifices. It was neither irrelevant nor unimportant. But nor was it at the epicentre of scribal practices or patrons' interests. As shown by Smith, a crucial moment in the evolution of the *Glossa ordinaria* was when scribes realised that they should follow the sequence of the gloss, rather than of the Bible, in their construction of the page's layout.

The emphasis on exegesis made the *Glossa ordinaria* a book relevant for readers of specialised interest, and skilled in the study of biblical exegesis. CUL MS Dd.4.25 is a unique glossed Psalter of the mid-twelfth century. Later readers, up to the fifteenth century, had added liturgical texts at the bottom of pages or on additional folios (e.g. sequences on fol. 155v, or the litany on fols 159r–164v). This, however, was unusual, as glossed Bibles were used nearly solely in the study of exegesis. Malleability, on the other hand, was key to the success of the LMB. Unlike the *Glossa ordinaria*, LMBs

28   For example, the double-gloss (as in CUL MS Ff.3.28, second half of the thirteenth century) or the Postil of the Parisian Master Nicholas of Lyra (†1349), which commented on the gloss and whose later manuscript and early print culture further divided the marginal space: Karlfried Froehlich and Margaret T. Gibson (eds), *Biblia latina cum glossa ordinaria: Facsimile reprint of the editio princeps, Adolph Rusch of Strasburg, 1480–81* (Turnhout: Brepols, 1992).

29   Smith, *Glossa ordinaria*, 238.

presented a different solution to the problem of linking Bible and exegesis. Rather than an ever-growing, complicated layout, the stationers embraced simplicity.[30] The minimalism of the LMB simplified the work of scribes and readers alike. Rather than linking Bible and exegesis, the newly integrated system of biblical divisions and references eased the way of readers in consulting exegetical works alongside a Bible. It also opened up an abundance of possible uses, enabling the LMB to become a highly versatile and accommodating tool. This was part of a wider transformation in the nature of scholarly tools. Mary and Richard Rouse have argued that the twelfth-century gloss 'represents efforts to assimilate and organize inherited written authority in a systematic form. In contrast, the tools of the thirteenth century represent efforts to search written authority afresh, to get at, to locate, to retrieve information.'[31]

The margins of many LMBs were wider than needed for binding, and are at odds with the miniaturisation of books. They serve as a testimony to the link between the glossed Bible and the LMB, and as a reminder of the importance of marginal space for scribes and readers. Nowadays, they allow us to trace a variety of uses by their diverse readers. At times they demonstrate a continuity with the glossed Bible. Engagement with biblical exegesis is evident in a variety of scholarly notes, whose proliferation in some manuscripts replicated the appearance of the glossed Bible.[32] Unlike the *Glossa ordinaria*, these notes exhibit a great degree of flexibility. Medieval readers were able to choose between several alternatives; some wrote full glosses, imitating those of the *Glossa ordinaria*. Such works rarely extend beyond a few books of the Bible, indicative of a selective process, if not the fatigue of readers-turned-scribes.

Many readers chose a less laborious route of engaging with biblical exegesis, and incorporated individual comments or indications of their interests, most commonly in the form of a pointing hand, known as a *manicule*, or the inscription of a marginal 'note' (*nota*). These provided an opportunity for medieval and early modern readers to identify elements most relevant for them, and to link the Bible to their individual concerns. For modern scholars such annotations open a window into practices of active reading informed by biblical knowledge. Thus, for example, in a Bible written in England *c*.1230, a reader added an extended note in a hand typical of *c*.1300; accompanying Revelation 13:17, it provides a detailed analysis of the Name of the Beast and

---

30   A similar strategy underpinned the success of Apple designs in the late twentieth and early twenty-first centuries.

31   Mary A. Rouse and Richard H. Rouse, *Authentic witnesses: approaches to medieval texts and manuscripts* (Notre Dame, IN: University of Notre Dame Press, 1991), p. 221.

32   Such as in BL Add. MS 15,253.

its Number, mentioned in that chapter.[33] A reader in Scotland *c.*1400 annotated a Bible written in Oxford a century and a half earlier. Employing the
marginal gloss to Ezekiel 33:6 from the *Glossa ordinaria*, he reflected on ways
of refuting Lollards, thus providing rare evidence for anti-Lollard polemics
north of the Border.[34] Some LMBs boast clean margins and a lavish iconography. Evidencing little use by early patrons and readers, these were possibly
treasured for their appearance rather than their practical value, rendering
them akin to modern collectors' items.[35] Some were used to refute heretics;
others contained legal works and medical treatises, recipes for ink or for
curing blindness.[36] Two of the most common uses of such Bibles, however,
were in preaching and in liturgical services.

Preaching the Late Medieval Bible

Alain of Lille, writing a treatise on the practice and theory of preaching
*c.*1200, likened one's ascent in faith to Jacob's Ladder, whose uppermost
rungs were the study of biblical exegesis and preaching.[37] Preaching was in
fact the continuation of exegesis. This was reflected in university education, where sermons were seen as the culmination of a university degree.
Theologians—from Augustine to Bernard of Clairvaux—wrote their exegesis in the form of sermons, and biblical commentaries were often compiled
for preachers.[38] Preachers found much use for glosses in their sermons, and
Giovanna Murano's deep analysis of an early thirteenth-century glossed Bible

---

33   Aberdeen University Library MS 217 fol. 258r.

34   Eyal Poleg, 'The earliest evidence for anti-Lollard polemics in medieval Scotland', *Innes Review* 64 (2013), 227–34.

35   This idea was raised by Laura Light and awaits further exploration. Some Bibles were kept in lavish aristocratic libraries which befitted such use. Thus, for example, in the late fourteenth century, the library of Thomas of Woodstock contained several Latin and Wycliffite Bibles: (Devine, 'A portable feast', pp. 337–8; Matti Peikola, 'The Sanctorale, Thomas of Woodstock's English Bible, and the orthodox appropriation of Wycliffite tables of lessons', in *Wycliffite Controversies*, ed. Mishtooni Bose and J. Patrick Hornbeck II, Medieval church studies 23 (Turnhout: Brepols, 2011), pp. 153–74.

36   On the variety of texts embedded in LMBs see Light, 'Non-biblical texts in thirteenth-century Bibles'.

37   Alanus de Insulis, 'Summa de arte prædicatoria', in *PL 210:111*; translated as Alan of Lille, *The art of preaching*, trans. Gillian R. Evans, Cistercian studies series 23 (Kalamazoo, MI: Cistercian Publications, 1981), pp. 15–16.

38   Some of the most important works in the field on medieval preaching are still Nicole Bériou, *L'avènement des maîtres de la Parole: la prédication à Paris au XIIIᵉ siècle*, Collection des études augustiniennes 31–32 (Paris: Institut d'études augustiniennes, 1998); H. Leith Spencer, *English preaching in the late Middle Ages* (Oxford: Clarendon Press, 1993); Beverly Mayne Kienzle (ed.), *The sermon*, Typologie des sources du Moyen Age occidental Fasc. 81–3 (Turnhout: Brepols, 2000). A summary is Eyal Poleg, ' "A ladder set up on earth": the Bible in medieval sermons', in *The practice of the Bible in the Middle Ages: production, reception & performance in Western Christianity*, ed. Susan Boynton and Diane J. Reilly (New York: Columbia University Press, 2011), pp. 205–27.

reveals the merging of the two disciplines in a graphic form.[39] Notes aimed at biblical studies, and those facilitating the compilation of sermons, are therefore all but indistinguishable in the margins of biblical manuscripts. Yuichi Akae's analysis of the use of the library in York by a medieval preacher has unearthed both the regulations and the practice of the use of Bibles by late medieval preachers.[40] The role of the LMB in preaching is often merged with its use within biblical exegesis. However, some links between preaching and the LMB could still be discerned.

An important transformation in medieval preaching coincided with the rise of the LMB. A new type of sermon was developed and practised in the nascent universities. Known as the 'New Form of Preaching' or the 'University Sermon', it presented a novel way of engaging with the biblical text. Earlier sermons took an entire biblical episode read during Mass (the *pericope* or *lection*) as their basis, which was then read and gradually elucidated in the course of the sermon. From *c.*1200 preachers often employed only a segment of the pericope, reflecting upon a sentence or even a single word from the Bible. This nucleus—known as the *thema* (plural *themata*)—was then submitted to an elaborate structure of major and minor divisions. The divisions broke down different aspects of the *thema*, employing its etymology, repetition of words, logical conjunctures and so forth. Each division or sub-division was verified by a 'proof', most commonly taken from the Bible, but at times taken from the writings of Church Fathers or the authors of antiquity.

A variety of aids were developed to assist in the task of creating these divisions and conflating the *thema* into a sermon.[41] Preachers were instructed to scrutinise the *thema*, look at its message and wording, exegesis and etymology, as means of developing their ideas and constructing their sermons. The most common addendum to the LMB was a biblical glossary known as the *Interpretations of Hebrew Names* (*Interpretationes nominum Hebraeorum*). This glossary evolved alongside the LMB, and gradually encompassed the entirety of the biblical text, unlike earlier glossaries which addressed only some biblical books (and thus better befitted multi-volume Bibles). The glossary provided

39   Giovanna Murano, 'The Epistles of St. Paul of the Convent of San Domenico (Bologna, Biblioteca Universitaria, MS 1545)', in *Form and function in the Late Medieval Bible*, ed. Eyal Poleg and Laura Light (Leiden: Brill, 2013), pp. 127–46; the link between the *Glossa ordinaria* and preaching was also explored by Gillian R. Evans, 'Gloss or analysis? A crisis of exegetical method in the thirteenth century', in *La Bibbia del xiii secolo. Storia del testo, storia dell'esegesi: Convegno della Società Internazionale per lo studio del Medioevo Latino (SISMEL) Firenze, 1–2 Giugno 2001*, ed. Giuseppe Cremascoli and Francesco Santi, Millennio medievale 49 (Florence: SISMEL, 2004), pp. 93–111.

40   Yuichi Akae, *A mendicant sermon collection from composition to reception: the Novum opus dominicale of John Waldeby, OESA*, Sermo 7 (Turnhout: Brepols, 2015), pp. 89, 93.

41   These are explored by Rouse and Rouse, *Authentic witnesses*, pp. 221–55, arguing for the supremacy of preaching in the development of thirteenth-century scholarly tools.

succinct etymologies for the Hebrew and Aramaic proper nouns mentioned in the Vulgate. Although often based on spurious etymologies of names not extant in the Bible, it became a treasure trove for medieval preachers in expanding biblical episodes and developing their arguments. The success of this often-incomprehensible glossary is linked to medieval preaching, and the way preachers integrated their message into the biblical narrative.[42] It thus provides a direct link between the LMB and the new form of preaching practised in the later Middle Ages.

New means of constructing sermons and the rise of the LMB are indicative of a major transformation in biblical knowledge and access, facilitated by the rise of the single-volume Bible. Texts accompanying (or relying upon) the LMB, as well as the biblical proofs in each sermon, indiscriminately employed elements from all books of the Bible. Dozens, if not hundreds, of biblical segments were deployed within a single sermon. They were taken from across the Bible, often detached from their original context. This practice attracted the criticism of medieval and early modern reformers, as well as that of modern scholars. John Wyclif saw in these sermons evidence of preachers' vainglory, while in 1926 G. R. Owst opined in his seminal study of medieval preaching that

> [t]he sacred page had clearly fallen, in the general decadence of preaching, to the mere level of any hand-book of collected narrations or moralized Properties of Things. Its living historic continuity of thought and action was being ruthlessly ignored. Its various characters and objects were being wrenched from their context, distorted or mutilated into mere passive conveniences for moral dilation, a mere lifeless framework to be set up and arranged, as the preacher pleases, to suit the formal superstructure of his discourse.[43]

Such criticism masks the novelty of this engagement with the Bible. The use of *themata* and proofs encouraged the dissociation of biblical components from their original contexts. The earlier homiletic form was based on the narrative unit of the pericope and its inherent story-like qualities. *Themata*, on the other hand, encouraged using sonic, etymological or exegetical principles, rather than following a biblical story. The reason a preacher was able to do with the biblical text 'as the preacher pleases' owed much to the rise

---

42   Poleg, 'The Interpretations of Hebrew Names in theory and practice'; Akae, *Mendicant sermon collection*, pp. 150–1.

43   Latin Sermons 30 and 31, Johann Loserth (ed.), *Iohannis Wyclif sermones: now first edited from the manuscripts* (London: Trübner & co., 1887–90), iv: 256–62, 262–75; G. R. Owst, *Literature and pulpit in medieval England: a neglected chapter in the history of English letters & of the English people*, 2nd rev. edn (Oxford: Blackwell, 1961), p. 66.

of the LMB. Its efficient retrieval system enabled preachers to move between diverse and seemingly unrelated biblical components. That these Bibles were single-volume books was also part of this transformation. Readers were able to navigate the entire biblical corpus at ease, and exegetical as well as preaching aids soon encompassed the Bible in its entirety. Preachers made use of biblical glossaries, concordances or thematic indices, which spanned the Bible and often relied on the new chapter division (and at times the sub-division as well).[44]

Cross-biblical aids which employed the new chapter- and sub-division assisted preachers in choosing the right *thema* to serve as the core of their sermons. Lists of biblical *themata* according to subject matter, either for refuting heretics or for admonishing audiences about their sins, assisted preachers in constructing their sermons. While the former has been examined by Laura Light,[45] the latter subject is evident, for example, in London, Victoria and Albert Museum, Reid MS 22, whose list of themes includes 'On pride', 'To pilgrims' and 'To merchants' (fol. 367v–368r, 'de superbia', 'ad peregrinos', 'ad mercatores'). In this Bible the list of *themata* is preceded by a table of lections—one of the most common addenda to the LMB—which supplied the biblical readings for each liturgical feast. This list merges two of the most common forms of biblical knowledge and dissemination: preaching and the liturgy.

Praying the Late Medieval Bible

Preaching is intrinsically linked to both exegesis and liturgy, two very different forms of biblical knowledge. The study of biblical exegesis had led medieval scholars to scrutinise the biblical text. Liturgical chants and rituals, on the other hand, gave priests and parishioners the opportunity to re-enact key biblical events, to chant or hear biblical and extra-biblical hymns and lections. Divine worship was integrated into sermons in several ways. Preachers were instructed to embed liturgical echoes into their sermons, which often began and ended with a prayer. Sermons were typically delivered alongside the Mass, hence the biblical reading at the core of the sermon had a strong

44 Akae, *Mendicant sermon collection*. For specific examples see Richard H. Rouse and Mary A. Rouse, 'Verbal Concordance of Scriptures', *Archivum Fratrum Prædicatorum* 44 (1974), 5–30. On aids incorporated into Bibles see Light, 'Non-biblical texts in thirteenth-century Bibles'. Such a view also fitted the scholastic adoption of alphabetical sequence and non-hierarchical view (see Rouse and Rouse, *Authentic witnesses*, pp. 221–55).
45 Laura Light, 'The new thirteenth-century Bible and the challenge of heresy', *Viator: Medieval and Renaissance Studies* 18 (1987), 275–88.

liturgical undertone. The pericope, or lesson, which was chanted during the Proper of the Mass, was then explicated in the subsequent sermon. The pericopes followed a complex liturgical calendar, which varied by region and monastic order. On most days there were two lessons: one taken from the Four Gospels (known as the *Gospel*) and another usually taken from the Epistles, but possibly from any other book of the Bible (the *Epistle*). In monasteries, continuous reading of the Bible took place in the Night Office, comprising an additional cycle of biblical time. In their sermons preachers not only engaged with the biblical text, but also explored the link between the biblical lesson and its liturgical occurrence, and probed the relationship between the biblical episodes and the event from the life of Christ or of a saint which was celebrated on that day. Yet, while liturgy permeated the very core of sermons and the preacher's treatment of the biblical text, preaching rarely influenced the liturgy.

Liturgy was one of the most important mediums through which lay and clerical audiences gained knowledge of the Bible.[46] It differed from preaching and exegesis in its attitude to tradition. Biblical exegetes and preachers saw themselves as 'dwarfs on the shoulders of giants' and willingly went back to the works of Church Fathers such as Jerome, Augustine or Hrabanus Maurus. Yet preachers and exegetes also celebrated the novelty of their work. A preacher repeating a sermon verbatim, or an exegete simply copying the works of his predecessor, would have been found lacking by their audience. Liturgical texts were markedly different. Their authors often masked any innovation so as to emulate the style of earlier chants, and primarily that of the Bible. This is reflected in their differing manuscript settings. Model sermons and glossed bibles (as in Figures 1.3 and 1.4) attempted to identify and reference different components and individual authors. This web of references was presented as weaving together (*texitur*) earlier works.

Liturgy had no such means of differentiation. All texts were given the same authoritative voice, seamlessly merging biblical, early Christian and medieval elements. The conservative nature of the liturgy also underpins the way liturgical texts were retrieved. Liturgical texts were known by their opening few words (the incipit). Numbered chapters became a standard feature of twelfth-century scholastic books, and a prominent means of identifying biblical sections in the LMB; yet these were not used in liturgical manuscripts. Books such as the Missal (containing readings and chants for the celebration of the Mass) or the breviary (for the celebration of the Divine Office, the day-long cycle of worship practised by monks and nuns, as well

---

46   Eyal Poleg, *Approaching the Bible in medieval England*, Manchester medieval studies (Manchester: Manchester University Press, 2013), ch. 1: 'The Bible and liturgy: Palm Sunday processions', pp. 14–58.

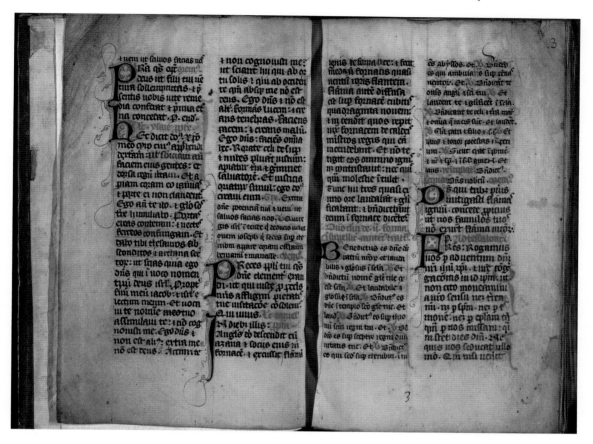

Figure 1.6 The more traditional layout of a fourteenth-century Missal. Liturgical books did not often incorporate novel finding aids and graphic features, common in other late medieval books. Cambridge, Trinity College MS B.10.14 fols 2v–3r. By permission of the Master and Fellows of Trinity College Cambridge.

as friars and canons), retained the older identification system by incipit, and do not contain chapter references. Thus, in Figure 1.6, from a fourteenth-century Missal following the Use of Sarum, the readings are identified only by the biblical books of Isaiah ('Lectio Ysaie prophete'), Daniel ('Lectio danielis propheta [*sic*]') and the (first) Epistle to the Thessalonians ('Ad tessalonicos'). This system is indicative of a pre- or partially literate society, and is more suitable for triggering one's memory than for navigating the text.[47] The two contrasting ways of accessing the biblical text—through incipit or through chapter number—appear in LMBs and can assist in unfolding the ways in which these books were used.

47   I wish to thank Scott Mandelbrote for this suggestion.

The Book of Psalms is the hinge around which innovative and traditional means of navigating Bible and liturgy rotated. The Psalms are uniquely written as poetry, unlike the narrative nature of most other biblical books. While most other biblical books recount biblical history, the Psalms are hymns, written in the first person and directly beseeching God. They became the backbone of the liturgy, chanted day and night by the clergy. In religious houses and churches, the entire Psalter was chanted in weekly or bi-weekly cycles. To both clergy and laity, the Psalms were the best-known book of the Bible. Clerks learned and recalled the Psalms as liturgical texts to be chanted, identifiable by their incipit. The first Psalm was known as *Beatus vir* ('Blessed is the man'), the second *Quare turbabuntur gentes* ('Why have the Gentiles raged') and so forth. Liturgical manuscripts, exegetical works, model sermons, chronicles and literary works all similarly identified the Psalms by their incipit.[48]

The unique nature of the Psalms, and the way they were known and recalled, impacted upon their appearance in the LMB. Several LMBs omit the Psalms altogether, most likely accommodating the many readers who retained that book in their memory. In nearly all other LMBs the layout of the Psalms is different from that of other biblical books. The Psalms appear as liturgical texts, without the above-mentioned innovative features introduced in the LMB. The layout of the Psalms reflected earlier manuscripts, as well as liturgical Psalters:[49] each verse is marked by an alternating red or blue initial, reflecting both the poetry of the Psalms and their chanted liturgical performance. Much like liturgical Psalters, the Book of Psalms has no running titles, and in this too it differs from other parts of the LMB. Large illuminated initials, which are reserved for the opening initial of other biblical books, are used in the Psalms to identify key Psalms, which facilitated the weekly or bi-weekly cycles of monastic Psalmody.[50]

To the modern eye, the most surprising feature of the Psalms' layout is the lack of chapter numbers. As each Psalm is a clear and distinct unit, the Psalms would have been the easiest biblical book to divide into enumerated chapters.[51] Yet, in all but a fraction of LMBs, the Psalms were

---

48   Paul Saenger, 'The impact of the early printed page on the reading of the Bible', in *The Bible as book: the first printed editions*, ed. Paul Saenger and Kimberly Van Kampen (London: British Library in association with The Scriptorium: Center for Christian Antiquities, 1999), pp. 31–51; Poleg, *Approaching the Bible*, pp. 129–38.

49   A useful survey of liturgical Psalms is Elizabeth Solopova, *Latin liturgical Psalters in the Bodleian Library: a select catalogue* (Oxford: Bodleian Library, 2013), especially, pp. x–xviii and Appendices 3, 5–6.

50   Solopova, *Latin liturgical Psalters in the Bodleian Library*, Appendix 4.

51   The only difficulty in such numbering being the discrepancy between Psalm numbering in Hebrew and Greek (Septuagint) manuscripts, the latter maintaining a lengthy tenth Psalm, while the former divides it into two: Psalms 10 and 11. This divide has separated the Psalms in Catholic and Protestant Bibles since the sixteenth century.

left unnumbered. This omission demonstrates how liturgical knowledge of the Psalms, identified by their incipits, had influenced their appearance in the LMB. As demonstrated throughout the following chapters, this way of knowing the Psalms was slow to change and lingered well into the early modern period.

Deep analysis of the manuscript setting of the LMB reveals slow and uncertain transformation. A small group of Bibles diverges from the tendency to preserve the liturgical nature of the Psalms. The *De Brailes Bible* (Oxford, Bodleian Library, Lat. bibl. e.7), for example, was written after 1234 and illuminated by William de Brailes, an illuminator active in Oxford in the second quarter of the thirteenth century.[52] In that Bible the Psalms are numbered in alternating red and blue, akin to any other biblical book. This was done as part of the original design of the book, rather than being a decision undertaken by a single craftsman. In Figures 1.7 and 1.7.1, from Psalm 38/39, fol. 183r, one sees the Psalm number and a large historiated 'D', in which King David is shown guarding his mouth in a literal depiction of the opening verse 'I have set guard to my mouth' ('Posui ori meo custodiam'). A cursive and confident hand noted down in the inner margins 'd'—the initial letter to be historiated—and '[xxx]viii'—the Psalm number to be provided in red (or rubricated). Remnants of the same hand are evident near several initials in the Bible, as in the red and blue minor initials of each verse of the Psalms, painted over by the rubricator. These marks were usually scraped out after use, and their rare survival attests to the means of communication used by craftsmen in creating the book. These marks were made either by the original scribe or by a stationer, who had used these to instruct the rubricator and illuminator in the layout of the book. They demonstrate that the Psalms' numbering was a decision undertaken as part of the book's original design, most probably to accommodate its patron.[53] The inclusion of a Mass for St Dominic in the Bible helps date it (Dominic was canonised in 1234), and suggests that this Bible—small, portable and innovative—was created in Oxford for a Dominican patron.

---

52   Light, 'Thirteenth-century pandects and the liturgy', pp. 202, 211–12 (with additional bibliography).

53   The opposite example is Cambridge, Gonville and Caius MS 350/567, where the craftsmen practised Psalm numbering which was not part of the original design of the book. This medium-sized Bible was written in Oxford by a professional team of scribes and illuminators at about the same time as the *De Brailes Bible*. This Bible, possibly produced for a monk (as suggested by the illumination accompanying the opening of the entire Bible and of the New Testament, unfoliated), presents the Psalms in their liturgical guise. However, Psalms' numbers were integrated as a local initiative, incorporated into the superscriptions for Psalms 22–24. This was most likely done by a new rubricator, as there are minor variations in the writing of 'p' (the gap between the two ascenders and the nature of the backwards slant). This identification, however, is hindered by a highly uniform script, characteristic of a professional group of craftsmen.

Figure 1.7 The layout of Psalm 38/9 in the *De Brailes Bible*. This unique Bible merges the common layout of the Psalms with the less traditional incorporation of chapter numbers. Oxford, Bodleian Library MS Lat. bib. e. 7, fol. 183r. By permission of the Bodleian Library, University of Oxford.

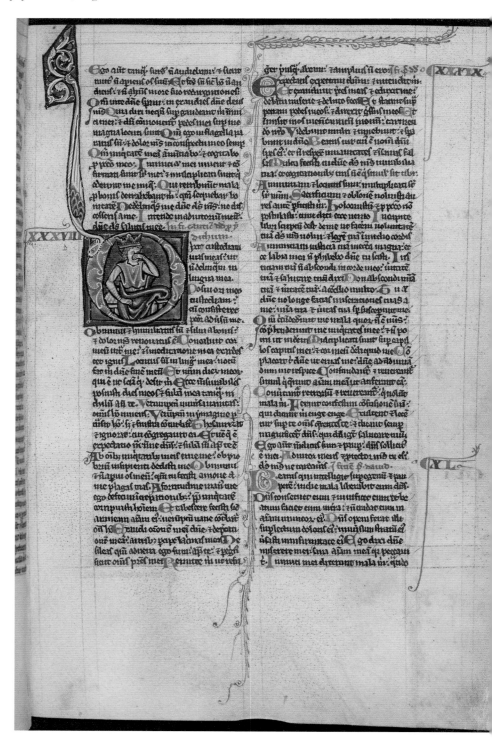

Figure 1.7.1 The layout of Psalm 38/9 in the *De Brailes Bible* (detail). The tiny letters in brown ink are a rare indication of the instructions that guided artists in the creation of books. Oxford, Bodleian Library MS Lat. bib. e. 7, fol. 183r (detail). By permission of The Bodleian Library, University of Oxford.

The numbering of Psalms is a useful prism for the study of the LMB. This feature is not mentioned in the descriptions of manuscripts in catalogues. However, a survey of over a hundred LMBs which were primarily made or used in England reveals a small group of manuscripts with numbered Psalms (see Appendix 1).[54] The analysis of this group reveals idiosyncrasies in presenting the Psalms' numbers, written in margins or preceding the Psalms; breaking off halfway through the Psalter, or continued by later readers. An extreme example is evident in two manuscripts. BL Arundel MS 303, written for a Dominican patron between 1228 and 1234, probably in Oxford,

54   I have surveyed LMBs produced or used in England. This, however, is inevitably a very porous criterion. Scribes and artists travelled across Europe, as did university students and members of the mendicant orders. LMBs produced in northern France and southern England are notoriously difficult to tell apart. I have therefore included in the survey manuscripts with uncertain provenance. For a full list of surveyed manuscripts see Poleg, *Approaching the Bible*, pp. 213–21.

and the 'William of Devon Bible' (BL Royal MS 1.D.i), probably written in Oxford in the third quarter of the thirteenth century and affiliated with the mendicant orders, present the Psalms as any other biblical book. The production team noted the number for each Psalm, omitted the liturgical verse identification and provided a running title identifying the alleged author (DA|VID or PSAL|TER). Most other manuscripts in this group provide the Psalm number alongside its more common liturgical layout. Other solutions were integrated into a handful of Bibles. In BL Burney MS 11, a table in a fifteenth-century hand links each Psalm's incipit with its ordinal number.[55] This was not uniquely English. Other Bibles, such as Philadelphia, University of Pennsylvania MS Codex 236 (Paris, *c*.1220–40), contain a Psalter numbered by the original production team; BL Add. MS 31,830 (Dominican, Naples, *c*.1253) contains Psalm numbers in ink made either by the original scribe or by a very contemporary reader (note the very minor variation in the 'x'). The producers of Cambridge, Fitzwilliam Museum, McClean MS 12, possibly of a Parisian Dominican house, embraced another solution, with the rubricator noting the Psalm number for every tenth Psalm.

Bibles incorporating Psalm numbers are the exception among LMBs. These Bibles, however, often share other innovative features such as Mass-texts and numbered Canticles (pp. 33–6 and thus constitute a unique class of LMBs. The provenance of this group of Bibles is surprisingly uniform. The vast majority of Bibles in this group are linked to the mendicant orders, primarily to the Dominicans and to Oxford. This is hardly surprising. The Dominicans were at the forefront of academic and liturgical creativity in the thirteenth century.[56] Their engagement with the Psalter resulted in a break with traditional liturgy, and a tendency to incorporate glossed or parallel Psalters (that is, Psalters with the differing translations of Jerome side by side) in their books. They offered a counter-intuitive layout of the Psalter, in an attempt to re-shape biblical knowledge. Hugh of St Victor (†1142) advocated learning the Psalms by number rather than by incipit. At the time, auditory memory (typical of liturgical chant) was deemed inferior to the visual. In

55   Fols 2r–v. This prefigures the presence of such tables in early modern English Bibles.

56   Malcolm B. Parkes, 'The compilation of the Dominican lectionary', in *Literarische Formen des Mittelalters: Florilegien, Kompilationen, Kollektionen*, ed. Kaspar Elm, Wolfenbütteler Mittelalter-Studien 15 (Wiesbaden: Harrassowitz, 2000; reprint, Malcolm B. Parkes, *Pages from the past: medieval writing skills and manuscript books*, ed. P. R. Robinson and Rivkah Zim (Farnham: Ashgate Variorum, 2012), §XIII), pp. 91–106; Eleanor Giraud, 'The Dominican *Scriptorium* at Saint-Jacques, and its production of liturgical exemplars', in *Scriptorium: Wesen, Funktion, Eigenheiten – CIPL XVIII. Kolloquium, St Gallen 11–14. September 2013*, ed. Andreas Nievergelt *et al.* (Munich: Bayerische Akademie der Wissenschaften, 2015), pp. 247–58; Eleanor Giraud, '"Totum officium bene correctum habeatur in domo": uniformity in the Dominican liturgy', in *Making and breaking the rules: discussions, implementation and consequences of Dominican legislation*, ed. Cornelia Linde (Oxford: Oxford University Press, 2018), pp. 153–72. On the Oxford Dominican engagement with the Hebrew and Greek Psalter see Saenger, 'British Isles', 80.

order to introduce new mnemonics, Hugh of St Victor suggested allocating a number to each Psalm. These were then to be placed on a mental grid, apart from their role in the liturgy, their musical or oral qualities.[57] These Dominican Bibles show a new way of engaging with the Psalms. The two conflicting ways of viewing the Psalter are evident in CUL MS Hh.1.3 (a Franciscan LMB, written in England in the third quarter of the thirteenth century). Its margins display a wealth of liturgical and exegetical annotations, and the Psalms have been numbered up to Psalm 12 (fol. 160r); another hand noted down antiphons to accompany each Psalm, and a third—medieval glosses. This Bible supports Laura Light's argument that '[s]ome mendicants studied at the university, some of them taught, and many of them preached— and for all these occupations, their Bibles could be useful [...], but all friars prayed'.[58] The margins of the Psalter became a meeting point for several forms of engagement with the biblical text.

Much like the *De Brailes Bible* and CUL Hh.1.3, several Bibles with numbered Psalms present another novel means of engaging with the liturgy: the inclusion of a Missal or Mass-texts.[59] These additional texts, inserted near the Book of Psalms or at the end of the volume, supply the Canon of the Mass and/or select Masses. They did not replace the traditional Missal, the book containing readings and chants for the celebration of the Mass, but provided a priest with the most recurring parts of the Mass, likely to support saying private Masses. Their parchment is stained from use. The smudge on the Crucifixion page facing the key prayer of the *Te Deum* in Huntington Library, MS HM 26061, fol. 178v, resulted from continuous rubbing by a priest while kissing and flattening the page in the course of the Mass.[60] These

---

57   Hugh of St. Victor, 'The three best memory aids for learning history', in *The medieval craft of memory: an anthology of texts and pictures*, ed. Mary Carruthers and Jan M. Ziolkowski (Philadelphia: University of Pennsylvania Press, 2002), pp. 32–40; William M. Green, 'Hugo of St. Victor: De tribus maximis circumstantiis gestorum', *Speculum* 18:4 (1943), 484–93. For the supremacy of visual memory see Mary Carruthers, *The book of memory: a study of memory in medieval culture*, Cambridge studies in medieval literature 10 (Cambridge: Cambridge University Press, 2008), pp. 100–6, with a discussion of the Psalms.

58   Laura Light, 'What was a Bible for? Liturgical texts in thirteenth-century Franciscan and Dominican Bibles', *Lusitania Sacra* 34 (2016), 165–82 at 173.

59   Light, 'Thirteenth-century pandects and the liturgy'. To Laura Light's list of manuscripts we can add CUL MS Ff.6.47, which has Mass-texts prefacing the Psalms (Nativity, St Stephen, St John). Immediately following the Book of Job, only a single side remains of the Mass-texts (fol. 16v). However, a codicological analysis reveals that the following leaves are missing, as is the majority of the Psalter. It is highly likely, therefore, that the Mass-texts extended beyond the single side. The readings, as well as the incorporation of Sts Stephen and John, link this Bible to the Franciscan order (as in https://digi.vatlib.it/view/MSS_ Arch.Cap.S.Pietro.E.1, accessed 24 August 2018). I thank Eleanor Giraud for suggesting this provenance. Lambeth Palace MS 534 (with the Dominicans of Arklow in the fifteenth century) contains short liturgical elements following the Psalms (fols 234r–v, by one of the original scribes), identifying chants sung in certain liturgical times.

60   http://dpg.lib.berkeley.edu/webdb/dsheh/heh_brf?Description=&CallNumber=HM+26061, accessed 29 November 2019.

Bibles were heavily used. Readers added, annotated and adapted them to new liturgical settings. The Mass-texts in CUL Hh.1.3 were begun by the original production team on fols 352v–354r with prefaces for a variety of liturgical occasions starting with the Nativity. A series of subsequent readers (fols 373v–404v, starting with the First Sunday in Advent) continued this work, adding and modifying chants. These readers, much like the users of Bible-Missals at large, belonged to a very specific section of Church and society. *All English pocket Bible-Missals explored by Light, and whose provenance could be ascertained, are linked to the Franciscans and Dominicans.* The unique combination of Bible and Missal suited their itinerant lifestyle. The small size made their use within the public liturgy unlikely. They were, however, ideal for saying private Masses away from one's convent.

The combination of Bible and Missal was not the amalgamation of two different books, but rather a way of merging two books that relied on one another. A large part of any Missal is the biblical lessons (*lections*) of the Gospels and Epistles, read during the Mass. When Mass-texts were integrated into an LMB, there was little reason for supplying them in full, as scribes and stationers gradually discovered. This was a novelty for the creators and readers of these Bibles. In BL Harley MS 2813, the scribe was inconsistent in providing the full lessons, leading Light to remark that '[t]he references to the biblical readings in this Missal usually include the biblical book, the chapter (identified by an Arabic numeral) and the opening words of the reading, although some readings, oddly, appear to be copied in full within the Missal'.[61] Cambridge, St John's MS N.1, is a unique witness to the liturgy of the small Gilbertine monastic order. Unlike its mendicant counterparts, this is a medium-size volume, whose Psalms are unnumbered. Yet its Mass-texts were written at the end of the volume by the original production team.[62] Biblical texts were identified, as is the custom in liturgical manuscripts, by their incipit, with the chapter numbers not being part of the original design. This was quickly augmented. A thirteenth-century reader (or possibly even the original scribe)[63] had added the chapter numbers in the margins. Thus, as can be seen in Figure 1.8, to the Epistle reading for the feast of Epiphany, starting 'Surge illuminare Iherusalem' and rubricated 'Epistola Ysaie prophete', the reader added Lx°, the modern chapter division (Is 60:1). The new method of chapter identification enabled a better retrieval of the biblical reading and was gradually accepted and integrated into the realm of liturgical texts in Bibles.

61   Light, 'Thirteenth-century pandects and the liturgy', 203.
62   Light, 'Thirteenth-century pandects and the liturgy', 201–2, 211.
63   I thank Tessa Webber for this suggestion.

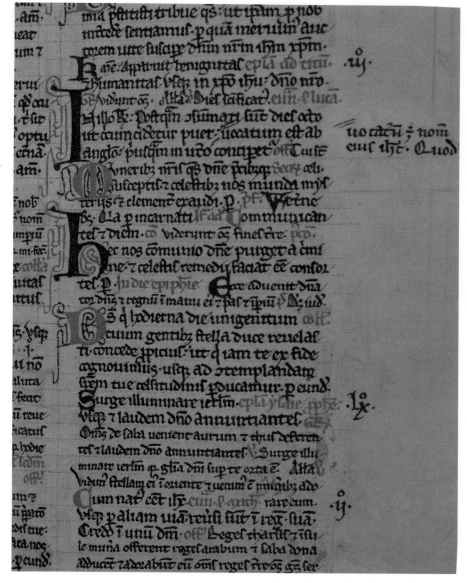

Figure 1.8 Mass texts. Chapter numbers were not part of the original design, but quickly integrated into the page. Cambridge, St John's College MS N1, unfoliated. By permission of the Master and Fellows of St John's College, Cambridge.

BL Harley MS 1748 presents another step in the evolution of Bible and liturgy. The original rubricator of this mid-thirteenth-century English Bible provided it with chapter and sub-division references as part of the rubrics of the Missal. The production process, however, did not fully support this innovative feature. At times the scribe did not leave enough space for these references, and the rubricator resorted to noting them above the line; the rubricator moved between Roman and Arabic numerals (e.g. fol. 172r). These idiosyncrasies, much like those of Harley MS 2813, suggest that scribes and rubricators were not following a template, but rather showed initiative in abbreviating and referencing the readings copied from a separate—and un-referenced—Missal. In some manuscripts the production team perfected the system of reference. Precise identification of the readings appears in CUL Hh.1.3, where the scribe noted both incipit and explicit, thus better demarcating the biblical lessons. The Gospel for the Second Sunday in Advent reads: 'According to Mt xi.a. [11:2–10] At that time. *when John had heard in prison*. Ending *before thee*' ('Secundum Mt xi.a. In ille T[empore]. Cum audisset Iohannes in vinculis. Fi[ne] ante te', fol. 373v). The scribes of McClean MS 16 took the link between Bible and addenda one step further. Much like other Bible-Missals, they had identified the lesson in the Missal through book, chapter and sub-division (made by the original rubricator). They then took to the biblical books themselves, where they had also provided an identification of the liturgical reading in the margins of the relevant section of the biblical text. Thus, for example, the reading for the Monday after Advent, 'Then there came two women that were harlots | ending to do judgment' ('venerunt due mulieres meretrices | finis ad faciendum iudicium III Rg iii e', fol. 530rb), is accompanied within the Bible itself: on fol. 136v, two marginal letters delineate the reading of 3 Rg 3:16–28 with the letters '.p.' for *principium* (*beginning*) and '.f.' for *finis* (*end*).[64] In this unique manuscript the retrieval system reached its fullest efficiency. Readers were able to follow and accurately retrieve the Mass-reading from the biblical text, with the cumbersome and less accurate biblical sub-divisions indicating a general area in which to look for the start- and end-markers of the lessons.

The gradual implementation of these more accurate retrieval systems is evident across the small group of Bibles with Mass-texts. It is also evident in subtle modifications made to a much wider group of Bibles, and to a more common addendum to the LMB—the table of lections. These tables identify the biblical readings of Gospel and Epistle lessons. These list liturgical occasions, each accompanied by the relevant lessons from the Gospels and the Epistles. They were common in a variety of Bibles, and were useful for liturgical performance, enabling priests to identify the correct chant, as well as for personal devotion and the preparation of sermons (the latter use made clear in positioning such tables near lists of themes, as in the above-mentioned example of Reid MS 22). In these tables, readings were generally identified by book and chapter reference, as well as by the more traditional incipit. Much like in the Bible-Missals, this retrieval system underwent further modifications to improve identification and ease consultation, evidencing

---

64   A similar system appears in BnF MS lat. 163. I thank Laura Light for bringing this to my attention.

the gradual reception of the LMBs' new textual divisions. At times references were accompanied by chapter sub-divisions. In some manuscripts the *explicit* was also provided to assist in identifying the end of a reading. This was evidently new ground. Some discrepancies within the production team appear in CUL MS Ee.1.16 (fols 349r–v). There, the original scribe provided space for writing the book, chapter and incipit, as well as the explicit. The latter, however, was not filled by subsequent scribes and stationers, who had kept to more traditional means of identifying the pericope by division and incipit alone.

These new methods for navigating the biblical text rarely appear in liturgical manuscripts. Missals and lectionaries continued to identify biblical readings solely based on their incipit within a given biblical book, with no reference to chapter and sub-division. This continued to the end of the Middle Ages, and even after the introduction of print. An important exception is a Dominican book, BL Additional MS 23,935. This portable book was made *c*.1260 for Humbert of Romans, Master General of the Dominican Order.[65] It is an all-encompassing liturgical book, including part of the Missal and collects, antiphons, saints' lives and a lectionary. In the lectionary (fols 141r–248v) the liturgical readings are provided in full, identified by their incipit. A contemporary hand, possibly that of the Master General himself, added references to chapter and sub-division, linking the new Dominican liturgy to new ways of navigating the biblical text.

Numbered Psalms, Mass-texts and references to biblical lections all introduced new ways of linking Bible and liturgy. Some Bibles, primarily of mendicant provenance and belonging to the new sub-group, also share another novel feature, hitherto unnoticed by scholars. An early reader of the *De Brailes Bible* noted at the end of the Psalter a list of the Canticles in a competent and slightly angular Gothic hand of *c*.1300. These Canticles are a group of biblical hymns, short poems from the Old and New Testaments. They were performed regularly in the liturgy, with the six ferial Canticles chanted at the Hour of Lauds, each on an ordinary day of the week. They were an integral part of liturgical Psalters, as well as of other liturgical books.[66] However, unlike in liturgical books, the list in the *De Brailes Bible* notes the biblical reference according to chapter and sub-division, alongside the Canticles' incipit, their habitual means of identification (fol. 204v):

---

65   Parkes, 'The compilation of the Dominican lectionary'; Simon Tugwell (ed.), *Humberti de Romanis Legendae Sancti Dominici: necnon materia praedicabilis pro festis sancti Dominici et testimonia*, Corpus hagiographicum Sancti Dominici 30 (Rome: Institutum historicum Ordinis fratrum praedicatorum, 2008).
66   Solopova, *Latin liturgical Psalters*, Appendix 7.

Ysa. xii.a. Confitebor (Isaiah 12.a [12:1–6] *I will give thanks*)

Ysa. xxxviii.c. Ego dixi (Isaiah 38.c [38:10–20] *I said*)

i Reg. ii.a. Exultavit (1 Regum 2.a [2:1–10] *Rejoiced*)

Exo. xv.a. Cantemus (Exodus 15.a [15:1–19] *Let us sing*)

Abacuc iii.a. Domine audivi (Habakkuk 3.a [3:2–19] *O Lord, I have heard*)

Deut. xxxii.a. Audite celi (Deuteronomy 32.a [32:1-43] *Hear, O ye heavens*)

This was a new way of engaging with the liturgy. Tables of lections were of great use for preachers, and Psalms were textual units easy to number. Liturgical chants, on the other hand, were known exclusively by their incipit. Apart from the Dominican exemplar already mentioned, no type of liturgical manuscript of the thirteenth or fourteenth century employs—to the best of my knowledge—chapter divisions for the identification of liturgical chant.

The system of reference for the Canticles evolved gradually. In a Bible written in Oxford *c.*1250, and employed in Scotland by 1400, a later hand had identified the Canticles by book and chapter, as well as by their page (e.g. '1st Page Prophet Isaiah chapter 12 *Confitebor*' 'Pagina i^m Ysaie prophete capitulo xii° confitebor').[67] This referencing system was new to the reader, as it was altered in subsequent Canticles from Roman to Arabic numerals. The process of change is also evident in Cambridge St John's College MS I.28. Like other Bibles produced in that decade, this book of *c.*1230 attests to the early evolution of the LMB, lacking running title and with chapter divisions appearing in the margins rather than within the textual column. The Canticles were integrated into the original design of the book, written (as is common in liturgical Psalters) in full after the Psalms with alternating red and blue initials, without any chapter or book reference. A hand of *c.*1300 added to this Bible a list of Canticles, with book and chapter number in Arabic numerals (see Figure 1.9).

A few other LMBs contain lists of Canticles (see Appendix 1). These have rarely been noted by cataloguers, so more examples are sure to appear. They are typically written at the end of the Psalms in a thirteenth- or fourteenth-century hand. Out of the fourteen Bibles I have identified with lists of Canticles, six contain a Missal or Mass-texts, and eleven have numbered Psalms. This suggests that these innovations should not be seen in isolation, but as part of new ways of engaging with the liturgy. Whenever provenance is known, affiliation with the mendicant orders is evident. Chicago, Newberry Library MS 19 is a small Bible, produced in Paris *c.*1250 for an English Franciscan, with a list of Canticles added in an early hand (at

---

67   The Bible is part of the library of Traquair House, Peeblesshire, and is unfoliated. For more information on the Bible see Poleg, 'Earliest evidence'. I thank Catherine Maxwell Stuart, 21st Lady of Traquair, for allowing me to inspect the manuscript.

Figure 1.9 Biblical Canticles. The list of canticles at the bottom of the page is a unique merging of two distinct spheres – liturgy and scholasticism. Cambridge, St John's College MS I.28, unfoliated. By permission of the Master and Fellows of St John's College, Cambridge.

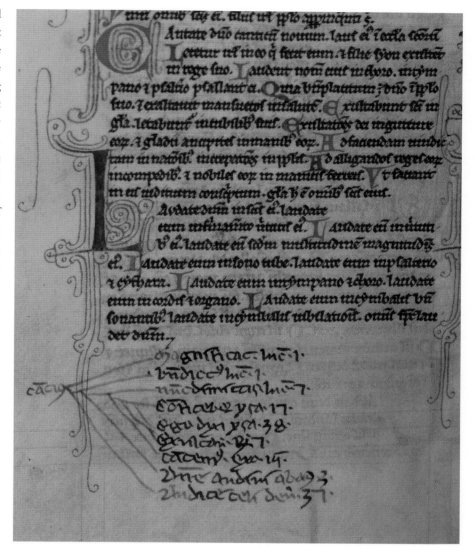

the end, following the table of lections).[68] A similar list exists in Edinburgh University Library MS 1 (fol. 203r), which was owned by the Dominicans of Carlisle in the fourteenth century. In BL Add. MS 35,085, a Dominican Bible containing numbered Psalms, the list of Canticles was written as part of the original design, employing red, blue and black ink. The Canticles are linked to their liturgical occurrence, with both the day and reference written

68   This is suggested by the attribution of the atelier responsible for the illuminations, combined with references to Francis and St Edmund in the table of lections (Paul Saenger, *A catalogue of the pre-1500 Western manuscript books at the Newberry Library* (Chicago: University of Chicago Press, 1989), pp. 35–6). I thank Paul Saenger for bringing this manuscript to my attention.

in alternating red and blue (e.g. 'Fferia ii canticum [that is *Monday Canticle*] Confitebor tibi Domine Ysa. xii.a'). The lists are far from uniform, as references and sub-divisions fluctuate from one Bible to the other. This suggests that these Bibles were not inspired by a sole exemplar, but all aimed towards a certain practical ideal type.

The layout of the Canticle list in St John's I.28 (see Figure 1.9, similar to the layout in Auct. D.4.9, McClean 16 and Pembroke 303) is worthy of special attention. The modest diagonal lines linking the title of 'Canticles' (*Cantica*) with the various Canticles merge two distinct realms. In medieval manuscripts this layout is common in the margins of scholarly works, preaching manuals and sermon collections (as in Figure 1.4). It embodies the late medieval aesthetics of the *divisio*, which underpinned the classification of exegetical, legal and medical knowledge. It is typical of the late medieval sermon, whose major and minor divisions were often depicted visually in similar ways. Such *divisiones* were often noted in the margins of biblical manuscripts, but reserved solely for preaching or exegesis. Ayelet Even-Ezra, who is the first to study them systematically, has concluded that these lines 'should be understood as an expression of a broader mode of thought that is typical of the culture of the medieval schoolmen: their perception of texts as non-sequential, modular, spatial entities rather than as linear running narratives' and that '[t]he use of these schemata betrays understanding of texts as modular and hierarchical structures, rather than linear stories or arguments'.[69] Liturgy, with its linear chant, was far removed from this aesthetics, yet the readers and scribes of this small group of primarily mendicant Bibles had eroded the boundaries between the liturgy and scholasticism. The link between preaching, exegesis and liturgy is made clear in the margins of McClean MS 16 (fol. 323v). There the list of Canticles is followed by a unique allegorical interpretation that linked each of them to a cardinal sin ('These morals: Pride, Wrath …' 'Hec moralia. Superbia, ira …'). This mindset is typical of preaching and exegesis, where each element could be interpreted in the light of the other; here it is made to work for the liturgy too.

A closer look at the innovative group of LMBs reveals highly educated and innovative readers, who combined liturgy, preaching and exegesis. The Mendicants were at the forefront of learning, but they were also active preachers, engaged in the care of souls; they celebrated Mass and took part in the daily Office. All these uses depended on the Bible and left traces on its pages. In Huntington MS HM 26061, alongside an actively used Missal, there

---

69   Ayelet Even-Ezra, 'Schemata as maps and editing tools in 13th century scholasticism', *Manuscripta* 61 (2017), 21–71; Ayelet Even-Ezra, 'Visualizing narrative structure in the medieval university: *Divisio textus* revisited', *Traditio* 72 (2017), 341–76 at 364, 369–70; Ayelet Even-Ezra, *Lines of thought* (forthcoming).

are signs of intricate and academic use: indexing symbols typical of the those employed by Robert Grosseteste (Chancellor of the University of Oxford and Bishop of Lincoln, †1253), while Arabic numerals link the Book of Job to Gregory the Great's *Moralia*.[70] McClean MS 16 contains, alongside a Missal with a list of Canticles and indications of lessons, a variety of exegetical notes with a clear interest in biblical etymology, a list of themes for sermons and a verbal concordance.

The *De Brailes Bible* lends itself to this kind of book archaeology. Alongside the variety of liturgical elements already discussed, one finds evidence of active academic engagement in the form of pointing hands (or *manicules*), *divisiones* and biblical cross-references. Its annotations move us away from a simple dichotomy of innovation and conservatism. Alongside novel means of engaging with the liturgy, its readers employed two more navigational systems, which facilitated liturgical performance in earlier times. A later hand, typical of the fourteenth century, added an alphabetical sub-division to accompany the biblical text, noting, for example, the letters A–H in the margins of the Book of Exodus. These letters do not correspond to the chapter division. Rather, they span larger units, as, for example, roughly the first three chapters of Exodus. These sub-divisions would have therefore been useless in dividing a chapter into equal length portions. Rather, they are a remnant from a time before the introduction of the modern chapter division. In this system the A–H letters are accompanied by the letters P, S, T—indication of 'First' (*Primus*), 'Second' (*Secundus*) and 'Third' (*Tertius*)—which assist in further dividing parts of the Bible. This is accompanied by annotations which direct use during meals in the refectory (*in refectorio*).[71]

This earlier system was designed to facilitate a continuous reading of the Bible. Whereas segments of the Gospel and Epistles were read during Mass, in the Night Office monks and friars heard the Bible in its entirety. Such marks, at times affiliated with the Carthusians, told readers when to break off the lesson in the Night Office and continue it during meals in the monks' refectory. They also facilitated the reading of the Bible in summer and winter, when Night Offices vary in length, or in different liturgical years.[72] Among

---

70   C. W. Dutschke and with the assistance of R. H. Rouse *et al.*, *Guide to medieval and Renaissance manuscripts in the Huntington Library* (San Marino, CA: Huntington Library, 1989, pp. 649–54); R. W. Hunt, 'Manuscripts containing the indexing symbols of Robert Grosseteste', *Bodleian Library Record* 4 (1952–53), 241–55.

71   These typically appear after the first textual portion of a biblical book (e.g. Gn 2:15 on fol. 5v, or Lv 4:14 on fol. 35v, where the same hand marked the beginning of the verse).

72   Teresa Webber, *Public reading and its books: monastic ideals and practice in England c. 1000–c. 1300* (forthcoming). An explanation for the system appears in the margins of the Book of Ezekiel in a large LMB: CUL MS Ee.2.23 fol. 255r (see Poleg, *Approaching the Bible*, p. 129). The association with the Carthusians is presented in Paul Needham, 'The changing shape of the Vulgate Bible in fifteenth-century printing shops', in *The Bible as book: the first printed editions*, ed. Paul Henry Saenger and Kimberly Van Kampen (London:

the pages of the *De Brailes Bible* they reveal how old and new, tradition and reform, came together. At large, the *mise-en-page* and array of annotations demonstrate the pliability of the LMB, employed in the performance of the liturgy, the compilation of sermons and the study of the *Sacra Pagina*. Unlike the *Glossa ordinaria*, the LMB became all things to a small group of highly innovative readers.

Conclusion

In this chapter we have seen the ways in which the LMB began a process of transforming reading practices and ways of engaging with the Bible. The Mendicants, the biblical avant-garde of the mid-thirteenth century, experimented with new ways of thinking about the liturgy, and linked modes of praying, preaching and studying in their use of the LMB. This conclusion provides a good opportunity to put these transformations in perspective. Beyond the small group of mendicant Bibles, the number of surviving LMBs at large allows us to rank them among the most popular books of the later Middle Ages. Yet this does not mean an equal distribution across society. Marks of ownership and use, evidence from wills, catalogues and inventories reveal that LMBs were commissioned for, and originally used by, the higher echelons of Church and society.[73] Wills and testaments in England before 1409 record thirty-six privately owned Latin Bibles: six owned by royalty; two by the aristocracy; and one by a London embroiderer. The remaining twenty-seven Bibles were owned by chaplains, monks, friars, bishops and university masters. This strongly suggests that in late medieval England Latin Bibles rarely existed beyond the realm of universities, cathedrals, monasteries and friaries, in whose library records they appear time and again. This accords with the nature of the LMB itself, as the tools incorporated by scribes and stationers anticipated highly professional readership, which could mentally divide chapter, navigate a complex tome or employ innovative tables of lections to link biblical text and liturgical occurrence.

The techniques developed in the schools and universities were not shared across late medieval English society. Tools that we now take for granted, such as tables, alphabetical lists, or chapter and sub-divisions, were foreign to many.[74] Even in the early fifteenth century, the scribes and stationers who

---

British Library in association with The Scriptorium: Center for Christian Antiquities, 1999), pp. 53–70 at 64 (without further reference).

73   See note 9 above, as well as Susan H. Cavanaugh, 'A study of books privately owned in England: 1300–1450' (Ph.D., University of Pennsylvania, 1980).

74   On the development of these tools, see Rouse and Rouse, *Authentic witnesses*, pp. 221–55.

produced Wycliffite Bibles (the topic of the following chapter) deemed it useful to explain how a table of lections, with its chapter and sub-divisions, was to be used. The LMB's novel layout was developed with preaching and exegesis in mind. As this chapter has shown, a small group of innovative and mostly mendicant Bibles attests to attempts at merging the new layout with a more traditional field—the liturgy. These attempts remained restricted to this small group of manuscripts, and were not embraced by the majority of medieval stationers and readers. Nevertheless, the way in which the single-volume Bible became the new standard, and in which biblical components were known and recalled, began a long process of transformation, which has altered biblical knowledge and harmonised elements within the Bible. As explored throughout this book, this process moved beyond the confines of universities and trained professionals to embrace female religious and the laity in the following centuries, reaching its full maturity centuries later, with the proliferation of Bibles facilitated by moveable-type print.

The LMB was also part of another prolonged transformation of biblical use and access. For a modern reader the medieval evidence seems foreign. Accustomed to the large tomes of parish Bibles, it is hard to realise that these simply did not exist in the Middle Ages. Surviving books and visitation records reveal that only a fraction of parishes had a Bible (about 1 per cent from churches in the dioceses of Ely, Exeter, Salisbury, London and Norwich), and that it has been mostly redundant in a parish setting.[75] The Bible was a long and expensive book, which had little use in parish liturgy. The lessons necessary for Mass were provided by Missals and lectionaries, while separate Psalters provided the backbone of divine worship. This reality was reflected in synodal legislation, which clearly stated the books necessary for parish churches: lectionary, antiphonary, gradual, Psalter, troper, ordinal and a Missal. Visitation records demonstrate that parish churches on the whole abided by these requirements with a profusion of liturgical books, and very few Bibles.

The mass production of LMBs in the mid-thirteenth century, combined with a decline in population following the Black Death, led to the proliferation of LMBs in fifteenth-century England. Some of these made their way beyond the confines of friaries, colleges, monasteries and cathedrals, and ended up in parish churches.[76] London, Guildhall Library deposited MS 4158A was given

75   For summary see Poleg, *Approaching the Bible*, pp. 66–9.

76   For fifteenth-century evidence for parish ownership see, for example, Pamela R. Robinson, 'A "prik of concience cheyned": the parish library of St Margaret's, New Fish Street, London, 1472', in *The medieval book and a modern collecto: essays in honour of Toshiyuki Takamiya*, ed. Takami Matsuda, Richard A. Linenthal and John Scahill (Woodbridge: D. S. Brewer, 2004), pp. 209–21; Michael Foster, 'John Hurte (d. 1476): A Nottingham Priest and his books', *Nottingham Medieval Studies* 53 (2009), 109–19.

by two chaplains to the parish church of St Peter-upon-Cornhill, London.[77] London, Lambeth Palace MS 1362, a thirteenth-century pocket Bible given to the parish church of St John the Baptist (Bredgar, Kent) by Sir John Mone (†1474, described as 'sometime vicar of Bredgar'), shows a gradual move through lay hands.[78] York Minster MS XVI.D.13 was written in England *c*.1250. It was annotated by subsequent readers, who employed it for academic study, as evident in a variety of *manicules*, gloss to Job in a thirteenth-century hand, summary notes in a cursive fourteenth-century hand and *distinctiones*. A note on fol. 325v reveals that in 1510 it was given to the church of St Martin, Coney St., in York by William Richardson, later vicar-choral of York Minster.[79] This was part of a thin stream of Bibles given to parishes. The following chapters will reveal how it was widened with the vernacular trans-lation of the Bible, to become a steady flow with the Great Bible of Henry VIII (the topic of Chapter 4) and the rise of the parish Bible in England.

77   These identifications follow N. R. Ker, *Medieval libraries of Great Britain: a list of surviving books*, 2nd edn, Guides and handbooks / Royal Historical Society 3 (London: Offices of the Royal Historical Society, 1964), pp. 221, 322. They were also noted by Christopher De Hamel, *The book: a history of the Bible* (London: Phaidon, 2001), p. 139.

78   An elaborate note in a late fifteenth-century hand explicates on Sir John's request (fol. iv.v). The note is transcribed in N. R. Ker, *Medieval manuscripts in British libraries. [vol.] 1: London* (Oxford: Clarendon Press, 1969), p. 95.

79   Bodl. MS Auct. D.5.19, an English LMB, appears to have gone in the other way, as in 1462 it was purchased by a fellow of Whittington College, London, from the priest of the adjacent parish church of St James Garlickhithe (Devine, 'A portable feast', p. 339).

2

Wycliffite Bibles and the
Limits of Orthodoxy

Evidence for the compilation, ownership and use of Wycliffite Bibles is scant and confusing. With over 250 surviving manuscripts, more Wycliffite Bibles survive than almost any other Middle English text. This first translation of the entire Bible into English has been ascribed to the followers of the Oxford theologian John Wyclif (†1384), whose views incurred the wrath of the English Church, and whose followers—known as Wycliffites or Lollards—were persecuted as heretics.[1] Access to the new Bible was restricted in Church legislation. In 1407 and 1409, Archbishop Arundel proscribed unlicensed use of the new translation, and possession of such Bibles by Lollards was often noted in heresy trials.[2] Church reformers in the sixteenth century saw Wyclif as the Morning Star of the Reformation, his Bible as a precursor to their own English translations and drew a direct line between Church reforms in the fourteenth and the sixteenth centuries.[3]

Wyclif is not mentioned once in the Bible that bears his name. Modern scholars ascribe the translation of the Bible to an Oxford circle of Wyclif's followers, yet, apart from the books themselves, there seems to be little record for the translation project itself.[4] Nor is the translation overtly anti-clerical. Cardinal Gasquet in the late nineteenth century, and Henry Ansgar Kelly who revived his argument in 2016, have both challenged this scholarly

---

1   For a summary of research and additional bibliography see J. Patrick Hornbeck, Mishtooni Bose and Fiona Somerset (eds), *A companion to Lollardy*, Brill's companions to the Christian tradition 67 (Leiden: Brill, 2016).

2   Most recently: Maureen Jurkowski, 'The selective censorship of the Wycliffite Bible', in *The Wycliffite Bible: origin, history and interpretation*, ed. Elizabeth Solopova, Medieval and Renaissance authors and texts 16 (Leiden: Brill, 2016), pp. 371–88.

3   Mark Rankin, 'Reading the Wycliffite Bible in Reformation England', in *The Wycliffite Bible: origin, history and interpretation*, ed. Elizabeth Solopova, Medieval and Renaissance authors and texts 16 (Leiden: Brill, 2016), pp. 426–49; Mark Rankin, 'The royal provenance and Tudor courtly reading of a Wycliffite Bible', *Journal of Medieval and Early Modern Studies* 47:3 (2017), 587–97.

4   Most recently: Anne Hudson, 'The origin and textual tradition of the Wycliffite Bible', in *The Wycliffite Bible: origin, history and interpretation*, ed. Elizabeth Solopova, Medieval and Renaissance authors and texts 16 (Leiden: Brill, 2016), pp. 133–61.

narrative, suggesting that the Bible was orthodox from its inception to its reception.[5] While this argument has clear shortcomings,[6] even its critics agree that the overwhelming majority of Wycliffite Bibles are devoid of any direct links with heterodoxy. Despite its theoretical censorship, the Wycliffite Bible is best seen as part of a wider rise in vernacular Bibles that swept across Europe in the later Middle Ages. The number of surviving manuscripts of Wycliffite Bibles, as well as their appearance, renders them akin to similar translations in France, Italy and the Low Countries, translations which were not opposed to, and often were actively supported by, the established Church.[7] Similarly, ownership marks in these Bibles (which are few and far between) place them in the hands of priests, nuns and members of the nobility.[8] The rituals and devotions encoded in their pages follow the most common liturgical rite in England: the Use of Sarum. The link between orthodoxy and manuscripts of the Wycliffite Bible has become commonplace, as evident in the works of Anne Hudson, J. Patrick Hornbeck II and Mary Dove.[9] Elizabeth Solopova, editor of *The Companion to the Wycliffite Bible*, agrees that 'the driving force

5   Francis Aidan Gasquet, 'The pre-Reformation English Bible', *Dublin Review* 115 (1894), 122–52; Francis Aidan Gasquet, 'The pre-Reformation English Bible (2)', in *The old English Bible and other essays* (London: J. C. Nimmo, 1897), pp. 156–78; Henry Ansgar Kelly, *The Middle English Bible: a reassessment*, The Middle Ages series (Philadelphia: University of Pennsylvania Press, 2016).

6   As unfolded respectively by Margaret Deanesly, *The Lollard Bible and other medieval biblical versions*, Cambridge studies in medieval life and thought (Cambridge: Cambridge University Press, 1920; reprint, 1966); and Kathleen E. Kennedy, 'Review of The Middle English Bible: A Reassessment by Henry Ansgar Kelly', *Journal of Medieval Religious Cultures* 43:2 (2017), 254–57.

7   For vernacular Bibles see the articles of Sabrina Corbellini (Italian), Margriet Hoogvliet and Guy Lobrichon (French) in Eyal Poleg and Laura Light (eds), *Form and function in the Late Medieval Bible*, The written word: the manuscript world 27:4 (Leiden: Brill, 2013). For the German example, including discussion of historiography and further bibliography, see Andrew Gow, 'The contested history of a book: the German Bible of the later Middle Ages and Reformation in legend, ideology, and scholarship', *The Journal of Hebrew Scriptures* 9 (2009), 2–37. For the Dutch see Suzan Folkerts, 'Reading the Bible lessons at home: Holy Writ and lay readers in the Low Countries', *Church History & Religious Culture* 93:2 (2013), 217–37. A view of French and Czech biblical translations as the background to the Wycliffite Bible is in the articles of Delbert Russell and Jakub Sichálekis in Elizabeth Solopova (ed.), *The Wycliffite Bible: origin, history and interpretation*, Medieval and Renaissance authors and texts 16 (Leiden: Brill, 2016). First steps in a pan-European analysis are the articles in the 2013 issue of *Church History and Religious Culture*, prefaced by Sabrina Corbellini *et al.*, 'Challenging the paradigms: Holy Writ and lay readers in late medieval Europe', *Church History & Religious Culture* 93:2 (2013), 171–88; as well as Andrew Gow, 'Challenging the Protestant Paradigm: Bible reading in lay and urban contexts of the later Middle Ages', in *Scripture and pluralism: reading the Bible in the religiously plural worlds of the Middle Ages and Renaissance*, ed. Thomas J. Heffernan and Thomas E. Burman, Studies in the history of Christian traditions 123 (Leiden: Brill, 2005), pp. 161–91.

8   Elizabeth Solopova, 'Medieval ownership and use of the manuscripts of the Wycliffite Bible', in *Form and function in the Late Medieval Bible*, ed. Eyal Poleg and Laura Light (Leiden: Brill, 2013), pp. 333–49.

9   Anne Hudson, 'Lollard book production', in *Book production and publishing in Britain 1375–1475*, ed. Jeremy Griffiths and Derek Pearsall, Cambridge studies in publishing and printing history (Cambridge: Cambridge University Press, 1989), pp. 125–42; J. Patrick Hornbeck II, *What is a Lollard? Dissent and belief in late medieval England* (Oxford: Oxford University Press, 2010), p. 41; Mary Dove, *The first English Bible: the text and context of the Wycliffite versions*, Cambridge studies in medieval literature 66 (Cambridge: Cambridge University Press, 2007), pp. 1–2.

behind the emergence of such a large number of professionally made or even luxury copies were not the threatened Lollard communities, evoked by early 15th-century trial records, but the wealthy and educated' and that 'there is very little evidence of Lollard ideology in both the translation itself and its manuscripts'.[10]

This chapter moves away from discussions of heterodoxy and orthodoxy, and the polarised views they entail. Building on earlier explorations of the link between the Wycliffite Bible and the Late Medieval Bible (LMB), I locate the former as a stage in the long history of the Bible in England.[11] It is fruitful to think of the Wycliffite Bible as an object in transition, with some elements revealing the hesitant reception of the LMB, alongside acts of simplification and scribal ingenuity. A closer look at the manuscripts of the Wycliffite Bible reveals a cohabitation of Latin and English and sheds light on the little-explored question of how these Bibles were used and by whom. Rather than the boundaries suggested by Church legislation, a close analysis of the manuscripts reveals a joint sphere, where nuns and devout laypeople employed their English Bibles as part of Church worship. This accords with a general rise in the use of English in the fifteenth century in many spheres of life, when lay devotions had led to the establishment of guilds, confraternities and chantries, and were manifested in the rich book culture of Books of Hours and vernacular theology.[12]

No Prologue nor Single Volume:
Away from the Origins of the Wycliffite Bible

The link between the Wycliffite Bible and lay readership is not a modern scholarly insight. It can be traced all the way back to the General Prologue, a tract prefacing the Wycliffite Bible and attesting to the origins of the

---

10   Elizabeth Solopova, 'Introduction: new directions in research on the first English Bible', in *The Wycliffite Bible: origin, history and interpretation*, ed. Elizabeth Solopova, Medieval and Renaissance authors and texts 16 (Leiden: Brill, 2016), pp. 1–8.

11   Eyal Poleg, 'Wycliffite Bibles as orthodoxy', in *Instructing the soul, feeding the spirit and awakening the passion: cultures of religious reading in the late Middle Ages*, ed. Sabrina Corbellini, Utrecht studies in medieval literacy 25 (Turnhout: Brepols, 2013), pp. 71–91; Anne Hudson and Elizabeth Solopova, 'The Latin text', in *The Wycliffite Bible: origin, history and interpretation*, ed. Elizabeth Solopova, Medieval and Renaissance authors and texts 16 (Leiden: Brill, 2016), pp. 107–32.

12   See, for example, Stephen Kelly and Ryan Perry, 'Devotional cosmopolitanism in fifteenth-century England', in *After Arundel: religious writing in fifteenth-century England*, ed. Vincent Gillespie and Kantik Ghosh, Medieval church studies 21 (Turnhout: Brepols, 2011), pp. 363–80; Kathryn Vulić, Susan Uselmann and C. Annette Grisé (eds), *Devotional literature and practice in medieval England: readers, reading, and reception* (Turnhout: Brepols, 2016); Elisabeth Salter, '"The dayes moralised": reconstructing devotional reading, c.1450–1560', in *Pieties in transition*, ed. Lutton Robert and Salter Elisabeth (Aldershot: Ashgate, 2007), pp. 145–62.

translation project. Alongside summaries of the books of the Old Testament (apart from the Books of Prophets, which have their own Prologue), its author comments upon the translation project, its goals, and the state of the English Church and society.[13] The author, identifying himself as 'Simple Creature', argues that the Bible should be read by all people, and that while the Old Testament is beneficial for 'simple men of wit' (§3, p. 7), the New Testament is particularly 'of full authority and open to the understanding of simple men' (§1, p. 5). In tune with the Lollards' emphasis on biblical truth and their rejection of clerical mediation, the General Prologue puts forward a view of laypeople's direct access to Scripture. Every person should be able to read the Word of God. Yet this claim is at odds with the contents of the General Prologue itself, and with key features of the Wycliffite Bible at large. Both the General Prologue and prologues to individual books of the Wycliffite Bible rely on the works of Jerome, which, as argued by Kantik Ghosh, 'would in large part be comprehensible only to those who were fully able to make sense of the Latin as well, not just in terms of the language but also of content'.[14] The layout of Wycliffite Bibles presents a complex view of the biblical text. There, within the textual column, or in its margins, one finds glosses and alternative readings of linguistic variants or etymologies. Michael Kuczynski has seen in these glosses 'many of the dilemmas of the Wycliffite movement itself, especially the difficulty of bridging "lerned" and "leued" [vulgar] cultures'.[15]

The gap between the ideal of lay access to Scripture and a sophisticated book culture typical of university books reveals an ambiguity at the core of the translation project.[16] The Bible's editors advocated a direct link between Bible and lay readers as a counter-reaction to clerical corruption and privilege. However, being university trained, they were unable to overlook the complexity of the biblical text, and the generations of Christian exegetes who had harmonised Bible and theology. The result was a Bible whose rhetoric addressed the uninitiated, while its practice favoured the learned.

---

13   The Prologue has been edited by Mary Dove (ed.), *The earliest advocates of the English Bible: the texts of the medieval debate* (Exeter: University of Exeter Press, 2010), pp. 3–85; For analysis see Kantik Ghosh, 'The prologues', in *The Wycliffite Bible: origin, history and interpretation*, ed. Elizabeth Solopova, Medieval and Renaissance authors and texts 16 (Leiden: Brill, 2016), pp. 162–82. All subsequent quotes are taken from Dove's edition.

14   Ghosh, 'The prologues', p. 181.

15   Michael P. Kuczynski, 'Glossing and glosses', in *The Wycliffite Bible: origin, history and interpretation*, ed. Elizabeth Solopova, Medieval and Renaissance authors and texts 16 (Leiden: Brill, 2016), pp. 346–67 at 366, and a similar sentiment at p. 354.

16   This gap is not confined to that treatise, but appears in prologues and glosses throughout the Wycliffite Bible. Thus it does not follow Kelly's suggestion that the General Prologue was a later interpolation: *The Middle English Bible: a reassessment*, ch. 2, 'Five and twenty books as "official" prologue or not', pp. 14–30.

This is indicative of reformed Bibles at large, and it demonstrates the innate difficulty of attempting to present the 'naked text' of the Bible to the uninitiated. Walden's analysis of the 1560 Bible created by exiled English reformers in Calvinist Geneva seems appropriate here as well: 'The Geneva Bible thus represented an uneasy tension between generosity towards and distrust of the common person to interpret scripture.'[17]

The summaries and arguments of the General Prologue are mostly mainstream Christian thought, relying on Augustine and Nicholas of Lyra (†1349), whose *Postillae* became the standard work for the study of the Bible. For example, the summary of Genesis leads to the conclusion that '[a]ll this process of Genesis should stir Christian men to be faithful, and for to dread and love God, and in all things do his will' (§3, p. 7). Yet the author also embeds criticism of Church and nobility into his narrative, merging biblical history and a heterodox view of current events. Following the summary of the biblical books of Chronicles, the author juxtaposes the merits of Old Testament protagonists with the sins of medieval priests: Jehosephat sending priests to every city to proclaim God's laws is contrasted with the greed of pardoners; Ezekiel cleansing the Temple with the purchase of Church offices (known as simony), and with priests taking up secular positions; Josiah preaching openly God's laws and burning idols with the fables of the Friars (§10, pp. 46–53). He continues to chastise secular lords, and dismisses oaths taken on relics. In the summary of Amos his criticism is acute and dire: 'But alas, alas, alas! The most abomination that ever was heard among Christian clerics is now proposed in England by worldly clerics and fiend religious, and in the chief university of our realm' (§13, p. 71). He also deplores the offerings made to images, and the pride and sodomy rife in the University of Oxford.

The strong heterodox stance of the General Prologue was not embraced by most producers and patrons of the Wycliffite Bible. The uneasy reception of its contentious elements is evident in CUL MS Mm.2.15. This Wycliffite Bible contains the General Prologue, placed in between the Old and the New Testament. In the General Prologue, the section about the University of Oxford in chapter 13 (fols 287v–288r) is written in a different contemporary hand and ink, on parchment whose whiteness suggests it had been erased and rewritten.[18] More widely, the General Prologue is lacking from the vast

---

17 Justine Walden, 'Global Calvinism: the maps in the English Geneva Bible', in *Shaping the Bible in the Reformation: books, scholars, and their readers in the sixteenth century*, ed. Bruce Gordon and Matthew McLean (Leiden: Brill, 2012), pp. 187–215 at 198–9.

18 This had been noted by Dove, *Earliest advocates*, p. xxvi. For general information on the manuscripts, suggesting more local production, see Lynda Dennison and Nigel Morgan, 'The decoration of Wycliffite Bibles', in *The Wycliffite Bible: origin, history and interpretation*, ed. Elizabeth Solopova, Medieval and Renaissance authors and texts 16 (Leiden: Brill, 2016), pp. 266–345 at 292–3. I thank both authors for their kind discussions of this mode of production.

majority of surviving manuscripts of the Wycliffite Bible, with only five manuscripts containing it in its entirety.[19] Seven additional manuscripts contain parts of the General Prologue, typically omitting the inflammatory materials of chapters 10 and 13. Such an omission is indicative of a gap between the origins and the reception of the Wycliffite Bible. While the Wycliffite Bible originated with the followers of Wyclif, most manuscripts were not created in, nor for, that circle. For the London stationers who were producing many of these manuscripts, as for the patrons who commissioned and used them, omitting inflammatory sections enabled them to accommodate the Bible into a more orthodox sphere and dissociate it from its heterodox origins.

The manuscript evidence of the Wycliffite Bible suggests another reason for the omission of the General Prologue. Modern scholars see the evolution of the Wycliffite Bible as a primarily textual one. They group manuscripts of the Wycliffite Bible based on their translation: the Early Version is a word-by-word rendering of the Vulgate; the Late Version presents a more idiomatic translation; several manuscripts elude this dichotomous view, either containing elements from both versions, or of an intermediary version.[20] Both Early and Late Versions encompass the entire Bible. The translation project began with the Old Testament, and the General Prologue views the Bible as a combination of Old and New Testaments. The material evidence, however, suggests another evolution, and another grouping. Most Wycliffite Bibles are not single-volume Bibles. Out of *c.*250 manuscripts, only twenty are single-volume Bibles, while another seventeen may have once formed part of such a book. The remaining manuscripts—the vast majority of Wycliffite Bibles—are a distinct category of books, at odds with the contents of the General Prologue. The inclusion of the General Prologue, with its summaries of biblical books that may not have been included in the same volume, would have therefore been redundant in that later stage in the evolution of the Wycliffite Bible.

New Testaments, in full or in part, comprise more than two-thirds of all extant manuscripts of the Wycliffite Bible, with Psalters the second-most popular book, in forty-two manuscripts.[21] This division challenges our definition

19   On manuscripts of the General Prologue see Dove, *Earliest advocates*, pp. xxv–xxx; Elizabeth Solopova, 'The manuscript tradition', in *The Wycliffite Bible: origin, history and interpretation*, ed. Elizabeth Solopova, Medieval and Renaissance authors and texts 16 (Leiden: Brill, 2016), pp. 223–45 at 233–6.

20   Dove, *The first English Bible*; Hudson, 'The origin and textual tradition of the Wycliffite Bible'; Anne Hudson, 'Editing the Wycliffite Bible', in *The Wycliffite Bible: origin, history and interpretation*, ed. Elizabeth Solopova, Medieval and Renaissance authors and texts 16 (Leiden: Brill, 2016), pp. 450–66; Conrad Lindberg, 'The Alpha and Omega of the Middle English Bible', in *Text and controversy from Wyclif to Bale: essays in honour of Anne Hudson*, ed. Helen Barr and Ann M. Hutchison, Medieval church studies 4 (Turnhout: Brepols, 2005), pp. 191–200.

21   For catalogues see Dove, *The first English Bible*, pp. 281–306; Kathleen E. Kennedy, *The courtly and commercial art of the Wycliffite Bible*, Medieval church studies (Turnhout: Brepols, 2014), pp. 197–208.

of the Wycliffite Bible. What is a Bible, if the majority of manuscripts are not single-volume Bibles, but rather New Testaments? What are the implications of such a truncation for the way manuscripts were used? What are the reasons for the move from translation to reception, from single-volume Bibles to New Testaments, a move that seems to reverse the thirteenth-century rise of the single-volume Bible, discussed in the previous chapter?

Wyclif and his followers had elevated the New Testament above any other part of the Bible to such an extent that Reginald Pecock (†c.1459) claimed that their devotion mirrored the Jews' reliance on the Old.[22] However, the heterodox origins of the project encompassed both Testaments, and manuscripts containing evidence of Lollard thought are typically single-volume Bibles.[23] The move from single-volume Bibles to New Testaments accorded with Church theology, which saw in the New Testament the culmination of history. It also had a very pragmatic outcome. It reduced the biblical text by 80 per cent, making these manuscripts smaller, more portable and significantly cheaper by saving on labour and parchment. It is indicative of a transition towards greater simplification, which also limited the variety of possible uses for the Wycliffite Bible. A comparison with the LMB, the predecessor of the Wycliffite Bible, helps contextualise this transformation.

The Wycliffite Bible and the Uncertain Reception of the Late Medieval Bible

I am writing this chapter in the manuscript reading room of Cambridge University Library with two books on my desk: CUL MS Ee.1.16 is an LMB, a single-volume Bible encompassing the books of the Latin Bible from Genesis to Revelation; CUL MS Ll.1.13 is a Wycliffite Bible, a full New Testament with additional selected lessons taken from the Old Testament. Both manuscripts are in size and contents typical of LMBs and Wycliffite Bibles, respectively. The two manuscripts are also similar in size to one

22   Reginald Pecock, *The repressor of over much blaming of the clergy*, ed. Churchill Babington, Rerum Britannicarum medii aevi scriptores 19 (London: Longman, Green, Longman, and Roberts, 1860), 1:69–70; addressed in Dove, *The first English Bible*, pp. 195–6; Anne Hudson, *The Premature Reformation: Wycliffite texts and Lollard history* (Oxford: Oxford University Press, 1988), p. 240.
23   This is most evident in manuscripts containing the General Prologue. Evidence from marginal marks adjacent to verses on idols or oaths (as suggested by Elizabeth Solopova, *Manuscripts of the Wycliffite Bible in the Bodleian and Oxford College Libraries*, Exeter medieval texts and studies (Liverpool: Liverpool University Press, 2016), pp. 28–30), for example, is much less conclusive as it could have been made as part of inner-ecclesiastical argument or by their opponents. For the use of marginal annotations in Bibles for anti-Lollard polemics see Eyal Poleg, 'The earliest evidence for anti-Lollard polemics in medieval Scotland', *Innes Review* 64 (2013), 227–34.

another (see Figure 2.1).[24] They have approximately the same number of folios and the same ratio of text area to margins.[25] They differ significantly in script and parchment, two notable characteristics of the LMB (Chapter 1, p. 4). The parchment of the Wycliffite Bible is 1.5 times thicker, leading to a great increase in its weight (more than twice that of Ee.1.16); its script is more than twice the height of that of the LMB.[26] Each manuscript is indicative of its time. In the thirteenth century the mendicants had revolutionised book culture with their *vademecum* books; in the fifteenth century, on the other hand, most scribes and parchmeners had moved away from the creation of minute volumes.[27] Written in larger script and on thicker parchment, Wycliffite Bibles are bulkier than their Latin predecessors. The shortening of the text by omitting the Old Testament had enabled scribes to keep both size and price in check. This should not, however, be seen only through the prism of decline in book production. The large script and robust parchment of Wycliffite Bibles made them more legible, easier to read for longer periods of time and more suitable for public recitation. Wycliffite Bibles reversed some of the innovative features of the LMB, and thus accorded less with the centrality of single-volume Bibles, or with the move from narrative to text discussed in the previous chapter.

Yet Wycliffite Bibles still depended on the LMB. Opening a Wycliffite Bible next to an LMB shows their similarity (see Figures 2.1 and 2.2). Both are usually written in two columns,[28] with running titles identifying the biblical book; large initials open each chapter, accompanied by the chapter number. The script of the Wycliffite Bible resembles that of Latin manuscripts, and as

---

24   Ee.1.16 measures 214x158x65 mm and MS Ll.1.13 250x180x95 mm. In comparison, the Wycliffite single-volume Bible CUL Mm.2.15 measures 380x270x75 mm, weight 6.80 kg, and is akin to a modern royal folio.

25   Ee.1.16: text area = 142x87 mm; page size = 208x152 mm; 350 folios. Weight = 1.35 kg.
Ll.1.13: text area = *c.*159x*c.*117 mm; page size = 235x179 mm; 362 folios. Weight = 3.05 kg.

26   Ee.1.16: 51 mm for 350 folios = 0.145 mm for each folio; 50 mm for twenty lines.
Ll.1.13: 84 mm for 362 folios = 0.232 mm for each folio; *c.*109 mm for twenty lines.

27   The wider question of changes in size and book culture between the thirteenth and the fifteenth century has not, to the best of my knowledge, been fully explored. Initial exploration on the size and discrete forms of fifteenth-century books in England, while advocating caution in associating these with printed book sizes, was made by Ralph Hanna, 'The sizes of Middle English books, ca. 1390–1430', *Journal of the Early Book Society* 8 (2015), 181–91, also alluding to the Wycliffite Bible. The use of thin parchment in a handful of Wycliffite Bibles has been addressed by Ralph Hanna, 'The palaeography of the Wycliffite Bibles in Oxford', in *The Wycliffite Bible: origin, history and interpretation*, ed. Elizabeth Solopova, Medieval and Renaissance authors and texts 16 (Leiden: Brill, 2016), pp. 246–65 at 254–6. Initial research carried out by Sarah Fiddyment of the BioArCh Research team (York and Cambridge) suggests a decline in the quality of parchment production from *c.*1300. I thank Sarah Fiddyment and Matthew Collins for sharing these findings.

28   Single column is the exception among Wycliffite Bibles, reserved for very short texts. It is employed, for example, in Edinburgh, National Library of Scotland MS 6127 (Pauline Epistles), Glasgow University Library MS Hunter. 191 (John, Catholic Epistles and Revelation), or MS Hunter. 337 (the Gospel of Mark).

Figure 2.1 Wycliffite Bible (CUL MS Ll.1.13, above) alongside a Late Medieval Bible (Ee.1.16, below). The books are roughly the same size, though the Wycliffite Bible contains only 20% of the text of the LMB. Reproduced by kind permission of the Syndics of Cambridge University Library.

Figure 2.2 Layout of a Wycliffite Bible. This was designed to replicate the layout of Latin Bibles. CUL MS Dd.1.27, fol. 435v. Reproduced by kind permission of the Syndics of Cambridge University Library.

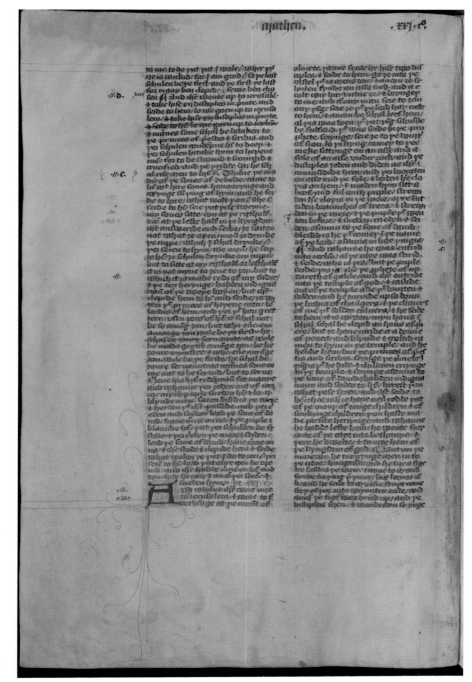

Ralph Hanna has argued, this was an intentional endeavour, and a counter-intuitive act of scribes and stationers:

> Thus, at the point the Wycliffite Bible entered circulation, the model biblical book was transmitted in a form alien at every stroke from what was deemed an appropriate local script strategy for vernacular productions. Perhaps the most striking thing about Wycliffite bibles is the general thoroughness with which book-producers adopted a script fundamentally alien to contemporary production.[29]

More luxurious Wycliffite Bibles had blue and red running titles and pen-work for initials, in a layout similar to that of the LMB.

The materiality of the Wycliffite Bible breaks away from the size of many LMBs, while still sharing other of its unique features, such as the chapter divisions. Such divisions, common in Latin Bibles from *c.*1230, were central to Wycliffite Bibles, and appear in all extant manuscripts. Some Wycliffite Bibles contain an abbreviated text of the Bible, which demonstrates how chapter divisions were instrumental in navigating the biblical text. Bodl. MS Laud. Misc. 182 contains only snippets of the biblical text. The principle of selection in this manuscript followed the chapter division, as specific chapters were chosen for inclusion, and others omitted altogether.[30] While chapter division appears as standard in Wycliffite Bibles, their layout allows us to trace the reception of this feature, revealing some unease about it, even two centuries after its introduction. The passing of time seems to have moved Bibles away from their initial uniformity, and Wycliffite Bibles show a variety and idiosyncrasy in presenting this device, unlike the uniformity of most LMBs.

In some Wycliffite Bibles the chapter division was overlooked by the rubricator, attesting to tensions within the production process. In Cambridge, St John's MS N.4, the rubricator did not integrate chapter numbers in the Gospels, in spaces left blank by the original scribe.[31] The same is true for the beginning of Cambridge, Sidney Sussex MS 99, where chapter numbers were noted by the scribe in faint ink in the margins, but ignored by the rubricator.[32] Such

---

29   Hanna, 'The palaeography of the Wycliffite Bibles in Oxford', pp. 258, 262. There is a need for a more in-depth study of Textura in fifteenth-century English manuscripts.

30   Discussed in Solopova, *Manuscripts of the Wycliffite Bible*, pp. 178–81; Mary Raschko, 'Taking apart the Wycliffite Bible: patterns of selective and integrative reading', *Journal of Medieval and Early Modern Studies* 47:3 (2017), 461–86 at 477–8. The same is true, though in a different way, of the biblical abbreviation of CUL MS Ee.1.10, discussed on pp. 76–8.

31   These appear only for Matthew 22, Mark 14, Luke 12–20. The rubricator had also left capitals lacking across the manuscript. Chapter numbers were noted inconsistently in Arabic numerals (in ink, top-right corner of each folio).

32   Only on fol. 23r (Matthew chapter 21) did the rubricator adhere to the scribe's instructions and integrate the chapter numbers both within the textual block and as part of the running title. This was done

omissions demonstrate that craftsmen in early fifteenth-century England were still somewhat unfamiliar with this device. Cambridge, Magdalene College Pepys MS 15 is a small and high-end manuscript comprising the Gospels and a lectionary. The rubricator had begun by prefacing each chapter with the formula of 'the XX chapter'. As the book progressed, he favoured the shorter 'C° XX', employing the abbreviation for chapter ('Capitulum') in Latin. Latin Bibles of the thirteenth century are uniform in their presentation, with running titles in alternating red and blue letters across an opening, chapter numbers in alternating red and blue roman numerals, and each chapter starting in a larger initial, again red and blue with some pen-work or illumination. Wycliffite Bibles display greater variation. Some imitate the layout of the LMB, while others provide a rudimentary single-colour scheme in red. These give the impression of a more diffused craftsmanship, or, possibly, a greater variety of end-products, to accommodate the taste and finance of different patrons.

The more flexible layout employed in Wycliffite Bibles enabled scribes and stationers to experiment with, and even improve upon, existing tools. While in LMBs chapter numbers are noted solely near the textual division, scribes and readers of Wycliffite Bibles also noted the chapter number as part of the running title.[33] This modification enabled quick and efficient identification of the chapter without the need to turn to the textual block itself. A century and a half later, English printers during the short reign of Edward VI likewise embraced this feature to accord with a newly founded centrality of chapter division in navigating the Bible (Chapter 5, pp. 158–60).

The comparison between the LMB and the Wycliffite Bible shows that by 1400 scribes and readers had grown more familiar with Arabic numerals.[34] The greater variety of layouts employed by scribes and stationers included Roman numerals, Arabic numerals, or a mixture of both as a form of numbering chapter divisions. At times it appears that the use of Roman numerals, much like the choice of script, was an intentional archaism, aimed at imitating the LMB. More expert fifteenth-century readers seem to have been quite familiar with Arabic numerals, used in biblical cross references in Cambridge, Emmanuel College MS I.4.33 (James §108) or Cambridge, Magdalene College Pepys MS 2073. Scribes seem to have been more familiar with Arabic numerals as well.

---

inconsistently, with chapter numbers still lacking for some chapters in the Gospel of John and the Epistle to the Romans.

33   As in Cambridge, Magdalene College Pepys MS 2073, a well-executed and high-end manuscript, in which the chapter numbers have been noted as part of the running title above the relevant column as part of the original design of the manuscript. On the production of the manuscript see Kennedy, *The courtly and commercial art of the Wycliffite Bible*, pp. 142–5.

34   On the gradual introduction of Arabic numerals see Mary A. Rouse and Richard H. Rouse, *Authentic witnesses: approaches to medieval texts and manuscripts* (Notre Dame, IN: University of Notre Dame Press, 1991), pp. 242–4.

In Sidney Sussex MS 99 the scribe had left chapter numbers in the margins for the rubricator to follow (as in the margins of fol. 13r). These were noted in Arabic numerals, but followed up by the rubricator in Roman ones.

A more substantial modification to the layout of Wycliffite Bibles reveals an important transformation in the way those Bibles were to be read. Prior to the introduction of verse divisions in the mid-sixteenth century, alphabetical sub-division helped readers in identifying sections within chapters. In the thirteenth century, readers were expected to divide a chapter into equal-length portions in their minds (A–G for longer chapters, A–D for shorter ones), and to link these to references in their concordances, tables of lections or preachers' aids. Only in a handful of Latin Bibles had scribes or readers noted the marginal sub-division. This tool was transformed in Wycliffite Bibles. Few Wycliffite Bibles contain the marginal sub-division in full, and even then this often peters out after a few chapters. The majority of Wycliffite Bibles, however, present the sub-division in a different form. They do not appear consecutively. Rather, scribes, rubricators and early readers noted them in the margins of chapters, primarily of the New Testament, without following a consecutive sequence. Thus, for example, Matthew chapter 21 is often affixed with letters A, C, F and G. The reason for this is found in the accompanying table of lections, where the choice of sub-divisions corresponds to the use of the Bible within the liturgy: Matthew 21 was read on the First Sunday in Advent and Palm Sunday (A); the Fifth Wednesday after the Octave of Epiphany (F); the Twenty-fourth Wednesday after Trinity (F); and the First Tuesday in Lent (C).[35] This somewhat disjointed way of noting the sub-division became the standard for Wycliffite Bibles, deployed by producers and readers alike. It simplified the previous system and had an evident appeal. Scribes no longer needed to note all marginal alphabetical letters, nor were less experienced readers expected to mentally sub-divide the chapter. Noting the liturgical sub-division enabled quick, efficient and accurate retrieval of the liturgical lections, especially when accompanied by a one-line capital letter or paragraph mark at the beginning of the lection. This simplification, however, came at a cost. The original tool opened a variety of reading strategies for expert readers, to be used in identifying liturgical lections, retrieving repeating words and biblical themes, or engaging in elaborate biblical exegesis alongside concordances, thematic compendia and other tools. In Wycliffite Bibles, the simplified tool lacked the flexibility to be used alongside a variety of aids. The malleability of the Late Medieval Bible was transformed

---

35   Based on CUL MS Kk.1.8. The unrelated 'G' could indicate that this was copied from an earlier model. This is not to say that highly literate and academic readers of the Wycliffite Bible did not use the complete virtual system. This is evident in William of Norton's tables, which rely on the work of Lyra. I thank Michael Kuczynski for this suggestion.

and harnessed. It was now to be used with a sole aim: accompanying the table of lections.

Table of Lections and New Modes of Reading

Much like other features of the Wycliffite Bible, the table of lections was a common addendum to the LMB (Chapter 1, pp. 32–3). These tables enabled readers to identify the Gospel and Epistles lections for the Mass according to their liturgical occasion. Starting with the First Sunday of Advent, they supplied the biblical reference, as well as the first few words for each reading. In LMBs, tables of lections vary greatly. They were often added by later readers, rather than being part of the book's original design. Their scope, design and entries are far from uniform: they refer inconsistently to the alphabetical subdivisions, and at times were integrated with Mass-texts. Wycliffite Bibles, on the other hand, despite their uneven general layout, embraced the table of lections as a standard and a much more uniform addendum.

Matti Peikola's careful analysis of this device has revealed a subtle transformation in the evolution of the table of lections in Wycliffite Bibles: a gradual move towards orthodoxy. As Wycliffite Bibles moved beyond the Oxford circle of Wyclif's followers, their tables of lections integrated more and more non-biblical saints, a custom frowned upon by Lollards: 'the general outline of this development was from tables of lessons which were more or less consonant with Wycliffite views to ones that conformed to orthodox ideas of saints and sanctity.'[36] As noted by Peikola, an earlier rendering of the table of lections is linked to the General Prologue, attesting to the heterodox nature of both early aids.[37]

Wycliffite tables of lections became increasingly uniform in both layout and contents (as can be seen in Figure 2.3). The entries are typically divided into several sections: the *Temporale* (the annual feasts of the Church), *Sanctorale* (saints' days) and *Commemorations* (votive Masses, that is private Masses said by a priest). Often an explanatory rubric, altogether lacking in Latin Bibles, precedes the table and explains its form and function to the reader:

---

36   Matti Peikola, 'The Sanctorale, Thomas of Woodstock's English Bible, and the orthodox appropriation of Wycliffite tables of lessons', in *Wycliffite controversies*, ed. Mishtooni Bose and J. Patrick Hornbeck II, Medieval church studies 23 (Turnhout: Brepols, 2011), pp. 153–74 at 168; Peikola, '"First is writen a clause of the bigynnynge therof": the table of lections in manuscripts of the Wycliffite Bible', in *Form and function in the Late Medieval Bible*, ed. Eyal Poleg and Laura Light (Leiden: Brill, 2013), pp. 351–78. I thank Matti Peikola for his kind and generous assistance throughout my work on the Wycliffite Bibles.

37   Of the three manuscripts to contain both aids, two include the earlier, more heterodox, version of the table of lections.

Figure 2.3 Table of lections in a Wycliffite Bible. This was the most common addendum to Wycliffite Bibles, linking them, time and again, to orthodox Church services. CUL MS Dd.1.27, fol. 420r. Reproduced by kind permission of the Syndics of Cambridge University Library.

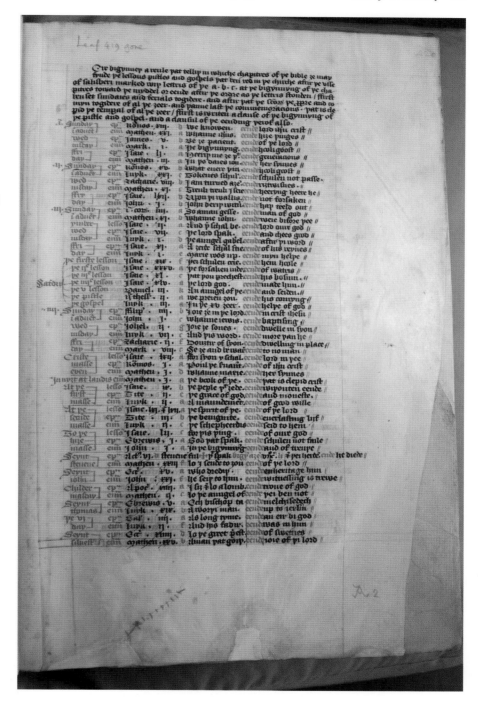

Here begins a rule that tells in which chapters of the bible ye may find the lessons, Epistles, and Gospels that been read in the church after the use of Salisbury, marked with letters of the abc at the beginning of the chapters, toward the middle or end, after the order as the letters stand in the abc. First been set Sundays and ferials together, and after that the sanctorum the proper and common [of saints] together of all the year; and then last the commemorations that is called the temporal of all the year. First is written a clause of the beginning of the Epistle and Gospel, and a clause of the ending thereof also.[38]

As narrated in the rubric, the entries of the table contain the list of lections, identified by book, chapter, sub-division, incipit and explicit. This uniform information is arranged graphically in five columns in red and black. A typical entry reads (as in the First Sunday in Advent from CUL MS Dd.1.27, fol. 420r, fig. 2.3):

			Beginnings	Ends
First Sunday in Advent	Romans xiii°	b	We know	Lord Jesus Christ
	Matthew xxi°	a	When Jesus	High things

Here we see the maturity of a device and a retrieval system that had been deployed in the LMB. It is more uniform, accurate and accessible than the experimental tables of lections found in thirteenth-century Bibles (Chapter 1, pp. 31–3). Alphabetical divisions were noted in the margins of the biblical chapters, and lections were typically demarcated within the text by a one-line capital or paragraph mark (opening) and double virgule ('//'—end). Anne Hudson and Elizabeth Solopova's seminal article on the Latin origins of the Wycliffite Bible provides an initial exploration into tables of lections in Wycliffite Bibles and in LMBs.[39] The idiosyncratic nature of tables of lections in LMBs suggests that further research, with careful attention to the presentation of these tables, would assist in better linking the two types of manuscripts, and in ascertaining the models used by scribes, patrons and stationers of the Wycliffite Bible.

The table of lections was central to the creators and users of the Wycliffite Bible. It appears in around 40 per cent of manuscripts and is its most common addendum. Tables of lections were actively used. As will be shown, scribes, rubricators and readers copied the lections in the margins of the biblical text, either with alphabetical sub-division or—less commonly—with the liturgical

---

38   Transcribed in Peikola, '"First is written a clause"', p. 366.
39   Hudson and Solopova, 'The Latin text'.

occurrence of the biblical pericope. Scribes also modified the table of lections to suit particular manuscripts. Thus, for example, the production team creating a manuscript of the Epistles of the New Testament (Cambridge, St John's MS E.13) made sure to incorporate only the relevant lections into the table. Manuscripts of the *Oon of Foure*—a Gospel harmony replacing the Four Gospels in some Wycliffite Bibles—contain a unique table of lections that refers to the *Oon* rather than the Four Gospels. In Wycliffite Bibles which did not have a table of lections, this was at times added by later readers. Thus, a fifteenth-century reader added to Bodl. MS Rawl. C.237/238 (a New Testament from the first quarter of the fifteenth century[40]) marginal annotations indicating the liturgical occurrence, as well as a rudimentary table of lections.[41]

A New Testament accompanied by a table of lections supplies all Gospel lections, and a large part of the Epistle lections for the Church calendar. In twenty-five manuscripts, the remaining Old Testament lections are provided by an additional lectionary. This lengthy addendum provides the full lections according to their liturgical order, at times encompassing all the Epistle lections (of both Old and New Testament, and thus replicating some of the text provided in the volume itself).

The centrality of the table of lections may shed light on the use of Wycliffite Bibles, a topic which has not been fully explored in modern scholarship.[42] The centrality of the tables of lections and the proliferation of Wycliffite New Testaments strongly suggests that these Bibles were employed in connection with the liturgical year. Here, however, opinions vary. Hudson raised the possibility of Lollards wishing to replace the Latin liturgy with an English one, while De Hamel envisioned parishioners consulting the manuscripts during the Latin service. Use in half-private meetings has been suggested by Dove, while Solopova and Raschko refer to unspecified liturgical use. Peikola has tried to reconcile these approaches, arguing that Lollards did not oppose the reading of Scripture in Church liturgy. He also alludes to the use of Wycliffite Bibles in private chapels, places of greater liturgical flexibility.[43] The evidence supplied below suggests locating some of the

---

40   Presented in Solopova, 'The manuscript tradition', p. 240; Solopova, *Manuscripts of the Wycliffite Bible*, pp. 201–5.

41   Liturgical occurrences accompany, for example, Mt 18, 21 and 22 (unfoliated). The table of lections appears on the last flyleaf of MS C.238.

42   This is evident, for example, in the lack of a chapter on the use of the manuscripts in the two most recent book-length studies of the Wycliffite Bible: Dove, *The first English Bible*; and Solopova, *The Wycliffite Bible*, where the section on 'reception' mainly addresses textual reception (with a chapter on the use of manuscripts during the Reformation).

43   Deanesly, *The Lollard Bible*, p. 176; Hudson, *The Premature Reformation*, p. 199; Christopher De Hamel, *The book: a history of the Bible* (London: Phaidon, 2001), pp. 184–6; Dove, *The first English Bible*, pp. 58–67; summarised in Peikola, '"First is writen a clause"', pp. 368–71; Raschko, 'Taking apart the Wycliffite Bible'; Solopova, *Manuscripts of the Wycliffite Bible*, pp. 6–17.

uses of these Bibles within religious establishments, often beyond the better-documented liturgical hubs in monasteries, colleges and cathedrals.

Lollard ideals and the rhetoric of the General Prologue advocate lay reading of Scripture. Some court records place Wycliffite New Testaments in Lollard hands. However, there is no direct evidence linking surviving manuscripts of the Wycliffite Bible to heterodox users. This may be indicative of fear of leaving one's name in such a book, or (though less likely) of the destruction of such manuscripts by the authorities. The manuscript evidence directs our gaze elsewhere. While identifying a Wycliffite Bible made for a nun in Barking, Elizabeth Solopova argues that

> [a]n almost unanimous assumption of modern scholarship is that the Wycliffite Bible was a book for laity, but there is growing evidence coming particularly from the study of the contents of the manuscripts of the Bible that contradicts this view. Such evidence, including the results of research presented here, shows that many copies were in clerical hands and many were probably made for clerical and religious patrons.[44]

Ownership marks, patterns of use and external evidence all support moving beyond a simple association of Wycliffite Bibles with the laity. Explicit evidence for ownership of Wycliffite Bibles is scant, yet its analysis, primarily carried by Solopova, has identified Bibles owned by monks, nuns and friars, as well as by the secular clergy.[45] The analysis of marginal annotations likewise suggests use within a variety of religious establishments. The snippets of surviving information lead us to rethink the separation of lay and clerical, and to look again at Church liturgy.

The Corpus of British Medieval Library Catalogues is an impressive tool that includes library catalogues, book lists and manuscript evidence from across medieval England, Scotland and Wales. It contains ample evidence for ownership of Latin Bibles, glossed and un-glossed, across religious establishments. The record for vernacular Bibles, on the other hand, is extremely scant.[46] This lack, however, should be taken in perspective. The survival

---

44   Elizabeth Solopova, 'A Wycliffite Bible made for a nun of Barking', *Medium Aevum* 85:1 (2016), 77–96 at 77.

45   Solopova, 'Medieval ownership and use'; Solopova, 'A Wycliffite Bible made for a nun of Barking'; Solopova, *Manuscripts of the Wycliffite Bible*, Appendix 5.

46   Richard Sharpe, *English Benedictine libraries: the shorter catalogues*, Corpus of British medieval library catalogues 4 (London: British Library in association with the British Academy, 1996):

- Ramsey, C14m 'Biblia in gallico' (B68.26; B68.413)
- Burton on Trent *c*.1175 'Evangelistas anglice', followed by 'Ymnarium, anglice' (B11.68)

Vincent Gillespie and A. I. Doyle, *Syon Abbey*, Corpus of British medieval library catalogues 9 (London: The British Library in association with the British Academy, 2001):

- London Smithfield Charterhouse, loans to Hull charterhouse 15ex/16in—Pauline Epistles, Wycliff's translation; Acts (C2.16, C2.17)

of book lists is partial and biased towards larger institutions. Such lists were not exhaustive inventories of all books within a religious establishment, but were compiled with specific aims in mind, such as commemorating donors or maintaining the library.[47] Several types of books rarely appear in library catalogues, as they were stored and used elsewhere in the institution. Thus, for example, two small volumes of the Pauline Epistles and Acts in the Wycliffite translation do not appear in a library catalogue, but rather in a list of books loaned by the London Charterhouse to the Charterhouse in Hull *c*.1500.

In the late fifteenth-century catalogue of St Augustine, Canterbury, an English Hexateuch (the first six books of the Bible: Genesis to Joshua) was not noted by the original scribe, but rather inscribed only later into the catalogue. This has led the modern editor to claim that this addition 'might itself suggest an earlier policy of exclusion'.[48] Such exclusion, which may explain the lack of vernacular Bibles more widely, was not the outcome of the censorship initiated by Archbishop Arundel in the early fifteenth century. The book in question is the renowned *Cotton Genesis*, an Anglo-Saxon translation of the Bible, and thus not subjected to the restrictions imposed by Arundel's Constitutions on new biblical translations. In editing the same catalogue, Barker-Benfield also suggests that a record for an English Gospel was lacking due to the fact that the book 'might have belonged with other gospels entries in the missing *Liturgica* section'.[49] This hints at the problem of preservation more widely. In religious establishments books were kept across the premises according to their function: books for study (and for preparing sermons) were typically kept in the library, for the performance of the liturgy in the choir, in the refectory for reading during meals, books for personal use in the cells of brothers and sisters, and volumes with lavish bindings in the sacristy.

- Syon, glossed Gospels 'Aquinas super lucam et Iohannem in anglico' (SS2.102)

B. C. Barker-Benfield, *St Augustine's Abbey, Canterbury*, Corpus of British medieval library catalogues 13 (London: British Library in association with the British Academy, 2008):

- *c*.1400 'Hexateuchus anglice' later addition (BA1.★95x)
- *c*.1400 'Euangel' anglice' (BA1.idx550)
- *c*.1400 'Genesis anglice' (BA1.★95)
- Old English Psalms (pp. 1661, 1836–7)
- Revelation in Latin and French with pictures (★225A)

Nigel Ramsay and James M. W. Willoughby, *Hospitals, towns, and the professions*, Corpus of British medieval library catalogues 14 (London: British Library in association with the British Academy, 2009):

- Keplier, hospital of St Giles 'alium librum vocatum a pistler; [...] a Ympner [...] a Gospeller' (p. 59)

James M. W. Willoughby, *The libraries of collegiate churches*, Corpus of British medieval library catalogues 15 (London: British Library in association with the British Academy, 20013):

- Eton, William Strete leaving English Bible in 7.06.1482 to John Pese, fellow & bursar (pp. 167–8).

47   I thank Tessa Webber for her insights on this topic.
48   Barker-Benfield, *St Augustine's Abbey, Canterbury*, 1:95.
49   Barker-Benfield, *St Augustine's Abbey, Canterbury*, 1:95.

How and where were Wycliffite Bibles used? There is some evidence for scholarly use in the margins of Wycliffite Bibles. A few manuscripts used in the study of biblical exegesis contain cross references and annotations made by early readers.[50] The table of lections, central to the Wycliffite Bible, ties the Bible to the liturgical year, but, as seen in the previous chapter, does not mandate use within liturgical performance. Bibles with tables of lections were valuable for preachers in preparing their sermons, as sermons typically expounded upon the biblical lection read during Mass. In Latin Bibles these tables appear at times alongside the list of themes for biblical lections such as confession, avarice, pride and others.[51] Such themes were of use for preachers, as they were for priests engaged in pastoral care more widely.

Cambridge, Corpus Christi College MS 147 is a Wycliffite Bible whose addenda and annotations reflect the way in which Latin Bibles were used by preachers. It is a single-volume Bible with the General Prologue and a table of lections. The original rubricator had noted down information to assist readers in navigating lengthy or repetitive lections.[52] Such engagement with lections is also evident in the marks made by the manuscript's subsequent users. A cursive fifteenth-century hand marked the Gospel and Epistle lections for Sundays and feast days in the margins. And so, the note accompanying Romans chapter 6 (fol. 411v) reads 'the Epistle for the 6th Sunday after Trinity' ('Epistola domenica 6ᵃ post trinitate'); it is followed a few lines later by a note of the lesson's end ('finis epistolis'). Written in Latin in a highly abbreviated fashion, this was clearly made by—and for—a trained professional, most likely a priest. The same cursive hand also identified themes within the biblical text: next to 1 Corinthians chapter 7 (fol. 416v) a note 'on virgins' ('de virginibus'), while on the next page (1Cor 9–10, fol. 417r) notes on themes and liturgical occasions: 'Epistle in Septuagesima', 'on idolatry' and 'on the adoration of images' ('epistola in septuagesima', 'de ydolatria', 'de adoratione ymaginis').[53] Much like in Latin Bibles, these annotations enabled

---

50   Cambridge, Emmanuel College MS I.4.33 (James §108), is a very small and neat New Testament with a table of lections *c.*1430–50. It contains fifteenth-century cross references in Arabic numerals in a very professional hand. According to a fifteenth-century note on the flyleaf, this had been the bequest of Thomas Hughes of Lincoln's Inn ('Ex dono Thome Hughes de Lincolnes Inne armigeri fratris mei charissimi'). Cambridge, Magdalene College Pepys MS 2073, a lavish New Testament, likewise has cross references in Arabic numerals in a very professional hand. In Cambridge, Sidney Sussex manuscript 99, a New Testament, there are cross references also to Old Testament books not in the volume (e.g. referencing Habakkuk chapter 2 in the Margins of Romans chapter 1 (fol. 96r)), suggesting use alongside other books.
51   As in V&A Reid MS 22 (fols 367v–368r).
52   At the beginning of Isaiah chapter 4 next to the marginal letter A (fol. 271r) the rubricator had noted 'And this is also the third lesson on Easter Eve & on Wittun [Pentecost] Eve'. Next to Isaiah chapter 18 (fol. 275v) a marginal note explains the complexity of varying-lengths lections, indicated by an additional set of marginal letters (.g. .c. .e. .f. .h. .i.), which are duly noted in the margins of the next chapter.
53   Lollards typically rejected several Church customs as idolatry. These notes could have therefore been used in these arguments, either by orthodox or heterodox. Likewise, 1 Corinthians chapter 13

readers to employ biblical lections within the liturgical year, and supported the tasks of preaching and pastoral care.

Wycliffite Bibles and Liturgical Plurality

In Cambridge, Sidney Sussex MS 99, a New Testament with an Old Testament lectionary, marginal themes were incorporated into the manuscript's original design. This was done either by the rubricator (in red) or by a contemporary hand before rubrication (in black and possibly by the original scribe). Some readings are identical to those we have just seen in CCCC MS 147, such as 'on virgins' ('de virginibus') in the margins of 1 Corinthians chapter 7 (fol. 110v). As a whole, the annotations reveal a clear engagement with women and the family: the silence of women in church, women's dress, widows, virgins, matrimony, temptation and so forth.[54] The notes were meant for an expert reader. Annotations such as the one accompanying Matthew chapter 20, for example, abbreviate the Latin verse 'Simile est regnum cælorum homini patrifamiliasis' ('The kingdom of heaven is like to an householder' Mt 20:1) into 'sil' e' reg' ce' hoi' pri'. This heavily abbreviated form could be deciphered only by someone well versed in the Latin Bible.

Sidney Sussex MS 99 is a Middle English Bible, whose design displays an interest in women, virginity and morality, and which was used by a reader well versed in the Latin Bible. Proficiency in Latin and English, alongside active engagement with the Bible and the centrality of female piety, are all typical of late medieval nunneries. The link between the Wycliffite Bible and nunneries has been noted by Deanesly and Solopova, with several manuscripts originating or used in nunneries such as Barking and Syon.[55] Studying book ownership and use across nunneries in late medieval England, David Bell has noted that '[e]ven at Thetford, a small and poor house, we find a Wycliffite translation of the New Testament'.[56] While there is no explicit evidence for the provenance of Sidney Sussex MS 99, its materiality assists

---

(fol. 418r) is accompanied by 'Epistle in quinquagesima' and 'on charity' ('epistola in quinquagesima', 'de caritate').

54   Mt 20:1: 'Simile est regnum cælorum homini patrifamilias' (fol. 22r); Mk 12:42: 'de vidua Luc 21' (fol. 43r, which indeed appears again in Luke 21 as 'de vidua Marc' xii', fol. 70r); Lk 11:2: 'Pater noster' (fol. 60r); 1 Cor 7:10: 'de matrimonio' (fol. 110r), 7:25: 'de virginibus' (fol. 110v); 1 Cor 10:13: 'nota temptacione' (fol. 112r); 1 Cor 14:34: 'mulieres non p[ermittitur] dic[ere] in ecclesia' (fol. 115r); 1 Tim 2:9: 'de ornatu mulierum' (fol. 140v); 1 Tim 3:2: 'Adam non est seductus', 'episcopatus cum uxor & fi' (fol. 140v); Tit 2:4: 'uxores amate' (fol. 145v).

55   Deanesly, *The Lollard Bible*, pp. 336–42, is still fundamental; Solopova, 'A Wycliffite Bible made for a nun of Barking'.

56   David Bell, *What nuns read: books and libraries in medieval English nunneries* (Kalamazoo, MI: Cistercian, 1995), pp. 72–3.

Figure 2.4 Tabs in a Wycliffite Bible. This seemingly unimportant feature strongly suggests the Bible was used at Syon Abbey. Cambridge, Sidney Sussex College MS 99 fol. 189r. By permission of the Master and Fellows of Sidney Sussex College, Cambridge.

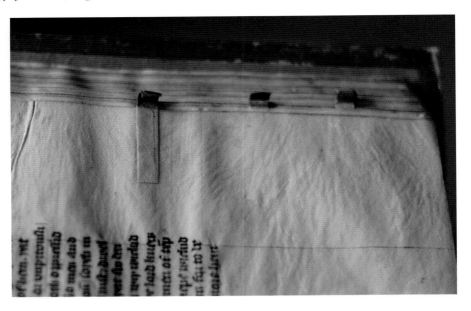

in further ascertaining its provenance. Navigation through the manuscript is eased by tabs at the beginning of each book of the Bible (see Figure 2.4). These leather tabs were pasted on both sides of the folio. The style of the tabs is typical of a specific establishment in late medieval England. Christopher De Hamel had traced tabs similar in their size and pasting to manuscripts produced and read in Syon Abbey.[57] This is corroborated by the nearly identical tabs in other Syon books such as Cambridge, St John's College MSS E.28 and F.2, or Bodl. MS Auct. D.3.1.[58] Established by Henry V in 1415, Syon Abbey was one of the wealthiest religious establishments in England, a unique house with sections for nuns and for monks. More of its books have survived than from any other nunnery, enabling a detailed analysis of its collections and reading habits.[59] The nuns in Syon appear to have embraced vernacular religion. Bell notes that while the brothers' library catalogue records only thirty non-Latin books out of a total of 1,421 books, the sisters' surviving manuscripts contain seventeen English books out of a total of twenty-four non-liturgical books.[60]

---

57   Christopher De Hamel, *Syon Abbey: the library of the Bridgettine Nuns and their peregrinations after the Reformation* (London: Roxburghe Club, 1991), pp. 103–4. The tabs were made using a strip of parchment 7 mm wide and with length varying between 37 and 42 mm (*c.*27 mm within the book, and from 10 to 15 mm projecting outwards).

58   All the tabs are glued on both sides of the folio. Their size is likewise similar. E.28: 7–9 mm wide, *c.*20 mm long (14 in-page + 6 protruding); F.2: 9–10 mm wide, *c.*27 mm long (22 in-page + 5 protruding).

59   De Hamel, *Syon Abbey*; Bell, *What nuns read*.

60   Bell, *What nuns read*, pp. 74–5. The discrepancy in the overall number of books is not due to a

Like other scholars of Syon and of Middle English literature more widely, Bell separates the nuns' interest in vernacular literature and theology from their Latin liturgy, seeing the two as distinct spheres. A closer study of their manuscripts reveals how these spheres overlapped. Syon is unique not only in the survival of its books, but also in the novelty of its rite, which combined the Benedictine rule with a distinct Brigittine liturgy. The nuns commissioned many manuscripts to support their distinctive devotions and liturgy. These often bear witness to a merging of Latin and vernacular in the liturgy. Unlike processionals from other institutions, the above-mentioned St John's MS F.2 is a processional whose prayers are in Latin, but whose rubrics are in English.[61] Thus, for example, the rubric prefacing the Responsory *Descendit de celis* (see Figure 2.5) reads in English 'Upon Christmas Day at the procession in going forth, R[esponsory]'. Other manuscripts contain even stronger evidence for vernacular liturgy in Syon. While the monks in Syon followed the Use of Sarum, the nuns followed that of the Brigittine Order. Cambridge, St John's College MS A.11 provides the rule in a volume suitable for public recitation. Most of the text is in Latin, yet on fols 25r–42v, the form of profession for one entering the order is provided in both Latin and English. The latter is rubricated as 'Anglice' (see Figure 2.6, containing explanatory rubric, liturgical texts and rubrics), and enables the dialogue with the entrant to take place in English, as the lengthy rubric explains:

> And note that nuns are always accustomed to professing in the mother tongue, as also lay brothers. Priests or deacons: in Latin if not in the mother tongue by the disposition of the bishop. The devotion of the people is accustomed to being more greatly satisfied in the mother tongue than any other language. The bishop shall therefore do (or esteem) over this, which shall seem better to him, with the advice of the general confessor.[62]

The rubric provides two options for the celebrant to choose from. Both were valid, and each accommodated the needs of a different audience and competency. Latin and English do not seem to oppose, but rather to

---

different size of each library, but rather due to the lack of any surviving library catalogue from the sisters' library.

61   This is part of a wider group of processionals, discussed by de Hamel, *Syon Abbey*. See also Oxford, St John's College MS 167 (Ralph Hanna, *A descriptive catalogue of the western medieval manuscripts of St. John's College, Oxford* (Oxford: Oxford University Press, 2002), pp. 232–4).

62   'Et notandum que moniales semper profiteri solent in lingua materna et etiam fratres laici. Sacerdotes vero et diaconi: in latina lingua sive materna pro dipositione episcopi. Devotio tamen populi magis exatari solet lingua materna quam alia lingua. Episcopus ergo faciat super hoc quod sibi melius videtur una cum consilio generalis confessoris' (fol. 25v).

Figure 2.5
Vernacular rubrics
in a processional.
The combination
of English rubrics
and Latin text is
indicative of the
merging of the
two languages
in liturgical
manuscripts from
Syon Abbey.
Cambridge,
St John's College
MS F.2, unfoliated.
By permission
of the Master
and Fellows of
St John's College,
Cambridge.

complement one another in the liturgy. This could be applied to Brigittine liturgy at large. The Brigittine Office and its commentary were translated into Middle English as the *The Myroure of Oure Ladye*.[63] Henry Hargreaves has shown that a short passage that prohibited the reading of the Office in English is a later interpolation. This leads him to conclude that 'without it, in the

---

63   Surviving in two parts: Aberdeen University Library MS 134 and Bodl. MS Rawlinson C.941. It was printed in 1530 by Richard Fawkes. The only modern edition is *The myroure of Oure Ladye: containing a devotional treatise on divine service, with a translation of the offices used by the Sisters of the Brigittine Monastery of Sion, at Isleworth, during the fifteenth and sixteenth centuries*, ed. John Henry Blunt, Early English Text Society ES 19 (London: Trubner for the Early English Text Society, 1873); assessed, and criticised, by Henry Hargreaves, 'The Mirror of Our Lady: Aberdeen University Library MS. 134', *Aberdeen University Review* 42:4 (1968), 267–80. For modern analysis see Nancy Bradley Warren, *Spiritual economies: female monasticism in later medieval England* (Philadelphia: University of Pennsylvania Press, 2001), pp. 44–54.

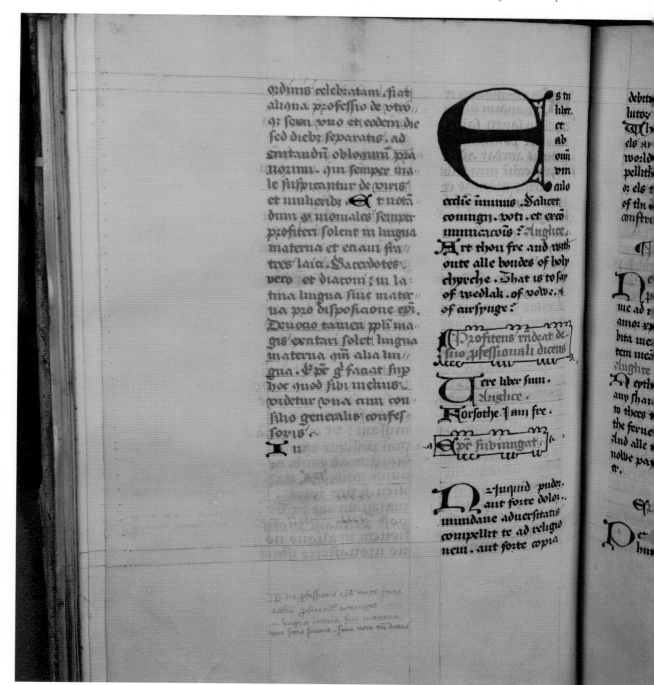

Figure 2.6 Brigittine Rule (Syon Abbey). When administering the profession into the order, the bishop is given the choice whether to perform the liturgy in English or in Latin. Cambridge, St John's College MS A.11 fol. 25v. By permission of the Master and Fellows of St John's College, Cambridge.

form in which it exists in the older version [...] it is even more liberal in its attitude to vernacular scriptures than has hitherto been realised'.[64]

Where and how did the nuns use their vernacular Bibles? A brother of Syon had translated a list commemorating the martyrs (the *martyrology*) into English, and De Hamel suggests that this was used 'semi-liturgically' in the Chapter House, where the community assembled daily to conduct its business. The rule also mandated spiritual readings in the Chapter House every night before Compline.[65] Such readings should be 'inwardly spiritual and easy to understand'. The layout of Sidney Sussex MS 99 suggests that it was designed to provide such materials. The rubrics identify sections on sin, women's behaviour and spirituality. The use of vernacular Scripture, taken either from the translated Office or from Wycliffite Bibles, could have also served in Syon's liturgy. While men and women took part in Mass and Office in the same church, its architecture separated the two parts of the community in the performance of two parallel liturgies: the men followed the Use of Sarum, and the nuns a unique simplified liturgy structured in a weekly cycle; monks were in the ground-level choir, nuns on a mezzanine floor; monks chanted their Office first, and the nuns followed.[66] The two levels could be seen as separate linguistic spheres. This, however, remains conjectural, and is indicative of a much wider problem regarding our knowledge of the use of the vernacular in the liturgy.

Liturgical manuscripts offer scholars a view of normative Latin rites, which were disseminated from cathedrals and monasteries. In fifteenth-century England the liturgy of Salisbury, or the Use of Sarum, became the dominant rite, replicated in liturgical manuscripts as well as in tables of lections in Wycliffite Bibles. However, David Chadd, Helen Gittos and Sarah Hamilton have all noted that liturgical manuscripts should not be taken as simply reflecting the performed rite.[67] These were also prescriptive objects, aimed at shaping a uniform liturgical experience. The gap between manuscript evidence and liturgical reality comes to the fore in the question of the language of the liturgy. Scholars of preaching accept that sermons preserved in Latin were often delivered in the vernacular, or in a mix of the

---

64   Hargreaves, 'The Mirror of Our Lady', 280.

65   Blunt, *myroure*, pp. xxxiii, 165–6; De Hamel, *Syon Abbey*, p. 72.

66   Richard William Pfaff, *The liturgy in medieval England: a history* (Cambridge: Cambridge University Press, 2009), pp. 532–3; De Hamel, *Syon Abbey*, pp. 52–4.

67   David Chadd, 'The ritual of Palm Sunday: Nidaros in context', in *The medieval cathedral of Tronheim: architectural and ritual constructions in their European context*, ed. Margrete Syrstad Andås et al. (Turnhout: Brepols, 2007), pp. 253–78; Helen Gittos, 'Researching the history of rites', in *Understanding medieval liturgy: essays in interpretation*, ed. Helen Gittos and Sarah Hamilton (Aldershot: Ashgate, 2015), pp. 13–37; Helen Gittos and Sarah Hamilton, 'Introduction', in *Understanding medieval liturgy*, pp. 1–10.

two. When it comes to liturgy, only recently has Helen Gittos embarked on gathering evidence for vernacular liturgy in England (primarily from the Anglo-Saxon period) arising from what have been considered as purely Latin liturgical texts.[68] Traces of such use are evident also in Littlehales and Wordsworth's 1904 survey, which reveals how in fifteenth-century England rites that involved the laity were conducted partially in English.[69] Wedding rituals and visitations of the sick were administered by the priest, but had to be understood by the laity, and hence incorporated elements in the vernacular (much like the above-mentioned profession). Both rites also appear under the 'Commemoration' section of the table of lections in Wycliffite Bibles. In Books of Hours the litany was at times supplied in English, likewise facilitating vernacular devotion for the laity. Syon's practices must be understood against this background.

The liturgy performed at cathedrals and monasteries, friaries and colleges, survives in numerous manuscripts, which portray a primarily Latin rite. For rites performed outside these centres, as for vernacular devotions, evidence is much more limited. As is the case for nunneries, the liturgy of chantries, private and guild chapels, which combined lay and female devotions, is seldom documented. The same is true of lay brothers and tertiaries, who shared only parts of monastic liturgy. The rubric from the Syon Processional (St John's MS A.11) explicitly equates nuns and lay brothers in their use of the vernacular ('And note that nuns are always accustomed to professing in the mother tongue, as also lay brothers').[70] Unlike male monastic, collegiate or mendicant communities, nuns, lay brothers and members of guilds and confraternities combined voluntary religious aspirations with an affinity to the vernacular and lower levels of Latin literacy.[71] This corresponds with the evidence from the Low Countries. Suzan Folkerts's study of biblical translations into Dutch, which are better documented and with a stronger record of provenance than the Wycliffite Bible, has revealed that 'Middle Dutch [biblical] manuscripts were mainly used by religious women: 167 out of 221 manuscripts, or 75 per cent, came from female religious institutions and individuals'.[72] The sparse evidence from Wycliffite Bibles likewise links

---

68 Helen Gittos, *English: the forgotten language of the medieval church* (working title, forthcoming). I thank Helen for numerous discussions about vernacular liturgy.

69 Christopher Wordsworth and Henry Littlehales, *The old service-books of the English Church* (London: Methuen, 1904), pp. 50–5. I thank Helen Gittos for this reference.

70 See note 62 above.

71 Another example for the role of the Bible in facilitating lay female devotion is evident in Anglo-Norman Apocalypses, whose audience was often noble women. See, for example, Renana Bartal, 'The Pepys Apocalypse (Cambridge, Magdalene College, MS Pepys 1803) and the readership of religious women', *Journal of Medieval History* 37:4 (2011), 358–77.

72 Folkerts, 'Reading the Bible', 228.

them to these milieus. The evidence above suggests use by female religious. Solopova's study of the calendar in BL MS Egerton MS 1171 positions it with the nuns of Barking.[73] Dove has linked BL MS Harley 1710 (a Wycliffite lectionary) with a chantry priest, and suggested that Thomas Woodstock's Bible (BL, MS Egerton 617) could have been used in his chapel alongside a Latin one.[74] If Wycliffite Bibles were used within the liturgy, this can also help explain their absence from our records. Liturgical books would not appear in catalogues or library records. They were commonly kept in the choir, whose book lists rarely survive.

CUL MS Ll.1.13 contains an Old Testament lectionary alongside a full New Testament. It has annotations in competent fifteenth-century hands, clear and heavily abbreviated; navigational tabs were sewn into the manuscript,[75] and all this suggests use within a bookish environment. The manuscript provides important evidence for the reception of the table of lections. Unlike other Wycliffite Bibles, it lacks the identification of the alphabetical chapter sub-division both in the table and in the margins of the biblical text. An early fifteenth-century reader corrected this absence by laboriously going through the book, marking liturgical occurrences in the margins of the biblical text (see Figure 2.7). These notes were written in a confident and highly abbreviated hand, similar to the ones employed by clerics in the margins of Latin Bibles or service books. In those books the annotations are almost solely in Latin. Here, on the other hand, the annotations are in English. Thus, we find on fol. 229r (1 Cor chapter 11) 'Corp^9 x^i day' for Corpus Christy day, or on fol. 142v (Lk chapter 6, fig. 2.7) 'þe s^o in v^s of dedicā of a churche' for the Sunday in the *utas* (octave, an eight-day liturgical period) of the dedication of a church.[76] Most references are even more highly abbreviated: the note near Matthew chapter 6 (fol. 72v) reads 'xv s^o af t^e', for the fifteenth Sunday after Trinity. A similar heavily abbreviated annotation in English for liturgical feasts is evident in the rubrics of the Syon processional, as in the reference to 'corp^9 xpi day' (St John's MS F.2, unfoliated). Here, the marginal annotations reveal a vernacular aspect of the liturgy, like that of Syon, in a Bible whose materiality suggests it was not a Syon book.

A clearer example for the use of Wycliffite Bibles in the course of vernacular liturgy is Cambridge, St John's College MS E.14. A small and profession-

---

73   Solopova, 'A Wycliffite Bible made for a nun of Barking'.
74   Dove, *The first English Bible*, pp. 64–6; Peikola, 'The Sanctorale'.
75   This was done in a way different from the tabs used in Syon. White thread was sewn into existing pricking holes, either in the upper or the outer margins of the book. Another manuscript with similar tabs is Cambridge, Pembroke College MS 141, an LMB. I thank James Freeman for this reference.
76   These are similar, but not identical to the ones used in the table of lections: 'Corp^9 dai x^i' (fol. 62r) and 'Sondai ī þe vtas' (fol. 63v).

Figure 2.7 Liturgical marginal annotations. These highly abbreviated indications of liturgical celebrations (the dedication of a church in this case) are uniquely provided in English. CUL MS Ll.1.13 fol. 142v. Reproduced by kind permission of the Syndics of Cambridge University Library.

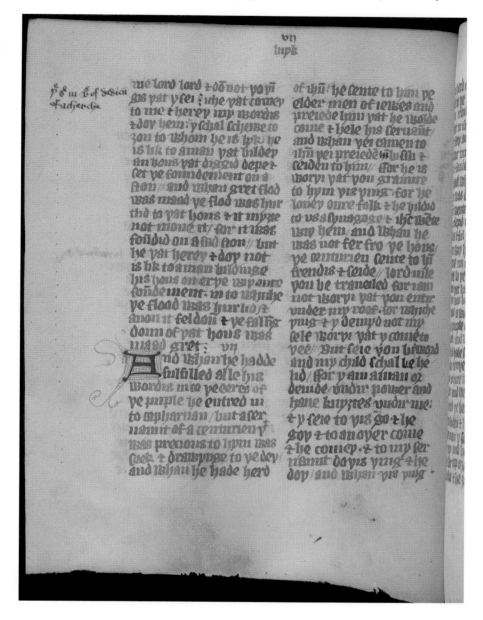

ally made volume, it comprises the Psalms, Canticles, Athanasian Creed and a few Sapiential Books (Proverbs to Ecclesiasticus).[77] On the last leaf of the manuscript, a slightly later fifteenth-century hand had noted down in English part of the Office for the Dead. These are taken from the first nocturne with

77 As explicit on ii.r, the manuscript was owned by Clemens Ridley, servant to Robert Shurton. It is most likely to have been Robert Shorton, Master of St John's College, Cambridge (†1535).

the first lesson (Job 7:16b–21), the subsequent responsory (relying on Job 9:25-6) and the second lesson (Job 10:1–7).[78] The text breaks away from the biblical sequence to follow the Latin Office. The last lesson is truncated, but the gathering suggests at least four leaves could be missing from the current manuscript, raising the possibility that a fuller Office had once existed. As in the previous manuscript, here too the liturgical elements are in English. The lections and responsory are taken from the Wycliffite Bible, although not from the current volume, which does not contain the book of Job. The end of the responsory in the manuscript once more suggests expert use. It truncates the very end of the responsory by substituting the last few words with an 'etc.'. Clearly the scribe expected the reader to be familiar with the Latin Office, and able to fill in the missing text. So here is an English part-breviary, which made use of the Wycliffite Bible in the creation of an English liturgy. It was made for a reader well versed in the liturgy, whose practice involved moving between Latin and English in the delivery of the liturgy. This does not evidence a confrontation between the two spheres, but rather indicates a cohabitation of the two languages, akin to that found in late medieval sermons.

Psalms and Competing Mnemonics

In its manuscript setting, St John's E.14 is more like an LMB than most other Wycliffite Bibles. As can be seen in Figure 2.8 (Psalm 109/110), it is immaculately written in clear black ink, with red and blue initials and pen-work, as well as rubrics and running titles. Although it has suffered over time, its parchment is significantly finer than that of most Wycliffite Bibles, more reminiscent of mid-thirteenth-century Latin Bibles. The presentation of the Psalms in the manuscript differs from that of Latin Bibles. The original rubricator had preceded each Psalm with a lengthy rubric providing

- the Psalm number in a Roman numeral;
- the biblical superscription (the verse preceding the Psalm in the Hebrew Bible, linking it to Temple worship or episodes from Old Testament history);
- the opening words of each Psalm in Latin (the Incipit); and
- occasionally a short commentary.

78   Christopher Wordsworth and Francis Procter (eds), *Breviarium ad usum insignis ecclesiae Sarum: juxta editionem maximam*, 3 vols (Cambridge: Cambridge University Press, 1879), vol. 2, cols 273–6.

Figure 2.8 Psalms in a Wycliffite Bible. This layout mirrors that of orthodox Bibles, and especially of the Dominicans', the Lollards' major adversaries. Cambridge, St John's College MS E.14, fol. 45r. By permission of the Master and Fellows of St John's College, Cambridge.

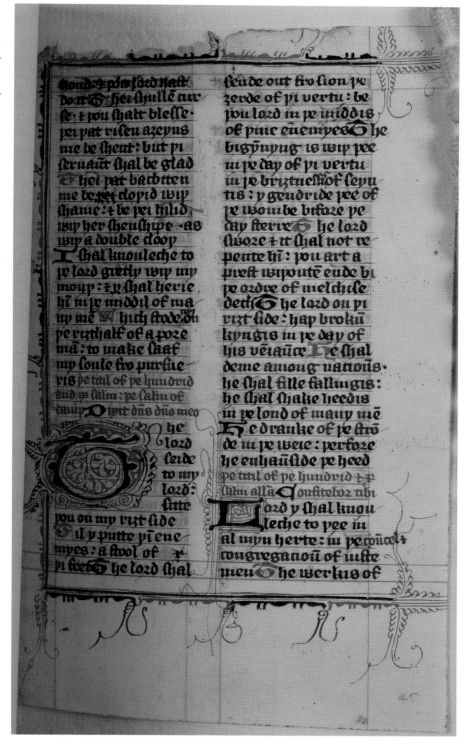

The rubric preceding the second Psalm reads 'the ij Psalm Quare fremuerunt. This Psalm hath no title in Hebrew and in Jerome's translation was made of David as the Apostle witnessed in the fourth chapter of Acts of the Apostles [Acts 4:25–6]'. This device appears to have been a novelty to the production team.[79] In the course of writing the manuscript the production team gradually began highlighting the Latin incipit—the opening words of the Psalm in the Latin. Initially less noticeable within the lengthy rubric, from Psalm 70/71 the rubricator directed attention to it by prefacing the Latin incipit with a minor red capital letter (see Figure 2.8, the capital 'D' beginning the verse 'Dixit Dominus Domino meo' for Psalm 109/110, or 'C' of 'Cofitebor tibi' of Psalm 110/111). As discussed in the previous chapter, the Latin incipit was central to the way the Psalms were retained in the memory of lay and clerical audiences in late medieval England. Now we can view how this extended to the Wycliffite Bible. In St John's MS E.14 another form of Psalm identification was introduced by a later reader. In the margins of the Psalter—at Psalms 40/41 to 91/92—a reader had noted the Psalm numbers in Arabic numerals in an accomplished fifteenth-century hand. Alongside the clear *nota* marks, these suggest a proficient and competent early reader, typical of a clerical milieu.

In the previous chapter the Psalms emerged as the site of competing mnemonics, in which two parallel systems of knowledge collided: one liturgical, vocal and musical, in which the Psalms were identified by their opening words; the other scholastic and visual, in which the Psalms were known by their numerical value. The first is common in liturgical Psalters and most LMBs; the second is typical of a small group of mendicant Bibles. Such competing mnemonics came to the fore in Wycliffite Bibles, whose language broke away from Latin liturgy and common Psalm mnemonics. Providing the Psalms in English moved vernacular translation and Latin performance onto a collision course. Much like St John's MS E.14, the layers of information embedded into Wycliffite Psalters—English text, Latin incipit, biblical superscription and Psalm number—had led scribes, stationers, rubricators and readers to omit or highlight specific components, thus taking a stance on the way they memorised and displayed the Psalms.[80]

Such tensions are evident in the layout of the Psalms in the earliest manuscripts of the Wycliffite Bible. Bodl. MS Bodley 959, a workshop manuscript copied *c.*1380–90, is one of the earliest Wycliffite Bibles,

---

79   Similar instances of unstable layout for the Latin incipits of the Psalms have been studied by Annie Sutherland, *English Psalms in the Middle Ages, 1300–1450* (Oxford: Oxford University Press, 2015), pp. 243–4, 259, 266–7.

80   For terminology see p. xvii. The most detailed study of Latin incipits in Middle English Psalters is Sutherland, *English Psalms in the Middle Ages*, pp. 248–72.

although most likely not the proto-Bible suggested by Forshall and Madden, or De Hamel.[81] The considerable scholarly attention given to the manuscript has unearthed the earlier stages of the production of the Wycliffite Bible. Unnoticed by scholars, however, is a moment frozen in the evolution of the English Psalms, which reveals a gradual accommodation of the Psalms' layout to common mnemonics and to Latin chant. The original scribe of the Psalms wrote the text in English; the Psalms were identified solely by their numerical value, entered by him in the margins in a mixture of Arabic and Roman numerals. The scribe also noted a guide-letter in the margins, indicating the capital letter to be rubricated. This instruction was followed by the rubricator, who preceded each Psalm with a three-line red capital. Shortly after the scribe and rubricator had concluded their labours, another hand added the Latin incipit, supplying another form of identification beyond that provided by the original creators. The timing of this can be ascertained by a close examination of the manuscript (see Figure 2.9). The ink of the Latin incipit prefacing Psalm 7 ('Domine Deus meus') was applied on top of the red of the capital letter, clearly indicating that this took place after the rubricator had concluded his role, and following the early production of the Psalter. The original production team aimed at presenting a fully English Psalter, which left little space for Latin mnemonics. However, the gap between inception and reception, between the competing Psalms mnemonics, was quickly filled.

A similar phenomenon is evident in CUL MS Add. 6681 (see Figure 2.10), another early Wycliffite Bible, in which the original scribe had not provided the Latin incipit. Once more, an early reader had filled the gap by providing the Latin incipit in the margins, and the Psalm number in Arabic numerals.[82] Much like Bodl. 959, this manuscript was written in a cursive hand. The Latin incipits, however, were written in a more angular script. Unlike its use in thirteenth-century manuscripts, such script was less common *c.*1400, and was reserved for specific genres, such as liturgical manuscripts and Latin Bibles. The scribe/reader of Add. 6681 noted the Latin incipit in a way that echoed the liturgy both aurally (the Latin recitation of the Psalms) and visually (the script of liturgical manuscripts). The

---

81   Josiah Forshall and Frederic Madden (eds), *The Holy Bible, containing the Old and New Testaments, with the Apocryphal books, in the earliest English versions made from the Latin Vulgate by John Wycliffe and his followers*, 4 vols (Oxford: Oxford University Press, 1850), 1:xvii; de Hamel, *The book*, 170–2. For a short description and summary of bibliography see Solopova, *Manuscripts of the Wycliffite Bible*, pp. 88–92. The Psalms of this manuscript were analysed, from the textual perspective, by Annie Sutherland, 'The Wycliffite Psalms', in *The Wycliffite Bible: origin, history and interpretation*, ed. Elizabeth Solopova, Medieval and Renaissance authors and texts 16 (Leiden: Brill, 2016), pp. 183–201 at 187–92.

82   It is possible this was done by the original scribe later in the production campaign, as the slightly different hand could be ascribed to the move between languages and scripts, rather than different individuals.

Figure 2.9 Psalms in an early Wycliffite Bible. This reveals how an early reader added the Latin incipits, tying the Psalms to orthodox Church services and common Psalms' mnemonics. Oxford, Bodleian Library, MS Bodl. 959 fol. 234r, detail. By permission of the Bodleian Library, University of Oxford (detail).

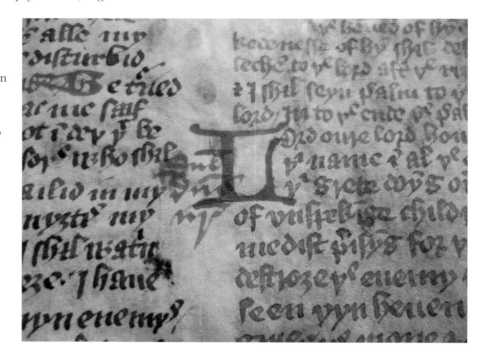

Latin incipit thus merges two spheres: Latin liturgy and vernacular Psalms, LMBs and Wycliffite Bibles. A subsequent reader noted the Latin incipit of the biblical Canticles with chapter numbers (fol. 223v) in a clear fifteenth-century hand, again reminiscent of Latin Psalmody and Bibles.[83] Both Bodl. 959 and Add. 6681 attest to an early transformation in the material history of the Wycliffite Bible. The original production of the two manuscripts suited a solely English Psalmody, befitting either the Wycliffite negation of Latin Psalmody or a lack of awareness of the complexity of Psalm mnemonics. This gap was bridged shortly after production, by users who drew the manuscripts closer to Latin liturgy.

Cambridge Corpus Christi College MS 147 is another example for competing mnemonics and their representation on the page. Like other Wycliffite Bibles, this single-volume Bible presents the Psalms through a multi-layered retrieval system, providing the Psalm number, biblical superscription and Latin incipit. Much like St John's MS E.14, the presentation of the Latin incipit was a novelty to the makers of this manuscript. The Latin incipit is written after the Psalm number and superscription, at times within the body of the Psalms, at times in the margins. While the number and superscription are rubricated, the Latin incipit is written in black with red underline—and

---

83   On the Canticles in Latin Bibles, Chapter 1, pp. 33–6; in Wycliffite Bibles, pp. 78–80.

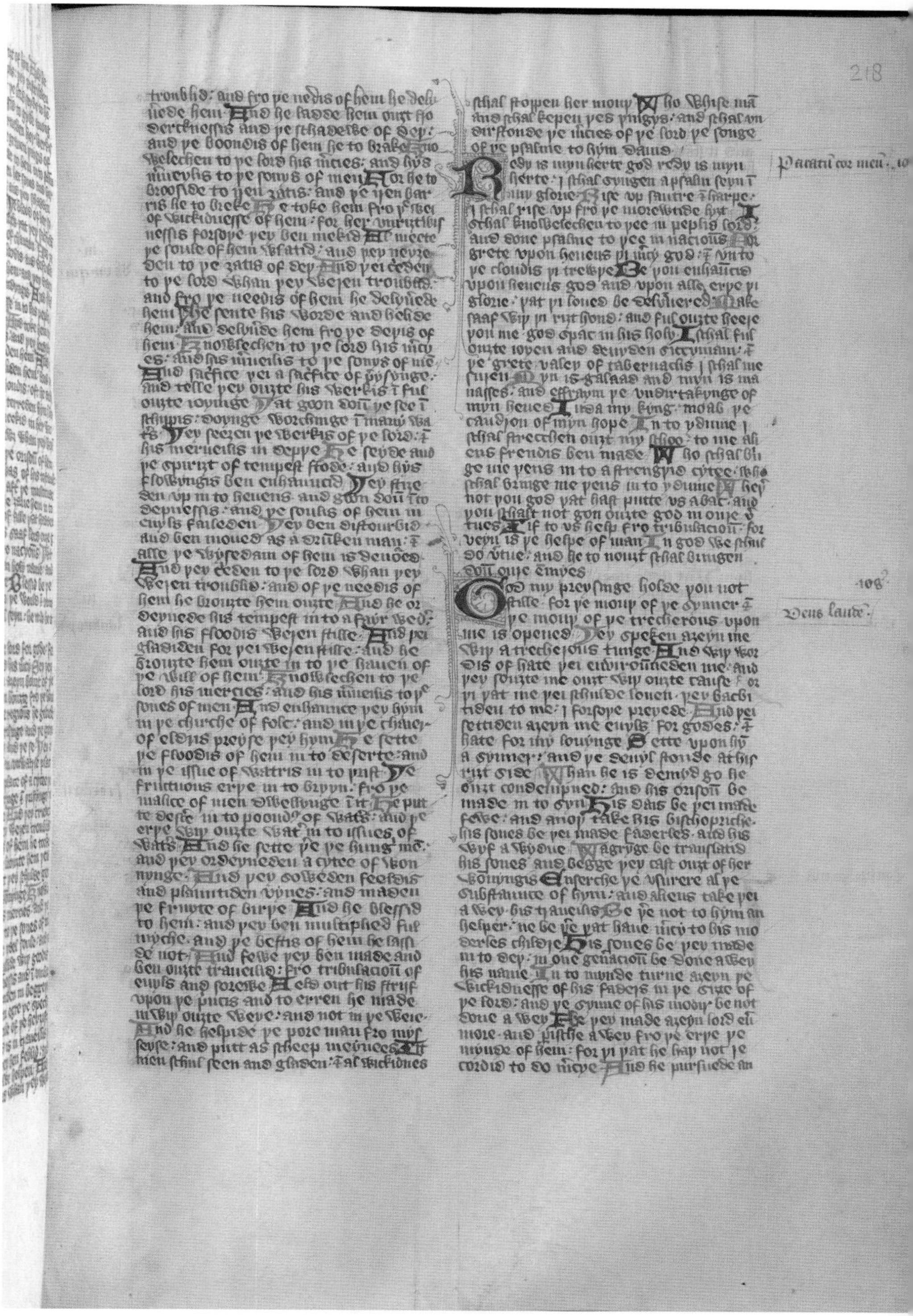

Figure 2.10 Psalms in an early Wycliffite Bible. This is another indication of the way the Latin incipits were not part of the original design of the book, but quickly affixed by an early reader, if not the original scribe. CUL Add. MS 6681 fol. 218r. Reproduced by kind permission of the Syndics of Cambridge University Library.

hence less noticeable. The original scribe sought to augment it, and to signal out the incipit: in several Psalms the first letter of the incipit was to be written as a distinct one-line initial. The scribe had noted the first letter faintly at a distance from the word, and expected the rubricator to scrape it out and write instead a coloured capital. This, however, was not followed up by the rubricator nor by the illuminator, leaving the Latin incipits in several cases to begin with their second letter (e.g. 'iserere' instead of 'miserere' for Psalm 50/51, fol. 218v),[84] or with the first letter written faintly and removed from the rest of the opening word.

Once the production of Wycliffite Bibles was established and manuscripts became more uniform, often the product of London stationers, these were created with Latin mnemonics as part of the Psalms' original design. Latin incipits are commonly an integral part of the layout, separated from the body of the Psalm by a marginal position, by red ink or red underline, thus enabling quick and efficient identification.[85] A more enmeshed view of English Bible and Latin liturgy is present in a small group of Wycliffite Psalters. In BL, Yates Thompson MS 52, for example, each English verse is preceded by the Latin opening word underlined in red (see Figure 2.11).[86] This layout enabled readers to follow the English translation alongside the Latin Psalms, either using a Latin Psalter, hearing the Latin chant or recalling it in their minds. Close affinity to the Latin liturgy is also evident in BL MS Add. 10,046, where the running titles identify the eightfold division of the Psalter: The running titles comprise of the Latin incipit of the Psalm which opens the division: *Beatus vir* (Ps 1) as the running title for Psalms 1–25/26;[87] *Dominus illuminatio* (Ps 26/27) for Psalms 26/27–37/38; and so forth.[88] Such layout linked the Wycliffite Psalter to the chant of Psalmody in the course of the Divine Office. This eightfold division is extant, albeit not as overtly, in Wycliffite Bibles in general, which, like LMBs, incorporate larger initials for Psalms 1, 26/27, 38/39, 52/53, 68/69, 80/81, 97/98 and 109/110, thus sub-dividing the Book of Psalms in accordance with its performance in the Divine Office.

CUL MS Ee.1.10 presents a more harmonious, yet enigmatic, view of English and Latin Psalmody. The manuscript is often described as a biblical

---

84   For a digital image see https://parker.stanford.edu/parker/catalog/hc524fk1795, accessed 12 November 2019.

85   De Hamel, *The book*, pp. 182–3; Hudson and Solopova, 'The Latin text', pp. 115–16.

86   Sutherland, *English Psalms in the Middle Ages*, pp. 136–58; Sutherland, 'The Wycliffite Psalms', 200N53.

87   The foliation of the manuscript is misleading, as many pages are mis-bound.

88   For this division in Latin liturgical Psalter see Elizabeth Solopova, *Latin liturgical Psalters in the Bodleian Library: a select catalogue* (Oxford: Bodleian Library, 2013), pp. 641–50. The eightfold division is typical of secular uses.

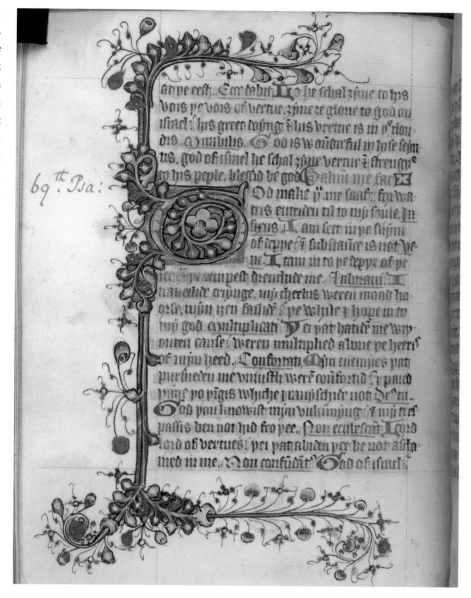

Figure 2.11 Wycliffite Psalter. This is an extreme example of the link between English Psalms and Latin performance, if not mnemonics. BL, Yates Thompson MS 52 fol. 96v. © The British Library Board.

summary.[89] Its function, however, is unclear, and it is far from serving as a useful summary in the modern sense. The manuscript does not present the

---

89 Studies of this manuscript have tended to concentrate on its text, which comprises an intermediate version of the Wycliffite Bible: Henry Hargreaves, 'An intermediate version of the Wycliffite Old Testament', *Studia Neophilologica* 28:2 (1956), 130–47, which acknowledges that the function of this book is unclear; Hudson and Solopova, 'The Latin text', p. 111; Sutherland, 'The Wycliffite Psalms', p. 191; Sutherland, *English Psalms in the Middle Ages*, pp. 152–5.

biblical text in its entirety. Rather, each biblical chapter comprises only a fragment of the text, a handful of verses grouped together, ending with the scribe noting '&c.'. Thus, for example, Psalm 2 (fol. 226r) comprises verses 1–3 followed by an '&c.', then verses 10–11 followed by another '&c.', before moving to Psalm 3. Such a device makes little sense in most chapters. Job chapter 1 (fols 212v–213r), for example, omits key elements such as the reply of Satan (1:8b–1:10a) or the start of Job's torments (1:12–16a). The Psalms' truncation likewise makes little sense and is hardly comprehensible on its own accord.

The presentation of the Psalms in the manuscript embraced another strategy of linking English and Latin Psalmody. Each Psalm begins with a two-line decorated initial in blue with red pen-work, with key Psalms opening with a three-line burnished gold initial on blue and pink background (see Figure 2.12). These introduce the Latin incipit, rather than the first English verse, which follows with a minor one-line red capital, like any other verse of the Psalms.[90] The effect is to create a visual echo to the Latin Psalter, with the large capital letters familiar to clergy and laity: the 'B' for the *Beatus* of Psalm 1, 'Q' for the *Quare fremuerunt gentes* of Psalm 2 (which begins with a W in the English), and so forth. The use of seemingly discrete elements of Psalm mnemonics extends even further in the presentation of the page, as the Latin incipit is written in black ink and is un-rubricated, presented as an organic part of the Psalm, rather than a separate tag.

Immediately following the Psalms in the manuscript is another feature familiar from the previous chapter: the biblical Canticles. These Old and New Testament hymns were integral to Latin liturgy and a common feature in Latin Psalters. Their affinity to the Psalter is evident in their Middle English name: *Psalms*.[91] Just as in mendicant Bibles, the Old Testament Canticles are referenced in our manuscript by their Latin incipit and biblical reference, as on fol. 74r: 'Confitebor tibi domino quoniam iratus es michi: Isaie.12.xii' ('I will give thanks to thee, O Lord, for thou wast angry with me').[92] As the New Testament is lacking in the volume, the Canticles derived from it, as well as extra-biblical Canticles, are provided in full on fols 74r–75v: *Te Deum Laudamus* (ascribed in the margins to Augustine and Ambrose); *Benedicite omnia opera* (the song of the Three Boys, Apocryphal, 'Psalmus' in rubric); *Benedictus dominus* (Lk 1:68–79, 'Zacharias'); *Magnificat* (Lk 1:46–55, 'Mary'); *Nunc dimittis* (Lk 2:29–32, 'Simeon'); *Quicumque vult* (Athanasian Creed, 'Athanasius'). Much like the Psalms, the English text is preceded by a Latin incipit with a two-line initial.

90   Similar to Bodl. MS Fairfax 2, presented by de Hamel, *The book*, p. 182. This was common in other Middle English translations explored by Sutherland.
91   For example, Blunt, *myroure*, p. 124.
92   Uniquely, the chapter number is given in both Arabic and Roman numerals.

Figure 2.12 Psalms in an abbreviated Wycliffite Bible. The capitals letters in this Bible direct the reader's attention not to the English text, but rather to the Latin incipits. CUL MS Ee.1.10 fol. 226r. Reproduced by kind permission of the Syndics of Cambridge University Library.

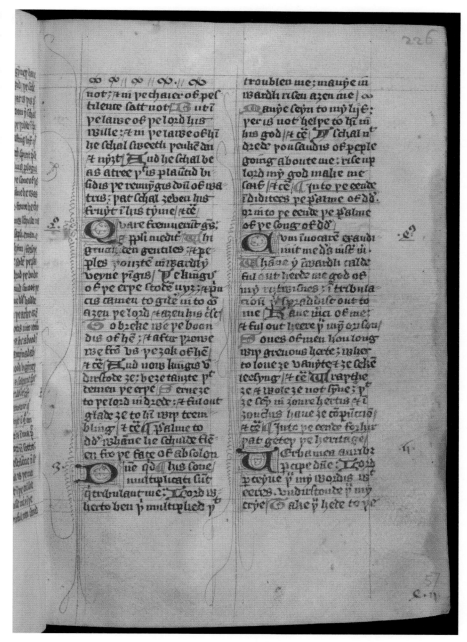

The link between layout and performance, English and Latin, extends from the Psalms to the Canticles. In Glasgow University Library Hunterian MS 189 (a New Testament in the Later Version), a fifteenth-century reader added the opening Latin words for each verse of the *Benedictus* (Song of Zechariah, Lk 1:68–79), connecting the English text to the performance of one of the most recurrent Canticles. Canticles often follow the Psalms in Wycliffite Bibles. In BL Add. MS 10,046 and in St John's E.14, for example, the Psalms are followed by the biblical Canticles in English, each prefaced by a Latin incipit. Like the mendicant Bibles discussed in the previous chapter, the Canticles are referenced by book and chapter. Nancy Bradley Warren argues that for the Brigittine translation of the Office, 'Latin lines [...] remind the women of the preeminence of Latin over the vernacular, reinforcing simultaneously the inferiority inherent in the nuns' inability to access the language of divine knowledge and their necessary dependence on clerical authorities'.[93] Against the background of competing mnemonics, such a hierarchy is less certain. We must think rather of bilingual chant and of liturgical mnemonics.

Conclusion

Little is known of the provenance and use of Wycliffite Bibles. The manuscript evidence examined in this chapter strongly supports their use within orthodox worship. A move is discernible in the evolution of the Wycliffite Bible—from single-volume Bibles to New Testaments and from a purely English text to one with traces of Latin cues, if not Church rituals. These are part of a wider transformation (evident also in the tables of lections explored by Matti Peikola) towards orthodox worship, towards accommodating common mnemonics and Latin Psalmody. As large-scale production of Bibles ensued, manuscripts adhered to the dominant liturgy of the English Church, the Use of Sarum, merging English and Latin. Placing the Bible within the liturgical year and Church worship became the underlying principle in the creation of the most prominent group of Wycliffite Bibles—New Testaments accompanied by a table of lections.

Wycliffite Bibles appear to be removed from the heterodox groups with which they have often been affiliated. Many manuscripts of the Wycliffite Bible were not annotated by early readers, and the identity of their early users remains a mystery.[94] Those that were annotated indicate use in nunneries, chantries and private chapels, where vernacular devotion was at the fore. Little evidence survives from the liturgy performed there, and the hegemonic nature of liturgical manuscripts hinders the full exploration of such uses of Wycliffite Bibles. However, the example from the relatively well-documented house of Syon reveals an affinity between Wycliffite Bibles and vernacular theology,

---

93   Warren, *Spiritual economies*, p. 49. A similar sentiment was presented by Sutherland, *English Psalms in the Middle Ages*, pp. 231, 234.
94   On the question of lay marks in books see Eamon Duffy, *Marking the hours: English people and their prayers 1240–1570* (New Haven, CT: Yale University Press, 2006).

which extended to the nuns' liturgical manuscripts. Their unique liturgy sometimes involved public recitation of vernacular texts, as in the Chapter House. I do not suggest that English took the place of Latin in the liturgy of the nuns at Syon, nor that full services were sung in the vernacular in such location. Neither do I suggest that one should confine vernacular devotions to 'para-liturgical' or 'semi-liturgical' elements, which were separated from the Latin liturgy. Rather, the manuscript evidence of the Wycliffite Bible and other fifteenth-century liturgical manuscripts reveals a cohabitation of Latin and English, in which—for specific elements and in specific times—the liturgy could be delivered in one language or the other. The surface uniformity of most liturgical manuscripts may mask a more fluid practice, in which, as suggested by the Syon profession ritual, officiants and participants could, at specific moments, move between linguistic spheres. The more seamlessly this was done, the less likely we are to trace it in the records. The merging of English and Latin in Church liturgy was not limited to Wycliffite Bibles. As we shall see in the exploration of the first Bible printed in England in the next chapter, this cohabitation continued well into the sixteenth century, once more eluding clear dichotomies of reform and conservatism.

3

The First Printed English Bible(s)

Transition—No Bible nor Printing

Johannes Gutenberg's celebrated 42-line Bible, printed in 1450s Mainz, was, in effect, a traditional form of innovation.[1] Gutenberg's Bible, the first European book printed in moveable type, imitated the Late Medieval Bible (LMB) in both text and appearance. Despite its atlas size, its text is heavily abbreviated, revealing its model to have been a thirteenth-century pocket Bible.[2] Its layout replicated the two columns of text, the chapter divisions and the running titles of biblical manuscripts from previous centuries. As in most LMBs, the Psalms are presented without their numerical value, attesting to the limits of the mendicant experimental group discussed in Chapter 1. As was the case with manuscript Bibles, patrons had to rely on a variety of crafts-men for the creation of the final product. The Bible, like other books printed in the following decades, left the printing shop unbound and lacking some of its key features. Scribes and artists were commissioned to provide rubrics, ini-tials and titles, and so gave a distinctive character to each copy. One aspect of Gutenberg's Bible broke away from its late medieval predecessor: the lack of biblical addenda. There is no table of lections nor any Mass-texts. Much like Wycliffite Bibles, it left the printer's shop without the *Interpretations of Hebrew Names*, which had accompanied most LMBs.[3]

---

1   The most recent exploration of the copies of the Gutenberg Bible, with a census and additional bib-liography, is Eric Marshall White, *Editio princeps: a history of the Gutenberg Bible*, Harvey Miller studies in the history of culture (Turnhout: Brepols, 2017). For a general introduction see Andrew Pettegree, 'Publishing in print: technology and trade', in *The new Cambridge history of the Bible*, vol. 3: *From 1450 to 1750*, ed. Euan Cameron (Cambridge: Cambridge University Press, 2016), pp. 159–86 at 159–64.
2   Paul Needham, 'The text of the Gutenberg Bible', in *Trasmissione dei testi a stampa nel periodo moderno*, vol. 2: *Il seminario internazionale Roma-Viterbo 27–29 giugno 1985*, ed. Giovanni Crapulli, Lessico intellet-tuale Europeo 44 (Rome: Edizioni dell'Ateneo, 1987), pp. 43–84.
3   This, however, was added in manuscript form in some copies of the Gutenberg Bible, as in a Carthusian copy currently at Aschaffenburg Hofbibliothek (see White, *Editio princeps*, pp. 93–4.). I thank Scott Mandelbrote for this suggestion.

In the early thirteenth century, the success of the LMB arose from the merging of technology and need: the new divisions befitted new means of engaging with the biblical text in schools and universities; the ability to produce minute volumes supplied the mendicants' need for portable books. By the mid-fifteenth century, the nascent technology and its deficiencies suited another need. Unlike many LMBs, Gutenberg's Bible was a very large volume. Moveable-type printing in its infancy involved numerous new processes and products. These restricted the kind of books that could be produced. The inability to cast minute type inevitably resulted in the creation of large tomes. Yet, as argued by Christopher de Hamel, by the mid-fifteenth century monastic reforms had made these restrictions a clear advantage.[4] The small Bibles of the thirteenth century were still in use and circulated in great numbers. Large lectern Bibles, however, were better suited for public recitation, if not public display, affiliated with the monastic revivals of the fifteenth century. Twelfth-century Romanesque Bibles were taken out of storage, rebound and displayed; new Bibles, large and lavish, were commissioned to equal them. Such changes once more brought to the fore folio Bibles, whose large type suited public reading. Gutenberg's 42-line Bible quickly sold out. In 1455 Enea Silvio Piccolomini (later pope Pius II, 1458–64) enthusiastically described it to cardinal Juan de Carvajal (†1469) as an exceptionally clear book, whose large size favoured legibility.[5]

The separation of the ways between manuscripts and printed books was a long process. It unfolded in a gradual decrease in the reliance on craftsmen to embellish half-finished books. Such mixed production made books more lavish, but also complicated their creation. Hand-added elements persisted,[6] yet within a generation of Gutenberg's invention these were no longer a necessity. Elements borrowed from the manuscript page were modified to better suit the new technology: rather than changes in ink and colour, it was the size of type or the deployment of a new typeface that differentiated between textual elements. Bibles produced in Venice from 1475 onwards employed black ink for running titles and rubrics (the etymology of whose name, originating from the Latin for 'red', was now lost). The material transformation also affected the ways Bibles were read. The size of the Gutenberg Bible dictated its intended audience. Like other Latin Bibles of the early incunabula period, it was a royal folio (height surpassing 50 cm): impressive and befitting public lections, but

4   Christopher de Hamel, *The book: a history of the Bible* (London: Phaidon, 2001), pp. 194–6.
5   Martin Davies, 'Juan de Carvajal and early printing: the 42-line Bible and the Sweynheym and Pannartz Aquinas', *The Library* series 6 XVIII:3 (1996), 193–215; White, *Editio princeps*, pp. 22–3.
6   See, for example, Lilian Armstrong, 'The hand illumination of Venetian Bibles in the incunabula period', in *Incunabula and their readers: printing, selling and using books in the fifteenth century*, ed. Kristian Jensen (London: British Library, 2003), pp. 83–113.

also expensive and cumbersome. It is therefore little wonder that many surviving Gutenberg Bibles were owned and used by religious houses (where they were often annotated for public recitation). Piccolomini's comment likewise shows the appeal of the Bible to the higher echelons of the Church. There was also a question of price: a lavish copy of the Gutenberg Bible cost a hundred Rhenish Guilders, which was equivalent to the price of a town house or a craftsman's wages for five years; an unbound paper copy cost 40 Rhenish Guilders, and a vellum one 90.[7] By the end of the century royal folio Bibles, produced primarily in Germany, gave way to new sizes as Venice became a major book-production hub. From 1475 Venetian Bibles were produced for the lower end of the book market. Cheaper chancery-folio books (height of *c*.30 cm) were more portable and saved the need for additional scribal labour. The diversification of sizes became more noticeable in 1491, when Johann Froben printed in Basel the first octavo Bible, equal in size to many small LMBs (in the 1520s and 1530s this was supplemented by even smaller duodecimo Bibles printed in Venice and Paris, the length of whose page was about 12 cm, Figures 5.3 and 5.4). This had a clear effect on prices. By the 1490s a small folio Bible would cost two guilders, and an octavo volume half a guilder. Within fifty years of Gutenberg's invention, Bibles proliferated in a staggering variety of sizes, layouts, addenda and costs. Leonhard Hoffmann concludes his study of book prices in the incunabula era with Sebastian Brant in 1498, saying that '[a] book, which formerly only the Empire and the King possessed, you can now find everywhere[,] also in the hut'.[8]

The rise of the early printed Bible had left England in the margins. The century between the heyday of the Wycliffite Bible and the first printed English Bibles (*c*.1425–1535) could be seen as a bleak period in the history of the English Bible. While on the Continent vernacular and Latin Bibles proliferated, not a single Bible was printed in England, and only a handful of Bibles were copied there.[9] The reasons for this absence are not yet understood. As seen

7   Leonhard Hoffmann, 'Die Gutenbergbibel: Eine Kosten- und Gewinnschätzung des ersten Bibeldrucks auf der Grundlage zeitgenössischer Quellen', *Archiv für Geschichte des Buchwesen* 39 (1993), 255–319 at 300–3; summarised by John L. Flood, 'Martin Luther's Bible translation and its German and European context', in *The Bible in the Renaissance: essays on biblical commentary and translation in the fifteenth and the sixteenth centuries*, ed. Richard Griffiths, St. Andrews studies in Reformation history (Aldershot and Burlington, VT: Ashgate, 2001), at 61.

8   'Was sonst nur der Reiche von einst und der König zu eigen besessen,/ Findet sich jetzt überall auch in der Hütte, ein Buch'; see Leonard Hoffmann, 'Buchmarkt und Bücherpreise im Frühdruckzeitalter', *Gutenberg-Jahrbuch* 75 (2000), 73–81 at 81.

9   See, for example, the scant evidence for a later production of Wycliffite Bibles in Elizabeth Solopova, *Manuscripts of the Wycliffite Bible in the Bodleian and Oxford college libraries*, Exeter medieval texts and studies (Liverpool: Liverpool University Press, 2016). On the reception of Gutenberg Bibles in England see Eberhard König, 'A leaf from a Gutenberg Bible illuminated in England', *British Library Journal* 9 (1983), 32–50. Snippets of biblical texts in printed books were surveyed by DMH, pp. xxx–xxxi.

throughout this book, direct evidence for the production of Bibles is scant, and indirect evidence is nearly always conjectural. The few scholars to note this lack have often seen in it the result of Arundel's 1407/09 Constitutions limiting the use of English Bibles, combined with a general unease with vernacular Bibles. In Daniell's history of the English Bible, the subtitle for the period between 1401 and the 1530s is 'A Century of Repression', primarily reiterating Arundel's Constitutions; Pettegree's concludes a brief survey of vernacular Bibles on the Continent with the claim that '[t]he only glaring exception to this trend was England, where the pre-Reformation tradition of the Bible rendered the vernacular text toxic'.[10] As the printing press was embraced by early reformers, the link between the new technology and religious dissent became intrinsic, leading to Henry VIII's legislation against the import of unlicensed religious books from the Continent (See p.87n27).

As much as theology, technology and economy were also major factors in this hiatus of Bible production in England. Not only Bibles, but the printing of books more generally lagged behind the Continent. Even a rudimentary analysis of book production in the incunabula era reveals that England produced only a fraction of books compared with those printed in France, Germany or Italy.[11] As argued by Philip Gaskell, in England 'printing had arrived late & [...] was deficient in technique and provincial in context'.[12] Even before the advent of print, the English book market had come to rely on the import of books such as illuminated Books of Hours, primarily from the Low Countries and France.[13] Continental craftsmen surpassed their English peers, leading monarchs and the nobility to recruit abroad for high-end projects.[14] As will be demonstrated in the following chapters, well into the sixteenth century English printers lagged behind their colleagues on the Continent in the quality, size and innovativeness of their books. Pettegree

10   David Daniell, *The Bible in English: its history and influence* (New Haven, CT: Yale University Press, 2003), pp. 108–10; Pettegree, 'Publishing in print', p. 168; S. L. Greenslade, 'English versions of the Bible, 1525–1611', in *The Cambridge history of the Bible*, vol. 3: *The West from the Reformation to the present day*, ed. S. L. Greenslade (Cambridge: Cambridge University Press, 1963), pp. 141–74; B. J. McMullin, 'The Bible trade', in *The Cambridge history of the book in Britain*, vol. 4: *1557–1695*, ed. John Barnard and D. F. McKenzie (Cambridge: Cambridge University Press, 2002), pp. 455–73 at 455.

11   This is evident from the following statistics based on the ISTC (http://istc.bl.uk/search/search.html, accessed 21 February 2019):
'Germany' & 'Latin' = 7284 hits; 'Germany' & 'German' = 3246 hits
'Italy' & 'Latin' = 7945 hits; 'Italy' & 'Italian' = 2426 hits;
'France' & 'Latin' = 3749 hits; 'France' & 'French' = 1688 hits
'England' & 'Latin' = 160 hits; 'England' & 'English' = 221 hits.

12   Philip Gaskell, *A new introduction to bibliography* (Winchester: Oak Knoll Press, 1995), p. 171.

13   Margaret Lane Ford, 'Importation of printed books into England and Scotland', in *The Cambridge history of the book in Britain*, vol. 3: *1400–1557*, ed. Lotte Hellinga and J. B. Trapp (Cambridge: Cambridge University Press, 1999), pp. 179–202.

14   See, for example, Kathleen E. Kennedy, *The courtly and commercial art of the Wycliffite Bible*, Medieval church studies (Turnhout: Brepols, 2014), ch. 6, 'Following the Corpus Master', pp. 127–58.

has even noted the unexpected benefits emanating from the need of Church reformers such as William Tyndale (†1536) to seek refuge abroad:

> 'The underdeveloped state of the English print industry was also a material factor in shaping events. When Cuthbert Tunstall, Bishop of London, refused to authorise an English translation of the Bible, this was perceived as a great set-back to the project. But it forced Tyndale to look abroad, which brought him into contact with the major centres of printing in Europe. Here he was able to deal with publishers far more suited to the production of large, complex pro-jects than the small, unimaginative and conservative London print industry.'[15]

The English reliance on the import of books, printers and technology has been well documented. The state of printing in England also depended on a very mundane commodity: paper. The use of paper manuscripts in England can be traced back to the thirteenth century, at first the reserve of mercantile, and then bureaucratic, circles.[16] Printers embraced paper to its full extent, with vellum-printed books gradually diminishing during the incunabula period, often reserved for high-end books or special audiences; vellum copies were also employed as lavish presentation books, whose other copies were printed on paper.[17] The price of paper was one of the key factors in determining the price of a book, constituting up to half of the printer's expenditure.[18] England differed from many Continental book-production centres in its reliance on imported paper. Apart from a very brief and localised spell in the last years of the fifteenth century, England had no paper mills. Printers had to rely on imported paper for the production of books, a fact that affected both price and availability. As argued by Bidwell for the sixteenth and seventeenth centuries, '[t]oo often [printers] had to cope with a sudden dearth of this commodity, a drop in quality, or a surge in price caused by political interference in overseas commerce, fluctuations in exchange rates, accidents at sea, adverse business conditions abroad, and other constraints on foreign trade'.[19]

15   Pettegree, 'Publishing in print', p. 180.
16   Orietta da Rold, *Paper in medieval England: from pulp to fictions* (Cambridge: Cambridge University Press, 2020). I thank Orietta for sharing an early draft of this book, as well as for many insightful conversa-tions on this topic.
17   Paul Needham, 'Book production on paper and vellum in the fourteenth and fifteenth centuries', in *Papier im mittelalterlichen Europa: Herstellung und Gebrauch*, ed. Carla Meyer, Sandra Schultz and Bernd Schneidmüller, Materiale Textkulturen 7 (Berlin: De Gruyter, 2015), pp. 247–74. One such copy, pre-sented to Henry VIII and Thomas Cromwell, is explored in Chapter 4, pp. 124–27.
18   John Bidwell, 'French paper in English books', in *The Cambridge history of the book in Britain*, vol. 4: *1557–1695*, ed. John Barnard and Donald Francis McKenzie (Cambridge: Cambridge University Press, 2002), pp. 583–601 at 587.
19   Bidwell, 'French paper in English books', p. 584; Lotte Hellinga, 'Printing', in *The Cambridge his-tory of the book in Britain*, vol. 3: *1400–1557*, ed. Lotte Hellinga and J. B. Trapp (Cambridge: Cambridge

More work is needed to ascertain the economy of paper-import and its impact on the English book market. However, it was not the only factor to have a bearing on the English market, as demand was also key in determining the fate of printers. On the Continent, well-endowed monastic houses became prime audiences for early printed books, and especially Bibles. In England, Mary Erler has argued that the patterns of book production and patronage in Syon Abbey (whose Bible and devotions are discussed in the previous chapter) made it 'the only English religious institution whose espousal of the new technology of printing is extensive enough to be described as adapting a continental model'.[20] Moreover, as demonstrated by Pettegree, in the incunabula era Latin Bibles were printed only in a handful of the largest printing centres of Europe, where printers and merchants had engaged with a multinational book market.[21] England's small print industry was ill-suited for such an endeavour. Its reliance on the import of paper and the more cumbersome means of exporting printed books to the Continent, in comparison with Italian, German or French printers, had left it to rely on Continental printers. For the English, up to the 1530s, Bible production was something that happened elsewhere.

1535

By 1535, religious reform had been simmering on the Continent for two decades, with Bibles serving as the battleground between religious factions. The centrality of biblical access for many reformers had led to a twofold approach to the Bible: attempts at engaging with the original languages of the Bible, and the dissemination of vernacular Bibles for the laity. In England change was slower and supported by the influx of reformed ideals and printed books from the Continent.[22] The religious landscape of the first decades of the sixteenth century in England was still primarily traditional. Liturgy followed, for the most part, the rites of previous centuries; parish Bibles were still a rare

---

University Press, 1999), pp. 65–108 at 95–7. Bidwell's argument differs from Hellinga's, the latter advocating a low impact of paper import on availability and price. However, Hellinga's argument is hindered by the general lack of evidence for the earlier period of printing in England.

20   Mary C. Erler, 'Pasted-in embellishments in English manuscripts and printed books c. 1480–1533', *The Library, 6th Series* 14 (1992), 185–206 at 204; quoted in Vincent Gillespie, 'Syon and the English market for Continental printed books: the Incunable phase', in *Syon Abbey and its books: reading, writing & religion, c.1400–1700*, ed. Edward Alexander Jones and Alexandra Walsham (Woodbridge: Boydell, 2010), pp. 104–28 at 111.

21   Pettegree, 'Publishing in print', pp. 165–6.

22   Paul Needham, 'The customs rolls as documents for the printed-book trade in England', in *The Cambridge history of the book in Britain*, ed. Lotte Hellinga and J. B. Trapp (Cambridge: Cambridge University Press, 1999), pp. 148–63; König, 'A leaf from a Gutenberg Bible illuminated in England'; Ford, 'Importation of printed books into England and Scotland', p. 190; Michael Carter, 'Brother Grayson's Bible: a previously unrecorded book from St Mary's Abbey, York', *Nottingham Medieval Studies* 57 (2013), 287–301.

exception; and no Bibles, Latin or English, had yet been printed in England.

Luther's September Testament (printed in 1522) manifests the reformed ideal. It was based on his Greek learning, but disseminated in the German.[23] In 1534, Luther's collaboration with the printer Hans Luft had led to the printing of an immaculately presented single-volume Bible.[24] The ideals of Bible and Reform had influenced English scholars too, first among them William Tyndale (†1536), who had left England in 1524 to print his New Testament in Cologne the following year (DMH§1; STC§2823).[25] Relying on Luther, among others, Tyndale produced a multitude of biblical books up to his arrest in 1535 and execution in the following year. His work was continued by others, with Miles Coverdale (†1568) editing an English single-volume Bible. It was printed in 1535, relying on the works of Tyndale, Luther and the Vulgate (DMH§18; STC§2063).[26]

The link between print and religious dissent informed Henry VIII's 1530 injunctions, which prohibited the printing or the import of any unlicensed English Bible or theological work.[27] However, by 1535, Henry's twenty-sixth year on the throne, attitudes had changed and allowed for greater tolera-tion of religious reform. Henry's engagement with the 'Great Matter' and his quest for a male heir had led to the annulment of his marriage to Catherine

23   On the materiality of reformed Bibles on the Continent see Wim François, 'The early modern Bible between material book and immaterial Word', in *The agency of things in medieval and early modern art: materials, power and manipulation*, ed. Grażyna Jurkowlaniec, Ika Matyjaszkiewicz and Zuzanna Sarnecka, Routledge research in art history (New York and London: Routledge, 2018), pp. 129–43. I thank Wim for sharing an early draft of this article.

24   *Biblia, das ist, die gantze Heilige Schrifft Deudsch / Mart. Luth.* (Wittemberg: begnadet mit kürfurstlicher zu Sachsen freiheit. Gedruckt durch Hans Lufft, 1534).

25   Tyndale had to flee Cologne and the edition was eventually printed in Worms the following year. For a fuller account see David Daniell, *Let there be light: William Tyndale and the making of the English Bible* (London: British Library, 1994). For Tyndale's reliance on Luther see Gerald Hammond, 'William Tyndale's Pentateuch: its relation to Luther's German Bible and the Hebrew Original', *Renaissance Quarterly* 33 (1980), 351–85.

26   For a survey see David Norton, 'English Bibles from c. 1520 to c. 1750', in *The new Cambridge history of the Bible*, vol. 3: *From 1450 to 1750*, ed. Euan Cameron (Cambridge: Cambridge University Press, 2016), pp. 305–44 at 305–11; and more elaborately in Daniell, *The Bible in English*, pp. 133–89. A useful and critical print-history perspective is given by Peter W. M. Blayney, *The Stationers' Company and the printers of London 1501–1557* (Cambridge: Cambridge University Press, 2013), pp. 228–9, 342–51. Other important studies include James Frederic Mozley, *Coverdale and his Bibles* (London: Lutterworth Press, 1953); S. L. Greenslade, *The Coverdale Bible, 1535* (Folkestone: Wm. Dawson & Sons, 1975); Guido Latré, 'The 1535 Coverdale Bible and its Antwerp origins', in *The Bible as book: the Reformation*, ed. Orlaith O'Sullivan and Ellen N. Herron (London: British Library, 2000), pp. 89–102; Gwendolyn Verbraak, 'William Tyndale and the clandestine book trade: a bibliographical quest for the printers of Tyndale's New Testament', in *Infant milk or hardy nourishment? The Bible for lay people and theologians in the early modern period*, ed. W. François and A. A. den Hollander, Bibliotheca Ephemeridum Theologicarum Lovaniensium 221 (Leuven: Peeters, 2009), pp. 167–89; Naomi Tadmor, 'People of the covenant and the English Bible', *Transactions of the Royal Historical Society* 22 (2012), 95–110.

27   Paul L. Hughes and James F. Larkin (eds), *Tudor royal proclamations*, vol. 1: *The early Tudors, 1485–1553* (New Haven, CT: Yale University Press, 1964), pp. 193–7. For reassessing the injunction, and for more localised initiatives, see Blayney, *Stationers' Company*, pp. 227–51, 326–39.

of Aragon and his union with Anne Boleyn in January 1533. The Act of Supremacy of November 1534 positioned Henry at the head of the English Church, constituting a major step in his break with Rome. This was accompanied by a royal mandate for the visitation of religious houses. Early in 1535 Thomas Cromwell (†1540) was appointed royal vicegerent, or vicar-general. He initiated the visitations of religious houses that eventually led to the suppression of small monasteries the following year. Opposition was met with a sharp royal response, employing oaths in support of the Act of Succession as a test of loyalty. The refusal of John Fisher, Bishop of Rochester, and Thomas More, previous Lord Chancellor, to take the oath had led to their execution in the summer of 1535. Alongside Cromwell, Thomas Cranmer (†1556), the Archbishop of Canterbury, supported the reformed cause and led the new demand for an English Bible.

In December 1534, the English higher clergy joined in a synod at Canterbury to petition Henry for an English Bible, followed by an early attempt at producing one.[28] Henry's newly gained control over religious establishments was accompanied by royal injunctions for the regulation of life and worship, and monks were instructed to hear chapters of the New or Old Testament during mealtimes.[29] The link between disseminating the Bible and royal hegemony was embraced by Cromwell, ushering in the rise of the parish Bible. State and Church legislation from 1536 had mandated the parish Bible (discussed in depth in the following chapter). This has often led scholars to adopt a narrative of the rise of the English Bible. It sees in the 1530s a movement towards the consolidation of the English Bible, culminating in the Great Bible of 1539, which we will explore in the next chapter.[30] Once more, the material history breaks away from any clear teleology. This accords with the political culture of the end of Henry VIII's reign, in which reform and conservatism were never far removed from each other, and a constant move in and out of Henry's favour left key players second-guessing Henry's desires regarding the English Bible and other matters.

The emphasis of this chapter will be on the first Bible printed in England. This peculiar Latin book was produced by the King's Printer in London in July 1535.[31] Unlike Coverdale's Bible, printed in English on the Continent in

28   Alfred W. Pollard, *Records of the English Bible: the documents relating to the translaton and publication of the Bible in English, 1525–1611* (London: Oxford University Press, 1911), pp. 175–7.

29   Gilbert Burnet and Edward Nares (eds), *The history of the reformation of the Church of England* (London: J. F. Dove, 1830), p. 218.

30   Most notably Daniell, *The Bible in English*. But see also De Hamel, *The book*, pp. 243–5. The exception is the print-based narrative of Blayney, *Stationers' Company*, pp. 342–8.

31   *Sacrae Bibliae tomus primus in quo continentur, Quinque libri Moysi, Libri Iosue, et Iudicum, Liber Psalmorum, Prouerbia Salomonis, Liber Sapientie, et Nouum Testamentum Iesu Christi* (London: T. Berthelte, 1535); STC§2055.

the same year, this Bible has attracted little scholarly attention.[32] Yet for our purposes, the Bible's position as a Latin book in a religious world gradually becoming English renders it the perfect witness to the uncertain course of change in mid-sixteenth-century England. Its seven surviving copies will shed light on the links between England and the rest of Europe, as well as on the nature of religious transformation in Henry VIII's reign, two aspects currently debated by Reformation historians.[33] The chapter will also explore the printing of the Bible, identifying models and presenting it as a traditional book carefully placed between conservatism and reform. A comprehensive survey of the book's text, layout and addenda will enable us to see its deficiencies not as signs of an aborted project (as suggested by Arthur Freeman),[34] but as evidence for the dependence of English printing on the importation of techniques, models and books. This bibliographical analysis corroborates Diarmaid MacCulloch's warning against dissociating the English Reformation from the rest of Europe.[35] Readers' marks and annotations will reveal how the Bible was employed by priests, scholars, children and crooks, by Catholic recusants and monastic houses shortly before the Dissolution. Hidden annotations in one copy will also reveal the merging of Latin and English in the liturgy at the end of Henry's reign. Much like the liturgical spheres explored in the previous chapter, these notes evidence a lack of clear boundaries of faith and language in early modern England.

Creation

There is no external evidence for the printing of the 1535 Latin Bible, apart from the information embedded in the book itself. However, unlike medieval manuscripts, sixteenth-century printed books incorporate direct evidence for

---

32   Walter Arthur Copinger, *The Bible and its Transmission. Being an historical and bibliographical view of the Hebrew and Greek texts, and the Greek, Latin and other versions of the Bible (both MS. and printed) prior to the Reformation* (London: Henry Sotheran & Co., 1897; reprint, Leipzig, 1972), p. 242; T. H. Darlow and H. F. Moule (eds), *Historical catalogue of the printed editions of Holy Scripture in the library of the British and Foreign Bible Society*, 2 (in 4 pts) vols (London: Bible House, 1903), ii:2, p. 929; Arthur Freeman, 'To guard his words: the selectivity, conservatism and startingly personal nature of a Bible designed by Henry VIII', *The Times Literary Supplement*, 12 December 2007, 13–14, followed by Freeman's letter of 8 February 2008; Blayney, *Stationers' Company*, pp. 352–6. This chapter builds on my article on this Bible: Eyal Poleg, 'The first Bible printed in England: a little known witness from late Henrician England', *Journal of Ecclesiastical History* 67:4 (2016), 760–80.

33   For a summary of research on the Reformation see Peter Marshall, '(Re)defining the English Reformation', *Journal of British Studies* 48:3 (2009), 564–86.

34   Freeman, 'To guard his words'. Freeman's suggestion that this is also indicative in the small number of extant copies was refuted by Blayney, *Stationers' Company*, pp. 353–4.

35   Diarmaid Macculloch, 'Protestantism in mainland Europe: new directions', *Renaissance Quarterly* 59:3 (2006), 698–706.

their production. The Bible's provenance is asserted by a colophon at its end, attributing production to Thomas Berthelet, the King's Printer, in London, July 1535, followed by an image of Lucretia holding a dagger to her chest.[36] The device is of Thomas Berthelet (or Berthelot, †1555), a London-based printer of French origins.[37] Berthelet began his London printing career in September 1524. In 1526 he was summoned before the vicar-general, the senior Church officer of the diocese of London, for printing works by Erasmus and a sermon by Bishop Fisher. He agreed not to print any book in the future without ecclesiastical approval. In 1530 Berthelet became the King's Printer, a position he held until the end of Henry VIII's reign. In this role he printed royal proclamations (including the above-mentioned prohibition on printing or importing English Bibles), as well as religious books endorsed by the Crown, such as the Bishops' Book (*The Institution of a Christian Man*, 1537, STC§5163–7) and the King's Book (*A Necessary Doctrine and Erudition for any Christian Many, Set Forth by the King's Majesty*, 1543, STC§5168–76).

Berthelet's Bible is a surprisingly modest book, given his royal connection.[38] It is a quarto volume (page size of 200x136 mm, width of 39 mm, weight 0.75 kg, Figures 5.3 and 5.4) written in two columns of Black Letter, with sparse marginal materials and notes in Roman type. Much like Continental Bibles (and following from the LMB), its running titles identify the biblical book, while chapters are noted within the textual column (each chapter preceded by 'caput' and chapter number in Roman numerals). Its iconography is simple, based not on the biblical text but rather on founts and woodblocks readily available in Berthelet's workshop. The seven-line illuminated initials at the beginning of each book do not correspond to its contents; rather, they are either floral or depict classical figures. A comparison with books printed in England in the 1530s reveals that these initials appeared in other books printed by Berthelet, as well as in books produced by other printers.[39] The recycling

36   'Londoni excudebat Thomas Bertheletus regius impressor, anno. M.D.XXV. mense Iul.', fol. 303r. For the device (fol. 303v) see R. B. McKerrow, *Printers' & publishers' devices in England & Scotland, 1485–1640*, Illustrated monographs 16 (London: Chiswick Press for the Bibliographical Society, 1913), §80 p. 27.

37   Clair Colin, 'Thomas Berthelet, royal printer', *Gutenberg Jahrbuch* (1966), 177–81; K. F. Pantzer, 'Berthelet, Thomas (d. 1555)', in *Oxford dictionary of national biography* (Oxford: Oxford University Press, 2008); Blayney, *Stationers' Company*, pp. 183–7, 245–8, 255–9, 374–5, 667–73 et passim.

38   For example, manuscript Bibles linked to English monarchs in previous centuries tend to be large and impressively illuminated volumes (as in BL MS Royal 1.E.ix, an early fifteenth-century LMB possibly owned by Henry IV and Henry V; BL MSS Egerton 617–618, a Wycliffite Bible owned by Thomas of Woodstock, son of Edward III; Wolfenbüttel, Herzog August Bibliothek, MS Guelf.Aug.A.2, a Wycliffite Bible owned by Thomas of Lancaster, brother of Henry V; Bodl. MS Bodley 277, a Wycliffite Bible of Henry VI; and BL MS Royal 1.C.viii, of Henry VII; this is also indicative of the Great Bible, explored in the following chapter).

39   The 'B' of the Psalms (295r) appears also in *Diuino implorato praesidio* (1532, STC§21310), *The addicions of Salem and Byzance* (1534, STC§21585, also presenting the 'S' of 3 John [294r]) and *The determinations*

of materials is most evident in the Bible's title page (see Figure 3.1), which has nothing to do with biblical themes. It portrays a medallion of a head crowned with laurels facing left between two sphinxes (top), and naked boys in procession (bottom). This title page was used extensively by Berthelet and other printers, both before and after 1535. It was first employed for Edward Fox's *Gravissimae, atque exactissimae illustrissimarum totius Italiae, et Galliae academiarum censurae*, printed in 1530 by Berthelet for Henry's marriage to Catharine of Aragon (STC§14286); over the next twenty years it was printed twenty-nine times, until John Bale's *The ymage of both Churches* (an English translation of Revelation, printed by John Wyer in 1550, STC§1299).[40]

This Bible contains some obvious errors, such as references to books not included in the volume.[41] Some of the pages are mis-numbered, as, for example, 146 for 149 and 148 for 151. The lack of attention to detail, a mark of haste or lack of printing expertise, is evident in the printing on wrinkled paper, which caused some lines to be illegible;[42] there is no collation formula or list of corrections. Two corrections were nevertheless made by hand: in all extant copies, at the end of the Epistle to the Reader (fol. [2]v) 'fortasse' was altered to 'fortassi' by crossing the 'e' and adding 'i' in the margins; the word 'honor' in the sentence 'honor et comes erit individuus' was crossed over by a single line. This was done in a similar hand and ink across all copies, suggesting a centralised correction, most probably in Berthelet's shop. This correction, apart from showing a small print run and rudimentary technique, reveals special attention to this opening section, which accords with its royal connection (pp. 99–100).

The material aspects of Berthelet's Bible reveal a book that lacks the innovative features common in Continental Bibles, which were produced in large formats with specially commissioned woodcuts depicting biblical scenes.[43] Berthelet's Bible contains the text of the Vulgate, the Latin Bible

---

of the moste famous and mooste excellent vniuersities (1531, STC§14287); the 'D' of Wisdom (172r) appears in *Diuino implorato praesidio* (1532, STC§21310) and *Kotser codicis R. VVakfeldi* (1533, STC§24943, which uses the same title page as the Bible, as well as the 'P' of Judges [114r] and Proverbs [161v], the 'V' of Leviticus [49r] and the 'S' of 3 John [294r]); the 'I' of Genesis (1r) appears also in *Howe one may take profite* (1531, STC§20052), *A dialogue betwene a knyght and a clerke* (1533? STC§12511a) and in several books of Robert Redman, such as *A proclamacyon of the hygh emperour Jesu Christ* (1534? STC§14561) and *The boke of Magna Carta* (1534, STC§9272); the 'I' of Mark (196r), John (222v) and Jude (294v) appears in *On Charity* (1535, STC§16940).

40   R. B. McKerrow and F. S. Ferguson, *Title-page borders used in England & Scotland, 1485–1640*, Illustrated monographs 21 (London: Printed for the Bibliographical Society at the Oxford University Press, 1932), §19 pp. 16–18.

41   For example, the notes to Genesis 36 refer to 1 Chronicles (fol. 19r); the notes to Genesis 41 refer to 1 Maccabees (fol. 22r); and the notes for Exodus 13 refer to Nehemiah (fol. 34v).

42   As in fol. 270 in the British Library copy, or fol. 38 in Lambeth Palace, Sion ARC 8o / A12.2/1535.

43   This is notable, for example, in the variety of Latin and vernacular Bibles printed in Antwerp in this period, which often include hundreds of specially commissioned illustrations, and a variety of biblical

Figure 3.1 Title page, *Sacrae Bibliae tomus primus in quo continentur [...]* (London: Berthelet, 1535). This Bible uses a generic and much recycled title page, evidence of the poor state of English printing at the time. © Lambeth Palace Library, London.

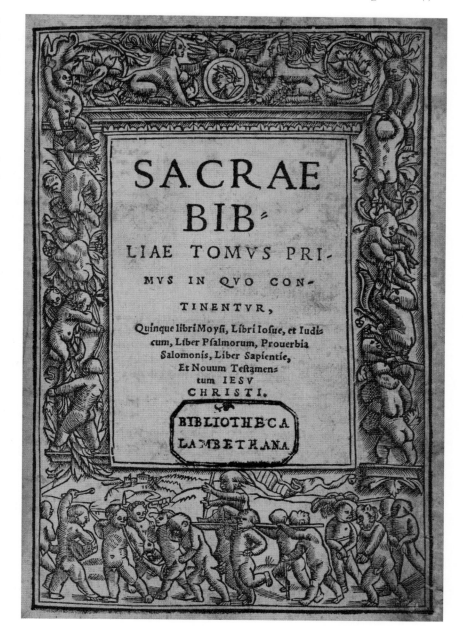

as translated by St Jerome in the late fourth century and employed throughout the Middle Ages (serving as the text of the LMB). By 1535, however,

---

devices: see Bart A. Rosier, *The Bible in print: Netherlandish Bible illustration in the sixteenth century*, 2 vols (Leiden: Foleor, 1997), 1:12–26 (study) and 149–208 (survey); 2: plates 31–185. I thank Scott Mandelbrote for suggesting this comparison. For other Bibles see note 64 below.

the Vulgate was not the only Latin Bible in circulation. In 1519 Erasmus completed a new Latin translation of the New Testament, relying on Greek manuscripts. It revealed important discrepancies between the Greek text and the wording of the Vulgate. This was followed by other translations such as Osiander the Elder's 1522 revision of the Vulgate, Pagninus's 1528 Latin literal translation or Sebastian Münster's 1534–5 new translation from the Hebrew.[44]

Berthelet's Bible preserved the traditional Latin of the Vulgate, despite the fact that the more recent translations were well known in England. Berthelet's choice of adhering to the text of the Vulgate was not necessarily a clear confessional matter, as some of the new translations were affiliated with the Roman Church. Although Münster was part of the Swiss Reform tradition, Pagninus was a Dominican, and the costs of his Bible were underwritten by Pope Leo X, the dedicatee of Erasmus's New Testament (whose fifth and last edition appeared in 1535 as well). Similarly, Bruce Gordon has demonstrated that in Reform strongholds the Vulgate was reserved for use by the less educated. This supports a better understanding of Berthelet's choice. The Vulgate would appeal to both reformed and conservative audiences.[45] It was not meant to facilitate high-end biblical exegesis, which relied on more innovative translations or devices, but was rather created with a more liturgical use in mind, as English rituals still, officially, relied solely on the Vulgate in 1535. This choice also had a practical reason. Gordon argues that even in the following decades, 'England possessed neither the depth of scholarship nor the printing resources adequate to such a gargantuan endeavour' as the production of a new Latin translation.[46]

Berthelet's Bible does not contain a table of lections. Unlike Wycliffite Bibles, whose standard addenda linked them to orthodox worship, Berthelet was more hesitant in linking his Latin Bible to Church ritual. Rather, the Bible replicated a standard addendum from Continental Bibles, and so eased the work of the printer. Its incorporation reveals something of Berthelet's tactics and his need to navigate conflicting religious affiliations. The Bible's reading aids are inferior to Continental models, and useless for sophisticated

---

44   Bruce Gordon, 'The authority of antiquity: England and the Protestant Latin Bible', in *The reception of Continental Reformation in Britain*, ed. Polly Ha and Patrick Collinson, Proceedings of the British Academy 164 (Oxford: Oxford University Press for the British Academy, 2010), pp. 1–22; Josef Eskhult, 'Latin Bible versions in the age of Reformation and post-Reformation: on the development of new Latin versions of the Old Testament in Hebrew and on the Vulgate as revised and evaluated among the Protestants', *Kyrkohistorisk årsskrift* 106:1 (2006), 31–67.

45   In this respect it is interesting to look at Josef Eskhult's measuring yard for reformed Vulgates, which often replace the intensive pronoun 'ipsa' of Gen. 3:15 with 'ipse' or 'ipsum'. Berthelet's Bible indeed reads 'ipsum', but this is most likely the result of a close reliance on his models (such as the 1526 Antwerp or the 1533 Venice editions).

46   Gordon, 'The authority of antiquity', p. 4.

exegetical use. In Continental Bibles biblical summaries, concordances and reading aids were by now the norm. Our Bible, on the other hand, provides only one table, named *Tabula historiarum*, eight folios long (sig. A.[i].r–[B. iv].v). The truncated title makes its identification difficult. The table is an alphabetical biblical summary. Unlike the *Interpretations of Hebrew Name*, common in LMBs, the current table does not provide etymologies, to be elaborated and developed by the reader. Rather, it supplies short headings for biblical narratives, accompanied by the biblical reference. Thus, for example, the first entry reads 'Aaron becomes High Priest, Exodus 18.a [rect. Exodus chapter 28]' ('Aaron fit summus sacerdos exodi.18.a').

A comparison with other Bibles reveals the origins of the table. It also suggests why Berthelet chose not to identify the author or nature of the table in his Bible. The table was taken from the *Tabula alphabetica historiarum Biblie* by the Franciscan Gabriele Bruno Veneto. Printed for the first time in Venice in 1490, it became popular in editions of the Vulgate well into the sixteenth century. Unlike Berthelet's Bible, each version of the table that I was able to inspect preserves the table's rubric,[47] which identifies its author, scope and methodology ('by Gabriele Bruno, the reverend master in Sacred scripture, Ordo minorum. Minister of the Holy Land', 'A reverendo in sacra scriptura magistro Gabriele bruno veneto ordinis minorum. Ministro prouincie terre sancte'). On its own, the table appears to be a tool for navigating the biblical text. Its rubric, however, links it with the very core of Catholic practice: the Franciscans, custodians of the Holy Land. Removed from the rubric, the table—much like the Bible as a whole—was detached from its Catholic roots. A similar phenomenon is evident in Wycliffite Bibles of the previous century, in which the removal of the more contentious General Prologue enhanced the appeal of that quintessentially non-polemical Bible to more orthodox audiences.

The table was modified in Berthelet's Bible. It was truncated, omitting entries from books that do not appear in Berthelet's Bible (thus narrowing its scope, as, for example, the entries for 'A' came down from 130 to 90). An analysis of the table's entries reveals copying done blindly and assists in establishing the Bible's model. It is unlikely that Berthelet used any of the early Venetian incunabula Bibles, which were the first to incorporate Veneto's table. These provide a slightly abbreviated version of the table that omits some of its entries and begins with *Abel*.[48] Much like French Vulgates printed in the 1520s and 1530s, Berthelet's Bible contains a more elaborate

---

47   Basle 1491; Venice 1492, 1494, 1496, 1497, 1498; Lyon 1497, 1519; Paris 1504, 1507, 1512, 1520, 1534; Nuremberg 1516.
48   This is evident in Bibles such as *Biblia cum tabula noviter edita* (Venice, 1494) or *Biblia cum summariis concordantiis: diuisionibus: quattuor repertoriis p[ro]positis* [...] (Lyons, 1497).

table, which begins with *Aaron*, and thus constitutes an obvious model for Berthelet's table.[49]

Berthelet's Bible contains a feature we have encountered in previous chapters. Like printers of Continental Bibles, Berthelet provided marginal letters sub-dividing each chapter. Whereas this system was rarely noted down in LMBs and was employed selectively to befit the identification of lections in Wycliffite Bibles, the new technology now made it possible to note the marginal sub-divisions in full. Each chapter of the Bible was divided using the letters A–D or A–G, written in the margins. This aided readers in navigating the Bible and demonstrates the benefits of the new technology. Print enabled the full incorporation of a medieval system, with readers no longer needing to employ the complex and expert mental sub-division explored in Chapter 1, pp. 11–13).

The system of sub-divisions has an unexpected value for the modern scholar. Unlike the later (and more accurate) system of verses, sub-divisions differed across Bibles and fluctuated across editions. Printers often refrained from modifying marginal cross references, preferring to copy them from their models, even when such copying diminished accuracy. These minute elements, together with marginal cross references, can therefore assist in the identification of Berthelet's model. Printed Bibles, either in quarto or folio, from Basle, Paris, Venice and Antwerp, present sub-divisions and marginal references that are markedly different to those he used.[50] Berthelet's model is found in an unexpected place. Among the variety of Latin Bibles printed on the Continent, there is a discernible group of small Bibles in duodecimo (Figures 5.3 and 5.4 present one such minute volume next to Berthelet's Bible). These tiny Bibles (at a page size of about 117x70 mm, the smallest for their time) constitute a unique group, with its own distinct devices. They were printed in multiple volumes and in Roman type by printers in Venice, Paris and Antwerp. And the marginal references and sub-divisions of this group are identical to those used by Berthelet.[51] Much like Berthelet's Bible, these duodecimo Bibles contain little additional material beyond Jerome's general prologues and a table of lections for the New Testament. This is not surprising, given that small Bibles were bound in multiple volumes, which made such aids of little use. This type of Bible was known in England; a

49   Berthelet's references to sub-division of the Psalms further limit the possible models, as these were not ubiquitous in editions of Bruni's table. A possible model is *Biblia sacra* (Paris: I. Preuel, 20 June 1528).

50   By and large, incunabula Bibles omit marginal references altogether, while some larger Parisian Bibles display a much fuller array of notes, references, summaries and etymologies than Berthelet's Bible.

51   This is corroborated through the examination of sample chapters across duodecimo of Bibles, commonly catalogued as *Pentateuchus Moysi* […] *Apocalypsis beati Ioannis* (Venice: L. Iuntę, 1533–8); (Paris: S. Colinæi, 1525–9); (Paris: S. Colinæi, 1531–5).

record of 13 January 1535 for parcels delivered to Henry VIII's court at Westminster by Mr Norres indicates 'Eight little books of the Bible', perfectly matching the type of Continental Bibles in question.[52]

This reliance on duodecimo volumes helps explain another feature of the 1535 Bible. The most uncommon facet of Berthelet's Bible is that it contains only some books: the Pentateuch, Joshua, Judges, the Psalms, Proverbs, Wisdom and the entire New Testament. Partial Bibles were common throughout the period explored in this book. Before 1200 Bibles were commonly multi-volume, and most Wycliffite Bibles comprise only the New Testament, in part or full. Most partial Bibles are comprised of a distinct biblical unit, commonly the Psalms, the Old or the New Testament. Berthelet's choice, on the other hand, is unique and I have yet to find a single Bible which shares his sequence of books.[53] The sequence of the duodecimo volume (as can be seen here in the Paris 1525–9 Bible) helps explain Berthelet's choice:

- Volume 1: the entire volume (The Pentateuch, Joshua and Judges) omitting Ruth
- Volume 3: the entire volume (Psalm)
- Volume 4: the entire volume (Works of Solomon)
- Volumes 7–8: the entire volumes (The New Testament)

Berthelet's Bible omits volumes two (History), five and six (Prophets and Maccabees) altogether, while employing all other volumes of that Parisian Bible in their entirety, with the exception of the omission of the Book of Ruth.

The Bible's sequence followed its Continental model. This sequence was so unusual that its creators anticipated objections. The Epistle to the Reader addresses this explicitly by confronting a possible complaint:

> We are anxious lest this alteration of the order of the books shall insufficiently please you, pious reader (who perhaps is religious), as it shall withdraw from the order of books, both sacred or traditional ones, or a little from ancient appearance if not from the customary form. If you shall look into our mind in this

---

52   James Gairdner (ed.), *Letters and papers, foreign and domestic, of the reign of Henry VIII: preserved in the Public Record Office, the British Museum, and elsewhere in England*, vol. 8: *January–July 1535* (London: Longman, Green, Longman, & Roberts, 1885), §44 p. 13. This could be British Library copy 219.a.15–20 (printed in Paris, 1525–9), which was part of the royal collection in the eighteenth century.
53   As corroborated by examination of works and catalogues of continental Bibles such as Bettye Thomas Chambers, *Bibliography of French Bibles: fifteenth and sixteenth century French language editions of the Scriptures*, Travaux d'humanisme et Renaissance 192 (Geneva: Droz, 1983); Darlow and Moule, *Historical catalogue* and the websites of *Biblia sacra* (http://www.bibliasacra.nl); the British Library Catalogue (http://explore.bl.uk); or the Incunabula Short Title Catalogue (http://istc.bl.uk).

issue and at the cause of this change, you shall think without doubt that this is laudable and made by right.[54]

The reader is then assured of the orthodox nature of the Bible and is informed of the printer's desire to publish the remaining books ('And we do not disregard other parts, lest anyone may rightly estimate that we have neglected or made [these] insignificant, but we have also put together these in another rightful volume: so that in that place it shall demand that we shall inquire into that accusation.').[55] This intention was alluded to on the Bible's title page, which presents the book as the Bible's first volume ('Sacrae Bibliae tomus primus').[56]

A second volume of the Latin Bible was never published, and closer analysis reveals that it had never been planned in earnest. The order of books and the structure of quires do not support the possibility of later integration of additional materials. Non-sequential books appear in the same quire, and the transition between Wisdom and the New Testament occurs on the same folio. This would have made it impossible to re-bind any new materials with the existing first volume while preserving the order of biblical books. Adding a second volume would have been cumbersome and illogical, necessarily breaking with the historical and doctrinal sequence (for example, presenting parts of the Old Testament after the New, detaching Ruth from Judges or the Song of Songs from the writings of Solomon). It would have also made redundant both the Epistle to the Reader and the prefatory table, since they refer to an incomplete Bible.

It is more likely that a second volume was a vague intention from the outset, without any concrete attempts at publication.[57] This accords with the choice of books, and the avoidance of more contentious books.[58] Berthelet's Bible contains all the key components of the biblical text: from the historical

---

54   'Subveremur autem ut ordinis librorum isthec immutatio pie lector tibi minus arrideat, cui fortasse religio est, ut in literis, saltem sacris aut earundem etiam ordine vel tantillum ab antiqua facie seu usitata forma recedat. Qui si mentem in hac re nostram et causam immutationis huius introspexeris, non dubium quin probabilem et iure factam esse censueris' (unfoliated).

55   'Neque enim alias partes ita seposuimus, ut neglexisse vel minoris fecisse quis recte debeat estimare, sed & ipsas in aliud iustum volumen compegimus: ut ubi locus id postularit, quod querendum sit illic inquiramus.'

56   This was replicated in modern catalogues, albeit often with the addition—as in the British Library's catalogue record—of 'General note: No more published'.

57   This inability becomes clearer when compared with the 1477 Delft Bible, whose five independent composition units were intended for the creation of a combined volume from the outset, giving readers a degree of flexibility in compiling their Bibles. See Mart van Duijn, 'Printing, public, and power: shaping the first printed Bible in Dutch (1477)', *Church History & Religious Culture* 93:2 (2013), 275–99.

58   On the question of the biblical canon in early modern England see Ariel Hessayon, 'The Apocrypha in early modern England', in *The Oxford handbook of the Bible in England, c. 1530–1700*, ed. Kevin Killeen, Helen Smith and Rachel Willie (Oxford: Oxford University Press, 2015), pp. 131–48.

events of the Pentateuch, through the omnipresence of the Psalms, to the salvation history and doctrine of the New Testament. As the Psalms and the New Testament constitute the backbone of the liturgy—the former in chant, the latter in biblical lessons—such an abbreviated volume was ideal for devotional or liturgical uses. Berthelet's choice mirrors the centrality of the Psalms and the New Testament in manuscripts of the Wycliffite Bible. Its truncated choices accord with other indicators of Berthelet's production, which differed from—if not lagged behind—Continental Bibles. Much like the printing in quarto (the only size, alongside octavo, for books printed by Berthelet at the time)[59] or the recycling of title page and illuminated initials, the brevity of the book reflects Berthelet's limited abilities, to suggest that he was not capable of printing a fuller, and more elaborate, Bible. The first printed Bible was indicative of the state of English printing.

The material aspect of Berthelet's Bible helps explain the hesitant royal link evident in the Bible's Epistle to the Reader. This short introduction (*Pio lectori*, two sides, unfoliated) justifies the appearance of the Bible, from the choice of font,[60] to the selection of books, before moving on to discuss the link between the Bible and the Crown. It presents the ideal of the King as disseminating Bibles. The King, it is said, like the sun in the sky and the soul in the body, is the ultimate ruler, whose authority is grounded in the Bible.[61] The King, whose ultimate responsibility is for the education of his people, is aided by the dissemination of the Bible to the laity and the clergy.[62] The ideal of a biblical monarch underpins much of Henry's attitude to the Bible, like a lynchpin uniting King, Scripture and people. The Epistle uses the 'royal we' when referring to the Crown. Following nineteenth-century scholarship, Freeman has suggested its author was no other than Henry himself, although it is more likely to have been Peter Vannes (Pietro Vanni, †1563), royal Latin secretary. Here is a new era for the English Bible, characterised by a closer involvement of the Crown with book production. Richard Rex has called

---

59   The only exception is royal proclamations, which were printed in folio but were limited in the number of leaves and the technique of printing.

60   Which indeed drew on a new fount, but Blayney doubts whether it was purchased for this Bible (*Stationers' Company*, pp. 354–6).

61   'We therefore, considering it to be our duty to God, have undertaken this task [publishing the Bible], so that we should be within our realm like the soul in the body, and the sun in the universe, and exercise judgment as God's representative in our kingdom.' ('Nos itaque consyderantes id erga deum officii nostri, quo suscepisse cognoscimur ut in regno simus sicut Anima in corpore et Sol in mundo, utque loco dei iudicium exerceamus in regno nostro.') The translation, as well as the following one, is based on Freeman, 'To guard his words'.

62   '[Y]et we have judged it our own concern to cherish the law of God in our own bosom, whence we shall constantly ascertain that both the people, and their spiritual fathers, faithfully and observantly execute their duties.' ('[N]ostra tamen nihilominus interesse iudicavimus, ut ipsam dei legem ipsi tanquam in sinu gestemus qua continue pervisuri simus uti tam plebs ipsa quam spirituales patres eius utrique quod debeant fideliter ac vigilanter adimpleant.')

this 'positive censorship', when 'censorship was accompanied by the deliberate use of king's name or authority to promote literature acceptable to the regime. A dedication to the king was already an accepted method of establishing the credentials of a book.'[63] Royal authorship is indeed a most efficient form of such censorship. Yet a closer look reveals only hesitant deployment of the royal connection. The Epistle to the Reader was left unsigned, and Henry's name was not mentioned in the Bible.

Berthelet's Bible does not fare well in comparison with Continental Bibles. Latin and vernacular Bibles are often large and imposing volumes, printed in folio or royal folio with a variety of Bible-specific illuminations, marginal annotations and reading aids.[64] One Continental Bible in particular stands as the material opposite to Berthelet's. Coverdale's Bible—the clandestine contemporary of Berthelet Bible—is a much more impressive book: a folio volume, whose elaborate title page depicts the enthroned Henry alongside diverse biblical episodes, and whose illuminated initials portray scenes from the biblical books they preface (see Figure 3.2). It suggests why Henry's support, if ever given in full, was withdrawn before the publication of Berthelet's Bible, leaving it without royal endorsement or a strong link to Henry in its prefatory materials or iconography. Berthelet's Bible, despite being printed by the King's Printer, recycled a generic title page, which has no connection to the biblical text, nor to Henry's reign. Worse yet, it employed the title page first printed for a book commemorating Henry's marriage to Catherine of Aragon. The title page of Coverdale's Bible, on the other hand, depicts both Bible and Henry, and celebrates the links between the two. Aspiring to royal approval, the title page was sketched by Holbein to impress upon the viewer the affinity between Henry and the Bible.

The title page of Coverdale's Bible presents a visual manifestation of the ideal link between monarch and Bible, the same one suggested in Berthelet's Epistle to the Reader. Holbein's visual narrative unfolds a history of salvation, from Creation to the triumphant Christ. Tatiana String has shown that

63   Richard Rex, *Henry VIII and the English Reformation*, 2nd edn, British history in perspective (Basingstoke: Palgrave Macmillan, 2006), p. 94.

64   For the high-level production of incunabula Bibles, of Dutch and of French Bibles see Paul Needham, 'The changing shape of the Vulgate Bible in fifteenth-century printing shops', in *The Bible as book: the first printed editions*, ed. Paul Henry Saenger and Kimberly Van Kampen (London: British Library in association with The Scriptorium: Center for Christian Antiquities, 1999), pp. 53–70; August den Hollander, 'Illustrations in early printed Latin Bibles in the Low Countries (1477–1553)', in *Shaping the Bible in the Reformation: books, scholars, and their readers in the sixteenth century*, ed. Bruce Gordon and Matthew McLean, Library of the written word 20 (Leiden: Brill, 2012), pp. 41–61; Bettye Chambers, 'What ever happened to Sola Scriptura? Text and paratext in sixteenth-century French Bibles', in *Infant milk or hardy nourishment? The Bible for lay people and theologians in the early modern period*, ed. W. François and A. A. den Hollander, Bibliotheca Ephemeridum Theologicarum Lovaniensium 221 (Leuven: Peeters, 2009), pp. 141–66; Chambers, *Bibliography of French Bibles*. Also see note 43 above.

Figure 3.2 Title page, Coverdale's Bible. The images and biblical scenes were carefully selected to appeal to Henry VIII (*Biblia. The Bible that is, the Holy Scripture […]* [Cologne?: Eucharius Cervicornus and Johannes Soter?, 1535]). Reproduced by kind permission of the Syndics of Cambridge University Library.

its details engage in subtle dialogue with theological controversies current in Henry's court: Christ gives keys to all the Disciples, rather than Peter alone, in direct opposition to papal doctrine; the reference to the Third Book of Ezra 9:7 was common among advocates of Henry's divorce.[65] As a whole, the sequence of pictures highlights Henry's position. He appears at the bottom of the page, his grandeur and centrality unmistakable. The iconography likens Henry to Old Testament monarchs: David is playing the harp on his right and Josiah proclaims the word of God on his left; enthroned, he is reminiscent of a second Solomon, distributing Bibles to bishops and kings.[66]

Coverdale started a long tradition of employing the Bible's title page to create an idealised view of the monarchy. As argued by String, the title page was a means of communicating complex ideology—if not propaganda—to wider audiences. It can also be seen to engage with one particular reader, Henry himself, in an attempt to influence his reception of the Bible through an idealised version of the Bible's contents, and its relevance to Henry's goals. Such a glorified view of Scripture extends to the Bible's preliminary material. Coverdale's Bible was printed on the Continent, most likely in Cologne.[67] Wishing to enhance the appeal of the Bible to Henry, its preliminary materials were quickly reprinted in London by James Nicolson. These were modified to enhance the link between Henry and the Bible. This Bible opens with a dedication to Henry:

> The right & just administration of the laws that God gave unto Moses and unto Joshua: the testimony of faithfulness that God gave of David: the plenteous abundance of wisdom that God gave unto Salomon: the lucky and prosperous age with the multiplication of seed which God gave unto Abraham and Sara his wife, be given unto you most gracious Prince, with your dearest just wife, and most virtuous Princess, Queen Anne, Amen. [sig. ✠.ii.r]

Henry is seen as a biblical ruler, like Moses, Joshua, David and Solomon (all of whom appear alongside him on the title page). The biblical link culminates in equating Henry and Anne Boleyn with Abraham and Sarah, whose devotion

---

65   Tatiana C. String, *Art and communication in the reign of Henry VIII* (Aldershot: Ashgate, 2008), pp. 88–91.

66   Seeing Henry as an Old Testament monarch reverberated also in the use of the Decalogue in his reign: Jonathan P. Willis, *The Reformation of the Decalogue: religious identity and the Ten Commandments in England, c.1485–1625*, Cambridge studies in early modern British history (Cambridge: Cambridge University Press, 2017), pp. 16–17, 74–9, 81 and 129. It is also the rationale for the frontispiece of the Great Bible, explored in Chapter 4.

67   For a summary of the printing of Coverdale's Bible see Blayney, *Stationers' Company*, pp. 344–51. A more detailed analysis is found in the earlier works of Greenslade, *The Coverdale Bible, 1535*, and Mozley, *Coverdale and his Bibles*.

had led Sarah to conceive Isaac. Coverdale and Nicolson used this simile since they knew how preoccupied Henry was with the production of a male heir. As time progressed, however, they probably realised the mistake of naming Henry's consort in print. Following the execution of Anne in 1536, the Preface was revised in 1537, replacing Anne with 'Queen Jane' (DMH§32–3; STC§2064–5). The reference to a consort was removed altogether in all subsequent editions.

The dedication in Coverdale's Bible adopts a godly stance, which likens the pope to the Antichrist, and supports vernacular Scripture. Invoking biblical precedents, the dedication advocates priestly obedience to the monarch, and argues that the Bible 'teaches all estates their office and duty' [sig. ✠.III.v]. The link between reform, Bible and authority was the brainchild of Thomas Cromwell, Henry's most influential minister. Richard Rex has indeed argued that Cromwell was the main advocate of the link between Scripture and obedience to Henry in the early 1530s.[68] Cromwell understood how the new Bible could be made to support the dual cause of reform and obedience to the monarch. In August 1535 he was approached by Nicolson to support the new Bible and provided his patronage to the English Bible from then on. Cromwell's 1536 injunctions made clear 'that every parson, or proprietary of any parish church within this realm, shall on this side the feast of St. Peter ad Vincula next coming [1 August 1536], provide a book of the whole Bible, both in Latin, and also in English'.[69]

As the royal printer, Berthelet was well aware of the religious turmoil of the mid-1530s. In 1535 he printed *A proclamation concerninge heresie* (STC§7785), in which Henry went against reformers who practised adult baptism, denied transubstantiation, and 'hold and teach other divers and sundry pestilent heresies against God and his holy scriptures … The king's most royal majesty, being Supreme head in earth under god of the church of England', requiring them to leave the realm within twelve days on pain of death. Following the 1534 clerical demand for a Bible, Berthelet took a chance on the production of a Latin Bible to the best of his limited abilities. He created a Bible that was marked by limitations and uncertainties, neither a reformed Bible nor a conservative one. The choice of text and books suggests a liturgical use, rather than an exegetical orientation, but it lacks any clear liturgical addenda.

---

68   Richard Rex, 'The crisis of obedience: God's Word and Henry's Reformation', *The Historical Journal* 39:4 (1996), 863–94 at 865.

69   Walter Howard Frere and William McClure Kennedy (eds), *Visitation articles and injunctions of the period of the Reformation*, vol. 2: *1536–1558*, Alcuin Club collections 15 (London: Longmans, Green, 1910), p. 9. For a reappraisal of the time of the injunctions, suggesting 1537 for the incorporation of the clause on Bible possession, see Paul Ayris, 'Reformation in action: the implementation of reform in the dioceses of England', *Reformation & Renaissance Review: Journal of the Society for Reformation Studies* 5:1 (2003), 27–53; refuted by Rex, *Henry VIII and the English Reformation*, pp. 190–1, n.28.

Despite Henry's supposed authorship of the Epistle to the Reader, royal support was quickly retracted. Berthelet's gamble had failed; it was Coverdale's Bible that showed the king the great potential of the printed Bible.

Reception

Berthelet's Bible survives in seven copies, three of which lack preliminary materials.[70] The marks and marginal annotations left in these copies reveal the world of sixteenth-century readers. The book's lack of any clear religious affiliation allowed it to be used by a variety of readers across the religious spectrum. The analysis of those annotations reveals the complex religious transformation of mid-sixteenth-century England, and accords with Christopher Haigh's view of multiple 'reformations', experienced along the lines of gender, class, religious affiliation and literacy.[71]

The British Library copy of Berthelet's Bible shows little to no sign of use, and has been traced by James Carley to Henry VIII himself.[72] It was described in the 1542 Inventory of books in the Upper library at Westminster (no. 446) as 'the first volume of a Bible printed by Thomas Berthelet' ('Primus tomus Bibliae impressus a Thoma Berthelet'), and its identity is reaffirmed by the British Museum stamp, indicative of George II's 1757 bequest to the British Museum.[73] Yet the volume lacks the grandeur evident in presentation Bibles (such as the vellum hand-painted copy of the Great Bible described in the next chapter). Here again the limits of Berthelet's capacities are manifest, casting doubt on whether the book was ever officially endorsed by Henry, or formally presented to him. Another renowned patron is allegedly linked

---

70   These are:
   – British Library C.36.e.19 (full)
   – Lambeth Palace Library Sion ARC 8o / A12.2/1535 (full)
   – Lambeth Palace Library SR2 E75 (1535) (full)
   – Cambridge University Library (Sel.5.176) (full)
   – Bodleian Library 4° B 1 Th.BS. (Lacking preliminaries)
   – Bridwell Library, Southern Methodist University, BRA2776 (Lacking preliminaries and Genesis 1–8)
   – A copy sold in the Harmsworth Sale of 8 July 1946 to Quaritch Booksellers, currently at the American Bible Society.
I was unable to inspect the last two copies in person.

71   Christopher Haigh, *English reformations: religion, politics, and society under the Tudors* (Oxford: Clarendon Press, 1993).

72   James Carley, *The libraries of Henry VIII*, Corpus of British medieval library catalogues 7 (London: The British Library in association with the British Academy, 2000), p. 95.

73   This is the typical octagonal blue British Museum stamp on the verso of the first folio (see P. R. Harris, 'Appendix I: identification of printed books acquired by the British Museum, 1753–1836', in *Libraries within the library: the origins of the British Library's printed collections*, ed. Giles Mandelbrote and Barry Taylor (London: British Library, 2009), pp. 387–423 at 392–4, 417, 423).

to the Sion College copy, currently in Lambeth Palace Library. This is a pre-dominantly unmarked copy, which bears the sign of the seventeenth-century Durdans Library, later given to Sion College. A signature on the title page invokes Hugh Latimer (†1555), Bishop of Worcester, and one of the Marian Martyrs. However, a comparison with Latimer's verified autograph reveals this to be spurious.

Further information on less prominent readers is evident in the Bodleian copy, which was bound using parchment from a high medieval Psalter (verses from Psalms 24 and 53 are visible near the front pastedown; Psalms 93 and 102 near the back). This suggests access to medieval manuscripts, though not necessarily a break with medieval tradition.[74] The book's annotations reveal signs of early engagement with the Bible. On the back paper pastedown a confident cursive sixteenth-century hand provided a table of contents, with special attention to the Gospels and Epistles. This was preceded by 'Dominus vobiscum et cum spiritu tuo' ('The Lord be with you and with your spirit'), giving clear evidence of conservative phraseology, if not affiliation.[75] A religious house, *studium* or university college may be a suitable home, also offering access to earlier manuscripts for re-binding. This affiliation and use, however, were short-lived. Later readers have also left their marks on the Bible, providing evidence of use by lay readers. Doodles on the back and front pages comprise pen-tests and signatures, noting 'William Beale is good man' and 'John Thomas' on the last page. The names of Edward and Peregrine Aldryche appear on a few pages in the book. The nature of Edward's script and its lack of uniformity (fols 152v, 153r and 184v) sug-gest that these were children practising their signatures, most probably two brothers—the children of George Aldriche, Esquire, who were naturalised in June 1604.[76]

Another copy likewise reveals a use within a more conservative setting. In the Bible kept in Cambridge University Library, a sixteenth-century reader, in a competent cursive hand, marked sections of interest, underlining them and writing 'nota' in the margins. The reader's knowledge of and reliance on the *Glossa ordinaria* are evident in a comment to the cryptic verse of Genesis 4:7, fol. 2v ('If thou do well, shalt thou not receive? but if ill, shall not sin forthwith be present at the door? but the lust thereof shall be under thee, and

---

74   Using scrap manuscripts in rebinding, even ones taken from a Bible or liturgical book, was practised in religious houses throughout the Middle Ages. It is also common in sixteenth-century English bindings made in Oxford.

75   The continuation is blurred, but most probably reads 'Sursum corda. Habemus ad Dominum. Gratias agamus Domino Deo nostro', the Salutations before the Prefaces of the Mass.

76   'House of Lords journal volume 2: 16 June 1604', in *Journal of the House of Lords*, vol. 2: *1578–1614* (London, 1767–1830), 321–2 (http://www.british-history.ac.uk/lords-jrnl/vol2/pp321-322, accessed 30 November 2019).

thou shalt have dominion over it.'), stating 'Note: he has dominion' ('Nota habet arbitrii'), a summary of the relevant gloss to the passage.[77] Much like the LMBs discussed in the first chapter, this copy shows active engagement with the biblical text and its exegesis, most likely within a classroom or a library. The religious affiliation of this reader is manifested on the title page (see Figure 3.3). The name of the reader and the Holy Name of Jesus (IHS) were inscribed below the book's title, crossed out by a later hand.[78] The crossing out makes the ownership mark less legible, probably 'This book of Thomas Atkinson, out of [the books] of Magister William White' ('Hic liber Thome Atcinson | ex [libris] Magistri Wi[l]hemi White').[79] Thomas Atkinson and William White are indeed recorded in mid-sixteenth-century Cambridge. The former received his BA in 1541/2 and his MA in 1547 from Trinity College, where he was a Fellow from 1546.[80] In the reign of Edward VI he displayed strong conservative tendencies during Nicholas Ridley's (church reformer and later Bishop of London, †1555) visitation of the university in June 1549. Atkinson's colleague and co-religionist Thomas Vavasour refuted Ridley's arguments using the biblical story of Adam's rib (Genesis 2:21–3), the same chapter that is marked with an underline and a 'nota' in this Bible as well.[81] The Magister is possibly William White, whose time in Cambridge spanned nearly thirty years. He was ordained as dean in Cambridge in 1510, and was warden of the Dominican order at the time of the Dissolution in 1538.[82] The Bible was used for active study despite its lack of Continental state-of-the-art biblical apparatus or more novel translation, demonstrating a continuing reliance on the text of the Vulgate, and one possible use for Berthelet's tome.

It is little wonder that sympathisers of a more traditional religion found use for a Latin Bible, even a partial one, and one only weakly linked to Henry VIII. However, hidden annotations in another copy of this Bible move away from a clear conservative affiliation and into the liturgy of the

---

77   Interlinear gloss to Genesis 4:7, in Karlfried Froehlich and Margaret T. Gibson (eds), *Biblia latina cum glossa ordinaria: facsimile reprint of the editio princeps Adolph Rusch of Strassburg 1480/81* (Turnhout: Brepols, 1992), vol. 1, p. 31.

78   On the English pre-Reformation veneration of the Holy Name see Rob Lutton, '"Love this name that is IHC": vernacular prayers, hymns and lyrics to the Holy Name of Jesus in pre-Reformation England', in *Vernacularity in England and Wales c. 1300–1550*, ed. Elisabeth Salter and Helen Wicker, Utrecht studies in medieval literacy 17 (Turnhout: Brepols, 2011), pp. 119–45.

79   Thomas's last name is the least legible word, with only the last three letters transcribed with full confidence.

80   *ACAD: A Cambridge Alumni Database* (http://venn.lib.cam.ac.uk, accessed 30 November 2019) unique identifier ATKN541T.

81   Richard Rex, 'Thomas Vavasour M.D.', *Recusant History* 20 (1990–1), 436–54.

82   John R. H. Moorman, *The Grey Friars in Cambridge, 1225–1538*, The Birkbeck lectures 1948–9 (Cambridge: Cambridge University Press, 1952), pp. 222–3.

Figure 3.3 Annotations on the title page of Berthelet's Bible. These reveal two early, and conservative, readers in sixteenth-century Cambridge (CUL copy Sel.5.176). Reproduced by kind permission of the Syndics of Cambridge University Library.

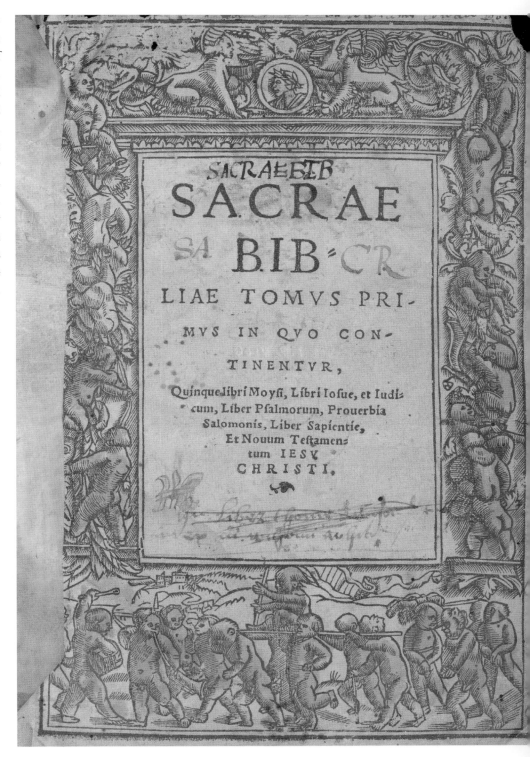

last years of Henry VIII. At first glance, a copy currently in Lambeth Palace (SR2 E75 [1535]) appears to be a 'clean' copy, with very few marginal annotations. A more detailed examination, however, reveals that heavy paper was carefully pasted over blank parts of the book, thus hiding densely annotated spaces. Backlight and long exposures assisted Professor Graham Davis (QMUL) and myself in bringing the annotations to view, which were then digitally subtracted from the printed text. Figures 3.4–3.6, of the black verso of the title page, reveal this process: the first is the image under regular light (see Figure 3.4), the second with backlight revealing the mixture of annotations and printed title page (see Figure 3.5), and the third after the digital subtraction, which removed the printed elements (see Figure 3.6).[83] Once revealed, the annotations are shown to be in two main hands that can be dated to the mid-sixteenth century. The bulk of the annotations is in a single hand, and appears on the blank verso of the title page and at the empty spaces at the bottom of the Epistle to the Reader, at the end of the table (sig. [B.4.]v) and the beginning of Genesis (fol. 1r). It comprises an element familiar from our earlier discussions: a table of lections, linking biblical episodes with the liturgical year. Each entry supplies the two biblical readings for a given occasion: Epistles (commonly the New Testament Epistles, but at times from other biblical books) and Gospels. It is written continuously, starting with the first Sunday of Lent, and identifies the biblical reading by chapter, sub-division and incipit. A typical entry reads 'On the iij Sunday [of Lent] | [E]phe. v. a. *be ye therfore follo.* | Lk. xi. b. *and he was casting out*', giving the sub-division and incipit referring to the Epistle to the Ephesians 5:1 and Luke 11:14.[84]

A detailed comparison with sixteenth-century devotional books reveals that the table of lections is based on that of the Great Bible of 1539, the first to disseminate such a table widely, following the Use of Sarum. In that Bible, the entry for the third Sunday in Lent reads '*Be ye therfore* the Ephe. v.a | *And he was castynge out* Luke. xi. b'. The layout of the two tables is also similar, presenting the information in two columns. The table was reprinted in Great Bibles throughout the 1540s, and can assist in dating the Lambeth annotations. They cannot have been made before the first printing of the table in the Great Bible of 1539 (DMH §46; STC§2068).[85] Nor could it have been

---

83   I thank Prof. Davis for his assistance and expertise, without which the notes would have stayed hidden from view.

84   The verso of the title page (unfoliated). The binding prevents the identification of some letters in the gutter.

85   The slightly earlier lists of biblical readings known as 'Pistles and Gospels' (incorporated into primers from 1537) differ from this table in both form and language. Those lists provide full biblical text, rather than reference and incipit; they rely on Tyndale's New Testament, whose wording deviates from that of the Great Bible and the Lambeth copy. For a study of the 'Pistles and Gospels' see Charles C. Butterworth,

Figure 3.4 To the naked eye this appears to be a blank page; but this hides multiple annotations (see Figure 3.5). The verso of the title page in Berthelet's Bible (Lambeth Library copy SR2 E75 [1535]). © Lambeth Palace Library, London.

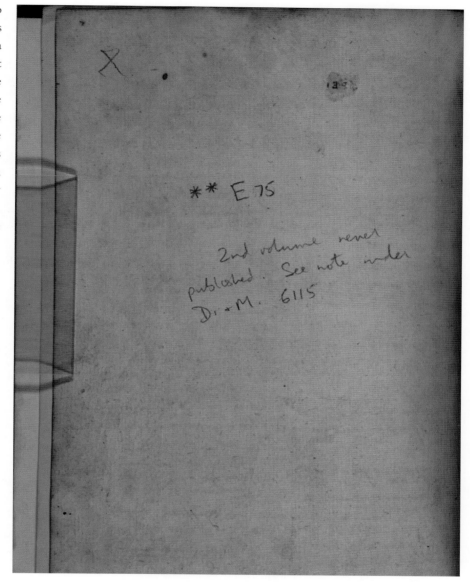

used after the introduction of the first Book of Common Prayer in 1549, which ushered in a table of lections slightly different to the one preserved in Lambeth.[86] The later table of lections appeared in subsequent reprints of the

---

The English primers, 1529–1545: their publication and connection with the English Bible and the Reformation in England (Philadelphia: University of Pennsylvania Press, 1953).

86   *The booke of the common praier and administracion of the Sacramentes, and other rites and ceremonies of the Churche: after the vse of the Churche of Englande* (London, 1549). Bible readings in the Book of Common Prayer are analysed in Chapter 5, 'Making Liturgical Sense'.

Figure 3.5 Hidden annotations with backlight. With a light source behind the page, annotations and printed text are mixed together. The verso of the title page in Berthelet's Bible (Lambeth Library copy SR2 E75 [1535]). © Lambeth Palace Library, London.

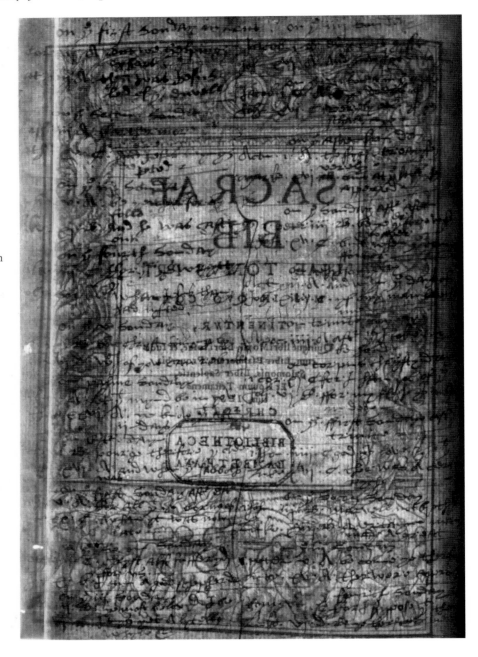

English Bible, such as the 1551 Great Bible (DMH§93; STC§2088). Thus, while both earlier Bibles refer to 'Palm Sunday', the Book of Common Prayer and subsequent prints refer to 'Sunday before Easter'; while the earlier table has only one communion on Easter, the later one has two. As the Great Bible's original table of lections became obsolete with the introduction of the

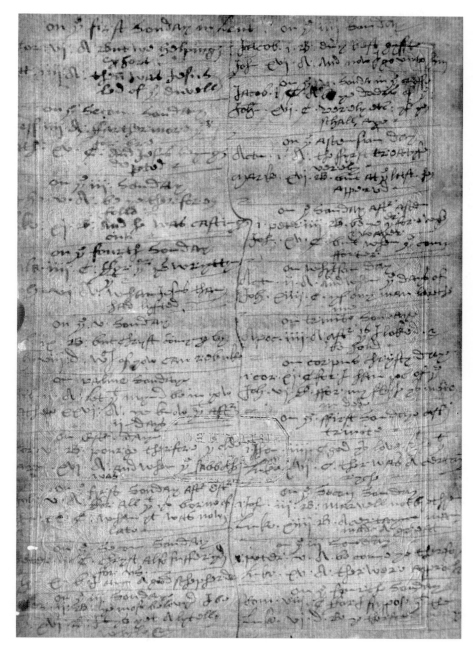

Figure 3.6 Hidden annotations following digital subtraction. An algorithm, developed by Prof. Graham Davis, QMUL, allows us to virtually 'peel' away the layers, revealing an English table of lections. The verso of the title page in Berthelet's Bible (Lambeth Library copy SR2 E75 [1535]). © Lambeth Palace Library, London.

Book of Common Prayer in 1549, it is evident that the table in the Lambeth copy was written between 1539 and 1549.[87]

87   The existence of a table of lections from the Great Bible in the last Bible printed during Edward VI's reign should be seen as an anomaly, stemming from unique circumstances (Chapter 5, p. 179).

Tables of lections were a common addendum to LMBs, and an integral part of Wycliffite Bibles. In the latter, they were modified by stationers to accommodate the contents of the manuscript they accompanied (Chapter 2, 'Table of Lections and New Modes of Reading'). A similar phenomenon is evident in this Bible. A comparison between its table of lections and that in the Great Bible reveals two peculiarities. Firstly, like other medieval and early modern tables of lections, that of the Great Bible follows the liturgical year from Advent to Michaelmas (29 September). In the Lambeth copy, however, the table of lections starts with the first Sunday after Lent (mid-February to early March). The earlier part of the table may have been on another folio, later removed from the book. However, as the page neatly begins with the first Sunday of Lent we can assume this was done intentionally, revealing that the copying did not encompass the full table, but possibly was done on a more ad hoc basis, to fill a specific need. The impression of improvised copying is reinforced by the second peculiarity of the table. While in the Great Bible the table provides lections for a variety of liturgical days, commonly Wednesdays, Fridays and major feasts, the Lambeth copy's table provides information only for Sundays. Surprisingly, this fits with the peculiarities of Berthelet's original Bible: non-Sunday lections often include readings from the Old Testament (with an affinity to the Books of Isaiah and Ezekiel). Sunday lections, on the other hand, were solely from the New Testament. As all books of prophets are lacking from Berthelet's Bible, keeping to Sunday lections assured the book at hand would be fully compatible with the table of lections.

The Lambeth copy helps unfold the complex reality of late Henrician liturgy. While the Bible is in Latin, the table of lections is in English, as Henry's legislation required. It shows how the Latin Bible was used in accordance with the new English liturgy. Cromwell's original injunction for a Latin and an English Bible to be used together was modified in legislation of 1538 (later reaffirmed in a royal injunction from 5 May 1541), for all parish churches to possess a copy of (solely) an English Bible.[88] However, the removal of Latin from the injunctions did not necessarily mean that it was removed from the living liturgy. The latter was surely the case in cathedrals and collegiate churches, where the liturgy was still chanted in Latin, as is evident in Cranmer's 1538 injunctions, as well as those for specific dioceses.[89] The inclusion of an English table of lections in a Latin Bible reveals how the Latin Bible was made to accommodate the new religious environment, moving away from a dichotomous view of Latin and English, conservatism and reform. Even where the liturgy was chanted in Latin it

88   Hughes and Larkin, *Tudor royal proclamations*, pp. 296–8.
89   Chapter 4, note .65.

did not simply continue old devotions, nor contest Henry VIII's new order. Rather, it adhered to the most updated liturgical order, preserving language, but reforming practice. This is reminiscent of the use of English in fifteenth-century liturgies throughout England, which likewise moves us away from a dichotomous view of English and Latin, reform and tradition (Chapter 2, 'Wycliffite Bibles and Liturgical Plurality').

The subsequent life of the Lambeth copy can be reconstructed with some accuracy. Shortly after the table of lections was written, the Bible left its ecclesiastical abode. Another mid-sixteenth-century hand on the last folio noted a transaction between two laymen (see Figure 3.7). I was not able to trace the first party—one William Cheffyn(?) of Bolengate (Calais). The other, however, had a more peculiar name—James Elys of London Cutpurse—which proved to be an accurate description. Cut-purse was quite a peculiar cognomen, if not affiliation. It describes the act of cutting another's purse, or, in its modern equivalent, a pickpocket. This dangerous trade assists in locating James Elys in our sources. A certain James Elys was hanged at Tyborn on 11 July 1552. He was described in the diary of Henry Machyn as 'the great pykke-purs that ever was, and cutt-purs'.[90] The unfortunate death of Mr Cutpurse supplies further insights into the fortune of the Lambeth copy. It provides a *terminus ad quem* for the annotation, assuring it was written before his death in 1552. This was a mere seventeen years after the printing of the Bible, and three years after the table of lections had become redundant. In our Bible, the merging of Latin and English in Henrician liturgy was indeed short-lived.

The last reader to leave his mark on this Bible attempted to wipe the slate clean by pasting heavy paper over all annotations. This, much like the crossing out of the Name of Jesus and Atkinson's name in the Cambridge copy, demonstrates how a later reader intended to transform the book to accommodate changing religious and cultural sensitivities. In comparison with the crossing-out of Atkinson's name and affiliation, the pasted paper is simultaneously a more and a less efficient way of obliterating the memory of previous readers. It gives the appearance of a 'clean' copy, and without the digital technology would have succeeded in hiding the annotations. Yet technology gives us a more complete view of the annotations and allows us to accurately date the transformation. Unlike the crossing out of names, paper can be analysed and dated. A single sheet of paper was cut and used to cover the verso of the first and last folios of the biblical text (fols 1v, 303v). It is possible to view, under backlight, the watermark on that sheet of paper, now cut in half

---

90 *The diary of Henry Machyn, citizen and merchant-taylor of London, from A.D. 1550 to A.D. 1563*, ed. John Gough Nichols, Camden Society publications 42 (London: Printed for the Camden Society by J. B. Nichols and Son, 1848), pp. 21–2.

Figure 3.7 Hidden
annotations
following digital
subtraction. These
contain reference
to the notorious
pickpocket James
Elys of London
Cutpurse. Fol. 303v
in Berthelet's Bible
(Lambeth Library
copy SR2 E75
[1535]). © Lambeth
Palace Library,
London.

between the two parts. This watermark is of a single-handed pot with flowers on top, inscribed with 'PD | B', similar to watermarks found in paper used in England between 1580 and 1610.[91] The date of the paper coincides with the possible dating of the arrival of the book to Lambeth Palace Library, suggesting the paper was pasted in the early seventeenth century by a bookseller or the librarian of Lambeth Palace.[92] This last act of transformation ended a volatile period of use in the history of the Lambeth copy, which had lasted about sixty years, from printing to pasting.

Conclusion

The study of Berthelet's Bible reveals less familiar facets of the English Reformation. History is written by the victors, and the rise of the English Bible has become an emblem of reform and language, leaving little space for other books or qualities. The course of reform was far from evident in 1535, when the royal printer employed his best, though limited, efforts to produce a Latin Bible, initially supported by Henry himself. He produced a book devoid of any clear religious affiliation, whose existence accorded with the legislation of the following year to furnish parish churches with both Latin and English Bibles. Yet such a Latin Bible was quickly put aside in the fast-paced transformations of the 1530s. As explored in the following chapter, the English Bible took on a more prominent role in Church legislation and book culture. Berthelet's Bible, however, was still in use, adapted to new environments. The digital analysis of one copy reveals how an English table of lections facilitated Latin chant according to the new English order in the 1540s. This unique merging of Latin and English defies the dichotomies of Latin–English and Catholic–Protestant which often underpin histories of the English Reformation. This plurality proved to be a temporary stage. As English took prominence, it was that other 1535 Bible which became a model for future books and modern historians. With the ascent of Edward VI, there was little place for a Latin Bible, except in the hands of Catholic recusants, children, laymen and criminals. Its past was crossed out or pasted over, adjusting it to the new religious environment and its sensitivities.

---

91   Although I was unable to find an exact match, the watermark is extremely similar to the ones used in 1583–99 (C. M. Briquet and Allan Stevenson, *Les filigranes: dictionnaire historique des marques du papier dès leur apparition vers 1282 jusqu'en 1600*, A facsimile of the 1907 edition (Amsterdam: Paper Publications Society, 1968), §12,793 2:638), 1590 (Folger Shakespeare Library L.a. 432 (http://www.gravell.org/record.php?&action=GET&RECID=882, accessed 30 November 2019) or *c*.1607 (Edward Heawood, *Watermarks mainly of the 17th and 18th centuries*, Monumenta chartae papyraceae historiam illustrantia 1 (Hilversum: Paper Publications Society, 1950), §3576).

92   I thank James Carley for this suggestion.

1535 marks a watershed in the history of the English Bible. At first glance, Berthelet's Bible seems removed from any transformation, an archaic remnant beside the nascent seeds of the English Reformation evident in that other English Bible of 1535, Coverdale's celebrated first single-volume Bible. Yet these two contemporary Bibles do not stand in opposition to one another. They both aimed to answer the desire for greater circulation of Bibles in England; they both promulgate the link between Crown and Bible; and they both testify to the state of English printing. The modesty and language of Berthelet's Bible have kept the first Bible printed in England out of sight. Its study reveals an important witness to a volatile era.

4

The Great Bible as a Useless Book

Introduction

The uncertainties surrounding Berthelet's Bible, explored in the previous chapter, were part of a wider phenomenon. The story of the English Bible at the end of Henry's reign does not follow a clear narrative of reform or retraction. Rather, it is a change that is far from uniform, when printers and reformers attempted to second-guess Henry's intentions, while parishioners and priests were handed a book which they were not quite sure how to use. Conflicting forces of reform and tradition, of innovation and technological limitations, all came to the fore in the development of Bibles. Without a clear direction, these years nevertheless revolutionised the landscape of sacred books in England, with the first attempts to produce a 'national' Bible. It was also the moment of inception for the parish Bible, the first time all parish churches in England were instructed to own one. Bibles at the end of Henry's reign, and predominantly Henry's Great Bible,[1] were in flux, constantly modified to accommodate evangelical or conservative sensibilities. They became a bellwether for moments of transformation and the uncertain course of Henrician reform. When explored in comparison with other contemporary Bibles, the Great Bible's title page, annotations, liturgical apparatus and use all reveal minute changes in emphases attuned to the religious and political transformations of the period.

Two years after Berthelet and Coverdale each endeavoured to create a royal Bible, another attempt at securing royal patronage was made. In 1537 two London merchants sought to provide the Bible that Cromwell's injunctions of the previous year had laid down for every parish. Given the unstable religious atmosphere in England, and the deficiencies of English printing, Richard Grafton (of the Grocers' Company, †1573) and Edward Whitchurch (of the Haberdashers' Company, †1562) sought a Continental printer to

---

1   DMH§46; STC§2068. For subsequent editions, see Appendix 2.

produce it. Its text relied on the works of Tyndale and Coverdale, edited and added to by John Rogers, Tyndale's close associate. It was eventually printed by Matthias Crom in Antwerp in 1537, using a pseudonym.[2] The Bible appealed to the reformed faction in Henry's court. A copy was inspected by Thomas Cranmer, Archbishop of Canterbury, who approved the translation and then passed it to Cromwell on 4 August 1537 for royal approval.[3] Consequently, its title page publicised the Bible as 'Set forth with the King's most gracious license', the very first Bible to attract royal support. The addenda to the Bible befitted its newly devised role: It begins with a calendar and almanac painstakingly printed in red and black, and ends with a table of lections. These devices enabled readers to link biblical lessons with the Sarum liturgy. Medieval aids were now put to use in English printed Bibles.

Unlike the portrayal of Henry as a biblical monarch in Coverdale's Bible, the title page of the Matthew Bible used a more generic Continental woodblock depicting salvation history from the Fall to Redemption. The preliminary materials contain a dedication to Henry (*To the moost noble and gracyous | Prynce Kyng Henry the eyght* [...], sig. [★.V.]v-[VI.]v), which likens him to biblical figures: like Hezekiah and Josiah, he is to proclaim God's Law and remove idolatry from the land. This simile was patently reformed, equating traditional religion with idol-worshipping. Such opposition to conservative practice extended beyond the Bible's preliminary materials. Its evangelical stance is most evident in its annotations, which link reformed theology with the biblical text. The Matthew Bible presents a wide array of explanatory materials, with long arguments preceding each chapter and notes in smaller Black Letter in the margins of the text. At times the editor's preoccupation with these annotations led him to overturn the balance of text and annotations: in Psalm 4, for example, the length of prefatory materials exceeds that of the Psalm text.[4] The prologue to the Epistle to the Romans, which reformers considered to be a summary of all Scripture,[5] is seven pages long (pt 5, fols LX.r–LXIII.r). Most notes explicate the Hebrew text or provide typological exegesis. So, for example, 1 Rg 14:27 'and his eyes received light' is accompanied by the note 'Thus speak the Hebrews for that we say. he recovered

---

2   *The Byble: which is all the holy Scripture: in whych are contayned the Olde and Newe Testament* (Antwerp?: Printed for R. Grafton and E. Whitchurch of London, 1537). DMH§34; STC§2066. For its history see Peter W. M. Blayney, *The Stationers' Company and the printers of London 1501–1557* (Cambridge: Cambridge University Press, 2013), pp. 356–9.

3   J. S. Brewer, R. H. Brodie and James Gairdner (eds), *Letters and papers, foreign and domestic, of the reign of Henry VIII: preserved in the Public Record Office, the British Museum, and elsewhere in England* (London: Longman, Green, Longman, & Roberts, 1864–1932), 12:ii:434, 512.

4   Preliminaries 36 lines (27+110 mm high); Psalm 24 lines (114 mm).

5   For the centrality of Romans for reformers' thought see Ralph S. Werrell, 'Tyndale's disagreement with Luther in the prologue to the Epistle to the Romans', *Reformation & Renaissance Review* 7:1 (2005), 57–68.

his strength / and was more cheerful.'; the note for Psalm 8:6 'To crown him &c is / to make him a king which thing was fulfilled in Christ after his resurrection, Mat. xxviii.d and of him doth the epistle to the Hebrews expound this verse. Hebr.ii.'; in the Song of Songs red rubrics identify the medieval 'voices', linking its often obscure biblical speakers to episodes from the life of Christ and the history of the Church.[6]

The notes to the Matthew Bible also reveal traces of theological strife and the editor's evangelical leanings. The note for the Epistle to the Romans 3:24 ('but are justified freely by his grace through the redemption that is in Christ Jesus.') reads 'S. Paul himself / in these words / freely without the law / without works / it is a gift' (pt 5, fol. LXIV.v). The letter of the Bible is seen as accommodating the reformist theology of justification by faith alone.[7] Such notes became one of the most controversial elements in the history of the English Bible. Seventy years later, the notes of the Geneva Bible were rejected by Crown and Church, contributing to the creation of the King James Bible.[8] Notes have attracted criticism in the period under investigation as well. The notes of the Matthew Bible did not escape unscathed. In a copy of the 1537 edition (Bible Society BSS.201.B37.6) an early modern reader systematically obliterated all the notes with brown paint (including entire folios from the prologue to the Romans), leaving only chapter summaries and cross references.[9] Herbert has suggested this followed the 1543 *Act for the Advancement of True Religion*, which required such notes to be removed or obliterated.[10]

---

6   The voices were printed in red—a highly difficult and innovative printing venture for the time, which required pulling the press twice for the same side. This had led to some inaccuracies, and the unseemly printing of black over red in Sg 2:16, 17. In all subsequent prints the voices for the Song of Songs were printed solely in back.

7   In this case the reformed tone of the notes differs from the translation itself. The translation of Rm 3:28 is often used to separate reformed and conservative Bibles. Unlike its notes, or many reformed Bibles, Matthew's translation of the sentence does not allude to justification by faith alone: cf. Wim François, 'The early modern Bible between material book and immaterial Word', in *The agency of things in medieval and early modern art: materials, power and manipulation*, ed. Grażyna Jurkowlaniec, Ika Matyjaszkiewicz and Zuzanna Sarnecka, Routledge research in art history (New York and London: Routledge, 2018), pp. 129–43.

8   See Femke Molekamp, 'Genevan legacies: the making of the English Geneva Bible', in *The Oxford handbook of the Bible in England, c.1530–1700*, ed. Kevin Killeen, Helen Smith and Rachel Willie (Oxford: Oxford University Press, 2015), pp. 38–53; Maurice S. Betteridge, 'The Bitter Notes: the Geneva Bible and its annotations', *The Sixteenth Century Journal* 14:1 (1983), 41–62; William W. E. Slights, '"Marginal notes that spoile the text": Scriptural annotation in the English Renaissance', *Huntington Library Quarterly* 55 (1992), 255–78.

9   Such obliteration is reflected in Books of Hours: Eamon Duffy, *Marking the hours: English people and their prayers 1240–1570* (New Haven, CT: Yale University Press, 2006), ch. 9: 'The break from Rome', pp. 149–70.

10   DMH§34, p. 19, following Brooke Foss Westcott, *A general view of the history of the English Bible* (London: Macmillan, 1868), p. 114. At the end of 3Rg (=CXXXIXv), a note identifies Spanish ownership in 1554, which may suggest another location for these erasures. For the Act see *The Statutes of the*

The Great Bible's Title Page, Preliminaries and Idealised Narratives

Cromwell became an ardent supporter of a new English Bible, a Bible worthy of royal patronage both in its content and in its material grandeur. Such a Bible would combine Cromwell's own evangelical leanings with the political aim of consolidating Henry's control over the English Church. In order to facilitate such an endeavour, Cromwell, Henry's chief minister, joined forces with Coverdale, whose 1535 Bible was the first single-volume Bible in English, and the merchant-publishers Grafton and Whitchurch, veterans of the Matthew Bible. The creation of the new Bible was beset by practical difficulties just as the previous ones had been. English printers were simply not equipped to produce a book of the magnitude sought by Cromwell, a large and complex volume worthy of royal support. There was simply no press big enough in England for printing such a large folio.[11] Likewise, England lacked the paper mills to furnish paper for printing such a Bible. As Cromwell sought the best-quality paper for his new Bible, the need to import paper further discouraged local production. Therefore, it is of little surprise that an early decision was made to move the printing of the Bible to the Continent.

The printer chosen for the project was François Regnault, who had been printing for the English market for some twenty years. Grafton and Whitchurch spent much of 1538 in Paris supervising the production, while Coverdale worked there on revising the translation of the new Bible. Their correspondence with Cromwell provides insight into the course of the project. Letters sent from Paris to England preserve valuable information regarding the production of the Bible. While the team in Paris was appreciative of the quality of printing, and especially of the high-grade paper available for Regnault in Paris, it quickly became clear that the project had run into difficulties.[12] Mounting political tensions between France and England led to French inquisitors being sent by the King of France to investigate the printing of the Bible. This was followed by the confiscation of the printed sheets of the Bible, which the French authorities refused to release. Nonetheless, they allowed (and, as suggested by Mozley, possibly even encouraged) the project to relocate

realm, printed by command of his majesty king George the third, in' pursuance of an address of the house of commons of Great Britain from original records and authentic manuscripts (London: Eyre and Strahan, 1817; reprint, 1963), 3:894–7. For the original draft, analysis and reappraisal see Blayney, *Stationers' Company*, pp. 550–5.

11   Blayney, *Stationers' Company*, p. 361.

12   See James Frederic Mozley, *Coverdale and his Bibles* (London: Lutterworth Press, 1953), pp. 202–60; A. J. Slavin, 'The Rochepot Affair', *The Sixteenth Century Journal* 10:1 (1979), 3–19; re-assessed by Blayney, *Stationers' Company*, pp. 360–74.

to England. Regnault's presses, types and paper made their way to London, where Grafton and Whitchurch assumed the role of printers of the Great Bible. Correspondence continued between England and Paris for the retrieval of the sheets; some sheets of the Paris printing have indeed been identified by Blayney, embedded into the second edition of the Great Bible (April 1540).

This move of men and materials had a lasting impact on English book production. It introduced advanced printing materials and techniques into England, which influenced the printing of subsequent editions of the Bible, and of other books as well. The unique circumstances of the printing of the Great Bible also shaped the appearance of its subsequent editions. As can be seen in Appendix 2, the 1538/9 printing was quickly followed by six editions printed by Grafton or Whitchurch (working individually rather than collaboratively on subsequent editions) between 1540 and 1541. The second edition replicated the first. Possibly in the hope of retrieving the confiscated sheets, exact page length was preserved, enabling the insertion of leaves from the first edition (printed either in Paris or London) into the second. This strategy continued into subsequent editions. Five of the seven editions (1st, 2nd, 3rd, 5th and 7th) were designed to allow the mixing of materials between them (printed at sixty-two lines per page, with care taken to preserve the length of each folio, thus enabling interchanging folios between the editions). The remaining two editions (4th and 6th editions, at sixty-five lines per page) also allowed the mixture of elements between them. Nowadays most surviving Bibles bring together components from different editions. Fry's survey of 146 copies of the Great Bible, still one of the most detailed analyses has revealed only thirty-one unmixed copies, scarcely more than 20 per cent, with the majority of surviving books each containing elements from at least two editions.[13] At times this was done during the compilation of the Bible (as, for example, in mixing sheets from Paris and London into editions); at other times it was done by later collectors.

All seven editions of the Great Bible share the same woodcut for their title pages (see Figure 4.1). Previous attributions of the title page to Holbein have been disproved, and the identity of the artist remains unknown.[14] Since there is '[n]o other printed visual statement [apart from the title page for

---

13   Francis Fry, *A description of the Great Bible, 1539, and the six editions of Cranmer's Bible, 1540 and 1541, printed by Grafton and Whitchurch: also of the editions, in large folio, of the authorized version of the Holy Scriptures, printed in the years 1611, 1613, 1617, 1634, 1640* (London: Willis and Sotheran, etc., 1865).
14   Myra Dickman Orth, 'The English Great Bible of 1539 and the French connection', in *Tributes to Jonathan J. G. Alexander: the making and meaning of illuminated medieval & Renaissance manuscripts, art & architecture*, ed. J. J. G. Alexander, Susan L'Engle and Gerald B. Guest (London: Harvey Miller Publishers, 2006), pp. 171–84 suggests execution in France by the Master of François de Rohan before production moved to England; String negates this suggestion, arguing that the design should be attributed to Lucas Horenbout or Giarolamo da Treviso (Tatiana C. String, *Art and communication in the reign of Henry VIII* (Aldershot: Ashgate, 2008), p96n19).

Coverdale's Bible] relating to the English Reformation from Henry's reign', the significance of the title page and its wide dissemination is evident.[15] The artist had been well instructed on his mission. String convincingly argues for a methodological difference between the title page of Coverdale's Bible (see Figure 3.2) and that of the Great Bible. While the former was based on a collection of texts given to Holbein to illustrate, the latter is the visual manifestation of Henry's authority. Henry reigns at the top of the page, distributing Bibles to laypeople and clerics, aided by Cromwell to his left and Cranmer to his right (each identified by his coat of arms). The Word of God then reaches the general public in the lower register, who duly proclaim 'vivat rex' and 'long live the king'. Iconographical omissions are likewise revealing. The three men imprisoned at the bottom-right corner do not praise the monarch; the laypeople in the lower register do not hold a Bible, but hear the Word of God through the sermon of a preacher in the bottom-left corner;[16] the Roman Church is absent from the dissemination of the Word of God, which flows from Henry to his people, aided by his ministers, the material artefacts and oral dissemination. This title page of the Bible masterminded by Cromwell distilled his theory of Scripture and obedience, although it set the Bible on a collision course with the reality of the English Church.

The iconographical shift from the title page of Coverdale's Bible to that of the Great Bible is seen by String as reflecting a change in the nature of authority. Coverdale's depicts the transmission of authority from God, at the top of the page, through the unfolding of divine history, all the way to Henry at the bottom of the page. In the title page of the Great Bible, on the other hand, Henry is at the top register, and thus 'the transmission of the Word of God … begins with God *and* Henry'.[17] We can now even extend this analysis further, to see in the new iconography a hierarchy of authority. In Coverdale's Bible God takes the form of a tetragrammaton (the divine name in Hebrew letters), befitting Coverdale's evangelical stance. In the Great Bible, on the other hand, the depiction of God is anthropomorphic. God assumes a human form, and so enhances the affinity between Henry and the Divinity. This is made explicit by their physical proximity, sharing the top register: Henry's outstretched arms distributing Bibles mirror God's posture of benediction. In the Great Bible, even God seems to be subjected to Henry's authority. The constraints of God's position between Henry's head and the top of the page forced the

---

15   String, *Art and communication*, p. 98.

16   As noted by Margaret Aston, 'Lap books and lectern books: the revelatory book in the Reformation', in *The Church and the book: papers read at the 2000 summer meeting and the 2001 winter meeting of the Ecclesiastical History Society*, ed. R. N. Swanson, Studies in Church history 38 (Woodbridge: Boydell for the Ecclesiastical History Society, 2004), pp. 163–89 at 178.

17   String, *Art and communication*, p. 97.

Figure 4.1 Title page of the first edition of the Great Bible. This iconic image distils Henry VIII's attitude to the English Bible (*The Byble in Englysh [...]* [Paris and London: Richard Grafton and Edward Whitchurch, 1539]). Reproduced by kind permission of the Syndics of Cambridge University Library.

artist to squeeze Him against the upper register of the frame, leaving God at a fraction of Henry's size (Henry's height is 4.6 times greater than Christ's). If in Coverdale's Bible Henry is a second Solomon, here he becomes a second Christ in Majesty. The break from Rome was complete with Henry as the *Vicar Christi* (the vicar of Christ), the title conferred on late medieval popes.

This woodcut was used in all seven editions of the Great Bible, demonstrating the appeal of its message to Henry, which is evident also in the choice to replace the earlier title page of the New Testament (from the second edition onwards) with this one as well. It also attests to the difficulties in procuring a new title page. Unable, or unwilling, to replace it completely, subtle modifications were nevertheless made to its appearance, adapting it to new environments. Such changes could be traced back to the time of the Great Bible's compilation in Paris. Two luxurious vellum copies were sent from Paris in 1538, as described in a letter from Coverdale and Grafton to Cromwell on 23 June 1538: '[W]e have here sent unto your lordship ii examples, on parchment, wherein we intend to print one for the king's grace, and another for your lordship.'[18] These have survived, one at the National Library of Wales, and the other in St John's College, Cambridge, with the latter Bible commonly seen as Cromwell's copy.[19]

While the copy at the National Library of Wales lacks some of its preliminary materials, the hand-painted title pages of that at St John's survive intact (see Figure 4.2). Its printed title pages were carefully painted over, with the original print at times peeping through, as in the brick background still visible through the red stockings of the green-clad figure at the bottom right of the opening title page, which diverges the most from the original print.[20] Its artist, constrained by the layout of the original printed page, still managed to introduce important modifications. The most evident omission in the painted title page, as noted by Orth, is the removal of the prison. Other modifications, so far unnoticed by scholars, were introduced by the artist to distance the image further from the original title page. In place of the prison, there is now a group of three people: a man in red hose and green cape holding an open book, another man in a blue coat in an *orans* posture, and behind them a woman with

18   Alfred W. Pollard, *Records of the English Bible: the documents relating to the translaton and publication of the Bible in English, 1525–1611* (London: Oxford University Press, 1911), p. 234.

19   The copies are mentioned in Orth, 'The English Great Bible of 1539 and the French connection', p. 178; Blayney, *Stationers' Company*, pp. 373–4. The best study is still Leslie A. Sheppard, 'A vellum copy of the Great Bible, 1539', *The National Library of Wales Journal* 1:1 (1939), 9–22. Blayney has argued that these Bibles utilise quires that were possibly produced in Paris and later confiscated by the French authorities. The association between Cromwell and the St John's copy rests on John Williams (†1650), Archbishop of York, and his possible family ties with Cromwell.

20   The examination of the page with a light-sheet reveals other instances of the printed page underneath the painted image.

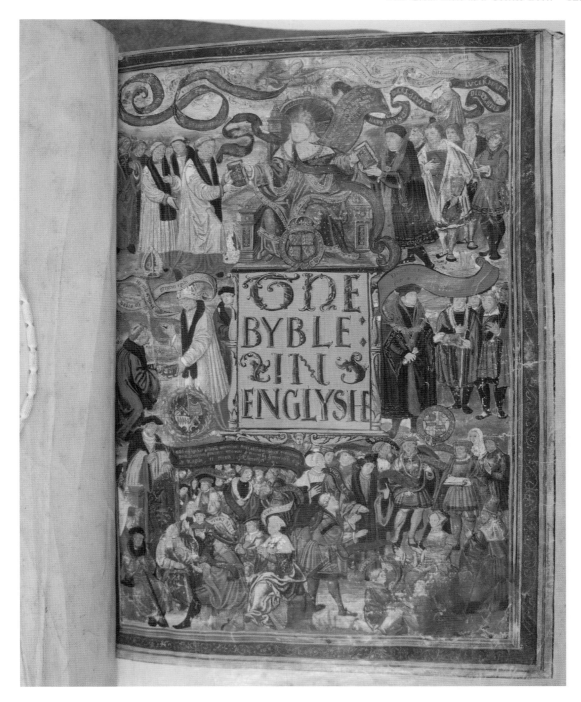

Figure 4.2 Hand-coloured title page of the Great Bible. This lavish image contains significant modifications of the original printed title page (Cambridge, St John's College, copy Bb.8.30). By permission of the Master and Fellows of St John's College, Cambridge.

a wimple or open-fronted veil. Aston noted the lack of books among the laity in the lower register, yet the unknown artist had changed this by having the three assemble around an open book, in what appears to be a presentation scene. Given the importance of the presentation copy, and the significant modification to the original layout, I believe this to be the presentation of the Bible to its patron, with the two men most likely Grafton and Whitchurch, and the woman possibly Ann Welles, Whitchurch's first wife (Grafton married only in 1545/47).[21]

The image of the woman below this small group (or adjacent to the prison in the printed title page) was also changed. In the original image, a woman is sitting next to a group of children, her hair in curls, possibly with a white undercap; her hands instruct the children, while her face is turned toward the man on her left (possibly the prison's warden). This was completely transformed in the painted title page. The woman now faces the children, and her features are clearer and more subtle. Her headgear has been turned into a lavish gable hood, worn by nobility and royalty.[22] This sumptuous short gable,

Figure 4.3 Hans Holbein the Younger's portrait of Jane Seymour (1536/37), Kunsthistoriches Museum Vienna. This portrait is similar to the modified title page of the Great Bible. ©KHM-Museumsverband.

in gold and possibly jewels, and the distinctive facial features are reminiscent of Holbein's portrait of Jane Seymour, painted in 1536 (see Figure 4.3). As demonstrated by Dolman, the portrait was well known at the time and had served to inspire other depictions of Jane Seymour, including one that was made in 1539, shortly after the hand-painted title page.[23] The integration of Jane into the title page combines with the newly devised presentation scene to transform our understanding of the St John's copy. Rather than Cromwell's Bible, this copy appears to have been Henry's own dedication copy. The prison scene and

---

21   For Ann Welles see Blayney, *Stationers' Company*, p. 357. This idea was first suggested to me by Richard Rex.

22   Georgine De Courtais, *Women's headdress and hairstyles in England from AD 600 to the present day*, rev. edn (London: B. T. Batsford, 1986), pp. 40–3.

23   Brett Dolman, 'Wishful thinking: reading the portraits of Henry VIII's queens', in *Henry VIII and the court: art, politics and performance*, ed. Thomas Betteridge and Suzannah Lipscomb (Farnham and Burlington, VT: Ashgate, 2013), pp. 115–29 at 121–2.

the penalty for disobedience gave way to an idealised scene of the royal family: the recently deceased Jane, whose memory was kept alive in numerous images, was seen in the company of children, alluding to the young Prince Edward, Henry's much sought-after heir.

Modifications of the title page continued into subsequent editions. While its iconography could not be easily changed in the course of mass production, the central text was changed effortlessly to accommodate a less evangelical stance. The title page of the first edition advertised a Bible that was '[t]ruly translated from Hebrew and Greek'. This mildly reformed sentiment detached the Bible from the Latin Vulgate and sent it back *ad fontes*, to its Greek and Hebrew origins. This claim was omitted from subsequent editions, and instead the revised title page told of a new prologue by Cranmer, as well as that '[t]his is the Bible appointed | to the use of the churches'.

The title page of the Great Bible presented an ideal state in which the kingdom functioned in harmony and the laity embraced a new appreciation of the monarch. Reality, however, was different. Like the appearance of Cranmer's prologue in the second edition, the title page of the Great Bible is indicative of the movement of people in and out of Henry's grace. Thomas Cromwell, the instigator of the Great Bible, appears on its title page supporting Henry by disseminating the Word of God to lay dignitaries. Shortly after the appearance of the Great Bible, Cromwell devised Henry's ill-fated marriage to Anne of Cleves in January 1540. The conservative faction in court used this opportunity to move against Cromwell, leading to his execution in July 1540. The printers of subsequent editions of the Great Bible faced the problem of retaining the image of a convicted traitor. The solution was not to replace the woodcut altogether—a cumbersome and very costly endeavour. Rather, they erased Cromwell's coat of arms from the fourth edition of November 1540 and all subsequent editions (see Figure 4.4). Rather than completely removing his memory, the lacking title page reminded readers of the fate of those seen to oppose Henry. In a later hand-painted vellum copy of the Great Bible presented to Henry VIII (see Figure 4.5), another solution was devised. There, the artist employed a similar colour palette to that of the St John's dedication copy. While the prison is in place, and the woman remains as in the printed edition, Cromwell's coat of arms is painted over, and his figure is modified to the likeness of an elderly man with white hair and beard. This is probably Anthony Marler, whose dedication is written on the blank page facing the image: 'This book is presented unto your most excellent | highness by your loving, faithful, and obedient | Subject and daily Orator[24] Anthony | Marler of London haberdasher'.

---

24   This phrase mirrors the 1535 dedication to Henry VIII in Coverdale's Bible, which ends 'Your graces humble subject and daily Orator, Myles Coverdale'.

Figure 4.4 Title page of the fifth edition of the Great Bible. Following the execution of Cromwell his coats of arms were obliterated from the title page (*The Byble in Englysh [...]* [London: Edward Whitchurch, 1541]). Reproduced by kind permission of the Syndics of Cambridge University Library.

Anthony Marler, a wealthy London haberdasher, supported Grafton and Whitchurch and took over the production of the Bible following Cromwell's execution, with Grafton and Whitchurch retaining their roles as printers. Unlike the two merchant-printers, Marler's commitment to the evangelical cause is not obvious. This has led Blayney to claim that 'however much

Figure 4.5 Title page of Marler's presentation copy of the Great Bible (BL Copy C.18.d.10). This was part of Marler's failed campaign to support his Bible-printing monopoly. © The British Library Board.

he [Marler] may have been prompted by evangelical zeal, his financing of reprints of the Great Bible was just one business deal among many'.[25] For

25   Blayney, *Stationers' Company*, p. 467. For Grafton and Whitchurch see their respective entries at the ODNB (Meraud Grant Ferguson, 'Grafton, Richard (1506/7–1573)', in *Oxford dictionary of national*

Marler this was a commercial enterprise above all. Producing the Bible, the largest and most elaborate book printed in England hitherto, was costly; at the agreed price of 10s. for unbound copies, and 12s. for bound copies, profit margins were small.[26] Later legal battles demonstrate the financial implications for Marler of printing the Bible: A record from October 1546 notes that Grafton owed £600 to Marler;[27] a court record from 1560 reveals Marler seeking 100 marks from John Fryer, doctor of medicine, and Philip Scapulis, alien member of the Stationers' Company, for the production of the Great Bible. They had been given 130 copies of the printed Bible as surety for the loan, and possibly for a share of the profits.[28]

Marler proceeded to secure an audience for his Bibles. On 1 May 1541, as the fifth edition was nearing completion, he petitioned the Privy Council to reissue the proclamation for the need of parish churches to own a Bible. The proclamation was made on 5 May 1541, under the pain of 40s. for non-compliance, and with half of the fine promised to any informant.[29] Ryrie demonstrates the effect of this proclamation, as churchwarden accounts testify to a rise in Bible acquisition.[30] Marler proceeded to secure his investment by seeking, and securing, a monopoly on printing the Bible. This was granted to him for four years under the royal seal on 11 March 1542.[31]

Further transformations of the title page reveal forces at work aimed at curbing the wave of vernacular Bibles. After Cromwell's execution, the title page of the fourth edition was treated more cautiously. Following the 1538 injunctions for the approval of biblical translations, the title page stated: 'overseen and perused at the commandment of the King's highness, by the right reverend fathers in God Cuthbert bishop of Durham, and Nicolas bishop of Rochester'. This note, however, was quickly removed, and does not appear in the fifth edition (though it is preserved in the sixth). Bishops

---

biography (Oxford: Oxford University Press, 2004); Alec Ryrie, 'Whitchurch, Edward (d. 1562)', in *Oxford dictionary of national biography* (Oxford: Oxford University Press, 2004)). Both printers were interrogated for religious dissent in 1543 and fell out of favour when Mary ascended the throne, which was not the case for Marler.

26   In the 1530s, a thresher's daily wage was 3.5p per day, hence requiring thirty-four days' salary for purchasing an unbound Bible. This is based on the wages supplied by Gregory Clark, 'The long march of history: farm laborers' wages in England 1208–1850', *Economic History Review* 60:1 (2007), 97–135 at 100.

27   Blayney, *Stationers' Company*, p. 530. I thank Jim Bolton for his assistance in this matter.

28   Henry R. Plomer, 'Anthony Marler and the Great Bible', *The Library*, 3rd Series 1:2 (1910), 200–6.

29   A copy of the proclamation, printed by Berthelet, is preserved in the British Library C.18.e.2.(21). It is printed in Pollard, *Records of the English Bible*, §43 pp. 261–5; Paul L. Hughes and James F. Larkin (eds), *Tudor royal proclamations*, vol. 1: *The early Tudors, 1485–1553* (New Haven, CT: Yale University Press, 1964), pp. 296–8.

30   Alec Ryrie, *The Gospel and Henry VIII: evangelicals in the early English Reformation*, Cambridge studies in early modern British history (Cambridge: Cambridge University Press, 2003), p. 43.

31   For the text see Blayney, *Stationers' Company*, p. 543.

Cuthbert Tunstal (†1559) and Nicolas Heath (†1578) grew closer to the conservative wing in the 1540s, giving credence to a claim made in 1546 that they requested their names to be removed from the Great Bible: '[B]ut when they saw the world somewhat like to wring on the other side they denied it, and said they never meddled therewith, causing the Printer to take out their names which were erst set before the Bible to certify all men that they had diligently perused it according as your highness had commanded.'[32] Both bishops denied any link to the Bible, and the title page was modified once more. This attests to a growing unease with the vernacular Bible. And indeed, despite Marler's best efforts, no Bible was printed in England after 1541 and until the end of Henry's reign.

The quick succession of editions may have led to market saturation, yet the reaction of Tunstal and Heath suggests that other forces were at play. Resistance to the English Bible was evident throughout Henry's reign. Tunstal's withdrawal from the Great Bible is indicative of the ways a mildly conservative bishop opposed reform while following Henry's injunctions. As the Bishop of London he rejected Tyndale's New Testament but was lenient towards heretics; he then supported the break from Rome and Henry's divorce, albeit at times reluctantly. A similar picture arises from Ryrie's study of Bishop Bonner, whose enthusiasm during the printing of the Bible in Paris weakened after he became the Bishop of London.[33] Ryrie suggests that a pragmatic stance, although strongly opposed by more ardent reformers, was typical of many bishops who disapproved of Cranmer's reforming tendencies and objected to vernacular Scripture, especially one prepared by evangelical translators such as Tyndale and Coverdale.[34] The matter came to a head at the same time that Marler secured his monopoly. In the Canterbury Convocation of February and March 1542, clergy and bishops assembled to discuss the English Bible.[35] They strongly opposed the Great Bible and advocated an episcopal revision. With Henry's support, Cranmer deferred the decision—indefinitely—by sending for consultation at the universities of Cambridge and Oxford. But Henry himself also came to oppose to the Bible, which ultimately frustrated Marler's efforts. Blayney even suggests that

---

32   *A supplication of the poore commons: Whereunto is added the supplication of beggers* (London: John Day and William Seres?, 1546), pp. 277–8; available at http://name.umdl.umich.edu/A00758.0001.001, accessed 19 November 2019; printed in Mozley, *Coverdale and his Bibles*, p. 253.

33   Bonner's changing attitudes were depicted in Foxe's account of a meeting between Bonner and Grafton the day after Cromwell's execution, when Bonner did not object to that act. The meeting and its reassessment are discussed by Ryrie, *The Gospel and Henry*, pp. 217–21.

34   Reflecting also David Scott Kastan, '"The Noyse of the New Bible": reaction and Reform in Henrician England', in *Religion and culture in Renaissance England*, ed. Claire McEachern and Deborah Shuger (Cambridge: Cambridge University Press, 1997), pp. 46–68.

35   Blayney, *Stationers' Company*, p. 542; Ryrie, *The Gospel and Henry*, p. 44. The Convocation's three evangelical bishops were in a clear minority.

granting Marler the patent for the printing of Bibles was aimed at thwarting attempts at printing the Bible during the remaining years of Henry's reign.

Henry grew disillusioned with the Bible as a vehicle towards conformity and obedience. Introducing vernacular Scripture was a major religious and social transformation. Henry's aim in this was clear, and received a visual manifestation on the Bible's title page: a godly monarch distributing Bibles, reaching a populace enthusiastically calling 'long live the king'. Early attempts were made to ensure conformity by directing and qualifying biblical access. In April 1539 the *Proclamation for Uniformity of Religion* decreed that the Bible should be read in low voices and not during service. The draft proclamation was amended by Henry himself, who added that he had permitted the use of English Scripture 'for his majesty's intent and hope was that they that would read the Scripture, would with meekness and wish to accomplish the effect of, read it, and not to maintain erroneous opinions and preach, nor for to use the reading or preaching of it in sundry times and places and after'.[36] Access to the Bible was not the right of the people; it was granted by the king, and hence could be revoked. The 1541 injunctions stated that Bible reading should lead people to keeping the commandments, and

> to obey their sovereign Lord and high powers [...] without murmur or grudgings [...] the purpose above rehearsed, humbly, meekly, reverently and obediently; and not that any of them should read the said Bibles with loud and high voices, in time of the celebration of the holy Masse and other divine services used in the church, nor that any his lay subjects reading the same should presume to take upon them any common disputation, argument or exposition of the mysteries therein contained.[37]

Henry feared that lay access to Scripture could lead away from the ideal expressed on the Bible's title page; that men and women might subject the biblical text to interpretations other than those intended by their king.

In 1543 the *Act for the Advancement of True Religion* alongside the *King's Book* curbed unrestricted access to Scripture. The former forbade private and public reading by women of the lower classes, artificers, apprentices, journeymen, yeomen and the lower classes; the latter subjected lay Bible reading to the wishes of the monarch. In effect, Henry replaced the Bible with the summary of doctrine in the *King's Book* as the means of instructing the laity.[38]

---

36   Hughes and Larkin, *Tudor royal proclamations*, pp. 284–6; discussed by Ryrie, *The Gospel and Henry*, p. 28.

37   See note 29 above.

38   See Ryrie, *The Gospel and Henry*, pp. 44–54; Richard Rex, 'The crisis of obedience: God's Word and Henry's Reformation', *The Historical Journal* 39:4 (1996), 863–94 at 891–3; and to a lesser extent Kastan,

The legislation was inspired by conservative Bishops such as Gardiner, and corresponded to the lack of new biblical prints for the remainder of Henry's reign. The image on the title page of the Great Bible had become reality: the hierarchy of the page, the absence of Bibles in the hands of the laity and the prison on the right all came into effect with the restrictions on Bible reading in 1543. From Henry's perspective, a four-year experiment in popular access to the Bible resulted in restrictive injunctions which aimed at moulding reality to the monarch's wishes. Nevertheless, Bibles were not retracted from parish churches, and the Act was followed by a single persecution (and, as shown by Ryrie, not a clear-cut one), which inevitably sent a mixed message regarding lay use of the Bible.[39]

Biblical Layout and Subduing Reform

In the Great Bible, as in the Matthew Bible before it and the Geneva Bible after it, notes turned into a battleground between reformed and conservative factions. Notes concerned theological interpretations of Scripture; they empowered individual readers to engage with the text and removed the need for clerical mediation. In the first edition of the Great Bible, the Prologue to the Reader, most likely written by Coverdale, explains the role of pointed hands, or *manicules*, in the Bible:

> We have also (as you may see) added many hands both in the margins of this volume, and also in the text, upon the which, we purposed to have made in the end of the Bible (in a table by them selves) certain godly annotations: but for so much as yet there hath not been sufficient time ministered to the king's most honorable council, for the oversight and correction of the said annotations, we will therefore omit them, till their more convenient leisure. Doing now no more but beseech the most gentle reader, that when you come at such a place where a hand does stand (or any other where, in the Bible) & you cannot attain to the meaning & true knowledge of that sentence, then do not rashly presume to make any private interpretation thereof: but submit your self to the judgement of those that are godly learned in Christ Jesus. To the which Jesus with the father and holy ghost be honour and praise for ever. Amen. [sig.★.[v].v]

"'The noyse of the new Bible'", p. 59. For the Act, N.10; For the King's Book see Henry VIII, *The King's book: or, A necessary doctrine and erudition for any Christian man, 1543*, ed. T. A. Lacey, Church Historical Society new series (London: Society for Promoting Christian Knowledge, 1932), pp. 5–6.
39   Ryrie, *The Gospel and Henry*, pp. 49–50.

Manicules indeed appear throughout the Bible (e.g. Figure 4.7, a page from the Psalms of the first edition of the Great Bible). According to the Prologue, their incorporation follows a simple rationale: they identify difficult places in the text, and were to be accompanied by a table of annotations at the back of the Bible. Due to lack of time and the need to have the notes approved by the Privy Council, the notes were put aside, to be integrated at a later time.

This short account conceals much debate about the notes, which we can glimpse from the correspondence between Paris and England, between Coverdale, Grafton and Whitchurch who oversaw the production of the Bible, and Cromwell, their sponsor, embedded in Henry's court. The notes are first mentioned in a letter from Coverdale and Grafton to Cromwell on 23 June 1538, in which they request additional funds for the printing of the Bible, whose material aspect (with paper 'of the best sort in France') and contents they praise. The Bible follows the original languages, and would contain a table 'with such annotations [...] as shall doubtless {d}elucidate and clear the same'.[40] At this early stage, the annotations were seen as integral to the new Bible. This, however, was immediately qualified, as they promised that the notes would contain no 'singularity of opinion', that is no religious dissent.

Cromwell's response has not survived, but a letter from Coverdale, Grafton and William Gray to Cromwell,[41] dated 9 August 1538, explains the marks and layout of the Bible. The *manicule* 'signifies that upon the same (in the later end of the book) there is some notable annotation; which we have written without any private opinion, only after the best interpreters of the Hebrews, for the more clearness of the text'. Despite Coverdale's assurance that the annotations were sound, the tone makes it clear that the notes had caused Cromwell unease. Coverdale's subsequent letter of 13 December 1538 adopts a very different tone:

> I humbly beseech your lordship, that by my lord elect of Hertford, I may know your pleasure, concerning the Annotations of this Bible, whether I shall proceed therein or no — Pity it were, that the dark places of that text (upon the which I have always set a hand ☞) should so pass undeclared. As for any private opinion or contentious words, as I will utterly avoid all such, so will I offer the annotations first to my said lord of Hertford; to the intent that he shall so examine the same, afore they be put in print, if it be your lordship's good pleasure, that I shall so do.[42]

---

40   Pollard, *Records of the English Bible*, pp. 234–6; discussed in Mozley, *Coverdale and his Bibles*, p. 256.

41   Gray was most likely Cromwell's man, who defended his reputation posthumously: Blayney, *Stationers' Company*, pp. 413, 421–2, 425–7.

42   BL Harley MS 604, fol. 112. Printed in Pollard, *Records of the English Bible*, pp. 245–6; Brewer, Brodie and Gairdner, *Letters and papers*, §1043, 13:2.

Clearly Cromwell had objected to the notes, leading Coverdale to assure him of their usefulness; he even suggested that Cromwell would scrutinise them before publication. This meant a great deal to Coverdale. Half of the short letter is dedicated to the matter of the notes, and only at its end does Coverdale raise the possibility of the Bible being confiscated 'if these men proceed in their cruelness against us'. For Coverdale, the political tensions surrounding the production of the Bible appeared secondary to the incorporation of notes.

We can now return to the Prologue and observe the tensions it reveals. Evelyn Tribble, and in her footsteps William Sherman, has seen this as an isolated moment, in which biblical segments were identified as 'Church property' to which lay readers should have no access.[43] A close reading of the Prologue, however, suggests this was a moment of transition: the notes had been compiled (as suggested in the letter of 9 August), and the editors were awaiting final approval. The Prologue's solution resembles the Bible's title page and its ideal of Bible reading: Henry's goal was the creation of an obedient populace, rather than encouraging a variety of opinions. Exegetical and interpretative notes, which could support individual opinions, did not serve this purpose. Their removal, and subjecting oneself 'to the judgement of those that are godly learned', better suited Henry's aims. Indeed, there is no indication that the notes had ever been submitted to the Privy Council or to Cromwell; nor were they inserted into the second edition of the Great Bible. Rather, the Prologue itself was removed from the third edition, as were the *manicules*.[44] The opportunity for lay empowerment was shut before it had been fully opened.

The story of the notes and their gradual erasure reflects tensions between reform and conservatism at Henry's court. It is also indicative of a growing distrust of lay reading. In a popular addendum to the second edition of the Great Bible, lay reading was actively encouraged. Thomas Cranmer, Archbishop of Canterbury, compiled a short treatise (*A prologue or preface made by the | most reverend father in God, Thomas Archbishop of Canterbury | Metropolitan and Primate of England*, sig. ★.ii.r–v.r in the second edition), preserved in all subsequent editions and advertised on its title page. The Preface was well received by Henry, who quoted from it in his 1545 Christmas speech.[45] Taking a

---

43   Evelyn B. Tribble, *Margins and marginality: the printed page in early modern England* (Charlottesville: University Press of Virginia, 1993), pp. 24–5; William H. Sherman, *Used books: marking readers in Renaissance England*, Material texts (Philadelphia: University of Pennsylvania Press, 2008), pp. 42–3.
44   Blayney (*Stationers' Company*, p. 382) suggests this was removed to avoid placing continuous blame on the Privy Council, an interpretation which sidelines the question of lay reading.
45   Diarmaid MacCulloch, *Thomas Cranmer: a life*, rev. edn (New Haven, CT: Yale University Press, 2016), pp. 258–60, 348.

strong stance on the value of lay reading, Cranmer encouraged all people to read the Bible. He admonished readers not to give in to lack of time or leisure, and advised them to consult the Bible even though 'thy wife provoketh thee to anger, thy child giveth thee occasion to take sorrow and pensiveness'. His call was made explicitly to the lower classes: to the publicans, the fishermen and the shepherds, who should read the Bible time and again. While the value—and even efficacious nature—of Bible reading was asserted, it was also qualified. Cranmer was weary of disputations and advised that readers consult the learned in difficult matters. His position was summarised in the famous dictum 'I forbid not to read, but I forbid to reason'.[46] Lay reading of the Bible was not to be done in private, but rather within parish churches. Cranmer's Prologue proved to be a rearguard action; its ideal of lay reading was eventually repealed in the injunctions of 1543.

The Great Bible's *manicules* reflect tensions between reform and conservatism, as well as Henry's disillusionment with lay reading. They also testify to the transition between two eras and the gradual assimilation of new technologies. The *manicules* were a medieval icon, commonly inserted by readers onto manuscript margins as means of identifying passages of interest. They are often accompanied—or replaced—by the letter NB (*nota bene*, 'note well'). This device was embraced by early modern readers, who often left *manicules* in the margins of their books.[47] None of the medieval Bibles surveyed for this book contain *manicules* written by the original scribe(s) as part of the initial design of the book. Rather, they were employed by active readers.

In printed Bibles, printers began to employ this device to guide readers through the biblical text. In Vorsterman's 1528 Dutch Bible,[48] Olivetan's French Bible of 1535 and the Matthew Bible of 1537 (the latter two serving as Coverdale's models in compiling the Great Bible), printed *manicules* accompany the text. They appear in the margins, or at times within the text box. Their role was, as Wim François has put it, to point at 'passages with a certain (theological) interest'. The editors of these reformed Bibles employed *manicules* to empower readers in their encounter with key biblical passages, alerting them to these sections and then leaving them to their own devices.

In the Great Bible, Coverdale attempted to use the *manicules* differently, breaking away from their medieval function. He introduced the

---

46   That is to discuss, argue or question.
47   Sherman, *Used books*, ch. 2: 'History of the manicule', pp. 25–52.
48   Wim François, 'Typology—back with a vengeance! Texts, images, and marginal glosses in Vorsterman's 1534 Dutch Bible', in *Imago exegetica: visual images as exegetical instruments, 1400–1700*, ed. Walter S. Melion, James Clifton and Michel Weemans (Leiden: Brill, 2014), pp. 89–136 at 94; followed by François, 'The early modern Bible', p. 132. I thank Wim François for his advice, and for supplying me with an early version of this article.

double-*manicule*: one in the margin and the other within the text block (see Figure 4.7). This enables the quick and accurate retrieval of a relevant passage, as the marginal *manicule* attracts the eye of browsing readers, while the in-text *manicule* supports precise identification. The number of *manicules* had also increased significantly, in the absence of other forms of marginal annotations in the Great Bible.[49] Coverdale's most notable innovation was the attempt to use *manicules* as tie-marks, linking text and commentary. This was unlike other early modern books which employed *manicules* alongside asterisks or stars to link text and marginal annotations, much like the use of footnotes in more modern books.[50]

Coverdale endeavoured to confine all annotations to the end of the book. This would have simplified the task of printers by clearing much of the marginal space; it would have enabled the compilation of lengthier annotations, not restricted by the marginal space;[51] and it would have enabled editors to modify notes without resetting the biblical page itself. This method drew upon Erasmus's *Novum instrumentum*, with its significant annotations section at the end of the book.[52] Whereas Erasmus's notes are indicated in the biblical text, Coverdale's *manicules* were to link text and annotation. This would have required much leafing between text and annotation across the book. Together with the use of a generic sign, it would have made retrieval cumbersome. This device would have also affected the very nature of the intended Bible. Dense annotation (as suggested by the sheer number of *manicules*) facilitated scholarly uses, as did Erasmus's Latin and Greek New Testament. Yet such a Bible would have been forbidding when used by untrained readers. This may have contributed to Cromwell's objection. The result was that the first two editions of the Great Bible became the exact opposite of what Henry had hoped for. They directed readers to the parts that were most theologically complex, without offering answers apart from the advice to consult the clergy.

The above-mentioned 1543 *Act for the Advancement of True Religion* took a clear stance against notes in Bibles. Conservatives also opposed the notes. The interrogation of Grafton and Whitchurch (8 April 1543) demonstrates that even after the removal of the *manicules* from the Great Bible, their memory persisted. Foxe's 1570 account recalls how

---

49   This is evident from the comparison with the Matthew and Olivetan's Bibles, which served as its models. Thus, for Deuteronomy chapter 6, the Great Bible has one (double) *manicule*, the Matthew Bible one and Olivetan's none; for Deuteronomy 12 2/1/0; 1 Regum 14 1/0/0; Psalm 3 3/0/0; Matthew 21 1/0/0.

50   Sherman, *Used books*, p. 43.

51   Avoiding, for example, the imbalance of text and annotations, evident in the Matthew Bible (p. 118)

52   Desiderius Erasmus, *Nouum Instrumentu[m] omne [...]* (Basilaeam: In ædibus Ioannis Frobenij, 1516), pp. 225–675.

Grafton was called, and first charged with the printing of Matthew Bible, but he being very fearful of trouble, made excuses for him self in all things. Then was he examined of the great Bible, & what notes he was purposed to make. To the which he answered, that he knew none. For his purpose was to have retained learned men to have made the notes, but when he perceived the king's majesty, and his clergy not willing to have any, he proceeded no further. But for all these excuses, Grafton was sent to the Fleet [Prison].[53]

This account, however, was written at a very different time. Twenty years after the introduction of the Great Bible, the Geneva Bible presented a plethora of notes, announced on its title page and preserved in many editions and reprints.

Parochial Difficulties

The *manicules* in the first two editions of the Great Bible reveal a book that—much like Berthelet's 1535 Bible—was in the process of a complicated and unintentional transition. Examining the Great Bible's liturgical role further removes its history from narratives of progress and reform. The complex reception of early modern Bibles has been explored by Margaret Aston in a seminal article on 'Lap books and lectern books'.[54] Aston saw the size of books as meaningful for their intended audiences, with large books being used by the clergy, and smaller lap books by the laity, and linked more closely to reform. Although some book types, such as the Late Medieval Bible (LMB), do not fit these categories, they help us understand the difficulty with the Great Bible. It was a book of a size hitherto reserved for liturgical perfor-mances (such as Antiphoners, hefty tomes for chants sung in connection with Psalms and Canticles) or for academic study (glossed books). With the Great Bible, a book of this size was put in lay hands. Aston briefly alludes to another tension within the Great Bible, the incompatibility of vernacular scripture with the primarily Latin rite of Henry's reign.[55] A closer investigation of the liturgical use of the Great Bible will allow us to expand Aston's understand-ing to reveal an innate contradiction in the use of the Great Bible, especially

---

53   John Foxe, *The first [- second] volume of the ecclesiasticall history contayning the actes and monumentes of thynges passed in euery kynges tyme in this realme, especially in the Church of England* (London: printed by Iohn Daye, 1570), https://www.johnfoxe.org/index.php; followed in Mozley, *Coverdale and his Bibles*, p. 284; Pollard, *Records of the English Bible*, p. 230. The more in-depth analysis is Blayney, *Stationers' Company*, pp. 548–50, which suggests Grafton and Whitchurch spent only twenty-five days in prison.
54   Aston, 'Lap books and lectern books'.
55   This is evident in the integration of the Bible's table of lections into a copy of Berthelet's 1535 Latin Bible, explored in Chapter 3, pp. 109–13.

when seen against the background of late medieval parishes, their book culture and liturgical customs.

The most stable addendum to the Great Bible is its liturgical apparatus, which appears in all seven editions. In four editions it is the only material additional to the biblical text, apart from Cranmer's Prologue.[56] As we have seen, the Bible opens with a calendar and an almanac printed in red and black, and ends with a table of lections. The calendar and table of lections function together to enable the identification and retrieval of biblical readings for liturgical feasts: One can find the feast for a specific date in the calendar, and then proceed to retrieve the lessons—the biblical texts read on that feast—in the table of lections. Marks in the biblical text itself correspond with the table of lections to indicate the beginning of the lesson (a full Maltese Cross ✠) and its end (half-cross ⸶), a system already at play in Wycliffite Bibles (discussed in Chapter 2). These devices, much like those of the Matthew Bible, facilitated the use of Bibles in liturgical rites. However, the Great Bible had little to no role to play within such services.

The Great Bible broke new ground in a way so far unnoticed by scholars. It was not only the first vernacular Bible actively supported by the state, but also the first Bible assigned to parish churches. There seems to have been much scholarly inaccuracy about this topic, and a general tendency to infer from modern book-cultures on medieval and early modern practice. Thus, in his study of book ownership in parish churches and by parish priests, Hunt argues that the 'polemical characterisation of pre-Reformation clerical learning—with the Bible "scarse to be found in one Priests studie of an hundred" was grossly inaccurate'.[57] Similarly Gee's study of parish libraries suggests that '[t]he Reformation injunctions concerning the provision of English Bibles in parish churches may have intended to extend and develop the already established tradition of providing Latin Bibles in churches', a sentiment echoing that of Fiona Kisby.[58] Even well-informed scholars such as Hudson and Solopova could claim, while tracing the origins of the Wycliffite Bible, that in the early fifteenth century 'lectern bibles [were] held, at least in theory, by any church'.[59] None of these articles, however, provide evidence

---

56   See Appendix 2.

57   Arnold Hunt, 'Clerical and parish libraries', in *The Cambridge history of libraries in Britain and Ireland*, vol. 1: *To 1640*, ed. Elisabeth Leedham-Green and Teresa Webber (Cambridge: Cambridge University Press, 2006), pp. 400–19 at 404.

58   Stacy Gee, 'Parochial libraries in pre-reformation England', in *Learning and literacy in medieval England and abroad*, ed. Sarah Rees Jones, Utrecht studies in medieval literacy 3 (Turnhout: Brepols, 2003), pp. 199–222 at 221; Fiona Kisby, 'Books in London parish churches before 1603: some preliminary observations', in *The Church and learning in later medieval society: essays in honour of R.B. Dobson; proceedings of the 1999 Harlaxton Symposium*, ed. Caroline M. Barron and Jenny Stratford, Harlaxton medieval studies. New series 11 (Donington: Shaun Tyas, 2002), pp. 305–26 at 324.

59   Anne Hudson and Elizabeth Solopova, 'The Latin text', in *The Wycliffite Bible: origin, history and*

for Church legislation for parish ownership of Bibles prior to the 1530s, nor to a considerable number of Bibles owned by parish churches. Another voice appears in Robert Whiting's study of the early modern parish, claiming that '[i]t is evident from the wardens' accounts and inventories, however, that before 1538 the possession of this book by a parochial community was virtually unknown';[60] his subsequent study prefaced a small survey of LMBs in parishes with Philip Nichols's 1548 claim that '[t]he bible was an unknown thing within these twenty year here in England'.[61] This comment was made by an ardent reformer, whose wish to demarcate a boundary between the medieval past and reformed present is obvious. Nevertheless, his claim concurs with the medieval injunctions and inventories explored at the end of Chapter 1, to suggest that only very few parish churches owned a Bible prior to Henry VIII's legislation.

The injunctions of 1536 and 1538, mandating that parish churches own a copy of the Bible, were a novelty. No one, however, had told priests and parishioners how exactly those new books were to be used. The injunctions of 1536 seem to be an uneasy combination of medieval legacies and reformed ideals. The Bible was to be kept in the choir, a usual location for non-liturgical books kept in medieval parish churches.[62] Thus, for example, in one of the rare instances of a Bible bequeathed to a parish church in the fifteenth century, a 1467 will specified it was to be chained in the choir of the church of St Martin, Saundby.[63] These, however, were books kept mostly for clerical use, and, as demonstrated by Margaret Aston, also for a lay elite.[64] This contradicted the reformed ideal of the 1536 injunctions for all parishioners to consult the Bible. And indeed, the 1537/8 Church decrees in the dioceses of Worcester, Lichfield and Coventry, York, Salisbury, Exeter and Hereford (for which Cranmer issued the injunction following the vacancy of the see), commonly placed the Bible in the nave, the area most accessible to the

---

interpretation, ed. Elizabeth Solopova, Medieval and Renaissance authors and texts 16 (Leiden: Brill, 2016), pp. 107–32 at 128.

60   Robert Whiting, *The blind devotion of the people: popular religion and the English Reformation*, Cambridge studies in early modern British history (Cambridge: Cambridge University Press, 1989), p. 190.

61   Robert Whiting, *The Reformation of the English parish church* (Cambridge: Cambridge University Press, 2010), p. 90.

62   Hunt, 'Clerical and parish libraries', p. 414. Gee has uncovered only one instance of a book kept in the nave (Gee, 'Parochial libraries', p. 207).

63   James Raine (ed.), *Testamenta Eboracensia: a selection of wills from the registry at York Part 2*, Publications of the Surtees Society 30 (London: J. B. Nichols, 1855), p. 283.

64   Margaret Aston, 'Segregation in church', in *Women in the church: papers read at the 1989 summer meeting and the 1990 winter meeting of the Ecclesiastical History Society*, ed. Diana Wood and W. J. Sheils, Studies in Church history 27 (Oxford: Blackwell, 1990), pp. 237–94 at 244–8; and, to a lesser extent, C. Pamela Graves, 'Social space in the English medieval parish church', *Economy and Society* 18:3 (1989), 297–322 at 301; Gee, 'Parochial libraries', pp. 205–6.

laity.[65] This accorded with Henry's initial injunctions to 'discourage no man from reading any part of the Bible'. The practical implications were addressed in Salisbury, where bishop Nicholas Shaxton (†1556) decreed that the Bible was to be chained to a desk, with similar devices extant in the diocese of York. Such a location also agrees with Cranmer's above-mentioned Prologue to the Great Bible, which advocates lay reading of the Bible as part of daily devotions. This broke with medieval custom in both location and intended audience. Parish books were typically directed at clerical use, often supporting preaching, liturgical use or pastoral care. A nationwide book directed explicitly at parishioners was a novelty.

The vague indication of lay access to the Bible was mirrored in the foiled incorporation of notes into the Great Bible, and the brief possibility of lay empowerment. Another use, however, was linked with the inception of the Great Bible. The new Bible had originally been intended to have a major liturgical role. At the end of 1538 and the beginning of 1539, as the Bible was being produced in Paris and London, Cranmer was drafting a new liturgy of the realm.[66] This comprised a cycle of continuous biblical reading, in which the Old Testament was to be read yearly, and the New Testament three times a year. The plan was not executed during Henry's reign, and the new liturgy had to wait until the accession of King Edward VI in 1549. Only then was the continuous reading of the Bible integrated into the liturgy of the English Church in the new Book of Common Prayer (as discussed in the following chapter). The intended use of the Great Bible within the liturgy is indicated in its addenda. The most stable non-biblical addition to the Bible is a table of lections according to the Use of Sarum, which supported a use within the liturgical year. Some bishops even tried to adopt the monastic custom of *lectio divina* to a parish setting, introducing the daily reading of a chapter of Scripture.[67] Such use, however, was in stark contrast to existing liturgical rites, which were still quintessentially medieval, as well as with church architecture. Consecutive daily reading of vernacular Scripture was not part of the parish liturgy, and continuous reading (or *Lectio continua*) of the Bible was all but unknown in parish churches. The Psalms were chanted in sequence

---

65   Walter Howard Frere and William McLure Kennedy (eds), *Visitation articles and injunctions of the period of the Reformation*, vol. 2: *1536–1559*, Alcuin Club collections 15 (London: Alcuin Club, 1910), pp. 9, 15, 20, 35–6, 44–6, 55–9, 63, 65.

66   Text: Francis Aidan Gasquet and Edmund Bishop, *Edward VI and the Book of Common Prayer: an examination into its origin and early history with an appendix of unpublished documents*, 2nd edn, The Catholic standard library (London: J. Hodges, 1891), pp. 373–4; Thomas Cranmer, *Cranmer's liturgical projects. Edited, from British Museum ms. Royal 7, B.iv, with introduction, appendix, notes, and indices*, ed. J. Wickham Legg, Henry Bradshaw Society 50 (London: Harrison, 1915), pp. lv, 15; and to a lesser extent xxvi, xxxv, xxxvii. Analysis: MacCulloch, *Thomas Cranmer: a life*, pp. 221–6, 332–4.

67   Worcester, York (four chapters), Salisbury, Exeter and Hereford.

in monasteries and cathedrals; continuous reading of specific biblical books in monasteries commonly took place during the sequence of prayers in the Night Office and during mealtimes in refectories. On the Continent reformed churches experimented with continuous reading, as part of their rejection of the non-biblical elements of the liturgy.

In England, a more conservative stance was taken by the Convocations of 1541 and 1543, which mandated 'that every Sunday and holy day throughout the year the curate of every parish church, after the *Te Deum* and *Magnificat*, should openly read unto the people one chapter of the New Testament in English without exposition and when the New Testament was read over, then to begin the Old'.[68] The withdrawal of Cranmer's draft liturgy, however, had left the new Bible in a liturgical vacuum. Without Cranmer's new liturgy, the worship in parish churches was ill-suited for the new Bible. In the first decade after its introduction, the Great Bible accorded neither with liturgical reading nor with performance. The primarily Latin service was carried out by the priest from the altar, hardly visible behind a rood screen; biblical lessons took place at lecterns near the altar, or from pulpits affixed to rood screens.[69] A vernacular book, laying on (and possibly chained to) a desk on the other side of the church, was simply unusable in the course of the liturgy. Despite its great cost and elaborate liturgical apparatus, the Great Bible was useless for church services, until significant changes to worship were introduced in subsequent decades.[70]

The discrepancy between the addenda to the Great Bible and its possible uses transforms the way we view the Bible in late Henrician England. Rather than simply seeing the use of the Bible as a bone of contention between evangelicals and conservatives,[71] its impracticality sheds a different light on the surviving evidence. Complaints about priests removing the Bible to the choir were interpreted by reformers—and by modern scholars—as an attempt to withhold the Word of God from the laity. The author of an anonymous reformed tract of 1546 explicitly claimed that 'many of this wicked generation, as well priests as other their faithful adherents, would pluck it other into the choir, either else into some Pew where poor men durst not presume to come'.[72]

---

68   21 February 1543: Gerald Lewis Bray, *Records of Convocation VII: Canterbury 1509–1603* (Woodbridge: Boydell in association with the Church of England Record Society, 2006), p. 271.
69   Susan Wabuda, 'Triple deckers and eagle lecterns: Church furniture for the book in late medieval and early modern England', in *The Church and the book: papers read at the 2000 summer meeting and the 2001 winter meeting of the Ecclesiastical History Society*, ed. R. N. Swanson, Studies in Church history 38 (Woodbridge: Boydell for the Ecclesiastical History Society, 2004), pp. 143–52.
70   It is possible that these changes were instituted, in part, by the availability of these Bibles, but more research is necessary in order to validate such a hypothesis.
71   As in Eamon Duffy, *The stripping of the altars: traditional religion in England c.1400–c.1580*, 2nd edn (New Haven, CT: Yale University Press, 2005), p. 361.
72   *A supplication of the poore commons*, p. 275; alluded to in Aston, 'Lap books and lectern books', p. 178; Ryrie, *The Gospel and Henry*, p. 50, n137.

We can now appreciate such a complaint as arising from the attempt to bring the Bible into the location common for books in the later Middle Ages, as well as into the sphere of liturgical performance. Priests not only followed the known liturgy by moving Bibles to pulpits, but were also forced to do so in order to facilitate any use of vernacular Scripture in liturgical services. Indeed, in 1542 Thomas Becon, reformed priest and tutor, lamented that

> [Henry the Eight supported the vernacular Bible] but how many read it? Verily, a man may come into some churches, and see the bible so enclosed and wrapped about with dust, even as the pulpit in like manner is both with dust and cobwebs, that with his finger he may write upon the bible this epitaph: *Ecce, nunc in pulvere dormio.*[73]

The Great Bible was in the wrong place at the wrong time for liturgical use. Priests taking it to 'their side' of the church incurred the wrath of Church reformers. Those leaving it unused did not fare better. When it was left in the nave, parishioners were faced with a book they were not accustomed to, nor instructed how to use. Such discrepancies can also explain the evidence for parishes failing to purchase the Great Bible. Apart from its cost, and the objections of conservative curates and parishioners, it was unusable. It was also unfamiliar. Priests did not find a use for these Bibles in liturgical rites, nor for the delivery of sermons,[74] two of their main duties. Seen through the eyes of parish priests, the Great Bible was both expensive and useless.

In the eyes of Henry and his officials, these were not the greatest threats arising from the Great Bible. A vernacular Bible with meticulous aids for identifying liturgical readings and following the Church calendar was chained in the church nave, where priests were unable to use it during divine services. The laity, supported by Church injunctions and encouraged by Cranmer and other reformers to read the Bible, took up the opportunity and actively consulted the Bible during liturgical services. And as they were responsible for paying for half of its costs, they may have even considered this their right. Such lay initiatives were strongly opposed by Henry. Within the context of liturgical impracticality, we can revisit the above-mentioned Church and

---

73   STC§1739, §1740: Thomas Becon, *Newes out of heauen: both pleasaunt [and] ioyfull, lately set forth to the great co[n]solacion [and] co[m]forte of all christen me[n]* (London: John Mayler for John Gough, 1542), unfoliated; reprinted with minor changes in Becon, 'The news out of heaven both pleasant and joyful', in *The early works of Thomas Becon: being the treatises published by him in the reign of King Henry VIII*, ed. John Ayre (Cambridge: University Press, 1843), pp. 35–58 at 38. While this treatise was written in Henry VIII's reign, its dating to 1541 by Mozley (*Coverdale and his Bibles*, p. 264) is unclear. The biblical quotation is from Job 7:21.
74   Although, like the Wycliffite Bible and the LMB, discussed in Chapters 1 and 2, this would have been of much use in the preparation of sermons.

State injunctions in the 1540s, such as the *Act for the Advancement of True Religion* and the *King's Book*, which repeatedly rejected the lay custom of consulting the Great Bible during services, especially when done out loud.

Opposition to lay reading during services is evident in local episcopal initiatives. Edmund Bonner, Bishop of London, placed six Bibles in St Paul's Cathedral. In 1541, however, he had Grafton and Whitchurch print a proclamation, which has survived bound in a copy of Berthelet's 1540 reprint of the Great Bible.[75] Bonner's proclamation accorded with royal ideology in encouraging lay reading as instilling greater obedience to the monarch. Reading, however, should not become a communal exercise, and especially 'no reading thereof be used (aloud and with noise) in the time of any divine service or sermon: or that in the same there be used any disputation, contention, or any other misdemeanor'. This was later reiterated in Bonner's now lost *Th'Advertisement of the Bishop of London Renewed Again to the Reader of This Bible*. If notes were seen as the bone of contention regarding the Bible's design, reading it during services was the crux of a controversy regarding its use. All this had led Henry to retract his support for general lay readership. This was the inevitable outcome of the contradiction between the Great Bible's liturgical apparatus and the reality of liturgical rites, putting it, once more, on a clear collision course with Church and State.

It is of little wonder that the Great Bible had not been met with considerable enthusiasm in many parish churches. In a 2004 DPhil dissertation, Gregory Duke has thoroughly traced the evidence for the purchase and possession of Bibles in East Anglia parish churches. He has tried to compensate for the limitation of traditional sources, such as churchwardens' accounts or court records, by deploying church-plate certificates, which supply important evidence for the purchase of church goods (and books) in Edward VI's time. He concludes that '[f]rom the point of view of the church-plate certificates and the churchwardens' accounts, the introduction of the English Bible into East Anglia may be concluded to be a partial failure'.[76] This has been reaffirmed by other scholars noting a widespread lack of Bibles in parishes in the first years following Cromwell's injunctions and the introduction of the Great Bible.[77] Such a lack gave rise to new means of enforcement, the

---

75   *The Byble in Englyshe, that is to saye, the content of all the holye scrypture, bothe of the olde and newe Testament, truly translated after the veryte of the Hebrue and Greke textes, by the diligent studye of dyuers excellent lerned men experte in the foresayde tongues* (London: Thomas Petyt and Roberte Redman for Thomas Berthelet, 1540), Bible Society Copy BSS.201.B40. This is reproduced in DMH §52, p. 29. For general discussion see Blayney, *Stationers' Company*, pp. 384–8.

76   Gregory Duke, 'Parish, people and the English Bible in East Anglia, 1525–1560' (Ph.D., University of Oxford, 2004), p. 151.

77   J. Charles Cox, *Churchwardens' accounts from the fourteenth century to the close of the seventeenth century*, The antiquary's books (London: Methuen, 1913), pp. 116–18, where the term 'half-bible' refers to the

above-mentioned penalty for its lack. This had only partial success. As shown by Duke, the Great Bible was more commonly purchased by churches in urban centres, and less so in rural parishes. This followed medieval patters of Bible ownership, when LMBs were commonly bequeathed to urban churches. It also had a more pragmatic logic as 'parishes which were further away from bookselling centres were forced to spend more for their copies of the Great Bible, owing to costs for portage'.[78] With no official distribution network, portage became a major expenditure, with parishes paying up to 30s. for a Bible whose cost was capped at 10s./12s.[79]

Psalms, Latin and a New Orthodoxy

The layout of the Great Bible is indicative of a book created to serve the wider population. While Coverdale's and the Matthew Bible were made as tools of reform, in the Great Bible concessions had to be made to current religious customs. Its calendar mirrored calendars of more conservative Books of Hours, often printed by or for Regnault himself.[80] As we have seen throughout this study, the Psalms' unique place within liturgical performance and private devotion have made them most susceptible to modifications of appearance and layout. They became the site of competing mnemonics, where opposing ways of recalling them had left their trace on the pages of the Bible. Late medieval Latin Bibles preserved a more archaic presentation of the Psalms, while a small group of mendicant Bibles experimented with numerical mnemonics; scribes and patrons of the Wycliffite Bibles, the first translation of the entire Bible into English, quickly began to integrate Latin elements into the English Psalter. Performative knowledge of the Psalms took a material form in these Latin incipits, which preceded each English Psalm with its opening words in Latin.

---

part of the cost covered by parishioners; Whiting, *Blind Devotion*, pp. 190–1; Whiting, *The Reformation of the English parish church*, pp. 90–1, 245. With an additional bibliography p. 257n12.

78   Duke, 'Parish, people and the English Bible in East Anglia', p. 140.

79   This adds credence to the complaint on the price of Bibles at the end of Henry's reign (Chapter 5, p. 157)

80   See, for example, the nearly identical calendars of: *This prymer of Salysbury vse is set out a long wout ony serchyng: with many prayers, and goodly pyctures in the kale[n]der, in the matyns of our lady, in the houres of the crosse in the. vii. psalmes, and in the dyryge* (Parys: Per Franciscum Regnault in vico sancti iacobi, e regione maturinorum. Ad signum Elephantis, 1531); *This prymer of Salysbury vse is set out a long withoutony serchyng, with many prayers, & goodly pyctures in the kalender, in the matyns of our lady, in the houres of the crosse, in the vij. psalmes, and in the dyryge* (And be newly enprynted at Parys: per Franciscum Regnault, 1533); *Here after foloweth the prymer in Englysshe sette out alonge: after the use of Sarum* (Rouen: Nycholas le Roux for Franchoys Regnault, 1538); *Thys prymer in Englyshe and in Laten is newly tra[n]slatyd after the Laten texte* (Paris: Francois Regnault, 1538). This is also reflected in the slightly less populated calendars of Regnault's Sarum Missal, such as *Missale ad usum insignis ac preclare ecclesie Sa[rum]* (Paris: François Regnault, 1533); *Missale ad vsum ecclesie Sarisburiensis* (Paris: F. Regnault, 1534).

Coverdale's Bible presented the Psalms in a uniform fashion. In the first English single-volume Bible, as in early manuscripts of the Wycliffite Bible, the Psalms were made to look like any other book of the Bible (see Figure 4.6). There are no Latin incipits and the Psalms are numbered, with the chapter numbers appearing both in a running title and preceding the Psalms (where they are merged with the biblical superscription, once more in a similar fashion to Wycliffite Bibles). Thus, for example, the second Psalm is preceded by: 'The II. A Psalme of Dauid'. The Psalms were also subjected to alphabetical sub-division, as any other biblical text, and composed in continuous textual blocks with verses distinguished only by short spaces. The layout of the Psalms in Coverdale's Bible breaks from that of medieval Bibles and presents an alternative to the Psalms' mnemonics. Their performative nature, evidenced in the distinctiveness of each verse as a unit of chant, or in their Latin incipits, was obliterated. A remark made by Coverdale at the end of the Book of Psalms explicates his view of the Psalms. There, an interpretation of the Hebrew word *sela* supplies evidence for the Psalms' unique qualities: 'In the Psalter this word sela comes very oft. and (after the mind of the interpreters) it is as much to say as, always, continually, for ever, forsooth, verily, a lifting of the voice, or to make a pause and earnestly to consider, and to ponder the sentence' (pt 3 fol. 37v). The interpretation of the Hebrew word enabled Coverdale to muse on how the Psalms should be read. Although the vocal qualities of the Psalms are acknowledged, they are secondary to their meditative reading, which the printed Psalms aimed to encourage. The Matthew Bible followed suit. It presented the Psalms surrounded in an interpretative frame (such as long summaries between the Psalm number and the superscription, or the above-mentioned elaborate marginal annotations [p. 118]), without Latin incipits. The two Bibles took a more evangelical stance by disconnecting the Psalms from their Latin performance, as befitting their editors.

The Great Bible's Psalms (see Figure 4.7) follow the Matthew Bible in text and headings, but present them in a new, simpler layout: most of the page is occupied by the text of the Psalms (with numbers and foliation); arguments and marginal commentary, apart from the above-mentioned *manicules*, are omitted. For the first time in an English printed Bible, the Psalms are introduced—alongside their number and superscription—by their Latin incipits. This was hardly a random decision, but must have been discussed and revised by the production team. The members of the team working on the production of the Great Bible in 1538 Paris—Coverdale, Grafton and Whitchurch—were responsible for the two earlier Bibles, which lacked such a device. Coverdale as editor, and Grafton and Whitchurch as publishers, had much influence on the appearance of these two earlier Bibles. No direct evidence exists for discussions surrounding the nature of the Psalms, but Cromwell's more grounded understanding of English religion and the limitations of reform suggests it was he who had made the decision to transform the layout of the Psalms.

The result has made the Latin incipits the most distinctive feature of the Psalms' layout. They were printed in Roman capitals on the background of Black Letter. The effect of the slender Roman type isolated from the body of the Psalm marked out the Latin incipits and directed the attention of readers, more accustomed to Black Letter, to this element. This was a novelty, and such a use of Roman capitals differed significantly from the English and Continental models of the Great Bible, as well as from other contemporary devotional books. While the Olivetan 1535 Bible mirrors Coverdale's Bible by omitting the Latin incipits altogether, these were incorporated into Lefèvre's French Bible of 1534. There, however, the Latin incipits are not distinguished typographically from the text of the Psalm; they were entered in the same type, size and colour alongside the Psalm number. In English primers, some printed by or for Regnault, Latin incipits are a standard element, although often not set apart by a distinct font or location.[81] When they are set apart, as in Regnault's 1531 Latin primer, this relies only on minor typographical variants, as the first line of each Psalm is written in a slightly larger type.[82] The centrality of Latin to the way the Psalms were recalled did not end with the Middle Ages, and Psalms were still known by their Latin incipits. Thus, for example, the title of a meditative work on Psalm 50/51, printed by Regnault in 1538 and bound with a primer printed that same year, clearly identifies the Psalm as 'the Ij. Psalm called Miserere mei Deus' (STC§21790–1).

The Great Bible's Psalter is a typographical conundrum. As Ian Green affirms, readers in early modern England were more accustomed to Black Letter.[83] English printers owned relatively few founts of Roman types, and typically printed in Black Letter. Roman type was common in scholarly books (as in Erasmus's New Testament), which were printed on the Continent and appealed to a more educated milieu. Black Letter, on the other hand, was seen as a traditional typeface, common in liturgical works. In the Psalter of the Great Bible we can see the reverse of this tendency, with the new translation provided in Black Letter, while the traditional Latin incipits are in Roman type. This was probably unintentional, arising from the technological limitations of early modern printers. Liturgical books could be printed in red and

---

81   See note 80
82   Type height (x-height) of 3 mm, in contrast to the regular height of 2 mm.
83   Ian Green, *Print and Protestantism in early modern England* (Oxford: Oxford University Press, 2000), pp. 61–5, 86–7.

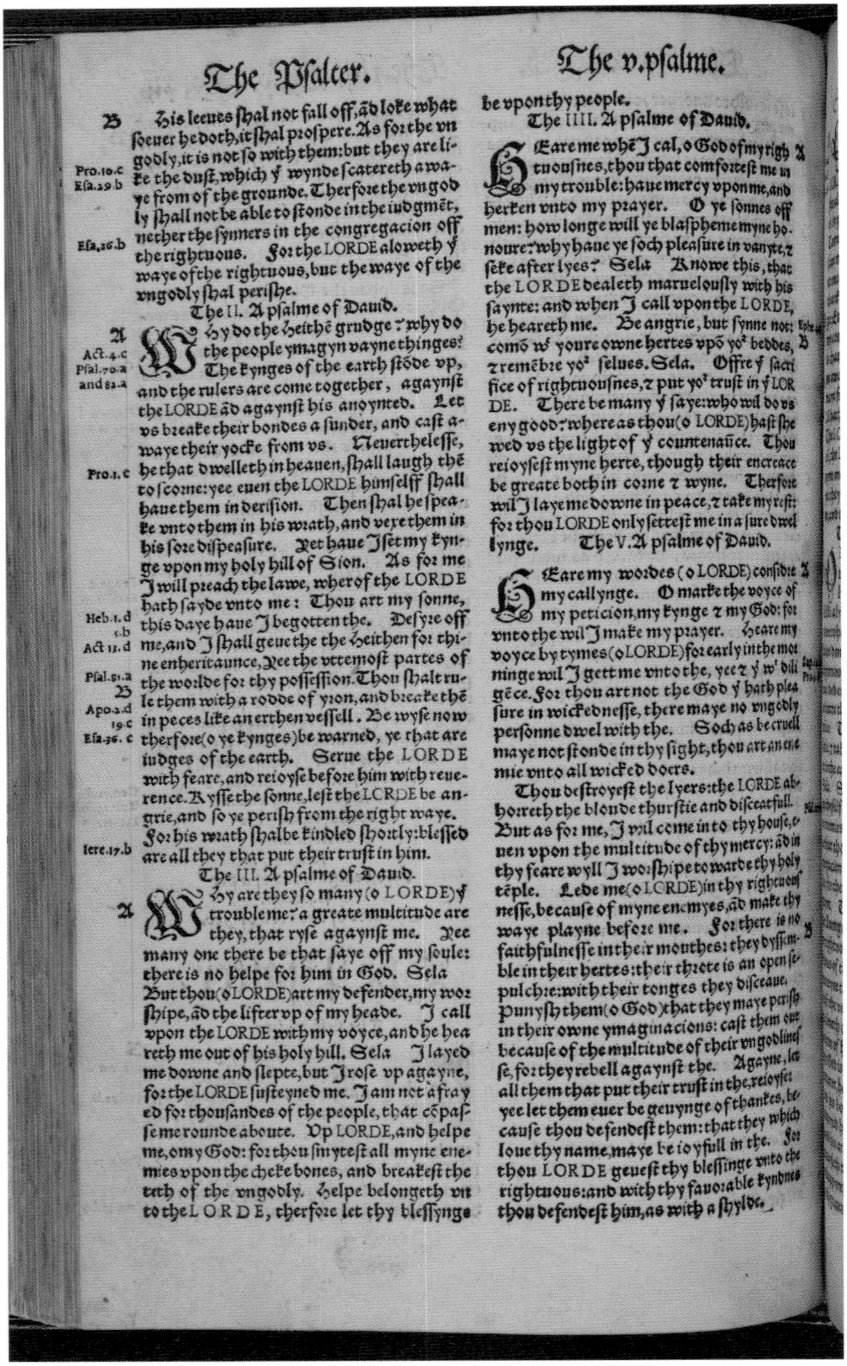

Figure 4.6 Psalms 2–5 in Coverdale's Bible. This layout exemplifies reformers' tendency to remove any Latin component from the English Psalms (*Biblia. The Bible that is, the Holy Scripture […]* (Cologne?: Eucharius Cervicornus and Johannes Soter?), pt.3 fol. 12v). Edinburgh University Library Special Collections.

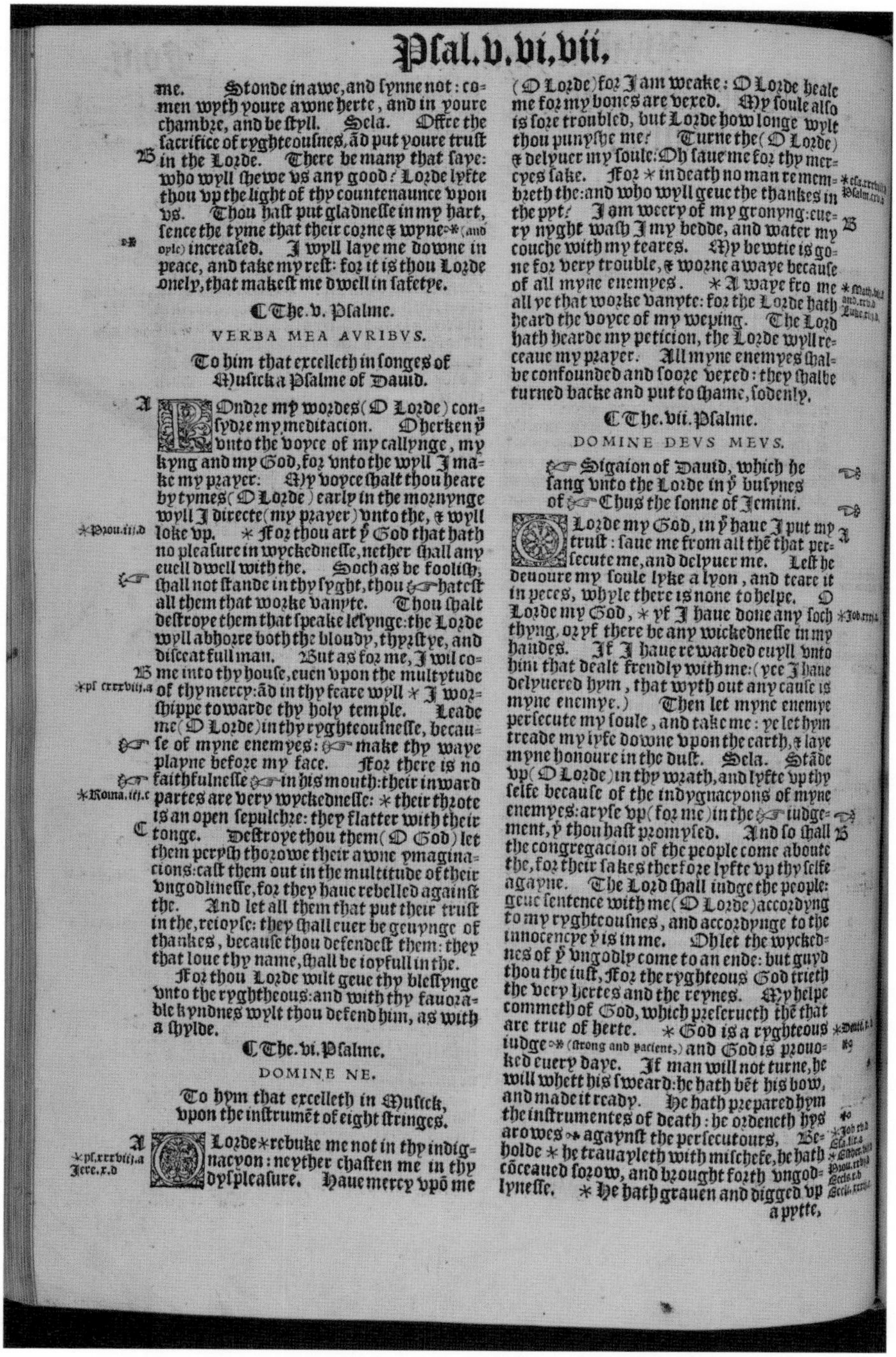

Psal.v.vi.vii.

me. Stonde in awe, and synne not: co=
men wyth youre awne herte, and in youre
chambre, and be styll. Sela. Offre the
sacrifice of ryghteousnes, ād put youre trust
B in the Lorde. There be many that saye:
who wyll shewe vs any good? Lorde lyfte
thou vp the light of thy countenaunce vpon
vs. Thou hast put gladnesse in my hart,
sence the tyme that their corne & wyne* (and
oyle) increased. I wyll laye me downe in
peace, and take my rest: for it is thou Lorde
onely, that makest me dwell in safetye.

¶ The.v. Psalme.

VERBA MEA AVRIBVS.

To him that excelleth in songes of
Musick a Psalme of Dauid.

A Ponder my wordes (O Lorde) con=
syder my meditacion. Oherken þ
vnto the voyce of my callynge, my
kyng and my God, for vnto the wyll I ma=
ke my prayer: My voyce shalt thou heare
by tymes (O Lorde) early in the mornynge
wyll I directe (my prayer) vnto the, & wyll
*Prou.iii.d loke vp. * For thou art þ God that hath
no pleasure in wyckednesse, nether shall any
euell dwell with the. Such as be foolish,
shall not stande in thy syght, thou hatest
all them that worke vanyte. Thou shalt
destroye them that speake lesynge: the Lorde
wyll abhorre both the bloudy, thryftye, and
disceatfull man. But as for me, I wil co=
B me into thy house, euen vpon the multytude
*ps.xxxviii.a of thy mercy: ād in thy feare wyll * I wor=
shippe towarde thy holy temple. Leade
me (O Lorde) in thy ryghteousnesse, becau=
se of myne enemyes: make thy waye
playne before my face. For there is no
faithfulnesse in his mouth: their inward
*Roma.iii.c partes are very wyckednesse: * their throte
is an open sepulchre: they flatter with their
C tonge. Destroye thou them (O God) let
them perysh thorowe their awne ymagina=
cions: cast them out in the multitude of their
vngodlinesse, for they haue rebelled against
the. And let all them that put their trust
in the, reioyse: they shall euer be geuynge of
thankes, because thou defendest them: they
that loue thy name, shall be ioyfull in the.
For thou Lorde wilt geue thy blessynge
vnto the ryghtheous: and with thy fauora=
ble kyndnes wylt thou defend him, as with
a shylde.

¶ The.vi. Psalme.

DOMINE NE.

To hym that excelleth in Musick,
vpon the instrumēt of eight stringes.

A *ps.xxxviii.a Iere.x.d O Lorde * rebuke me not in thy indig=
nacyon: neyther chasten me in thy
dysplesure. Haue mercy vpō me
(O Lorde) for I am weake: O Lorde heale
me for my bones are vexed. My soule also
is sore troubled, but Lorde how longe wylt
thou punyshe me? Turne the (O Lorde)
& delyuer my soule: Oh saue me for thy mer=
cyes sake. For * in death no man remem=
breth the: and who wyll geue the thankes in
the pyt? I am weery of my gronyng: eue=
ry nyght wash I my bedde, and water my B
couche with my teares. My bewtie is go=
ne for very trouble, & worne awaye because
of all myne enemyes. * Awaye fro me
all ye that worke vanyte: for the Lorde hath
hearde the voyce of my weping. The Lord
hath hearde my peticion, the Lorde wyll re=
ceaue my prayer. All myne enemyes shal=
be confounded and soore vexed: they shalbe
turned backe and put to shame, sodenly.

¶ The.vii. Psalme.

DOMINE DEVS MEVS.

Sigaion of Dauid, which he
sang vnto the Lorde in þ busynes
of Chus the sonne of Iemini.

O Lorde my God, in þ haue I put my A
trust: saue me from all thē that per=
secute me, and delyuer me. Lest he
deuoure my soule lyke a lyon, and teare it
in peces, whyle there is none to helpe. O
Lorde my God, * yf I haue done any soch *Iob.xxxi.
thyng, or yf there be any wickednesse in my
handes. If I haue rewarded euyll vnto
him that dealt frendly with me: (yee I haue
delyuered hym, that wyth out any cause is
myne enemye.) Then let myne enemye
persecute my soule, and take me: ye let hym
treade my lyfe downe vpon the earth, & laye
myne honoure in the dust. Sela. Stāde
vp (O Lorde) in thy wrath, and lyfte vp thy
selfe because of the indygnacyons of myne
enemyes: aryse vp (for me) in the iudge=
ment, þ thou hast promysed. And so shall B
the congregacion of the people come aboute
the, for their sakes therfore lyfte vp thy selfe
agayne. The Lord shall iudge the people:
geue sentence with me (O Lorde) accordyng
to my ryghteousnes, and accordynge to the
innocencye þ is in me. Oh let the wycked=
nes of þ vngodly come to an ende: but guyd
thou the iust, For the ryghteous God trieth
the very hertes and the reynes. My helpe
commeth of God, which preserueth thē that
are true of herte. * God is a ryghteous
iudge * (strong and pacient,) and God is prouo=
ked euery daye. If man will not turne, he
will whett his sweard: he hath bēt his bow,
and made it ready. He hath prepared hym
the instrumentes of death: he ordeneth hys
arowes * agaynst the persecutours. Be=
holde * he trauayleth with mischefe, he hath
cōceaued sorow, and brought forth vngod=
lynesse. * He hath grauen and digged vp
a pytte,

Figure 4.7 Psalms 5–7 in the first edition of the Great Bible. The Latin incipits, printed in Roman type, became the most noticeable feature of the Psalms' layout (*The Byble in Englysh [...]* [Paris and London: Richard Grafton and Edward Whitchurch, 1539], pt. 3 fol. 2v). Edinburgh University Library Special Collections.

black, providing printers with clear means of singling out texts; wishing to avoid the complications of dual-colour printing (which necessitated pulling the press twice and, as shown above, had clear limitations in the Matthew Bible), Regnault resorted to the next available tool for singling-out textual elements.[84] The need to mark out and direct attention to the Latin incipit was obvious to the printer, and the Bible was to be linked to living (Latin) liturgy from its onset.

Conclusion

The Great Bible is a large book. Its weight in a sixteenth-century binding is 6.80 kg. Its margins, however, are narrow, with a text area of 338x232 mm and a page size of 375x252 mm.[85] This was not only a practical issue, arising from the need to accommodate the largest type into a royal folio. In the Great Bible, the marginal space provides a clear view of the book's intended function. On the pages of the Great Bible marginal annotations were discouraged. This was not a book to be used in disputations, nor to furnish the laity with materials for theological arguments. How the book was to be used, however, remained unclear throughout Henry's reign. It was mandated to all parish churches, but with little understanding of how to employ it. Cranmer's liturgical draft of 1538/9 would have been a perfect match for the Great Bible and its liturgical apparatus, but it was retracted before implementation. The Great Bible had to await the reform of the liturgy under Edward VI and the introduction of the Book of Common Prayer to make liturgical sense.

The story of the Great Bible is that of uncertainties and material transformations. It contradicts Bernard's view of the Reformation as a major force directed and controlled by Henry himself,[86] to suggest a more jagged course, where conditional support was first given and then retracted at the sovereign's will. Hesitation surrounds all the main actors responsible for the Great Bible as they implemented their religious convictions, while trying to guess Henry's intentions. The title pages of Coverdale's and the Great Bible, the only two visual manifestations of an English Reformation, were not created by Henry, nor under his direct authority. They were introduced by stationers

---

84   Employing Roman type as a means of differentiation was used in Coverdale's 1535 Bible for singling out the divine name ('LORDE'), in a custom parallel to the Second Temple Jewish writing of the tetragrammaton in a different script, evident in the Dead Sea Scrolls.

85   While some later trimming in rebinding may have occurred, these measurements are common across existing Bibles, and also apply to those with contemporary bindings, such as Bible Society BSS.201.B39.2.

86   G. W. Bernard, *The King's Reformation: Henry VIII and the remaking of the English Church* (New Haven, CT: Yale University Press, 2005), pp. 521–7.

who tried—with the support of Henry's ministers, especially Cromwell—to represent in a graphic form Henry's understanding of the Bible, and the biblical roots of obedience to the monarch. Throughout the creation of Bibles in the 1530s we can see how these books engaged with two types of readers simultaneously: the general population; and that very special reader—King Henry himself.

Unlike earlier Bibles, which were more reformed in nature, the Great Bible reflected the mixed reality of the English Church. At a time when Church doctrine was intrinsically linked to the complex politics of Henry's reign, the Great Bible was supposed to cater for the needs of people in every parish church, as well as in cathedrals and colleges. It accommodated knowledge of the Psalms, which was oral and performative; it followed the Psalms' appearance in Books of Hours, one of the most popular books in the later Middle Ages. Its incipits enabled readers to tie the English text, new to many, to the familiar Latin Psalms, known through their performance.

In 1541/2, Marler's investment finally failed. He was trapped between the bishops' rejection of the Great Bible and Cranmer's stalling of the revised orthodox translation. Marler and his books were in limbo. After the quick succession of the seven editions, no other Bible was printed in Henry's reign, the outcome of the combination of market saturation and a shift towards conservatism. The tortuous story of the Great Bible looks different when we regard the Bible's title page. There, Henry's hesitant stance towards lay reading prefigured the retraction of Bibles in 1543. But, although access to the Bible was denied to the lower classes, no order was issued for recalling these Bibles. They remained in parish churches, part of a gradual process of transformation in parish religion. This process gained momentum after Henry's death, when reformed printers and clergy engaged afresh with transforming Bibles and religion.

5

Into Fast Forward:
The Bibles of Edward VI

Introduction

Henry VIII died on 28 January 1547, after nearly thirty-eight years on
the throne. His reign saw the emergence of the English printed Bible, but
also its curtailment. Single-volume Bibles produced during his reign were
highly uniform: the partnership of Whitchurch and Grafton (at first under the
powerful patronage of Thomas Cromwell) provided parish churches, colleges
and cathedrals with impressive folio Bibles, which were still incompatible
with their liturgies.

Henry was succeeded by his son Edward, who acceded to the throne at
the age of nine and died before his fifteenth birthday. The six years of Edward
VI's short reign (1547–53) are usually brushed aside in histories of the English
Bible. Yet, from the perspective of the production and use of Bibles, this was
a pivotal period, which saw an explosion in Bible printing, variety and uses.[1]
While Whitchurch and Grafton continued to produce Bibles, they no longer
controlled the market. New printers came to the fore: John Day experimented with layout and size; William Hill innovated in liturgical addenda;
and Bibles were printed abroad and by consortia of printers. This was a time
of transformation and growth, with eleven full Bibles printed in diverse formats and by different printers. Bibles now came in various sizes, aimed at
different audiences and uses. Some Bibles began to resemble the small tomes
of the Late Medieval Bible (LMB), and therefore befitted private ownership.
The size and apparatus of such books set them apart from the parish Bibles of
the previous reign and ushered in a new era of printed Bibles.

Edward ruled first under the protectorate of Somerset (Edward Seymour,
†1552) and then under the leadership of Northumberland (John Dudley,
†1553), both supporters of the evangelical cause. Thomas Cranmer retained

---

1   Appendix 3 summarises the Bibles produced during the reign of Edward VI.

his position as the Archbishop of Canterbury and, unhampered by Henry VIII's restrictions and hesitations, was free to move the country in the direction of reform. Bibles came to hold a prominent role in churches. During Henry's reign, as explored in the previous chapter, the introduction of the parish Bible created a conundrum: a book made for, and denied to, the laity; the wrong book in the wrong place at the wrong time for public recitation. It was during Edward's reign that the Bible began to make liturgical sense. The resulting transformation had a long and lasting impact on English religion.

The emphasis of scholars on the text of the Bible has veered them away from this period, in which they saw no 'new edition' of the Bible.[2] The reign of Edward is often seen by historians as a period of confrontation between evangelicals and conservatives over religion. Unlike the heated debates surrounding the Mass or the veneration of saints, the Bible was a common ground for differing factions. It did not occupy a central place in early modern polemics, nor in their modern scholarly analysis.[3] Still, Stephen Alford has commented that '[b]iblical translations and commentaries, sermons, books of devotion, iconographical representations of godly, reforming, and imperial kingship represent, collectively, one of the most successful and enduring achievements of the Edwardian years'.[4] This chapter will support this insight by analysing the Bibles of Edward VI's reign both in their material aspects and for their liturgical use. The quick succession of Bibles reveals the reign's

2   The period receives a single sentence in David Norton, 'English Bibles from c. 1520 to c. 1750', in *The new Cambridge history of the Bible*, vol. 3: *From 1450 to 1750*, ed. Euan Cameron (Cambridge: Cambridge University Press, 2016), pp. 305–44 at 315 (unaware of Day's octavo Bible). It does not occupy a significant place in the book's other chapters, nor in the earlier work of S. L. Greenslade (ed.), *The Cambridge history of the Bible*, vol. 3: *The West from the Reformation to the present day* (Cambridge: Cambridge University Press, 1963). Printed Bibles of the reign take up a single page in David Daniell, *The Bible in English: its history and influence* (New Haven, CT: Yale University Press, 2003), pp. 245–6, and are omitted altogether from Christopher de Hamel, *The book: a history of the Bible* (London: Phaidon, 2001). The period is likewise overlooked in nearly all articles in Kevin Killeen, Helen Smith and Rachel Willie (eds), *The Oxford handbook of the Bible in England, c. 1530–1700* (Oxford: Oxford University Press, 2015), with the only exception being Ian Green, 'Hearing and reading: disseminating Bible knowledge and fostering Bible understanding in early modern England', pp. 272–86, whose emphasis on hearing and reading has led him to identify the important transformation of the period (albeit with a lesser interest in the materiality of Bibles).
3   See for example Diarmaid MacCulloch, *Tudor Church militant: Edward VI and the Protestant Reformation* (London: Penguin, 2001); Eamon Duffy, *The stripping of the altars: traditional religion in England c.1400–c.1580*, 2nd edn (New Haven, CT: Yale University Press, 2005); Peter Marshall, *Reformation England, 1480–1642*, 2nd edn, Reading history (London: Bloomsbury Academic, 2012), p. 84; Andrew Pettegree, 'Printing and the Reformation: the English exception', in *The beginnings of English Protestantism*, ed. Peter Marshall and Alec Ryrie (Cambridge: Cambridge University Press, 2002), pp. 157–79 at 174–5; Norman L. Jones, *The English Reformation: religion and cultural adaptation* (Oxford: Blackwell, 2002). Two studies of iconography and politics in the reign of Edward VI have paid more attention to the use of biblical imagery: Margaret Aston, *The King's bedpost: art, Reformation and iconography in a Tudor group portrait* (Cambridge: Cambridge University Press, 1993); Stephen Alford, *Kingship and politics in the reign of Edward VI* (Cambridge: Cambridge University Press, 2002).
4   Alford, *Kingship and politics in the reign of Edward VI*, p. 116.

religious and political aims. Size, readership and addenda demonstrate how printers were free to experiment with their Bibles, as well as a greater acceptance of the evangelical cause. Nowhere was this more evident than in the creation of a new liturgy, codified in the Book of Common Prayer. Cranmer put into practice his draft liturgy composed during Henry VIII's reign and placed the Bible at the heart of liturgical rite. This transformed the use of the Bible within the liturgy, its role in parish churches, and its content and appearance. While the new liturgy was swiftly deployed, its impact on printed Bibles was a more gradual process, linked with the implementation of new technologies.

Addenda

Continuity and change are evident at the onset of Edward's reign. At his coronation, Archbishop Cranmer identified the new king as a second Josiah, the biblical monarch and reformer. Comparisons between the English monarchy and biblical kings were common.[5] A preface written by Edmund Becke to one of the first Bibles printed during the reign, a revision of the Matthew Bible published by John Day and William Seres in 1549, recommends that the king read the Bible since

> [i]t lieth not now in a king's choice to study or not to study in God's book. He must not let the book of this law depart out of his mouth, but study it day and night.[6] Then his wisdom and highness must not suffer it to lie unoccupied and be thrown about in corners, that a man may write upon it with his finger. ECCE NUNC IN PULVERE DORMIO [Job 7:21]. But he must read it (sig. [AA.v].r–[AA.vi].r).[7]

The keen reader may hear in this the echo of Thomas Becon's criticism of the neglect of the Bible in churches during Henry's time.[8] Using the same verse from Job, Becon's description of dust-covered Bibles, deserted in corners of churches, was now employed to exhort the young king. The reign of the boy king, however, was asserted with little acceptance of such

---

5   The link between Edward VI and Josiah has been explored most extensively by Aston, *The King's bedpost*, pp. 26–53. See also Alford, *Kingship and Politics in the Reign of Edward VI*, pp. 51–2, 100.

6   cf. Josh. 1:8, common also in Henrician texts.

7   DMH§74; STC§2077. This section is alluded to by Alford, *Kingship and Politics in the Reign of Edward VI*, p. 41, without referencing its origins or afterlife. As demonstrated by Alford, this verse was deployed repeatedly during Edward's reign.

8   Chapter 4, p. 143.

Figure 5.1 Becke's dedication in Day's 1551 Bible: *The Byble […]* (London: Jhon Daye, 1551), unfoliated. Becke kneeling in front of a majestic Edward may be his attempt to appease the monarch following the condescending tone deployed at the first printing of this dedication. Reproduced by kind permission of the Syndics of Cambridge University Library.

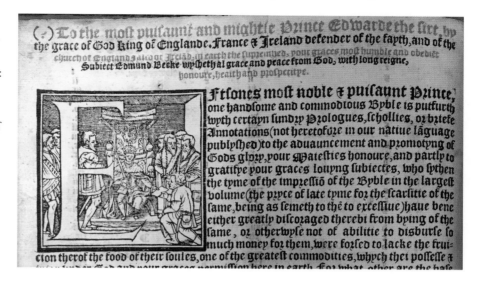

condescendence. We have no record for the reception of the preface at Edward's court. However, when the Bible was reprinted by Hill in 1551 (DMH§92; STC§2083–6) the preface was omitted altogether; when Day reprinted the Bible the same year (DMH§93; STC§2092, sig. ★.iii.v-[★.iv].v), the preface was reprinted without the contentious paragraph. Moreover, the opening words of the preface were modified. In the revised version the newly integrated first word 'Eftsones' ('once more', implicitly alluding to the first printing of the Bible) enabled the printer to start the text with the capital letter 'E'. This was depicted in a large and elaborate thirteen-line historiated initial,[9] in which Becke kneels before an enthroned and majestic Edward, presenting him with the book (see Figure 5.1). The image depicts a clear hierarchy of power, and expresses a lesson learnt.

Few of the elements added to Bibles during Edward's reign were innovative. Becke's *A Perfect Supputation of the Years & Time from Adam unto Christ* (providing the years from Creation to Nativity), or the liturgical addenda discussed in this chapter, are exceptions. As can be seen in Appendix 3 (single-volume Bibles printed in the reign of Edward VI), most addenda were recycled from earlier Bibles.[10] At times this was done to the point

9   The initial was reproduced in facsimile in John N. King, 'John Day: master printer of the English Reformation', in *The beginnings of English Protestantism*, ed. Peter Marshall and Alec Ryrie (Cambridge: Cambridge University Press, 2002), pp. 180–208 at 200–1, alongside its reuse by Day in 1563 for the printing of the *Actes and Monuments*. It is presented in Alford, *Kingship and Politics in the Reign of Edward VI*, p. 51; Aston, *The King's bedpost*, pp. 158–9.

10   Alford discusses the affinity between the reign and Day's inclusion of the Table of the Principal Matters in his 1549 Bible (*Kingship and Politics in the Reign of Edward VI*, p. 33), but does not mention that the table was recycled from the Matthew Bible of 1537.

of obsoleteness. A quarto Bible printed in 1550 by Froschover in Zurich reproduces Coverdale's 1535 dedication to Henry VIII with only minor alterations.[11] It blesses Edward 'with the multiplication of seed which God gave Abraham and Sari [sic] his wife, be given to you most gracious prince', a blessing more for the forty-four-year-old Henry seeking a male heir than for the twelve-year-old king. Prefatory materials testify to the removal of the restrictions imposed by Henry VIII on reformed theology and its dissemination. In the first year of Edward's reign, parliament repealed legislation that had limited the 'printing, uttering, selling, giving, or delivering' of Bibles.[12] Prefaces and dedications were therefore taken from the works of Tyndale, the Matthew Bible (as also his table of principal matters, in itself taken from Olivetan French Bibles) and Coverdale, all censored during the previous reign. The ever-popular prologue by Cranmer once more opened English Bibles, reflecting a renewed emphasis on biblical access. The array of preliminary materials differs significantly from that of the Great Bible and its reprints. It shows a greater variety of Edwardian Bibles, as well as a reformed environment that enabled printers to adopt more evangelical materials without fear.

Size Matters (2)

At the onset of Edward's reign parliament re-instituted the requirement for parish churches to own a Bible. The state-controlled production of Bibles of Henry VIII was a thing of the past, as was also the now-expired four-year monopoly granted to Marler in 1542. Printers were free to print Bibles and fully embraced this opportunity. The market that had been cornered by Whitchurch and Grafton (and to a lesser extent Berthelet) was opened to new players and to competition.[13] While much prefatory material was replicated, Edwardian Bibles broke new ground in matters of size. Vernacular single-volume Bibles had hitherto been in folio: Wycliffite Bibles and early sixteenth-century printed English Bibles were both large and cumbersome

---

11   DMH§84; STC§2080 sig. [✣.ii].v-[✣.iiii].r. For discussion of the original dedication, see Chapter 3 pp. 102–3.
12   Act of Repeals (1 Edward VI, c.12), *The statutes of the realm: Volume the fourth* (London: George Eyre and Andrew Strahan, 1819), p. 19.
13   The most important discussion of the period's printed Bibles is Peter W. M. Blayney, *The Stationers' Company and the printers of London 1501–1557* (Cambridge: Cambridge University Press, 2013), pp. 673–82. The collaboration between printers was explored by Alford, *Kingship and Politics in the Reign of Edward VI*, pp. 116–19.

objects.[14] Their size suited a public function rather than private readership; the price of the large reams of paper or parchment had led to the creation of expensive books which only institutions or well-off patrons could afford. This had also been the outcome of the technological restrictions faced by English printers, not having the type nor the expertise to replicate the achievements of their contemporaries abroad; literacy rates and Henry's rejection of biblical access for the lower classes likewise served to hinder the creation of smaller and cheaper volumes.

Little had changed in the first years of Edward's reign. The first Edwardian Bibles were three folio Bibles, all printed in 1549. With legislation allowing for the printing of Bibles, which were also required by a new liturgy, printers rushed to supply the market. The first was John Day (in partnership with William Seres), whose Bible appeared in August 1549.[15] It incorporates the above-mentioned prologue by Edmund Becke, which also bewails the dearth of Bibles in the last years of Henry's reign. This scarcity of Bibles had driven prices up, so that people 'have been either greatly discouraged thereby from buying of the same, or otherwise not of ability to disburse so much money for them, were forced to lack the fruition thereof, the food of their souls' (sig. [AA.v].r). Day's Bible was quickly followed by that of Thomas Raynald and William Hill (October 1549),[16] and then by another folio, whose title page names Edward Whitchurch, the acclaimed printers of the Great Bible, but which had begun in Germany, continued in England by William Hill and finished by Whitchurch (December 1549).[17]

The three Bibles adopted different textual traditions: Day's first Bible was the most innovative, with Becke's revision of Matthew; the second was a closer reprint of Matthew; and the third was a reprint of the Great Bible. Each Bible proclaimed its origins on its title page, appealing to new audiences: Day's advertised its novelty ('translated [...] lately with great industry and diligence'), despite relying heavily on Matthew; Hill's its link to the Matthew Bible ('purely translated into English by Thomas Matthew in 1537'); and Whitchurch linked the newly printed Bible to his Great Bible ('after the translation appointed to be read in the churches'). Title pages were employed as advertising devices.

Comparing the three Bibles, it is clear that Day's is the most innovative. His reliance on a more recent textual revision is reflected in the book's appearance, which uses a lighter and more legible variant of Black Letter

---

14   The only exception is a poor-quality large quarto copy of Coverdale's Bible printed by Nicholson in 1537 (DMH§33; STC§2065) with a page size measuring 204x144 mm.
15   DMH§74; STC§2077.
16   DMH§75; STC§2078.
17   DMH§76; STC§2079.

(textura no. 78), thus also reducing its size (see Figure 5.2).[18] Day did not use this innovation to make a smaller object.[19] Rather, he expanded the marginal space. As was the case with the LMB, the ability to condense the textual area did not necessarily lead to the creation of smaller objects, but rather to the expansion of the marginal space, giving readers a greater ability to engage with the biblical text through the incorporation of marginal annotations, glosses, references and pointing hands. Day's Bible turned away from the narrow marginal spaces of Henry VIII's Great Bible. Growing apart from Henrician Bibles, this move was accompanied by annotations and prologues. Tyndale's prologues preceded each biblical book; Becke's shorter notes were provided in the margins, and lengthier ones followed each biblical chapter. Together with short summaries preceding each chapter, an array of auxiliary devices eased the reader's way through the text, while presenting the literal sense espoused by evangelical theology. In the third chapter of the Epistle to the Romans, for example, the reformed article of justification by faith alone is embedded into the biblical text through a variety of means: the summary ('and are justified only through the free mercy of God in Christ'); the marginal headings ('Justifying comes by faith | Faith justifies | Faith maintains the law'); and the notes at the end of the chapter ('This saying does St Ambrose expound in this wise. They working nothing, nor acquitting him anything at altar[,] justifies by faith alone, by the gift of God. This word alone (though many men be therewith unjustly offended) is also evidently expressed by Paul himself in these words. Freely without the law, without works, it is the gift and such like.') [part v, fols lxx.r–v].

The layout of Day's Bible broke new ground in the presentation of chapter numbers (see Figure 5.2). His competitors' Bibles replicated the running titles of previous Bibles: they identify the biblical book, folio number and at times provide a one-word summary of the biblical story. Day's Bible, for the first time in England, integrates chapter numbers into the running titles.[20] Using his lighter type, Day was able to supply more information in a clearer way, and his running titles include a summary, book and chapter identification, as well as a folio number (e.g. for 1Rg14: 'Saul | i.Samuel | The.xiiii.Chapter. | fol. xxvi.'). As we have seen, chapter division had gradually shaped biblical layout and knowledge. It had led medieval readers to adopt new reading strategies, preferring fragmented reading and browsing to continuous reading. Day's Bible now enabled readers to identify the chapter division without

18   At 77 mm for twenty lines, unlike his competitors' 93 mm, it enabled Day to print sixty-two lines per column, whereas Hill was able to cram only fifty-three to fifty-four lines into an equal-sized column.
19   All three volumes are approximately the same size, see Appendix 3.
20   Chapter numbers appear in the titles of several Wycliffite Bibles, but this was far from the norm in the production of these Bibles.

Figure 5.2 Layout of Day's 1549 folio Bible. Innovative type and layout deployed in the first Bible printed in the reign of Edward VI. *The Byble […]* (London: Jhon Daye, 1549), pt. 1 fol. 9r). Reproduced by kind permission of the Syndics of Cambridge University Library.

recourse to the textual block itself. The late medieval system of navigation reached its maturity with this innovation, enabling faster and more efficient identification of a necessary chapter by skimming through the running titles. This was of use for any reader practising fragmented reading, not least priests adapting to the new liturgy.

While Day was producing his folio Bible he was also involved in another innovative project. In 1549 he printed three part-Bibles in octavo, constituting half of a six-part Bible, whose other three volumes were printed over the next two years.[21] This was the smallest Bible printed in England hitherto, and remained so until Barker's octavo Geneva Bible of 1577. The first part of the Bible has survived only as a fragment, recently identified by Blayney (currently Bible Society copy BSS.201.B48.7). The gradual damage incurred to a capital 'A' in the course of printing has served Blayney to demonstrate that the fragment was printed after the completion of Day's folio Bible. This book shows the innovative nature of Day's printing, as well as its limitation. Day used a traditional Black Letter type, which was only slightly smaller (though heavier) than the one used in his folio Bible.[22] The effect is underwhelming, especially when compared with the minute French volumes of the previous generation (see Figures 5.3. and 5.4). English printers had neither the expertise nor the type for printing very small books; beyond the intellectual elite, the English market was unaccustomed to Roman type, necessary for true miniaturisation of books. The thick strokes, typical of Black Letter, differed considerably from the lighter strokes of the Roman type, which required far less ink, and hence was better suited for smaller volumes. With its heavier Black Letter type, Day's Bible is printed in a textual block of 117x62 mm (with the weight of the first volume 540 g, based on CUL copy BSS.201.B51.10). The text is in a single column with little marginal space, and with no separation between text and running title. This is in stark contrast to the French duodecimo Bibles of the first decades of the sixteenth century, which acted as textual template for Berthelet's Latin Bible in 1535. These minute French Bibles employ Roman type for greater legibility; their clearer type measures 61 mm for twenty lines (including more leading between the

---

21   The best study of these is Blayney, *Stationers' Company*, pp. 676–81.
  1. Pentateuch printed probably in 1549 and surviving in a fragment; reprinted in 1551 (DMH§94; STC§2087)
  2. Joshua–Job (1549, DMH§81; STC§2087.2)
  3. Psalms–Song of Songs (1550, DMH§86; STC§2087.3)
  4. Prophets: Isaiah–Malachi (1550, DMH§87; STC§2087.4)
  5. Apocrypha (1549, DMH§82; STC§2087.5)
  6. New Testament (1551?). Several octavo New Testaments were printed by Day, none explicitly linked to this project.
22   70 mm for twenty lines, in comparison with 77 mm in the folio Bible.

lines), leading to a text block of 83x45 mm, nearly half the size of Day's octavo Bible.[23]

The small format meant that Day could no longer keep all the features of his folio Bible. The importance of Becke's notes to Day's Bible comes to the fore as we examine the move from folio to octavo size. Even in these diminutive volumes, Day made sure to preserve the notes in full, supplied after each chapter.[24] The running titles are much shorter, and omit chapter numbers. In the first volume (the fragment identified by Blayney) they contain one-word summaries, book and folio number. This experimental volume was later modified, with subsequent volumes proving more legible: Day was able to separate the running titles, thus making them more reader-friendly, containing only summary and book identification.

Day did not create a miniature single-volume Bible. Combining all six volumes together into one tome would have created a book difficult to consult or to bind, whose thickness would have exceeded its height (the combined thickness of the six books is *c*.210 mm, while the height of the page is 140 mm). In effect, Day created a cheap and affordable lay library, a collection of books to be bought gradually and consulted individually. His endeavours not only replicated the French duodecimo Bibles, but also raised an earlier, medieval, idea of the Bible as a library rather than a single volume. Like the monastic Bibles preceding the LMB (and the French minute volumes), the printing of the Bible in multiple volumes inhibited the integration of cross-biblical addenda. There are almost no preliminary materials in these volumes. Cross-references in the margins of these volumes replicated those of earlier Bibles but were of less use since they required consulting different volumes.

Day's multi-volume Bible contained minimal marginal space.[25] This did not stop zealous readers from annotating extensively. One such reader owned Day's 1551 Pentateuch (housed in the Bible Society, BSS.201.B51.10); this reader annotated in minute script on key passages, underlined the biblical text and inserted well-formed *manicules*. Other readers were less scholarly. Some copies contain rough doodles, and in the 1549 fragment marginal annotations for the book of Numbers in a sixteenth-century hand attest that one William Wayt had his book witnessed by John West and others (fols ccxxiv.v–ccxxv.r and repeated in fol. ccxiii.r).

23   With the page size of the French 12o Bibles being 3735 sqmm, in comparison with 7254 sqmm of Day's octavo. The dimensions of the French 12o is *c*.117x70 mm, based on *Pentateuchus Moysi: Genesis, Exodus, Leuiticus, Numeri, Deuteronomium. Iosue, Liber Iudicum, Ruth* (Parisijs: In officina Simonis Colinæi, 1527).
24   This is similar to the preservation of notes across editions of the Geneva Bible.
25   With a page size of 139x97 mm and text block of 124x64 mm, leaving outer margins of only *c*.20 mm, at times occupied by printed notes.

Figure 5.3
Some of the
smallest Bibles
of the sixteenth
century. This
also reveals the
supremacy of
Continental
printers. A Parisian
duodecimo
Bible: bottom,
*Pentateuchus Moysi
[...]* (Parisijs: In
officina Simonis
Colinæi, 1527);
Day's octavo Bible:
middle, *The second
parte of the Byble
[...]* (London: Day
and Seres, 1549);
and Berthelet's
Latin Bible: top,
*Sacrae Bibliae
tomus primus [...]*
(London: Berthelet,
1535). Reproduced
by kind permission
of the Syndics
of Cambridge
University Library.

Figure 5.4
The size of the Bibles when closed. A Parisian duodecimo Bible: right, *Pentateuchus Moysi [...]* (Parisijs: In officina Simonis Colinæi, 1527); Day's octavo Bible: middle, *The second parte of the Byble [...]* (London: Day and Seres, 1549); and Berthelet's Latin Bible: left, *Sacrae Bibliae tomus primus [...]* (London: Berthelet, 1535). Reproduced by kind permission of the Syndics of Cambridge University Library.

Blayney's analysis demonstrates that Day's first octavo volume followed the Great Bible both in its text and its printing. It employed four woodcuts which had been used in the Great Bibles of 1539–41, indicating the approval of Whitchurch or Grafton, if not their involvement in the project. Subsequent volumes of Day's octavo Bible rely on Taverner's Bible and contain Becke's annotations, thus constituting a 'new' book, in terms of subsequent printing. This allowed Day and Seres to claim privileges and stop unlicensed reprinting. The movement from the earlier fragment to the 1551 reprint also reveals a clear rise in evangelical emphases. In the earlier fragment woodcuts portray God the Father and angels, all rejected by the reform-minded. Indeed, an early modern reader did not approve of the woodcut accompanying Exodus chapter 25, which depicts the Ark of the Covenant and the cherubim (made from a woodblock used in the printing of the Great Bible) and crossed it out with ink (see Figure 5.5). This sentiment was shared by Day, so these images were removed from its 1551 reprint. Rather, Day incorporated into the latter edition the prologues of

Figure 5.5 Crossed image in Day's 1549 octavo Bible reveals the reformed leanings of an early reader: *First Part of the Bible [...]* (London: Day and Seres, 1549), fol. cxxvi.v. Reproduced by kind permission of the Syndics of Cambridge University Library.

William Tyndale. The book thus mirrors the transition from Henry's reign to a more outspoken reformed environment under his son Edward.

No Bible of similar dimensions appeared during the rest of Edward's reign. Other printers were more traditional in their choices. Following the folio and octavo Bibles of 1549, two Bibles were printed in the following year.[26] Catalogued as in quarto, their size does not differ considerably from

26   DHL§84; STC§2080, printed in Zurich for Andrew Hester; DHL§85; STC§2081, printed in Rouen for Whitchurch.

a small folio. In fact, one of these Bibles has exactly the same type-size as Day's folio edition of 1549 (77 mm for twenty lines). Both 1550 Bibles were printed on the Continent, demonstrating that their size was not due to lack of means. For most of Edward's period larger volumes prevailed. Yet there is also a gradual move towards smaller, more personal Bibles, possibly for the use of lay people. This was a gradual process, as printers grew in confidence, and readers began to embrace volumes other than the parish tomes. The smallest single-volume Bibles appeared at the very end of the period. Hill's 1552 attempt at a volume in quarto (which measures 195x146 mm, weighing 1.3 kg) was followed by an even smaller book. Printed by Grafton in 1553, the last year of Edward's reign, it has a page size of 173x128 mm and weight of 1.0 kg (see Figure 5.7). Both volumes were suited to personal devotion rather than to public performance of the liturgy. Both volumes innovated by linking liturgy and Bible, which will be discussed at length at the end of the chapter.

The reasons for producing books in varying sizes arose from both commercial and devotional rationales. The first volume of Day's octavo Bible(s) contains a short address, *The Printer to the Reader*, on the verso of the title page.[27] There Day explains his reasons for printing the series. He argues that Bibles 'being together in any one volume, either are of so high price that the poor, to whose chief comfort and consolation, the holy ghost hath caused them to be written, are not able to buy them'. Therefore, 'I (furthered by the honest request of divers) have to the commodity of these poor, printed the whole Old Testament in iiii sundry parts,[28] that they which are not able to buy the whole, may buy a part, which he delights most in, and exercise him in the same till God's increase make him able (as no doubt but it will) to buy the rest' [sig. [c.ii.]v]. Day envisioned this to be a biblical library for the poor, enabling them to purchase even a single volume out of the six available tomes. The mention of poverty may have been a literary flourish, rather than a reflection of reality. The poorest were not likely to consult the Bible for reasons of illiteracy, as well as cost.[29] The preface demonstrates how Day, in the words of Pratt and King, had engaged with a 'demographically stratified vernacular readership'.[30] Day was providing simultaneously for

27   In the 1551 reprint of the Pentateuch. As the original 1549 volume exists only in a fragment, it is not possible to ascertain its existence in that edition.
28   Separating the Old Testament from the Apocrypha.
29   I thank Ian Green, once more, for this suggestion.
30   John N. King and Aaron T. Pratt, 'The materiality of English printed Bibles from the Tyndale New Testament to the King James Bible', in *The King James Bible after 400 years: literary, linguistic, and cultural influences*, ed. Hannibal Hamlin and Norman W. Jones (Cambridge: Cambridge University Press, 2010), pp. 61–99 at 71; a similar claim was also made by Elizabeth Evenden, *Patents, pictures and patronage: John Day and the Tudor book trade*, St Andrews studies in Reformation history (Aldershot: Ashgate, 2008), p. 15.

the rich and the middling sorts, for churches and for individuals. He printed both large folios and minute octavos, the former aimed at communal use, to serve in the mandatory state-wide rituals celebrated in every parish church; the latter, for personal use. Books in folio could be left on tables and lecterns; books in octavo, on the other hand, necessitate a close personal touch to keep them open and to follow their words. Margaret Aston explored the different reading culture of lap books and lectern books;[31] Day produced both. An understanding of English religion and its practices led Day to create two distinct objects for two distinct audiences, thus maximising profit and mitigating risk.

The diversification of editions had clear economical gains. It also followed reformed ideology. Day's evangelical affiliation, explored by Evenden and King, supported the printing of smaller and more personal Bibles. As claimed explicitly in Day's address, these books offered the Bible to wider sections of society. Tyndale, who (like Luther) also produced smaller tomes of individual biblical books, introduced the ideal of the ploughboy consulting the Bible, which echoes in Day's address.[32] It may have been inspired by Henry's 1543 legislation that limited biblical access to the lower classes. Just as printers re-integrated elements of Tyndale, Coverdale or Rogers, all rejected during the last years of Henry's reign, the ideal and practice of biblical access was embraced in the Bibles made under Edward VI. This was done with the support of the political and religious leadership. Day's address was not only aimed at the poor; it also assisted him in seeking patronage for the production of his Bibles. He found such a patron in Frances Grey, duchess of Suffolk, Edward's cousin and a supporter of the evangelical cause. Her arms were indeed printed in several volumes of the octavo Bible.[33]

Making Liturgical Sense

During Edward's reign, the governance of the realm was primarily in the hands of those sympathetic to the evangelical cause. Archbishop Cranmer was now free to move the country in the direction of reform. Liturgy was central to Cranmer's attempts at religious change. Already in the first year

---

31   See page 138 above.

32   Reformed leanings were not the only reason for producing minute volumes, as could be seen from the above-mentioned duodecimo copies of the Latin Vulgate.

33   As, for example, in the verso of the title page in the second part of the Bible (DMH§81; STC§2087.2); see also King, 'John Day: master printer', pp. 186–90; slightly curtailed by Blayney, *Stationers' Company*, p. 679 N. B. The duchess's eldest daughter was Lady Jane Grey, whom Edward attempted to have succeed him.

of Edward's reign, royal injunctions reiterated the need for parish churches to own 'one book of the whole Bible, of the largest volume, in English', as well as Erasmus's Paraphrases of the Gospels. The Mass was to include readings from the Gospels and Epistles in English, and Sundays and holy days were occasions for biblical readings: a chapter from the New Testament at Matins, and one from the Old Testament at Evensong.[34] Cranmer proceeded to implement the draft liturgy he had compiled a decade earlier by introducing a novel, reformed and experimental liturgy to England.[35] For the first time the entire kingdom was expected to adhere to a single vernacular rite, whose language and performance were more akin to the liturgies of Continental reformers than to Catholic sacraments.[36] In regard to the Bible, Cranmer's new liturgy surpassed many of the Continental rites. It was the first national liturgical experiment for the reading of the Bible in its entirety.

The new liturgy was disseminated on a larger scale than ever before. The Book of Common Prayer, the embodiment of Cranmer's liturgical transformation, now replaced the multitude of liturgical books priests had consulted, as well as the variety of liturgical customs which differed from diocese to diocese. The Act of Uniformity ordered each parish to own a Book of Common Prayer (priced at 2s.2d. unbound and up to 4s. bound in calf) from 9 June 1549.[37] The new book was printed by Whitchurch in May 1549, with assigns deployed to deliver the vast quantity needed.[38] Modern analyses of the Book of Common Prayer tend to engage with specific elements within the new liturgy, and to concentrate on discussions of the Eucharist, the epicentre of

34   A 31 July 1547 declaration printed by Grafton: Paul L. Hughes and James F. Larkin (eds), *Tudor royal proclamations*, vol. 1: *The early Tudors, 1485–1553* (New Haven, CT: Yale University Press, 1964), pp. 393–403; Gerald Lewis Bray (ed.), *Documents of the English Reformation* (Cambridge: James Clarke, 1994), pp. 247–57.

35   Bryan Spinks, 'The Bible in liturgy and worship, c. 1500–1750', in *The new Cambridge history of the Bible*, vol. 3: *From 1450 to 1750*, ed. Euan Cameron (Cambridge: Cambridge University Press, 2016), pp. 563–78; Green, 'Hearing and reading', pp. 275–80; Brian Cummings (ed.), *The Book of Common Prayer: the texts of 1549, 1559, and 1662* (Oxford: Oxford University Press, 2011), pp. xxii, 4, 690; Kate Narveson, '"Their practice bringeth little profit": clerical anxieties about lay Scripture reading in early modern England', in *Private and domestic devotion in early modern Britain*, ed. Jessica Martin and Alec Ryrie (Farnham: Ashgate, 2012), pp. 165–87.

36   The reformed reading also drew on the revised Catholic Breviary of Cardinal Francesco de Quiñones (Green, 'Hearing and reading', pp. 275–6).

37   Bray, *Documents of the English Reformation*, pp. 267–71. For the June 1549 legislation on the price of the Book of Common Prayer see Hughes and Larkin, *Tudor royal proclamations*, p. 464.

38   *The booke of the common prayer and administracion of the Sacramentes, and other rites and ceremonies of the Churche: after the vse of the Churche of England* (London: Edward Whitchurch, 1549); Cummings, *Book of Common Prayer*; The special issue of *Revue Française de Civilisation Britannique French Journal of British Studies* 22:1 (2017): 'The Book of Common Prayer: studies in religious transfer', and especially Aude de Mézerac-Zanetti, 'A reappraisal of liturgical continuity in the mid-sixteenth century: Henrician innovations and the first Books of Common Prayer' (http://rfcb.revues.org/1218).

controversies between reformers and conservatives. Thus, biblical lessons are hardly discussed by Brian Cummings in his indispensable modern edition of the Book of Common Prayer, or in the 2017 special issue of the *Revue française de civilisation britannique* dedicated to the Book of Common Prayer. This emphasis matches the historiography of this period, which sees Edward's reign through tensions between reform and tradition. Yet when we examine the Book of Common Prayer, we find that most of its 168 folios are dedicated to biblical texts, with only a fraction (fols cx.r–cxxi.v) presenting the Eucharist, now called 'The supper of the Lord and the holy communion, commonly called the Mass'.[39] Moreover, many texts chanted and spoken during the sacraments and rites of passage comprise biblical passages, or those closely paraphrasing it.[40] The Bible was essential to the new Book; Cranmer's prologue to the book (sig. A.ii.r–v) celebrates access to the Bible and biblical knowledge:

> for they [the ancient fathers] so ordered the matter, that all the whole Bible (or the greatest part thereof) should be read over once in the year [...] And further, that the people (by daily hearing of holy scripture read in the Church) should continually profit more and more in the knowledge of God, and be the more inflamed with the love of his true religion.

The shift from the previous reign was dramatic indeed. No longer is obedience to the monarch presented as the overarching rationale for religious practice, as it had been in Henry VIII's time. Edification of the people and a return to the ways of the Ancient Church are presented as all-important guiding principles. Cranmer further explores this in his discussion of the Psalter:

> [T]he ancient fathers had devised the psalms into seven portions:[41] whereof every one was called a nocturne: now of late time a few of them have been daily said (and oft repeated) and the rest utterly omitted. Moreover, the number & hardness of the rules called the pie [Ordinale], and the manifold changings of the service, was the cause, that to turn the book only, was so hard and intricate a matter, that many times, there was more business to find out what should be read, then to read it when it was found out.

---

39   This is based on CUL copy Sel. 3.218 of *The booke of the common prayer and administracion of the Sacramentes, and other rites and ceremonies of the Churche: after the vse of the Churche of England* (London: Whitchurch, 1549).

40   Green, 'Hearing and reading', p. 283.

41   This is the rationale behind the divisions of the medieval Psalter, presented in Chapters 1 and 2.

A clear dichotomy is presented between medieval rites, customs and books, on the one side, and the clear, simple and ancient rites, on the other. Like many other medieval and early modern reformers, Cranmer presents his innovations as a return to the glorified past of the Early Church, in the course of which he rids the people of unnecessary medieval accretions. The source of the ancient rites, as well as of Cranmer's revision, was the Bible, which was to become again the cornerstone of Church rites. The new liturgy was constructed around a new order of reading, which restored the *lectio continua*, the uninterrupted sequence of biblical reading:

> [H]ere is set forth such an order, whereby the same shall be redressed. And for a readiness in this matter, here is drawn out a calendar for that purpose, which is plain and easy to be understood, wherein (so much as may be) the reading of holy scripture is so set forth, that all things shall be done in order, without breaking one piece thereof from another. For this cause be cut of Anthems, Responses, Invitatories, and such like things, as did break the continual course of the reading of the scripture.

The Bible is simple and clear, the opposite of convoluted medieval rites. The underlying moral implications of this divide aided Cranmer in presenting the liturgy to a fragmented country. Cranmer employed the Bible as a middle ground, appealing to reformers and conservatives alike, both accepting the centrality of Scripture. He was aware of the need for a gradual introduction of change into a divided society. Although reform was supported by the leadership of Church and State alike, many of the gentry, clergy and the general population did not share Cranmer's ideals. This became clear during the revolts of the summer of 1549, following the introduction of the Book of Common Prayer.[42] Such opposition was anticipated by Cranmer. In his preface, new liturgy and Bible were one and the same; the removal of medieval chant was a return to the simplicity of the Bible.

For Cranmer the centrality of the Bible was not empty rhetoric, but rather at the core of the new liturgy. Spanning 136 folios, biblical lessons constituted the bulk of the book's 168 folios. These largely followed the older liturgical cycles of Gospel and Epistles lessons, in which biblical readings were read on Sunday and major feasts. These biblical lessons are provided in full in the new book, according to the liturgical occasion. As is common in medieval liturgical manuscripts, the cycle begins with the first Sunday in Advent and continues throughout the liturgical year.[43]

42　On the precarious nature of Edward VI's religious reforms see Alford, *Kingship and Politics in the Reign of Edward VI*, especially p. 61.

43　Fols vii.r–clx.r, followed by the moveable Sundays of Lent (fols clii.v–clv.v).

This medieval remnant of Gospel and Epistle lections was only a fraction of the biblical revision instigated by Cranmer. It is the supremacy of the *lectio continua* that reverberates throughout the Book of Common Prayer. Cranmer's Preface is followed by two tables which explain this innovative manner of reading Scripture, each accompanied by explanatory notes. 'THE ORDER how the Psalter is appointed to be read' (sig. A.iii.v–A. iiii.r, Fig. 5.6) explicates how the Psalms were to be read in monthly cycles, including how to manage longer or shorter months. The presentation of Psalms in the book constitutes a break with traditional Psalm mnemonics, as it omits the Psalms' Latin incipits, the opening words of each Psalm in the Vulgate and the common way the Psalms were referenced in the liturgy. Like the works of other Church reformers depicted throughout this study, from the earlier Wycliffite Bibles to Coverdale's Bible, Cranmer did away with the way Psalms were retained in the memory of priests and laity. The Book of Common Prayer follows the numbering 'after the great English Bible', and hence was incompatible with the Vulgate and its numbering.[44]

'THE ORDER how the rest of holy Scripture (beside the Psalter) is appointed to be read' (sig. A.iiii.v–[A.x.]v) accompanies a more complex table, which provides the reading sequence for the entire year, during which time the Old Testament is read in its entirety and the New Testament is read three times. A few books were to be avoided, as 'certain books and chapters, which be less edifying, and might best be spared, and therefore are left unread'. Among those omitted are the Song of Songs, with its erotic imagery, and the puzzling mystical vision of the Book of Revelation.[45] Two decades later the editors of the Bishops' Bible had scrutinised the Bible for unsuitable narratives, omitting episodes whose morality could be misinterpreted. Cranmer, on the other hand, appears to have omitted primarily materials of lesser interest: chapters of archaic law, genealogies and of repetitive nature (causing the omission of 1 and 2 Chronicles in their entirety, as these biblical books mostly retell earlier narratives).[46] These omissions simplified the biblical reading and provided the audience with a clearer narrative. Cranmer undertook another major amendment to the biblical sequence, which shows the lingering of medieval perceptions. This had to do with the time when the Prophecies of Isaiah were to be read. In the Bible, the Book of Isaiah is

44   Some movement between the two was facilitated by the incorporation of the following note: 'both from the .ix. Psalm unto the .c.xlviii. Psalm (following the division of the Hebrews) doeth vary in numbers from the common Latin translation.'

45   Chapters from Revelation were nevertheless read on All Saints' (1 November, chapter 19), and on the Feast of John the Evangelist (27 December, chapters 1 and 23).

46   The readings were not modified when the Book of Common Prayer was revised in 1552.

located among the Old Testament prophets. All other Old Testament prophets were read in the summer months. Isaiah, on the other hand, was placed as the last book of the Old Testament, to be read in November and December. This followed common allegorical interpretations of Isaiah's prophecies as prefiguring the arrival of Christ, and hence Cranmer's choice of reading this book at the time of Advent and Christmas. This mirrored the season when biblical lections from the Book of Isaiah had been read in medieval churches and monasteries.

In this revised form the Bible was read throughout the year. The system of reading may appear impenetrable to the modern reader, as it no doubt did to early modern priests and parishioners. Starting in parallel with Genesis, Matthew and the Pauline Epistles, a complex sequence was created. Two services—matins (later renamed 'Morning Prayer') and evensong—each had two lessons, one from the Old Testament and the other from the New. The Old Testament lessons ran sequentially, typically one chapter for each lesson, from matins to evensong. New Testament readings were different: matins was reserved for readings from the Gospels and Acts, and evensong for the Epistles. Thus, as demonstrated in Figure 5.6 (the order of reading for January), the readings for 5 January comprise:

- Matins: the fifth Psalm; Genesis chapter 7; and the Gospel of Matthew chapter 4
- Evensong: Genesis chapter 8; and the Epistle to the Romans chapter 4.

The next day, being Epiphany, was marked out by readings from Isaiah 9 and Luke 3 (matins); Isaiah 49 and John 2 (evensong). The sequence was resumed the following day, with the readings for 7 January taken from Genesis, Matthew and Romans.

The rubrics to the table of lections in the Wycliffite Bible (discussed in Chapter 2) suggest that fifteenth-century readers found challenging a system of two lessons for each Sundays. The system introduced by Cranmer in the sixteenth century was as complex as could be. The experimental liturgy attempted the difficult task of following four different cycles—Old Testament, Gospels, Epistles and Psalms—one yearly, two tri-yearly and the last monthly. These were often interrupted by key feasts and their unique lessons. And this was to be done on a national scale, in each and every parish church. To facilitate reading, Cranmer innovated in the use of chapter divisions. This centuries-old device now became the foundation of liturgical performance. For the first time in their history, chapter divisions were embedded into the heart of Church services. They now took the place of the earlier pericopes, those shorter and non-numerical narrative units which had been the

Figure 5.6 Table
of Lections in the
Book of Common
Prayer. This was
the first time the
Bible was to be
read (nearly) in its
entirety in every
parish church.
The booke of the
common prayer and
administracion of
the sacramentes […]
(London: Edward
Whitchurch, 1549),
sig. A.iv.v–A.v.r.
Reproduced by
kind permission
of the Syndics
of Cambridge
University Library.

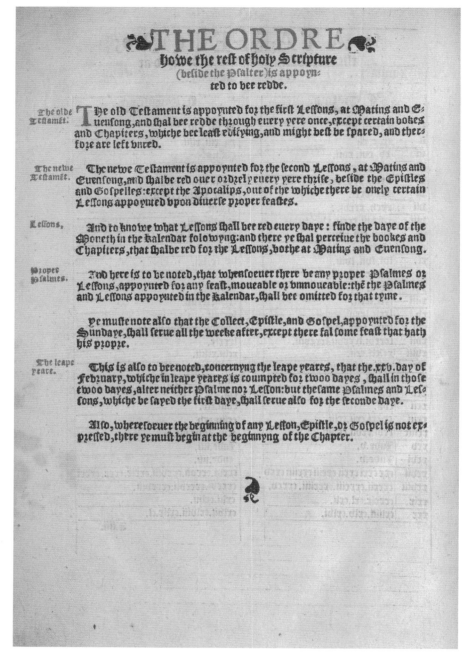

backbone of medieval liturgical readings.[47] The new *lectio continua* embraced
the numerical, more uniform chapter division, with one chapter typically read

47   The pericope nevertheless continued to structure the Gospel and Epistle Mass lessons.

January.

January.		Psalmes.			Matins.		Evensong.	
					i.Lesson.	ii.Lesson	i.Lesson.	ii.Lesson
A	kalend.	i	Circumci.	i	Gen.xvii	Roma.ii	Deut. x	Collof.ii.
b	iiii.No	ii		ii	Gene. i	Math. i	Gene. ii	Roma. i
c	iii.No.	iii		iii	iii	ii	iiii	ii
D	Prid No	iiii		iiii	v	iii	vi	iii
e	Nonas.	v		v	vii	iiii	viii	iiii
f	viii.Id.	vi	Epiphani.	vi	Esai.lx.	Luke. iii	Esai.xlix	John. ii.
g	vii.Id.	vii		vii	Gen.ix.	Math. v	Gen. xi.	Roma v
A	vi.Id.	viii		viii	xii	vi	xiii	vi
b	v.Id.	ix		ix	xiiii	vii	xv	vii
c	iiii.Id.	x		x	xvi	viii	xvii	viii
D	iii.Id.	xi		xi	xviii	ix	xix	ix
e	Prid.Id.	xii		xii	xx	x	xxi	x
f	Idus.	xiii		xiii	xxii	xi	xxiiii	xi
g	xix. kl.	xiiii		xiiii	xxiiii	xii	xxv	xii
A	xviii kl.	xv		xv	xxvi	xiii	xxvii	xiii
b	xvii.kl.	xvi		xvi	xxviii	xiiii	xxix	xiiii
c	xvi.kl.	xvii		xvii	xxx	xv	xxxi	xv
D	xv.kl.	xviii		xviii	xxxi	xvi	xxxiii	xvi
e	xiiii.kl.	xix		xix	xxxiii	xvii	xxxv	i.Cor. i
f	xiii.kl.	xx		xx	xxxvi	xviii	xxxvii	ii
g	xii.kl.	xxi		xxi	xxxviii	xix	xxxix	iii
A	xi.kl.	xxii		xxii	xl	xx	xli	iiii
b	x.kl.	xxiii		xxiii	xlii	xxi	xliiii	v
c	ix.kl.	xxiiii		xxiiii	xliiii	xxii	xlv	vi
D	viii.kl.	xxv	Con.Pauli.	xxv	xlvi	Act.xxii.	xlvii	Act.xxvi
e	vii.kl.	xxvi		xxvi	xlviii	mat xxiii	xlix	i.Cor.vii
f	vi.kl.	xxvii		xxvii	l	xxiiii	Exod. i	viii
g	v.kl.	xxviii		xxviii	Exod. ii	xxv	iii	ix
A	iiii. kl.	xxix		xxix	iiii	xxvi	v	x
b	iii.kl.	xxx		xxx	vi	xxvii	vii	xi
c	Prid.kl.	xxxi		i	viii	xxviii	ix	xii

A.v.

at each lesson. These divisions became instrumental in the complex structure created by Cranmer and its four parallel cycles of biblical readings. The link between the liturgy and the new chapter division, the subject of experiment in mendicant Bibles of the mid-thirteenth century, was fully realised.

The new liturgy was challenging for the officiating priest. It had the potential to be nearly indecipherable to the laity. When it was introduced in 1549, the vast majority of parishioners were only able to hear the liturgy without having a book in front of them.[48] They would have therefore found it extremely puzzling. Even if they did attend all services, they would still need to follow differing monthly and yearly cycles stretching across morning and evening prayers. To ease this difficulty, Cranmer employed the chapter division once more in an unprecedented way:

> And before every lesson, the minister shall say thus. The first, second .iii. or .iiii. Chapter of Genesis or Exodus, Matthew, Mark or other like as is appointed in the Calendar. And in the end of every chapter he shall say. 'Here endeth such a chapter of such a book'.[49]

This is a key moment in the parallel evolution of Bible and liturgy. For the first time in English history, priests were instructed to utter the chapter division in the performance of the liturgy. In the past, they were only required to identify the book, as in 'here begins the Gospel according to …'. This innovation was aimed at mitigating the confusion caused by the new reading system, to help hearers identify their place within the *lectio continua*. It also anticipated personal Bibles, which were indeed created during the reign, and whose users would benefit from proclaiming the chapter number as a cue to follow in one's book. The result was to present the chapter division to every member of the community, easing navigation and retention of the biblical text. More than three and a half centuries after their introduction, chapter divisions were presented to the entire population.

With the new order of reading in the Book of Common Prayer, the parish Bible which had been mandated during Henry VIII's reign began to make liturgical sense. Bibles were integrated into the liturgy and were read continuously throughout the year. This, however, was not yet reflected in church architecture. The Bible was to be made accessible for parishioners to consult, and biblical lessons were to be read in a way that was heard and understood by the congregation. The priest, however, still performed much of the liturgy in the choir or from the pulpit. Only in the reign of Elizabeth was the 'Low Pulpit' or 'Lector Pulpit' introduced, to create a space for the Bible shared by parishioners and clergy. A table in the nave was used in many churches for consultation of Bibles, as well as for Bible lessons.[50]

48   The introduction of smaller, cheaper and personal Bibles could be seen to alleviate this problem.
49   'Order for Matins daily through the year' (fol. i.v).
50   G. W. O. Addleshaw and Frederick Etchells, *The architectural setting of Anglican worship: an inquiry into the arrangements for public worship in the Church of England from the Reformation to the present day* (London:

Liturgy into Bibles—A More Gradual Change

The Prologue to the Book of Common Prayer makes clear that 'the curates shall need none other books for their public service, but this book & the Bible' (sig. A.ii.v). The printing of the three folio Bibles in 1549 testifies to a rush to supply parish churches with the latter. Liturgical addenda proliferated in these Bibles, as indeed in the reign's Bibles more widely. During Edward's short reign we can discern a transformation of liturgical addenda, and a gradual amalgamation between Bibles and liturgical rites.

The novelty of the new liturgy only gradually influenced the appearance of Bibles. All three 1549 Bibles contain a table of lections for the Gospels and Epistles. The printers had begun work on these Bibles in the previous year, prior to the publication of the Book of Common Prayer, so they were unable to incorporate much of its unique liturgy. In the two earlier Bibles the table of lections refers to the now-obsolete Use of Sarum. Only the last Bible of that year correctly refers to that of the Book of Common Prayer. Printed on 29 December, its printer had caught up with the new liturgy. Whitchurch, responsible for this Bible, was well aware of the liturgy of the Book of Common Prayer, whose printing he had overseen earlier that year.

The table of lections in its entirety became somewhat archaic in the context of the new parish book culture. All three 1549 Bibles, in their folio tomes, suited public worship in parish churches. The worship their layout and addenda facilitated, however, was that of Henry's reign, rather than that of the Book of Common Prayer. For the Gospels and Epistles lections, they employed a centuries-old system, common in both LMBs and Wycliffite Bibles. It provides a table of liturgical readings (commonly at the end of the volume); the readings themselves are delineated in the biblical text with Maltese Crosses marking the beginning of lections, and half-crosses marking their end. With the coming of the Book of Common Prayer, such devices were no longer needed. The new Book of Common Prayer supplied the liturgical readings of the Gospels and Epistles in full, saving priests the need to consult a Bible for these non-sequential readings. While the three Bibles provide the now-redundant Gospel and Epistle readings, they do not address the most innovative feature of Cranmer's liturgical creation. The new *lectio continua* does not appear in full in the Book of Common Prayer, and requires an accompanying Bible. That reading, however, is not mentioned in these

Faber and Faber, 1948), pp. 22–4, 68–70; Robert Whiting, *The Reformation of the English parish church* (Cambridge: Cambridge University Press, 2010), pp. 94–7; on reading and the transformation of English churches more generally see Margaret Aston, *Broken idols of the English Reformation* (Cambridge: Cambridge University Press, 2016), p. 916.

Bibles. This is also true for the new monthly Psalmody, whose new division is likewise lacking in these three Bibles. Early modern readers often inserted the day and indication of 'matins' or 'evensong' in the margin of the Psalter in these Bibles, augmenting this omission.

Tables of lections, now redundant for officiating priests, continued to appear in Bibles throughout Edward's reign. The 1551 Zurich quarto Bible goes even further and incorporates a unique calendar, which identifies for each Sunday or feast the reading from the Gospels and Epistles, possibly in an attempt to target lay readers, who would benefit from a clearer means of identification, as well as a smaller Bible. No reference, however, is made to the Book of Common Prayer's *lectio continua* in that calendar. A slightly later Bible, and another calendar, began linking Bible and new liturgy. A folio Bible printed by Hill in 1551 for a consortium of publishers replicated the detailed calendar of the Book of Common Prayer to help readers identify the biblical reading for each day of the year.[51] This was the first step towards providing the biblical readings according to the *lectio continua*, that part of the liturgy for which an additional Bible was required. In the same Bible another table identifies the Psalms to be read according to the Book of Common Prayer's monthly cycle (sig. A.ii.r). Liturgy and Bible were now intertwined.

The new way of linking liturgy and Bible through the incorporation of the table into Bibles eased the task of priests (and possibly of well-to-do parishioners too), but was not embraced by all printers. While it was replicated in Hill's quarto Bible of the following year (1552, DMH§98; STC§2089), and in the preliminary materials for a reprint of the Zurich quarto Bible printed for Jugge (1553, DMH§101; STC§2090), it was not taken up in Bibles printed by Day (1551, DMH§93; STC§2088) or Whitchurch (1553, DMH§102; STC§2091). Some printers were more traditional (such as Whitchurch, whose Bibles mostly replicated the appearance of the Great Bible), while others embraced specific facets of change. Hill printed Bibles of more traditional size, but experimented with liturgical addenda. Day's Bibles were of innovative size, but did not integrate elements from the Book of Common Prayer. One aspect in Day's Bibles was nevertheless valuable for priests performing the new liturgy. The rise in the centrality of chapter division for liturgical performance is mirrored in the layout of Day's folio Bible, which provides the chapter divisions as part of the running title. This identification was of great value when navigating the book in the course of the new liturgy. As the Book of Common Prayer's *lectio continua* was facilitated by chapter division, priests were able to retrieve the correct segment without consulting the textual block itself.

---

51   Sig. A.ii.r-[A.vi].v in DHL§92; STC§2086. The printing for the consortium is discussed in Blayney, *Stationers' Company*, p. 675.

Day's octavo Bibles were personal books, well suited for use by parishioners wishing to follow the *lectio continua*. No device linked these books with the new liturgy. Yet this did not stop readers from employing its volumes within a liturgical setting. A reader of the Psalter in Day's octavo Bible (the third volume, which is kept at the British Library, BL b.51.a.12) had identified the day of the month and matins/evening prayer in the margins (e.g. '4 ad matu'' near Psalm 19, indicating this Psalm is sung in matins on the fourth day). This is likely to have been done within two years of the Bible's printing. In the liturgical reform of 1552, matins was renamed 'Morning Prayer', making the marginal terminology archaic, if not obsolete. A later reader indeed rectified this in the margins, correcting each 'matins' to 'Morning Prayer'. Printers saw new possibilities in the creation of personal Bibles which would assist parishioners in following the new liturgy. Day's multi-volume octavo Bible would have been quite cumbersome for such a use, as the liturgy often engaged with texts in three or four of its different volumes. A single-volume Bible, on the other hand, better suited Cranmer's continuous reading. The creation of private Bibles evolved alongside new liturgical needs. Priests were equipped with the Book of Common Prayer and a large Bible to facilitate biblical readings. Parishioners were to benefit from a new-found ability to follow the complex cycles of reading in their own books. This fitted the reformed emphasis on an active laity, which differed from the restrictive legislation at the end of Henry VIII's reign.

Commerce and reform once more combined in the creation of a new personal Bible, whose novel size and features linked Bible and liturgy, ushering in a new era of English Bibles. Size and a new liturgical adaptability came together in two Bibles printed at the end of Edward's reign, the smallest single-volume Bibles hitherto printed in England. Hill's innovation in liturgical addenda was crystallised in his quarto Bible of 1552, which provides a wide array of prefatory materials, including 'The Order of the Common Prayer, for Matins and Evensong throughout the whole year'.[52] This lengthy addendum combines Bible and the Book of Common Prayer by providing much of the material included in the Book of Common Prayer itself (without replicating the now-redundant biblical readings of Gospels and Epistles), and facilitating the use of the Bible in the course of the liturgy. Hill's innovation was confined to the Bible's preliminary materials. Readers still needed to identify the readings based on the table, and then to continue consulting it while leafing through the book to retrieve the relevant lessons.

The last Bible printed during Edward's reign brought the link between liturgy and Bible to a new level. Printed by Grafton in 1553, this highly

---

52   Fols i.r–xii.v in DMH§98; STC§2089.

Figure 5.7 Layout of Grafton's 1553 Bible. Although a rushed production, this was the strongest manifestation for the link between Bible and liturgy. *The Bible in Englishe [...]* (London: Richarde Grafton, 1553), fols viii.v–ix.r. Reproduced by kind permission of the Syndics of Cambridge University Library.

portable quarto volume introduced a minute gothic type to create the smallest single-volume Bible printed hitherto.[53] It also broke new ground by identifying the readings of the Book of Common Prayer within the text itself. Unlike previous Bibles, here the liturgy was reflected in the design of each page, not limited to preliminary addenda. On each page a running title identifies the month in which the biblical lesson should be read, while marginal notes name the day and prayer (see Figure 5.7). For 1 Samuel chapter 14, for example, the running title directs the reader to April while the marginal annotation reads 'the .xv. day. Matins'). The Psalter likewise blends biblical text and liturgical performance by identifying the day and matins/evensong in the margins,[54] while the running title reads 'moneth', that is following a monthly cycle.

Such a device was highly innovative, even for the Bible's printers themselves. Blayney has identified how the printing of the Bible was begun by Hill, and only later taken over by Grafton. This is evident in the use of Hill's distinctive five-line initial 'I' at the opening of the Book of Genesis.

53   DMH§103; STC§2092. At 51 mm for twenty lines, a page size of 173x128 mm and weight of 1.0 kg, it was significantly smaller than its closest contemporary (Hill's 1552 quarto, at 53 mm for twenty lines, page size of 195x146 mm, and weight of 1.3 kg). This is also true when we consider the books' thickness (without the binding boards): 38 mm for Grafton's and 48 mm for Hill's.
54   With 'matins' preserving the pre-1552 terminology.

However, as Hill and Grafton employed identical type, Blayney has been unable to tell where Grafton took over from Hill. The new liturgical device may provide an answer. The first gathering of the biblical text (fols i–viii) does not supply the unique liturgical apparatus. Rather, it presents the standard running titles with their one-word summaries of biblical events ('Adam' for fols i.v–ii.r; 'Noe' for fols ii.v–iii.r; etc.). These very titles appear in Hill's other Bibles. Only from the second gathering, on fol. ix.r (Genesis chapter 25), does the new liturgical information appear with 'January' in the running title and 'evensong' and 'the .xv. day. Matins' in the margins for Genesis 25 and 26 respectively (see Figure 5.7). It stands to reason, therefore, that this is the point where Grafton took over from Hill.

The size and liturgical apparatus of Grafton's Bible inaugurated new reading strategies and engaged with new types of users. Here was a personal book, a lap book to use Aston's terminology, that was intrinsically linked to liturgical performance. Its size did not conform to the clerical use of Bibles in the course of the liturgy, nor to the legislation mandating a 'Bible of the larger size' for parish churches. This was a personal Bible. Its type and size required close handling and constant touch to keep its pages open. Much like Day's octavo Bible, this Bible encouraged biblical exploration by the laity. The small and personal Bibles, born in the clerical circles of the thirteenth century, had now become available for lay people to own and handle.

Grafton's Bible can be seen as the fruition of the link between Bible and liturgy, which Cranmer sought to establish. It also marks its (temporary) end. This was the last Bible to be printed in Edward's reign, and its layout and addenda reveal the uncertainties which prevailed at the end of that reign. Despite the emphasis on liturgical performance and the new links between the Bible's layout and the Book of Common Prayer, the Bible lacks any additional material apart from a table of contents at its beginning and a table of lections at its end. In a Bible so enmeshed with the liturgy, it is most surprising to find the now-obsolete table of lections according to the Use of Sarum, which differed in important ways from that of the Book of Common Prayer. By that time virtually all Bibles came to include the new table of lessons, and this incompatibility demands an explanation.

For all its innovation, Grafton's Bible was produced in a rush. The attention to detail is lacking: it has a generic and mostly empty title page; it was printed on wrinkled paper;[55] and its foliation is lacking, leading Herbert to comment that '[t]he numbering of the leaves is most incorrect'.[56] Historical circumstances can help explain these idiosyncrasies. Edward VI fell ill in

---

55   E.g. fols ix, xvi in Bible Society BSS.201.B53.4 copy.
56   DMH, p. 59.

February 1553 and died on 6 July that year. The evangelicals feared that reform would be halted, and attempted to crown Lady Jane Grey, whose proclamation was printed by Grafton himself. But this attempt failed. Princess Mary, a lifelong adversary of the evangelical cause, acceded the throne and steered the realm back into alliance with Rome. Grafton, as the King's Printer, was also the one printing Princess Mary's proclamation. He knew what this regime change could mean for his business as for his religious cause. The new Bible depended completely on Cranmer's new liturgy and on the reformed ideal of lay access to Scripture. Grafton therefore rushed to produce his new and reformed Bible before production could be halted.

Conclusion

The Bibles of Edward VI's reign were more diverse than any before. They were printed by a variety of printers, who had competed (as well as collaborated) with one another, leading to constant modifications to the Bible's size, layout and addenda. Cranmer's introduction of a new liturgy made the Bible a true necessity in parish churches, where it began to make—for the first time—liturgical sense. In this new liturgy chapter divisions were instrumental, accelerating the process of transforming biblical reading and knowledge. The rise of personal Bibles resulted from the combined effect of the new liturgy, a reformed ideology and commercial interests.

Edward's short reign transformed the appearance of English Bibles. The first large folio Bible of 1549 seems of a different era when compared with the small quarto printed by Grafton in 1553. Bible production was going into fast forward with the diversification of trade, of size and audiences, and the enmeshing of Bible and new liturgy, all leading to the creation of innovative books. This came to an abrupt end with the death of Edward VI, as evident in Grafton's 1553 Bible. Mary's reign, however, was only a temporary hiatus, and the Bibles of Edward VI had a lasting effect on English Bibles. Reformers fleeing persecution found refuge in Calvinist Geneva. Tapping into the latest innovations in book technology and reformed theology, they created the 1560 Geneva Bible. One of the most popular books in early modern England, it was the first to be printed in Roman type and to integrate a variety of notes, as well as the verse division.[57] Its small format (in quarto) reflected the editors'

---

57   DMH§107; STC§2093. For facsimile and introduction see Lloyd E. Berry (ed.), *The Geneva Bible, a facsimile of the 1560 edition* (Madison: University of Wisconsin Press, 1969); Maurice S. Betteridge, 'The Bitter Notes: the Geneva Bible and its annotations', *The Sixteenth Century Journal* 14:1 (1983), 41–62. In-depth examinations of subsequent prints, editions and reception are Ian Green, *Print and Protestantism in early modern England* (Oxford: Oxford University Press, 2000), ch. 2: 'English Bibles and their owners',

explicit wish for a wide dissemination of the Bible. Placed side by side with Day's octavo Bible, or with Grafton's quarto Bible, we can put their innovation in perspective, seeing the same reformed ideals, and the same implementations in print (albeit curbed by deficient techniques) during the reign of Edward VI. Such dependency is even more evident in the first Bible printed in Elizabethan England. Printed in royal folio, the Bishops' Bible of 1568 was to serve as a new parish Bible.[58] It was deeply embedded in the liturgy in the Book of Common Prayer, with its layout mirroring that of Grafton's 1553 quarto, but now on a much grander scale.

pp. 42–100; Femke Molekamp, 'Using a collection to discover reading practices: the British Library Geneva Bibles and a history of their early modern readers', *The Electronic British Library Journal* (2006); Femke Molekamp, 'Genevan legacies: the making of the English Geneva Bible', in *The Oxford handbook of the Bible in England, c. 1530–1700*, ed. Kevin Killeen, Helen Smith and Rachel Willie (Oxford: Oxford University Press, 2015), pp. 38–53; Thomas Fulton, 'Toward a new cultural history of the Geneva Bible', *Journal of Medieval and Early Modern Studies* 47:3 (2017), 487–516.

58   DMH§125; STC§2099. Relatively little has been written on this Bible: Margaret Aston, 'The Bishops' Bible illustrations', in *The Church and the arts*, ed. Diana Wood, Studies in Church history 28 (Oxford: Blackwell, 1992), pp. 267–85; C. Clair, 'The Bishops' Bible 1568', *Gutenberg Jahrbuch* (1962), 287–90; Green, *Print and Protestantism*, ch. 2: 'English Bibles and their owners', pp. 42–100; a recent monograph adds little new information: Jack P. Lewis, *The day after Domesday: the making of the Bishops' Bible* (Eugene, OR: Wipf & Stock, 2016).

Conclusion

This book's aim has been to examine both the creation of Bibles and the evidence for their use. We can now appreciate how these two processes—creation and reception—are interlinked. Decisions undertaken by the makers of books determined size, layout, type and colour. These encouraged, if not determined, the ways in which subsequent readers have used their Bibles. The Late Medieval Bible's (LMB) chapter divisions and running titles facilitated quick browsing favoured by preachers and scholars, as revealed in many marginal annotations. Berthelet's 1535 Bible, carefully placed between conservatism and reform, appealed to a variety of readers, from priests and Catholic recusants to laymen, women and children. Other books directed their readers more closely. The standard addition of a table of lections or the selective deployment of marginal sub-divisions in Wycliffite Bibles linked those Bibles with the chanting of lections during divine services.

Size also influenced readership and introduced discrete uses for the Bible. Aston's distinction between lectern and lap books points at one way in which books were made to fit their users: large books were inevitably more expensive and could be read from afar; smaller ones required personal touch and were more commonly owned by individuals.[1] The book's layout was designed to facilitate specific uses, evident, for example, in the size of the book's margins. The LMB's wide margins were at odds with attempts to make it small and portable but allowed readers to inscribe annotations and engage in dialogue with the biblical text. The Great Bible's narrow margins, on the other hand, reflected Henry VIII's discomfort with Bible reading by laypeople. Despite its immense size, its very narrow margins reveal that readers were not meant to annotate their books, an attitude aligned with Henry's distrust of lay readership but at odds with the reformed ideal of lay access to Scripture.

---

1   Margaret Aston, 'Lap books and lectern books: the revelatory book in the Reformation', in *The Church and the book: papers read at the 2000 summer meeting and the 2001 winter meeting of the Ecclesiastical History Society*, ed. R. N. Swanson, Studies in Church history 38 (Woodbridge: Boydell for the Ecclesiastical History Society, 2004), pp. 163–89.

A twofold attitude towards lay access to Scripture is evident throughout this book. Surprisingly it appears in some of the books most strongly associated with a reformed cause. Both the General Prologue to the Wycliffite Bible, and, centuries later, the Geneva Bible, merge the rhetoric of lay access with devices aimed at a narrow elite. The Wycliffite Prologues, much like early modern diagrams, drew on cutting-edge biblical scholarship. These were tools well known to the editors of these Bibles, yet foreign to the majority of lay readers. Marginal notes—one of the most contested elements in the history of the English Bible—likewise demonstrate means of controlling lay perception of the biblical text. The correspondence between members of the production team of the Great Bible demonstrates that notes were the single most important issue for Coverdale; and as Day created miniature Bibles in the reign of Edward VI, he omitted many of the features appearing in his larger Bibles, but kept the notes intact. This corroborates Alec Ryrie's argument that 'the intellectualism of early Protestantism is hard to overestimate'.[2]

Notes were key to Bibles also beyond the period under investigation. They were central to the Geneva Bible of 1560 (DMH§107; STC§2093). Advertised on its title page ('With most profitable annotations upon all the hard places'), they persevered across editions and reprints. And, like the notes of the Great Bible, those of the Geneva Bible also incurred the criticism of Church and State leaders. During the reign of James I the notes of the Geneva Bible were criticised, and were one of the factors leading to the inception of the King James Version.[3] Much like diagrams and maps, notes empowered the readers of Scripture while simultaneously limiting their interpretations to a single theological direction dictated by the editor. These practices differ considerably from the malleability of the LMB, which offered a variety of understandings and opportunities for use. Such openness also characterised the Great Bible, where the disorderly removal of annotations had left readers to their own devices, in ways of which Henry VIII would have disapproved.

The material aspects of the English Bible lead us to re-think the nature of reform and religious change. Looking at manuscripts and early printed books, the course of the Reformation is anything but a straight line. Wycliffite Bibles followed the models set by the Bibles of the Dominicans, their proclaimed adversaries, and their layout shows little evidence for the beliefs of that Shining Star of the Reformation. The same is true of the use of Wycliffite Bibles in nunneries and chantries. The evidence for vernacular Scripture and liturgy shows that we cannot use the fifteenth century to draw the battle lines

2   Alec Ryrie, *Being Protestant in Reformation Britain* (Oxford: Oxford University Press, 2013), p. 261; see also Ian Green, 'The laity and the Bible in early modern England', in *The English Bible in the early modern world*, ed. Robert Armstrong and Tadhg Ó hAnnracháin (Leiden: Brill, 2017), pp. 53–83 at 58–9.
3   See Chapter 4, note 8.

between 'proto-Catholics' and 'proto-Reformers'. This was a time of mixed linguistic spheres, which existed alongside restrictive Church legislation. The cohabitation of Latin and English in medieval and early modern Bibles is a clear manifestation of the need to re-imagine the division between reform and conservatism in England. The hidden annotations and the use of Berthelet's 1535 Bible, where Latin and English coexisted in the liturgy of Henry VIII's late years, likewise followed patterns that had prevailed for at least a century.

Clear turning points in the history of the English Bible are less sharp when viewed from the material perspective. This is true of religion as it is of technology. Change takes time, and its full extent is often revealed only after a period of trial and error. Moveable-type print is a case in point. The late medieval lay stationers' shops were models for early modern printers, who likewise replicated the layout of manuscripts in early printed books. Gutenberg's Bible was clearly based on the layout and text of the LMB. Key material features, such as presenting the text in two columns, or the centrality of chapter- and sub-division, were preserved in Bibles across the period we have studied.

Change takes time, and the scope of this book enables us to trace some facets of its long history. The rise and incorporation of chapter- and sub-divisions is a thread running throughout the current book. One of the most prominent features of the LMB, the fragmentation of the biblical text, assisted the work of preachers and exegetes as they combined biblical segments into sermons or tracts, often aided by innovative tools such as biblical concordances. A small group of mendicant Bibles also made use of these divisions in re-imagining the liturgy (an attempt not taken up in the majority of LMBs). It was 300 years later that the link between chapter division and the liturgy came to the fore. In the reign of Edward VI and with the introduction of the Book of Common Prayer, Cranmer had used chapter divisions in new ways to link Bible and liturgy, easing navigation through his complex cycle of liturgical readings. The same was not true of marginal sub-divisions. The LMB's complex and virtual system was simplified in Wycliffite Bibles, but also subjected to the aim of retrieving Gospel and Epistle lections. The sub-division was later used in early modern printed Bibles, but it soon became stagnant, copied blindly from one book to the other. Other divisions proved more enduring. In the second half of the sixteenth century the more uniform and accurate verse division came to the fore and has been embedded into Bibles ever since.

The Bible (or, more specifically, Gospel and Epistle lections) was read during the medieval Mass and explicated in the subsequent sermon. Tables of lections linked biblical text with the liturgical calendar and were instrumental in retrieving Gospel and Epistle readings. They became a common feature in LMBs, where they were often added in by early readers rather than by the original scribes. In these tables readers experimented with evolving retrieval systems, enabling them to achieve greater accuracy and efficiency. In Wycliffite Bibles tables of lections became a standardised addendum, typically copied by the original scribe(s), who adhered to a much more uniform layout and reference system. Such tables remained a key feature of Bibles well after the introduction of the Great Bible, in which their presence makes clear the incompatibility between the Bible's addenda and late Henrician liturgy. The centrality of the table of lections as a means of navigating the biblical text led to its incorporation into a copy of Berthelet's 1535 Latin Bible. At the end of Edward VI's reign, the link between liturgical time and biblical layout was consolidated as liturgical reading cycles, chapter divisions and biblical layout came together in the last Bible of the reign in 1553.

The Psalms emerge as one of the most versatile—and revealing—elements in the long history of the Bible. As laypeople, nuns, monks and clerics chanted them in private devotions and in the Divine Office, their knowledge was shaped by their performance. In biblical manuscripts and early prints their layout veered between reflecting their liturgical distinctiveness and subjecting the Psalms to the layout of any other biblical book. The latter strategy was adopted by Church reformers and innovators, from the small group of mendicant LMBs, through the earlier manuscripts of the Wycliffite Bible, to the Bibles of Coverdale and Matthew, and the Book of Common Prayer. All of these subjected the Psalms to the numerical chapter division, while omitting or marginalising their Latin incipits, in an attempt to shape a new experience of the Psalms. Reformed Bibles across the centuries aimed at innovating the Psalms' layout. This study has demonstrated how, time and again, they have failed to do so. The mendicant group remained an isolated minority; Latin incipits were added to earlier Wycliffite Bibles shortly after their compilation, becoming a standard feature in later Wycliffite Bibles and a prominent device in Wycliffite Psalters. In the sixteenth century Coverdale was made to integrate the Latin incipits back into the Great Bible, attesting to the need to accommodate previous liturgical knowledge. This phenomenon extended into the sixteenth and seventeenth centuries, but now with a new orthodox twist. The 'prose' Psalms employed in the Book of Common Prayer, themselves copied from the Great Bible, became the crux of Anglican liturgy. They therefore proliferated in subsequent Bibles, despite the inferiority of their translation, and against the judgement of Church reformers.[4]

---

4   See Eyal Poleg, 'Memory, performance and change: the Psalms' layout in late medieval and early modern Bibles', in *From scrolls to scrolling: sacred texts, materiality, and dynamic media cultures in Judaism, Christianity, and Islam*, ed. Bradford Anderson (Berlin: de Gruyter, 2020), pp. 119–51.

In each chapter of this book we have explored specific questions and emphases, indicative of distinct periods in English history. Chapter 1 followed the single-volume Bibles made for clerics who prayed and studied in Latin. Their Bibles were a versatile working tool. As Chapter 2 has shown, 150 years later Wycliffite Bibles evidence vernacular Scripture and rites, directing our gaze to the liturgies beyond cathedrals and universities: in nunneries, chantries and guilds. Wycliffite Bibles encode the merging of linguistic spheres, foreign to the evidence preserved in the overwhelmingly unilingual manuscripts of the LMB.

Chapters 3 and 4 addressed the dramatic changes at the end of Henry VIII's reign. Those responsible for the creation of Bibles attempted to address two audiences simultaneously: the English populace and the King. Printers, ministers and editors aimed to please Henry with the Bibles they devised, and to anticipate his reactions. Richard Rex's 'positive censorship' is manifested in the Epistle to the Reader to Berthelet's 1535 Bible. It also accords with the strong visual depiction of Henry's system of authority in the title pages of Coverdale's and the Great Bible. These Bibles were not commissioned by Henry but were rather shaped to appeal to his authority. The desire to appease the monarch had also led to failed attempts. I began this investigation while envisioning Henry's attitude to the Bible as a see-saw, wavering between reform and conservatism. However, the period's Bibles tell another story, that of Henry's consistency. Little had changed, from Henry's perspective, between a laity deprived of Bibles depicted on the title page of the Great Bible, and the restrictions on lay access to Scripture he announced in 1543. As the Bibles of the reign demonstrate, it was for other agents to learn and adhere to the royal disposition. Chapter 5 showed the free rein given to printers and reformers for the creation of Bibles under Edward VI. Printers competed in an ever-growing market, and in the process revolutionised the appearance and use of the Bible.

The ability to appreciate the unique features of Bibles from different periods underpins the structure of this book. Its chronological sequence enables the examination of Bibles as part of the transformation of Church, society and politics. The story of the late medieval and early modern Bible, however, could have been told differently. Some Bibles feature across this book's chapter boundaries, as with LMBs in parish churches, or copies of Berthelet's 1535 Bible which were used throughout Henry VIII's reign, as well as during those of Edward VI, Mary and Elizabeth I. This is part of a much wider phenomenon, largely overlooked in this book. Bibles had no expiry date. Liturgical books became obsolete with the change of rites, and scholastic and canon law books were destroyed en masse during the sixteenth-century dissolution of the monasteries. Scripture, on the other hand, retained its appeal, and possibly even a sacral value, in the face of religious and cultural change. Some Bibles even became relic-like objects. Wycliffite Bibles were cherished by Church reformers. CUL MS Mm.2.15 (see Figure 6.1), an early fifteenth-century deluxe Wycliffite Bible, was employed at the court of Edward VI, linking the most reformed monarch with evidence for that Shining Star of the Reformation.[5] Wycliffite Bibles were read across the early modern period, as shown by Mark Rankin and Alec Ryrie.[6] Ryrie has even traced a Wycliffite New Testament, which contains marginal annotations copied from Coverdale's 1538 New Testament. These allowed a sixteenth-century reformed reader to engage in dialogue with Wycliffite theology. LMBs were likewise used across the period. A mid-thirteenth-century Bible was used to refute Lollards in *c.*1400 Scotland,[7] while Edinburgh, The National Library of Scotland Advocate MS 18.1.2 was used at St Giles, Edinburgh, in the sixteenth century. The use of earlier Bibles in late medieval Durham has been explored by Richard Gameson, and suggests a different way of writing the long history of the Bible in England.[8] Tracing the antecedents of specific Bibles would be a much-needed addition to the history of the Bible, as well as an opportunity to reassess change and continuation within English culture and religion. It would also, however, have made for a very different book from the current one.

The survey of distinct eras in the history of the English Bible reveals important links and gradual changes across the period under investigation. The introduction of the LMB in the early thirteenth century ushered in the spread of Bibles to new audiences. The LMB was aimed at a small clerical elite, with its aids anticipating the needs (and capacities) of trained professionals. The sheer number of LMBs meant that such Bibles reached beyond the original target readership, with a small number of Bibles making their way to lay nobility or parish churches. Its layout was emulated in vernacular Bibles across Europe, providing new audiences with means of accessing the Bible. Its features were now deployed to popularise access and in ways not necessarily anticipated by the trained professionals who had created and used the LMB. This transformation had impacted the layout of Bibles, as sub-divisions and lengthy explanatory rubrics were integrated to assist less proficient readers in

---

5   Mark Rankin, 'The royal provenance and Tudor courtly reading of a Wycliffite Bible', *Journal of Medieval and Early Modern Studies* 47:3 (2017), 587–97.
6   Rankin, 'Reading the Wycliffite Bible in Reformation England', in *The Wycliffite Bible: origin, history and interpretation*, ed. Elizabeth Solopova, Medieval and Renaissance authors and texts 16 (Leiden: Brill, 2016), pp. 426–49; Alec Ryrie, *The Gospel and Henry VIII: evangelicals in the early English Reformation*, Cambridge studies in early modern British history (Cambridge: Cambridge University Press, 2003), pp. 235–6.
7   Eyal Poleg, 'The earliest evidence for anti-Lollard polemics in medieval Scotland', *Innes Review* 64 (2013), 227–34.
8   Richard Gameson, 'Durham's Paris Bible and the use of communal Bibles in a Benedictine Cathedral Priory in the later Middle Ages', in *Form and function in the Late Medieval Bible*, ed. Eyal Poleg and Laura Light (Leiden: Brill, 2013), pp. 67–104.

Figure 6.1
Wycliffite Bible
(right) with
sixteenth-century
additions (left).
The later elements,
which mimic
late medieval
manuscripts,
attest to the way
reformers saw
Wyclif as the
Shining Star of the
Reformation. CUL
MS Mm.2.15,
fols 274v–275r.
Reproduced by
kind permission
of the Syndics
of Cambridge
University Library.

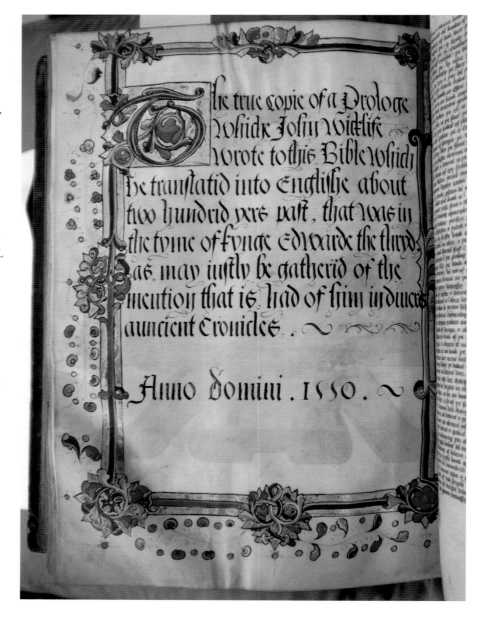

navigating the Wycliffite Bible. Most evidence for ownership of Wycliffite Bibles comes from Church institutions, but not necessarily the cathedrals and universities which saw the rise of the LMB.[9] The vernacular Bible now supported devotions by religious women, lay brothers and devout laypeople.

9   This may be due to the fact that laymen and women were less accustomed to signing their books, and so left most manuscripts unattributed. More research is needed to explore this possibility.

This is part of a gradual move, which this study unfolds: the gradual move of biblical books, as well as means of approaching and navigating them, which took place throughout the period under investigation. At first the reserve of ecclesiastical and academic centres, Bibles were then employed in nunneries, chapels and confraternities, and later, in the sixteenth century, were disseminated en masse to parish churches and lay individuals.

While some transformations are undermined in this study, one moment is seen as a major revolution in the history of the Bible, albeit one not often noticed by scholars of the medieval and early modern Bible. Injunctions in the reign of Henry VIII led to the creation of the parish Bible, and thus transformed biblical knowledge and dissemination.[10] Churches that had hitherto needed only to provide a handful of liturgical books were now mandated to purchase a large vernacular Bible. The trickle of LMBs and Wycliffite Bibles became a flood, albeit at times a hesitant one. Henry's injunctions were not retracted even after he had withdrawn access to the Bible from the lower classes in 1543. During the next reign, printers' commercial interests and reformed ideals joined to extend biblical readership to a broader section of the population.[11] Parish churches, hesitant to purchase a Bible during Henry's reign, were now bent on owning one.

This book has shown that access to Scripture owed as much to commerce as it did to theology. The mass production of manuscripts by thirteenth-century lay stationers met the demand for Bibles in universities, mendicant convents and monasteries. In the hands of stationers concerned with commercial viability, Wycliffite Bibles were modified, increasing their appeal to heterodox and orthodox patrons alike. Printers were likewise keen to ensure that their books would sell. Anthony Marler lobbied King and Convocation to guarantee that his investment in the Great Bible would pay off. Day's engagement with a 'demographically stratified vernacular readership', to employ Pratt and King's term, had both a theological and a commercial rationale.[12]

Time does not seem to move at the same pace across the period. The Bibles explored in this book dominated the English market and book culture for a certain period. The layout and addenda of the LMB were largely codified by the 1250s and were replicated in Latin Bibles for the next two centuries. The overwhelming majority of Wycliffite Bibles were produced over three decades, with no other Bible created in England for the following century.[13] The Great Bible, printed in seven quick editions over two years, dominated

---

10   More work is needed on the rise of the parish Bible, especially from a cross-national perspective.

11   This was also the underlying rationale for providing part of Scripture, as in Gospel and Epistle lections. Byddell's 1537 edition of the *Pistles&Gospels* (STC§15997.5) explicitly states: 'And because the word of god may the better go forward | and for as much as the price of the whole new testament is somewhat high, and specially for them that have little money.' Charles C. Butterworth, *The English primers, 1529–1545: their publication and connection with the English Bible and the Reformation in England* (Philadelphia: University of Pennsylvania Press, 1953), p. 156.

12   John N. King and Aaron T. Pratt, 'The materiality of English printed Bibles from the Tyndale New Testament to the King James Bible', in *The King James Bible after 400 years: literary, linguistic, and cultural influences*, ed. Hannibal Hamlin and Norman W. Jones (Cambridge: Cambridge University Press, 2010), pp. 61–99 at 71.

13   This was noted for the LMB and the Wycliffite Bible by Anne Hudson and Elizabeth Solopova, 'The Latin text', in *The Wycliffite Bible: origin, history and interpretation*, ed. Elizabeth Solopova, Medieval and Renaissance authors and texts 16 (Leiden: Brill, 2016), pp. 107–32 at 129.

the Bible market for the next decade. The rise of print caused one of the most significant transformations in Bible production: an acceleration of the rate of change. In the manuscript era specific Bibles had dominated the market for centuries and generations. With the introduction of print, Bibles could become obsolete within decades, or even years. The new technology and constant competition led printers to keep modifying their Bibles, seeking new audiences and unique selling points. The result was an ever-faster pace in the material history of the Bible in England. The first two chapters of the book cover the period from the 1230s to the 1430s; the last three chapters plot the transformations between 1535 and 1553, a mere eighteen years, which saw an immense transformation in the appearance and dissemination of Bibles. The following decades were even more distinctive in their pace: introduced in 1560, the Geneva Bible became the most popular Bible of its time, with over a hundred editions and reprints in a staggering variety of sizes and layouts.

The reaction of civic and ecclesiastical officials to the Bible varied greatly, as did attempts at controlling production and readership. This was hardly necessary for the LMB—the *correctoria* employed to identify textual variants was far removed from a uniform or regulatory device.[14] But in the wake of the Wycliffite Bible, the 1407/9 Constitutions of Archbishop Arundel aimed at curbing unregulated lay readership of Scripture. While court records indicate some adherence to the Constitutions, the manuscript evidence suggests these were not fully implemented. Wycliffite Bibles have survived in great numbers, and with little evidence for the licence their readership required in theory. A stronger form of control was introduced in the sixteenth century. Nationwide state legislation at the time of Henry VIII mandated against the printing or importation of unlicensed religious texts, and later against access to Scripture by the lower classes. Both these laws, however, had clear shortcomings: a stream of reformed Bibles flowed from the Continent to England, and almost no evidence exists for attempts at enforcing Henry VIII's restrictive legislation on Bible reading.

Another type of censorship emerged in late Henrician England. 'Positive censorship' in Bibles from this period led printers and editors to display affinity to the King through dedications and titles pages. Royal Bibles were hardly a novelty.[15] However, royal patronage for an edition of the Bible, rather than for a craftsman or an author, was a sixteenth-century phenomenon in England. The editors and printers of these Bibles commonly employed the themes of Old Testament kingship, favoured by Henry, to appeal for royal

14   Cornelia Linde, *How to correct the Sacra scriptura? Textual criticism of the Latin Bible between the twelfth and fifteenth century*, Medium Aevum monographs 29 (Oxford: SSMLL, 2012).

15   BL Royal MS 1.E.ix, the LMB *Magna Biblia*, is likely the one belonging to Henry IV, Henry V and Henry VI; Wycliffite Bibles were owned by Henry IV, Henry VI and Henry VII.

favour. Bibles became intrinsically linked with the Court, not only as a result of the break from Rome, but as a manifestation of new systems of royal authority. The Great Bible, with the visualisation of obedience to Henry on its title page, was not only the first parish Bible in England. It was also an early and substantial attempt to disseminate visually a royal message across all of England.

The Bibles at the opposite ends of the period under investigation seem the most similar. Both the 1230s and the reign of Edward VI saw the miniaturisation of Bibles to unprecedented sizes: one in manuscripts, the other in print. Both periods saw experimentation with liturgy, biblical divisions and layout. In the thirteenth century the Mendicants only needed a Bible and a breviary to perform most of their roles.[16] In the mid-sixteenth century, Archbishop Cranmer introduced his new Book of Common Prayer by claiming that 'the curates shall need none other books for their public service, but this book & the Bible'.[17] Both periods ushered in a new ideal of the Bible, and across the years in between we clearly witness the similarities and differences, the long transformation and the gradual dissemination of the English Bible.

---

16   Laura Light, 'What was a Bible for? Liturgical texts in thirteenth-century Franciscan and Dominican Bibles', *Lusitania Sacra* 34 (2016), 165–82.
17   Chapter 5, p. 175.

Appendices

Appendix 1 Innovative LMBs

Shelfmark	Numbered Psalms
Cambridge, CUL Ee.1.16	+
Cambridge, CUL Ff.6.47	-
Cambridge, CUL Hh.1.3	+ (C14 hand) Pss. 1-11
Cambridge, Fitzwilliam Museum, McClean 16	+
Cambridge, Gonville and Caius 350/567	Pss. 22-24 – numbered by original rubricator as part of the rubric
Cambridge, Pembroke 303	+
Cambridge, St John's I.28	-
Cambridge, St John's N.1	-
Cambridge, St John's N.8	+ (part of the Psalms' superscriptions)
Cambridge, Trinity B.10.21	+ (mostly truncated by a later binder)
Chicago, Newberry Library, 19	+
Edinburgh, NLS MS 1901	+ (probably by rubricator)
Edinburgh, UED 1	-
Edinburgh, UED 313	+ (red only)
London, BL Add 35085	+ (numbering breaks off after Psalm 116)
London, BL, Arundel 303	+
London, BL, Harley 1748	+ (C14 hand)
London, BL, Harley 2813	+ (C14 hand)
London, BL, Royal 1.D.i	+
London, Lambeth Palace 534	+ (originally written by the rubricator (in the margins, in red).From Psalm 6 (fol. 220v) tiny contemporary hand had noted them in the margins, at times with matching tie-marks linking numbers and text. From Psalm 120 (fol. 231r), the same hand noted the numbers near the text of the relevant Psalm)
Oxford, Bod., Auct. D.4.11	+ (written by the second rubricator, responsible for later books; redder hue of ink; Upper diagonal slant of 'v')
Oxford, Bod., Auct. D.4.9	-
Oxford, Bod., Auct. D.5.9	+
Oxford, Bod., Lat. bibl. e. 7	+
Paris, BnF, lat. 10431	+ (C14 hand for Pss 2-30)
Paris, BnF, lat. 163	+
Paris, BnF, lat. 215	+
San Marino, California, Huntington Library, HM 26061	+ (C14 hand)
San Marino, California, Huntington Library, HM 51	+ (numbered in Arabic numerals)

Galican Canticles	Mass texts	Affiliation	Provenance
–	–		
–	+	Franciscan	
+	+	Franciscan	C13 3/4; York
+	+	Dominican	
–	–		C13 2/4; Oxford
+ (C14/15 reader)	–	Dominican	
+ (C14 reader)	–		
–	+	Gilbertine	
– (other hymns)	–		
+	–	Dominican	
+	–	Franciscan	Written in Paris for English use
–	–		
+	–	C14 Dominicans	C14 Carlisle
–	–		
+	–	Dominican	
–	–	Dominican	Oxford
–	+		
+	+	Franciscan	Oxford
–	–	Friars (illumination fol. 1r)	Oxford
–	– liturgical instructions following Psalms		C15 Dominicans of Arklow (Ireland)
–	–	Franciscan	Oxford
+	–		C16 Exeter College
+	–	Dominican	Dominican Table of Lections by original production team; C14 Lincoln Cathedral
–	+	Dominican	Oxford
+ (C13 hand)	+	Cistercian	
–	+	Dominican → Franciscan	
–	+	Dominican	
+	+	Regular Canons?	
+	+		

Appendix 2 Editions of the Great Bible in the Reign of Henry VIII

DMH STC	§46 §2068	§53 §2070	§54 §2071
Cromwell's arms	+	+	+
Overseen by Bishops Cuthbert and Nicolas	–	–	–
Date of (according to colophon)	April 1539	April 1540	July 1540
Printed by	Richard Grafton and Edward Whitchurch	Edward Whitchurch	Richard Grafto
page	375★252 (slightly truncated)	380★250	400★253
printed area	338★232	337★233	337★237
column	323★91	317★90	320★93
20 lines	103	103	103
lines / column	62	62	62
Table of contents	1	6	3
Calendar and almanak	2	1	1
Exhortation	3	2	–
Sum and content	4	3	–
Prologue	5	–	–
Succession of Kings	6	4	–
Judgement on reading the Bible	7	–	–
Cranmer's Prologue	–	5	2
End – table of lections	+	+	+

§60 §2072–3	§61 §2074	§62 §2075	§63 §2076	§52 §2069
–	–	–	–	n/a
+	–	+	–	n/a
Nov. 1540	May 1541	Nov. 1541	Dec. 1541	April 1540
Richard Grafton	Edward Whitchurch	Edward Whitchurch	Richard Grafton	Thomas Petyt and Robert Redman, for Thomas Berthelet
SIZE				
407★275	363★256	406★270	392★273	318★220
358★240	336★233	360★248	340★233	289★200
336★100	317★91	337★97	323★91	270★80
103	103	103	103	95
65	62	65	62	57
PRELIMINARIES				
1	1	1	7 [not in BL copy]	2
2	3	2	1	1
–	–	–	2	–
–	–	–	3	–
–	–	–	4	3
–	–	–	5 [not in BL copy]	–
–	–	–	–	–
3	2	3	6 [not in BL copy]	–
+	+	+	+	+

Appendix 3 Single-Volume Bibles Printed in the Reign of Edward VI

DMH STC	§74 §2077	§75 §2078	§76 §2079	§84, §101 §2080, §2090
Date of (according to title / colophon)	August 1549	October 1549	December 1549	August 1550 / 1553
Printed for	John Day and William Seres	Thomas Raynald and William Hill	Edward Whitchurch	Christopher Froschover for Andrew Hester / Richard Jugge
Place of printing (other than London)				Zurich (preliminary leaves reprinted 1550 and 1553)
Textual model	Becke's revision	Matthew Bible	Great Bible	Coverdale's Bible
SIZE				
page	309★197	298★200	308★198	237★188
printed area	260★162	270★177	290★180	202★171
column	250★61	250★70	266★73	190★65
20 lines	77 mm	94 mm (no leading)	93	77 mm (no leading)
lines per column	62	54/3	57	50
Weight (kg)	3.75	4.25	3.85	2.35
Measurements based on CUL copy	BSS.201.B49.4	BSS.201.B49.6	BSS.201.B49.10	Young.86
PRELIMINARIES				
Table of contents		1		
Calendar and almanak	1 (r&b)	2		4 (with Gospel & Epistle Readings in the calendar)
Exhortation	2	3	3	
Sum and content	3	4	2	
Coverdale's dedication				2
Becke's Dedication	4			
Prologue – Tyndale		9		
Prologue – *shewing the use*	8			
Coverdale's To the Christian Reader				3
Cranmer's Prologue			1	
Succession of Kings	5	5		
Books and chapters	9	7		1
A Perfect Supputation of the years (Becke's)	7	8		
Register of names	9			
Book of Common Prayer (BoCP)				
Principal matter	6	6		
NT glossary (Aba)				
Order of Psalms				
End – Table	+ (Use of Sarum)	+ (Use of Sarum)	+ (BoCP)	+ (Use of Sarum)

§85 §2081	§92 §2083–6	§93 §2092	§98 §2089	§102 §2091	§103 §2092
1550	May 1551	May 1551	1552	1553	1553
Edward Whitchurch	Consortium of Printers	John Day	Nicholas Hill	Edward Whitchurch	Richard Grafton
Rouen					
Great Bible	Matthew Bible	Becke's revision	Great Bible	Great Bible	Great Bible
220★155	300★198	273★186	195★146	314★212	173★128
205★146	280★180	246★160	172★128	292★194	167★120
193★58	260★72	234★63	161★50	275★79	157★45
62	94 mm (no leading)	70 mm (no leading)	53	95	51
61/2	54/5	67	61	58/9	62
1.6	4.20; 4.35	2.35	1.3	4.4	1.0
BSS.201.B50.6	BSS.201.B51.4; BSS.201.B51.3	BSS.201.B51.8	BSS.201.B52.1	BSS.201.B53.2	BSS.201.B53.4
	4		3	1	1 (‖ §102)
	1 (Alman); 3 (Calendar with OT lesson)	1 (r&b)	1 (Alman); 4 (Calendar with OT lesson)		
	5	5			
2	6	6			
		2			
	10	11			
1					
3	7	10			
	11	8			
	9	7			
	12	9			
			5 'Order of Commen prayer, […] throwe oute the whole yere'; 'The Letany and Suffrages'		
	8 (with intro before succession)	3	6		
		4			
	2		2		
+ (BoCP)	+ (BoCP)	+ (BoCP)	+ (BoCP)	+ (BoCP)	+ (Use of Sarum)

Bibliography

The following bibliography provides primarily secondary literature, with a few select primary sources. Editions of the Great Bible are presented in Appendix 2; Bibles from the reign of Edward VI are presented in Appendix 3. Manuscripts are presented in Index 1 and Appendix 1.

Primary Sources

Alanus de Insulis. 'Summa de arte prædicatoria.' In *PL 210:111*.

—. *The art of preaching*, trans. Gillian R. Evans, Cistercian studies series 23 (Kalamazoo, MI: Cistercian Publications, 1981).

Becon, Thomas. *Newes out of heauen: both pleasaunt [and] ioyfull, lately set forth to the great co[n]solacion [and] co[m]forte of all christen me[n]* (London: John Mayler for John Gough, 1542).

—. 'The news out of heaven both pleasant and joyful', in *The early works of Thomas Becon: being the treatises published by him in the reign of King Henry VIII*, ed. John Ayre (Cambridge: Cambridge University Press, 1843), pp. 35–58.

Biblia. The Bible that is, the Holy Scripture [...] (Cologne?: Eucharius Cervicornus and Johannes Soter?, 1535).

The booke of the common prayer and administracion of the Sacramentes, and other rites and ceremonies of the Churche: after the vse of the Churche of England (London: Edward Whitchurch, 1549).

The book of common prayer: the texts of 1549, 1559, and 1662 , ed. Brian Cummings (Oxford: Oxford University Press, 2011).

Bray, Gerald Lewis, ed. *Documents of the English Reformation* (Cambridge: James Clarke, 1994).

—. *Records of Convocation VII: Canterbury 1509–1603* (Woodbridge: Boydell in association with the Church of England Record Society, 2006).

Brewer, J. S., R. H. Brodie and James Gairdner, eds. *Letters and papers, foreign and domestic, of the reign of Henry VIII: preserved in the Public Record Office, the British Museum, and elsewhere in England* (London: Longman, Green, Longman, & Roberts, 1864–1932).

The Byble: which is all the holy Scripture: in whych are contayned the Olde and Newe Testament (Antwerp?: Printed for R. Grafton and E. Whitchurch of London, 1537).

The Byble in Englyshe, that is to saye, the content of all the holye scrypture, bothe of the olde and newe Testament, truly translated after the veryte of the Hebrue and Greke textes, by the diligent studye of dyuers excellent lerned men experte in the foresayde tongues (London: Thomas Petyt and Roberte Redman for Thomas Berthelet, 1540).

'The Clementine Text Project', http://vulsearch.sourceforge.net.

Cranmer, Thomas. *Cranmer's liturgical projects*. Edited, from British Museum ms. Royal 7, B.iv, with introduction, appendix, notes, and indices, ed. J. Wickham Legg, Henry Bradshaw Society 50 (London: Harrison, 1915).

Dove, Mary, ed. *The earliest advocates of the English Bible: the texts of the medieval debate* (Exeter: University of Exeter Press, 2010).

Erasmus, Desiderius. *Nouum Instrumentu[m] omne [...]* (Basilaeam: In ædibus Ioannis Frobenij, 1516).

Forshall, Josiah, and Frederic Madden, eds. *The Holy Bible, containing the Old and New Testaments, with the Apocryphal books, in the earliest English versions made from the Latin Vulgate by John Wycliffe and his followers*, 4 vols (Oxford: Oxford University Press, 1850).

Foxe, John. *Actes & monuments of these latter and perillous dayes [...]* (London: John Day, 1563).

—. 'The first [- second] volume of the ecclesiasticall history contayning the actes and monumentes of thynges passed in euery kynges tyme in this realme, especially in the Church of England' (London: Printed by Iohn Daye, 1570).

Frere, Walter Howard, and William McClure Kennedy, eds. *Visitation articles and injunctions of the period of the Reformation*. Vol. 2: *1536–1558*, Alcuin Club collections 15 (London: Longmans, Green, 1910).

Froehlich, Karlfried, and Margaret T. Gibson, eds. *Biblia latina cum glossa ordinaria: facsimile reprint of the editio princeps Adolph Rusch of Strassburg 1480/81* (Turnhout: Brepols, 1992).

Henry VIII. *The King's book: or, A necessary doctrine and erudition for any Christian man, 1543*, ed. T. A. Lacey, Church Historical Society new series (London: Society for Promoting Christian Knowledge, 1932).

Hugh of St Victor. 'The three best memory aids for learning history', in *The medieval craft of memory: an anthology of texts and pictures*, ed. Mary Carruthers and Jan M. Ziolkowski (Philadelphia: University of Pennsylvania Press, 2002), pp. 32–40.

Hughes, Paul L., and James F. Larkin, eds. *Tudor royal proclamations*. Vol. 1: *The early Tudors, 1485–1553* (New Haven, CT: Yale University Press, 1964).

Humberti de Romanis Legendae sancti Dominici: necnon materia praedicabilis pro festis sancti Dominici et testimonia, ed. Simon Tugwell, Corpus hagiographicum Sancti Dominici 30 (Rome: Institutum historicum Ordinis fratrum praedicatorum, 2008).

Machyn, Henry. *The diary of Henry Machyn, citizen and merchant-taylor of London, from A.D. 1550 to A.D. 1563*, ed. John Gough Nichols, Camden Society publications 42 (London: Printed for the Camden Society by J. B. Nichols and Son, 1848).

The myroure of Oure Ladye: containing a devotional treatise on divine service, with a translation of the offices used by the Sisters of the Brigittine Monastery of Sion, at Isleworth, during the fifteenth and sixteenth centuries, ed. John Henry Blunt, Early English Text Society ES 19 (London: Trubner for the Early English Text Society, 1873).

Pecock, Reginald. *The repressor of over much blaming of the clergy*, ed. Churchill Babington, 2 vols, Rerum Britannicarum medii aevi scriptores 19 (London: Longman, Green, Longman, and Roberts, 1860).

Pollard, Alfred W., ed. *Records of the English Bible: the documents relating to the translaton and publication of the Bible in English, 1525–1611* (London: Oxford University Press, 1911).

Raine, James, ed. *Testamenta Eboracensia: A selection of wills from the registry at York Part 2*, Publications of the Surtees Society 30 (London: J. B. Nichols, 1855).

Pentateuchus Moysi [...] *Apocalypsis beati Ioannis* (Venice: L. Iuntę, 1533–8); (Paris: S. Colinæi, 1525–9); (Paris: S. Colinæi, 1531–5).

Sacrae Bibliae tomus primus in quo continentur[...] (London: Berthelet, 1535).

The statutes of the realm, printed by command of his majesty king George the third, in' pursuance of an address of the house of commons of Great Britain from original records and authentic manuscripts (London: Eyre and Strahan, 1817; reprint, 1963).

The statutes of the realm: Volume the fourth (London: Printed by George Eyre and Andrew Strahan, 1819).

A supplication of the poore commons: Whereunto is added the supplication of beggers (London: John Day and William Seres?, 1546).

Wordsworth, Christopher, and Francis Procter, eds. *Breviarium ad usum insignis ecclesiae Sarum: juxta editionem maximam* (Cambridge: Cambridge University Press, 1879).

Wyclif, John. *Iohannis Wyclif sermones: now first edited from the manuscripts*, ed. Johann Loserth (London: Trübner & co., 1887–90).

Secondary Literature

Addleshaw, G. W. O., and Frederick Etchells. *The architectural setting of Anglican worship: an inquiry into the arrangements for public worship in the Church of England from the Reformation to the present day* (London: Faber and Faber, 1948).

Akae, Yuichi. *A mendicant sermon collection from composition to reception: the Novum opus dominicale of John Waldeby, OESA*, Sermo 7 (Turnhout: Brepols, 2015).

Alford, Stephen. *Kingship and politics in the reign of Edward VI* (Cambridge: Cambridge University Press, 2002).

Armstrong, Lilian. 'The hand illumination of Venetian Bibles in the Incunabula period', in *Incunabula and their readers: printing, selling and using books in the fifteenth century*, ed. Kristian Jensen (London: British Library, 2003), pp. 83–113.

Aston, Margaret. 'The Bishops' Bible illustrations', in *The Church and the arts*, ed. Diana Wood, Studies in Church history 28 (Oxford: Blackwell, 1992), pp. 267–85.

—. *Broken idols of the English Reformation* (Cambridge: Cambridge University Press, 2016).

—. *The King's bedpost: art, Reformation and iconography in a Tudor group portrait* (Cambridge: Cambridge University Press, 1993).

—. 'Lap books and lectern books: the revelatory book in the Reformation', in *The Church and the book: papers read at the 2000 summer meeting and the 2001 winter meeting of the Ecclesiastical History Society*, ed. R. N. Swanson, Studies in Church history 38 (Woodbridge: Boydell for the Ecclesiastical History Society, 2004), pp. 163–89.

—. 'Segregation in church', in *Women in the church: papers read at the 1989 Summer Meeting and the 1990 Winter Meeting of the Ecclesiastical History Society*, ed. Diana Wood and W. J. Sheils, Studies in Church history 27 (Oxford: Blackwell, 1990), pp. 237–94.

Ayris, Paul. 'Reformation in action: the implementation of reform in the dioceses of England', *Reformation & Renaissance Review: Journal of the Society for Reformation Studies* 5:1 (2003), 27–53.

Barker-Benfield, B. C. *St Augustine's Abbey, Canterbury*, Corpus of British medieval library catalogues 13 (London: British Library in association with the British Academy, 2008).

Bartal, Renana. 'The Pepys Apocalypse (Cambridge, Magdalene College, MS Pepys 1803) and the readership of religious women', *Journal of Medieval History* 37:4 (2011), 358–77.

Bell, David N. *What nuns read: books and libraries in medieval English nunneries* (Kalamazoo, MI: Cistercian, 1995).

Belt, Henk van den. 'Sola scriptura: an inadequate slogan for the authority of Scripture', *Calvin Theological Journal* 51:2 (2016), 204–26.

Bériou, Nicole. *L'avènement des maîtres de la Parole: la prédication à Paris au XIIIᵉ siècle*, Collection des études augustiniennes 31–32 (Paris: Institut d'études augustiniennes, 1998).

Bernard, G. W. *The King's Reformation: Henry VIII and the remaking of the English Church* (New Haven, CT: Yale University Press, 2005).

Berry, Lloyd E., ed. *The Geneva Bible, a facsimile of the 1560 edition* (Madison: University of Wisconsin Press, 1969).

Betteridge, Maurice S. 'The Bitter Notes: the Geneva Bible and its annotations', *The Sixteenth Century Journal* 14:1 (1983), 41–62.

Bidwell, John. 'French paper in English books', in *The Cambridge history of the book in Britain*. Vol. 4: *1557–1695*, ed. John Barnard and Donald Francis McKenzie (Cambridge: Cambridge University Press, 2002), pp. 583–601.

Blayney, Peter W. M. *The Stationers' Company and the printers of London 1501–1557* (Cambridge: Cambridge University Press, 2013).

Bloom, Harold. *The shadow of a great rock: a literary appreciation of the King James Bible* (New Haven, CT: Yale University Press, 2011).

Boffey, Julia. 'From manuscript to print: continuity and change', in *A companion to the early printed book in Britain, 1476–1558*, ed. Susan Powell and Vincent Gillespie (Woodbridge: Boydell & Brewer, 2014), pp. 13–26.

Branner, Robert. *Manuscript painting in Paris during the reign of Saint Louis: a study of styles*, California studies in the history of art 18 (Berkeley: University of California Press, 1977).

Briquet, C. M., and Allan Stevenson. *Les filigranes: dictionnaire historique des marques du papier dés leur apparition vers 1282 jusqu'en 1600*, A facsimile of the 1907 edition (Amsterdam: Paper Publications Society, 1968).

Brown, Catherine. *Contrary things: exegesis, dialectic, and the poetics of didacticism*, Figurae (Stanford, CA: Stanford University Press, 1998).

Burnet, Gilbert, and Edward Nares, eds. *The history of the Reformation of the Church of England* (London: J. F. Dove, 1830).

Butterworth, Charles C. *The English primers, 1529–1545: their publication and connection with the English Bible and the Reformation in England* (Philadelphia: University of Pennsylvania Press, 1953).

Campbell, Gordon. *Bible: the story of the King James Version, 1611–2011* (Oxford: Oxford University Press, 2010).

Carley, James P. *The libraries of Henry VIII*, Corpus of British medieval library catalogues 7 (London: The British Library in association with the British Academy, 2000).

Carruthers, Mary. *The book of memory: a study of memory in medieval culture*, Cambridge studies in medieval literature 10 (Cambridge: Cambridge University Press, 2008).

Carter, Michael. 'Brother Grayson's Bible: a previously unrecorded book from St Mary's Abbey, York', *Nottingham Medieval Studies* 57 (2013), 287–301.

Cavanaugh, Susan H. 'A study of books privately owned in England: 1300–1450' (Ph.D., University of Pennsylvania, 1980).

Chadd, David. 'The ritual of Palm Sunday: Nidaros in context', in *The medieval cathedral of Trondheim: architectural and ritual constructions in their European context*, ed. Margrete Syrstad Andås *et al.* (Turnhout: Brepols, 2007), pp. 253–78.

Chambers, Bettye. *Bibliography of French Bibles: fifteenth and sixteenth century French language editions of the Scriptures*, Travaux d'humanisme et Renaissance 192 (Geneva: Droz, 1983).

—. 'What ever happened to Sola Scriptura? Text and paratext in sixteenth-century French Bibles', in *Infant milk or hardy nourishment? The Bible for lay people and theologians in the early modern period*, ed. W. François and A. A. den Hollander, Bibliotheca Ephemeridum Theologicarum Lovaniensium 221 (Leuven: Peeters, 2009), pp. 141–66.

Clair, Colin. 'The Bishops' Bible 1568', *Gutenberg Jahrbuch* (1962), 287–90.

—. 'Thomas Berthelet, royal printer', *Gutenberg Jahrbuch* (1966), 177–81.

Clark, Gregory. 'The long march of history: farm laborers' wages in England 1208–1850', *Economic History Review* 60:1 (2007), 97–135.

Copinger, Walter Arthur. *The Bible and its transmission. Being an historical and bibliographical view of the Hebrew and Greek texts, and the Greek, Latin and other versions of the Bible (both MS. and printed) prior to the Reformation* (London: Henry Sotheran & Co., 1897; reprint, Leipzig, 1972).

Corbellini, Sabrina, Mart van Duijn, Suzan Folkerts and Margriet Hoogvliet. 'Challenging the paradigms: Holy Writ and lay readers in late medieval Europe', *Church History & Religious Culture* 93:2 (2013), 171–88.

Cox, J. Charles. *Churchwardens' accounts from the fourteenth century to the close of the seventeenth century*, The antiquary's books (London: Methuen, 1913).

Crawford, Matthew R. *The Eusebian Canon Tables: ordering textual knowledge in Late Antiquity*, Oxford early Christian studies (Oxford: Oxford University Press, 2019).

Crystal, David. *Begat: the King James Bible and the English language* (Oxford: Oxford University Press, 2010).

Da Rold, Orietta. *Paper in medieval England: from pulp to fictions* (Cambridge: Cambridge University Press, 2020).

Daniell, David. *The Bible in English: its history and influence* (New Haven, CT: Yale University Press, 2003).

—. *Let there be light: William Tyndale and the making of the English Bible* (London: British Library, 1994).

Darlow, T. H., and H. F. Moule, eds. *Historical catalogue of the printed editions of Holy Scripture in the library of the British and Foreign Bible Society*, 2 (in 4 pts) vols (London: Bible House, 1903).

Davies, Martin. 'Juan de Carvajal and early printing: the 42-line Bible and the Sweynheym and Pannartz Aquinas', *The Library* series 6 XVIII:3 (1996), 193–215.

De Courtais, Georgine. *Women's headdress and hairstyles in England from AD 600 to the present day* (London: B. T. Batsford, rev. edn 1986).

De Hamel, Christopher. *The book: a history of the Bible* (London: Phaidon, 2001).

—. *Glossed books of the Bible and the origins of the Paris booktrade* (Woodbridge: D. S. Brewer, 1984).

—. *Syon Abbey: the library of the Bridgettine Nuns and their peregrinations after the Reformation* (London: Roxburghe Club, 1991).

de Mézerac-Zanetti, Aude. 'A reappraisal of liturgical continuity in the mid-sixteenth century: Henrician innovations and the first Books of Common Prayer', *Revue française de civilisation britannique* 1 (2017), http://rfcb.revues.org/1218.

Deanesly, Margaret. *The Lollard Bible and other medieval Biblical versions*, Cambridge studies in medieval life and thought (Cambridge: Cambridge University Press, 1920; reprint, 1966).

Dennison, Lynda, and Nigel Morgan. 'The decoration of Wycliffite Bibles', in *The Wycliffite Bible: origin, history and interpretation*, ed. Elizabeth Solopova, Medieval and Renaissance authors and texts 16 (Leiden: Brill, 2016), pp. 266–345.

Derolez, Albert. *The palaeography of Gothic manuscript books: from the twelfth to the early sixteenth century* (Cambridge: Cambridge University Press, 2003).

Devine, Alexander L. 'A portable feast: the production and use of the thirteenth-century portable Bible 1200–1500' (Ph.D., University of Pennsylvania, 2016).

Dolman, Brett. 'Wishful thinking: reading the portraits of Henry VIII's queens', in *Henry VIII and the court: art, politics and performance*, ed. Thomas Betteridge and Suzannah Lipscomb (Farnham and Burlington, VT: Ashgate, 2013), pp. 115–29.

Dove, Mary. *The first English Bible: the text and context of the Wycliffite versions*, Cambridge studies in medieval literature 66 (Cambridge: Cambridge University Press, 2007).

Duffy, Eamon. *Marking the hours: English people and their prayers 1240–1570* (New Haven, CT: Yale University Press, 2006).

—. *The stripping of the altars: traditional religion in England c.1400–c.1580*, 2nd edn (New Haven, CT: Yale University Press, 2005).

Duke, Gregory. 'Parish, people and the English Bible in East Anglia, 1525–1560' (Ph.D., University of Oxford, 2004).

Dutschke, C. W., with the assistance of R. H. Rouse *et al.*, *Guide to medieval and Renaissance manuscripts in the Huntington Library* (San Marino, CA: Huntington Library, 1989).

Erler, Mary C. 'Pasted-in embellishments in English manuscripts and printed books c. 1480–1533', *The Library, 6th Series* 14 (1992), 185–206.

Eskhult, Josef. 'Latin Bible versions in the age of Reformation and post-Reformation: on the development of new Latin versions of the Old Testament in Hebrew and on the Vulgate as revised and evaluated among the Protestants', *Kyrkohistorisk årsskrift* 106:1 (2006), 31–67.

Evans, Gillian R. 'Gloss or analysis? A crisis of exegetical method in the thirteenth century', in *La Bibbia del xiii secolo. Storia del testo, storia dell'esegesi: Convegno della Società Internazionale per lo studio del Medioevo Latino (SISMEL) Firenze, 1–2 Giugno 2001*, ed. Giuseppe Cremascoli and Francesco Santi, Millennio medievale 49 (Florence: SISMEL, 2004), pp. 93–111.

Even-Ezra, Ayelet. *Lines of thought* (forthcoming).

—. 'Schemata as maps and editing tools in 13th century Scholasticism', *Manuscripta* 61 (2017), 21–71.

—. 'Visualizing narrative structure in the medieval university: *Divisio textus* revisited', *Traditio* 72 (2017), 341–76.

Evenden, Elizabeth. *Patents, pictures and patronage: John Day and the Tudor book trade*, St Andrews studies in Reformation history (Aldershot: Ashgate, 2008).

— and Thomas S. Freeman. *Religion and the book in early modern England: the making of Foxe's 'Book of Martyrs'*, Cambridge studies in early modern British history (Cambridge: Cambridge University Press, 2011).

Ferguson, Meraud Grant. 'Grafton, Richard (1506/7–1573)', in *Oxford dictionary of national biography* (Oxford: Oxford University Press, 2004).

Fiddyment, Sarah, Bruce Holsinger, Chiara Ruzzier, Alexander Devine, *et al.* 'Animal origin of 13th-century uterine vellum revealed using noninvasive peptide finger-printing', *Proceedings of the National Academy of Sciences* 112:49 (2015), 15066–71.

Flood, John L. 'Martin Luther's Bible translation and its German and European con-text', in *The Bible in the Renaissance: essays on biblical commentary and translation in the fifteenth and the sixteenth centuries*, ed. Richard Griffiths, St Andrews studies in Reformation history (Aldershot and Burlington, VT: Ashgate, 2001).

Folkerts, Suzan. 'Reading the Bible lessons at home: Holy Writ and lay readers in the Low Countries', *Church History & Religious Culture* 93:2 (2013), 217–37.

Ford, Margaret Lane. 'Importation of printed books into England and Scotland', in *The Cambridge history of the book in Britain*, vol. 3: *1400–1557*, ed. Lotte Hellinga and J. B. Trapp (Cambridge: Cambridge University Press, 1999), pp. 179–202.

Foster, Michael. 'John Hurte (d. 1476): a Nottingham priest and his books', *Nottingham Medieval Studies* 53 (2009), 109–19.

François, Wim. 'The early modern Bible between material book and immaterial Word', in *The agency of things in medieval and early modern art: materials, power and manipulation*, ed. Grażyna Jurkowlaniec, Ika Matyjaszkiewicz and Zuzanna Sarnecka, Routledge research in art history (New York and London: Routledge, 2018), pp. 129–43.

—. 'Typology—back with a vengeance! Texts, images, and marginal glosses in Vorsterman's 1534 Dutch Bible', in *Imago exegetica: visual images as exegetical instruments, 1400–1700*, ed. Walter S. Melion, James Clifton and Michel Weemans (Leiden: Brill, 2014), pp. 89–136.

Freeman, Arthur. 'To guard his words: the selectivity, conservatism and startingly personal nature of a Bible designed by Henry VIII', *The Times Literary Supplement*, 12 December 2007, 13–14.

Fry, Francis. *A description of the Great Bible, 1539, and the six editions of Cranmer's Bible, 1540 and 1541, printed by Grafton and Whitchurch: also of the editions, in large folio, of the authorized version of the Holy Scriptures, printed in the years 1611, 1613, 1617, 1634, 1640* (London: Willis and Sotheran; etc., 1865).

Fulton, Thomas. 'Toward a new cultural history of the Geneva Bible', *Journal of Medieval and Early Modern Studies* 47:3 (2017), 487–516.

Gameson, Richard. 'Durham's Paris Bible and the use of communal Bibles in a Benedictine Cathedral Priory in the later Middle Ages', in *Form and function in the Late Medieval Bible*, ed. Eyal Poleg and Laura Light (Leiden: Brill, 2013), pp. 67–104.

Gaskell, Philip. *A new introduction to bibliography* (Winchester: Oak Knoll Press, 1995).

Gasquet, Francis Aidan. 'The pre-Reformation English Bible', *Dublin Review* 115 (1894), 122–52.

—. 'The pre-Reformation English Bible (2)', in *The old English Bible and other essays* (London: J. C. Nimmo, 1897), pp. 156–78.

— and Edmund Bishop. *Edward VI and the Book of Common Prayer: an examination into its origin and early history with an appendix of unpublished documents*, 2nd edn, The Catholic standard library (London: J. Hodges, 1891).

Gee, Stacy. 'Parochial libraries in pre-Reformation England', in *Learning and literacy in medieval England and abroad*, ed. Sarah Rees Jones, Utrecht studies in medieval literacy 3 (Turnhout: Brepols, 2003), pp. 199–222.

Ghosh, Kantik. 'The prologues', in *The Wycliffite Bible: origin, history and interpretation*, ed. Elizabeth Solopova, Medieval and Renaissance authors and texts 16 (Leiden: Brill, 2016), pp. 162–82.

Gillespie, Vincent. 'Syon and the English market for Continental printed books: the Incunable phase', in *Syon Abbey and its books: reading, writing & religion, c.1400–1700*, ed. Edward Alexander Jones and Alexandra Walsham (Woodbridge: Boydell, 2010), pp. 104–28.

— and A. I. Doyle. *Syon Abbey*, Corpus of British medieval library catalogues 9 (London: The British Library in association with the British Academy, 2001).

Giraud, Eleanor. 'The Dominican *Scriptorium* at Saint-Jacques, and its production of liturgical exemplars', in *Scriptorium: Wesen, Funktion, Eigenheiten – CIPL XVIII. Kolloquium, St Gallen 11.–14. September 2013*, ed. Andreas Nievergelt, Rudolf Gamper, Marina Bernasconi Reusser, Birgit Ebersperger and Ernst Tremp (Munich: Bayerische Akademie der Wissenschaften, 2015), pp. 247–58.

—. '"Totum officium bene correctum habeatur in domo": uniformity in the Dominican liturgy', in *Making and breaking the rules: discussions, implementation and consequences of Dominican legislation*, ed. Cornelia Linde (Oxford: Oxford University Press, 2018), pp. 153–72.

Gittos, Helen. *English: The Forgotten Language of the Medieval Church* (working title, forthcoming).

—. 'Researching the history of rites', in *Understanding medieval liturgy: essays in interpretation*, ed. Helen Gittos and Sarah Hamilton (Aldershot: Ashgate, 2015), pp. 13–37.

— and Sarah Hamilton. 'Introduction', in *Understanding medieval liturgy: essays in interpretation*, ed. Helen Gittos and Sarah Hamilton (Aldershot: Ashgate, 2015), pp. 1–10.

Gordon, Bruce. 'The authority of antiquity: England and the Protestant Latin Bible', in *The reception of continental Reformation in Britain*, ed. Polly Ha and Patrick Collinson, Proceedings of the British Academy 164 (Oxford: Oxford University Press for the British Academy, 2010), pp. 1–22.

Gow, Andrew. 'Challenging the Protestant paradigm: Bible reading in lay and urban contexts of the later Middle Ages', in *Scripture and pluralism: reading the Bible in the religiously plural worlds of the Middle Ages and Renaissance*, ed. Thomas J. Heffernan and Thomas E. Burman, Studies in the history of Christian traditions 123 (Leiden: Brill, 2005), pp. 161–91.

—. 'The contested history of a book: the German Bible of the later Middle Ages and Reformation in legend, ideology, and scholarship', *The Journal of Hebrew Scriptures* 9 (2009), 2–37.

Graves, C. Pamela. 'Social space in the English medieval parish church', *Economy and Society* 18:3 (1989), 297–322.

Green, Ian. 'Hearing and reading: disseminating Bible knowledge and fostering Bible understanding in early modern England', in *The Oxford handbook of the Bible in England, c. 1530–1700*, ed. Kevin Killeen, Helen Smith and Rachel Willie (Oxford: Oxford University Press, 2015), pp. 272–86.

—. 'The laity and the Bible in early modern England', in *The English Bible in the early modern world*, ed. Robert Armstrong and Tadhg Ó hAnnracháin (Leiden: Brill, 2017), pp. 53–83.

—. *Print and Protestantism in early modern England* (Oxford: Oxford University Press, 2000).

Green, William M. 'Hugo of St. Victor: De tribus maximis circumstantiis gestorum', *Speculum* 18:4 (1943), 484–93.

Greenslade, S. L., ed. *The Cambridge history of the Bible*. Vol. 3: *The West from the Reformation to the present day* (Cambridge: Cambridge University Press, 1963).

—. *The Coverdale Bible, 1535* (Folkestone: Wm. Dawson & Sons, 1975).

—. 'English Versions of the Bible, 1525–1611', in *The Cambridge history of the Bible*. Vol. 3: *The West from the Reformation to the present day*, ed. S. L. Greenslade (Cambridge: Cambridge University Press, 1963), pp. 141–74.

Haigh, Christopher. *English reformations: religion, politics, and society under the Tudors* (Oxford: Clarendon Press, 1993).

Hammond, Gerald. *The making of the English Bible* (Manchester: Carcanet New Press, 1982).

—. 'William Tyndale's Pentateuch: its relation to Luther's German Bible and the Hebrew original', *Renaissance Quarterly* 33 (1980), 351–85.

Hanna, Ralph. *A descriptive catalogue of the western medieval manuscripts of St. John's College, Oxford* (Oxford: Oxford University Press, 2002).

—. 'The palaeography of the Wycliffite Bibles in Oxford', in *The Wycliffite Bible: origin, history and interpretation*, ed. Elizabeth Solopova, Medieval and Renaissance authors and texts 16 (Leiden: Brill, 2016), pp. 246–65.

—. 'The sizes of Middle English books, ca. 1390–1430', *Journal of the Early Book Society* 8 (2015), 181–91.

Hargreaves, Henry. 'An intermediate version of the Wycliffite Old Testament', *Studia Neophilologica* 28:2 (1956), 130–47.

—. 'The Mirror of Our Lady: Aberdeen University Library MS. 134', *Aberdeen University Review* 42:4 (1968), 267–80.

Harris, P. R. 'Appendix I: Identification of printed books acquired by the British Museum, 1753–1836', in *Libraries within the library: the origins of the British Library's printed collections*, ed. Giles Mandelbrote and Barry Taylor (London: British Library, 2009), pp. 387–423.

Heawood, Edward. *Watermarks mainly of the 17th and 18th centuries*, Monumenta chartae papyraceae historiam illustrantia 1 (Hilversum: Paper Publications Society, 1950).

Hellinga, Lotte. 'Printing', in *The Cambridge history of the book in Britain*. Vol. 3: *1400–1557*, ed. Lotte Hellinga and J. B. Trapp (Cambridge: Cambridge University Press, 1999), pp. 65–108.

Herbert, A. S., ed. *Historical catalogue of printed editions of the English Bible, 1525–1961* (London: British and Foreign Bible Society, 1968).

Hessayon, Ariel. 'The Apocrypha in early modern England', in *The Oxford handbook of the Bible in England, c. 1530–1700*, ed. Kevin Killeen, Helen Smith and Rachel Willie (Oxford: Oxford University Press, 2015), pp. 131–48.

Hoffmann, Leonhard. 'Buchmarkt und Bücherpreise im Frühdruckzeitalter', *Gutenberg-Jahrbuch* 75 (2000), 73–81.

—. 'Die Gutenbergbibel: Eine Kosten- und Gewinnschätzung des ersten Bibeldrucks auf der Grundlage zeitgenössischer Quellen', *Archiv für Geschichte des Buchwesen* 39 (1993), 255–319.

Hollander, August den. 'Illustrations in early printed Latin Bibles in the Low Countries (1477–1553)', in *Shaping the Bible in the Reformation: books, scholars, and their readers in the sixteenth century*, ed. Bruce Gordon and Matthew McLean, Library of the written word 20 (Leiden: Brill, 2012), pp. 41–61.

Hornbeck II, J. Patrick. *What is a Lollard? Dissent and belief in late medieval England* (Oxford: Oxford University Press, 2010).

—. Mishtooni Bose and Fiona Somerset, eds. *A companion to Lollardy*, Brill's companions to the Christian tradition 67 (Leiden: Brill, 2016).

Hudson, Anne. 'Editing the Wycliffite Bible', in *The Wycliffite Bible: origin, history and interpretation*, ed. Elizabeth Solopova, Medieval and Renaissance authors and texts 16 (Leiden: Brill, 2016), pp. 450–66.

—. 'Lollard book production', in *Book production and publishing in Britain 1375–1475*, ed. Jeremy Griffiths and Derek Pearsall, Cambridge studies in publishing and printing history (Cambridge: Cambridge University Press, 1989), pp. 125–42.

—. 'The origin and textual tradition of the Wycliffite Bible', in *The Wycliffite Bible: origin, history and interpretation*, ed. Elizabeth Solopova, Medieval and Renaissance authors and texts 16 (Leiden: Brill, 2016), pp. 133–61.

—. *The premature Reformation: Wycliffite texts and Lollard history* (Oxford: Oxford University Press, 1988).

— and Elizabeth Solopova. 'The Latin text', in *The Wycliffite Bible: origin, history and interpretation*, ed. Elizabeth Solopova, Medieval and Renaissance authors and texts 16 (Leiden: Brill, 2016), pp. 107–32.

Hunt, Arnold. 'Clerical and parish libraries', in *The Cambridge history of libraries in Britain and Ireland. Vol. 1: To 1640*, ed. Elisabeth Leedham-Green and Teresa Webber (Cambridge: Cambridge University Press, 2006), pp. 400–19.

Hunt, R. W. 'Manuscripts containing the indexing symbols of Robert Grosseteste', *Bodleian Library Record* 4 (1952–53), 241–55.

Johnston, Michael, and Michael Van Dussen, eds. *The medieval manuscript book: cultural approaches*, Cambridge studies in medieval literature 94 (Cambridge: Cambridge University Press, 2015).

Jones, Norman L. *The English Reformation: religion and cultural adaptation* (Oxford: Blackwell, 2002).

Jurkowski, Maureen. 'The selective censorship of the Wycliffite Bible', in *The Wycliffite Bible: origin, history and interpretation*, ed. Elizabeth Solopova, Medieval and Renaissance authors and texts 16 (Leiden: Brill, 2016), pp. 371–88.

Kastan, David Scott. ' "The noyse of the new Bible": reaction and Reform in Henrician England', in *Religion and culture in Renaissance England*, ed. Claire McEachern and Deborah Shuger (Cambridge: Cambridge University Press, 1997), pp. 46–68.

Katz, David S. *God's last words: reading the English Bible from the Reformation to fundamentalism* (New Haven, CT: Yale University Press, 2004).

Kelly, Henry Ansgar. *The Middle English Bible: a reassessment*, The Middle Ages series (Philadelphia: University of Pennsylvania Press, 2016).

Kelly, Stephen, and Ryan Perry. 'Devotional cosmopolitanism in fifteenth-century England', in *After Arundel: religious writing in fifteenth-century England*, ed. Vincent Gillespie and Kantik Ghosh, Medieval church studies 21 (Turnhout: Brepols, 2011), pp. 363–80.

Kennedy, Kathleen E. *The courtly and commercial art of the Wycliffite Bible*, Medieval church studies (Turnhout: Brepols, 2014).

—. 'Review of the Middle English Bible: a reassessment by Henry Ansgar Kelly', *Journal of Medieval Religious Cultures* 43:2 (2017), 254–57.

Ker, N. R. *Medieval libraries of Great Britain: a list of surviving books*, 2nd edn, Guides and handbooks/Royal Historical Society 3 (London: Offices of the Royal Historical Society, 1964).

—. *Medieval manuscripts in British libraries. [vol.] 1: London* (Oxford: Clarendon Press, 1969).

Kienzle, Beverly Mayne, ed. *The sermon*, Typologie des sources du Moyen Age occidental Fasc. 81–3 (Turnhout: Brepols, 2000).

Killeen, Kevin, Helen Smith and Rachel Willie, eds. *The Oxford handbook of the Bible in England, c. 1530–1700* (Oxford: Oxford University Press, 2015).

King, John N. 'John Day: master printer of the English Reformation', in *The beginnings of English Protestantism*, ed. Peter Marshall and Alec Ryrie (Cambridge: Cambridge University Press, 2002), pp. 180–208.

— and Aaron T. Pratt. 'The materiality of English printed Bibles from the Tyndale New Testament to the King James Bible', in *The King James Bible after 400 years: literary, linguistic, and cultural influences*, ed. Hannibal Hamlin and Norman W. Jones (Cambridge: Cambridge University Press, 2010), pp. 61–99.

Kisby, Fiona. 'Books in London parish churches before 1603: some preliminary observations', in *The Church and learning in later medieval society: essays in honour of R.B. Dobson; proceedings of the 1999 Harlaxton Symposium*, ed. Caroline M. Barron and Jenny Stratford, Harlaxton medieval studies. New series 11 (Donington: Shaun Tyas, 2002), pp. 305–26.

König, Eberhard. 'A leaf from a Gutenberg Bible illuminated in England', *British Library Journal* 9 (1983), 32–50.

Kuczynski, Michael P. 'Glossing and glosses', in *The Wycliffite Bible: origin, history and interpretation*, ed. Elizabeth Solopova, Medieval and Renaissance authors and texts 16 (Leiden: Brill, 2016), pp. 346–67.

Latré, Guido. 'The 1535 Coverdale Bible and its Antwerp origins', in *The Bible as book: the Reformation*, ed. Orlaith O'Sullivan and Ellen N. Herron (London: British Library, 2000), pp. 89–102.

Lewis, Jack P. *The day after Domesday: the making of the Bishops' Bible* (Eugene, OR: Wipf & Stock, 2016).

Light, Laura. 'The new thirteenth-century Bible and the challenge of heresy', *Viator: Medieval and Renaissance Studies* 18 (1987), 275–88.

—. 'Non-biblical texts in thirteenth-century Bibles', in *Medieval manuscripts, their makers and users: a special issue of Viator in honor of Richard and Mary Rouse*, ed. Christopher Baswell (Turnhout: Brepols, 2011), pp. 169–83.

—. 'The thirteenth century and the Paris Bible', in *The new Cambridge history of the Bible: from 600 to 1450*, ed. Richard Marsden and E. Ann Matter (Cambridge: Cambridge University Press, 2013), pp. 380–91.

—. 'Thirteenth-century pandects and the liturgy', in *Form and function in the Late Medieval Bible*, ed. Eyal Poleg and Laura Light (Leiden: Brill, 2013), pp. 185–215.

—. 'What was a Bible for? Liturgical texts in thirteenth-century Franciscan and Dominican Bibles', *Lusitania Sacra* 34 (2016), 165–82.

Lindberg, Conrad. 'The Alpha and Omega of the Middle English Bible', in *Text and controversy from Wyclif to Bale : essays in honour of Anne Hudson*, ed. Helen Barr and Ann M. Hutchison, Medieval church studies 4 (Turnhout: Brepols, 2005), pp. 191–200.

Linde, Cornelia. *How to correct the Sacra scriptura? Textual criticism of the Latin Bible between the twelfth and fifteenth century*, Medium Aevum monographs 29 (Oxford: SSMLL, 2012).

Lutton, Rob. ' "Love this name that is IHC": vernacular prayers, hymns and lyrics to the Holy Name of Jesus in pre-Reformation England', in *Vernacularity in England and Wales c. 1300–1550*, ed. Elisabeth Salter and Helen Wicker, Utrecht studies in medieval literacy 17 (Turnhout: Brepols, 2011), pp. 119–45.

MacCulloch, Diarmaid. 'Changing historical perspectives on the English Reformation: the last fifty years', in *The Church on its past: papers read at the 2011 summer meeting and the 2012 winter meeting of the Ecclesiastical History Society*, ed. Peter D. Clarke and Charlotte Methuen, Studies in Church history 49 (Woodbridge: Published for The Ecclesiastical History Society by The Boydell Press, 2013), pp. 282–302.

—. 'Protestantism in mainland Europe: new directions', *Renaissance Quarterly* 59:3 (2006), 698–706.

—. *Thomas Cranmer: a life*, rev. edn (New Haven, CT: Yale University Press, 2016).

—. *Tudor Church militant: Edward VI and the Protestant Reformation* (London: Penguin, 2001).

McKerrow, R. B. *Printers' & publishers' devices in England & Scotland, 1485–1640*, Illustrated monographs 16 (London: Chiswick Press for the Bibliographical Society, 1913).

McKerrow, R. B., and F. S. Ferguson. *Title-page borders used in England & Scotland, 1485–1640*, Illustrated monographs 21 (London: Printed for the Bibliographical Society at the Oxford University Press, 1932).

McMullin, B. J. 'The Bible trade', in *The Cambridge history of the book in Britain*. Vol. 4: *1557–1695*, ed. John Barnard and D. F. McKenzie (Cambridge: Cambridge University Press, 2002), pp. 455–73.

Marshall, Peter. '(Re)defining the English Reformation', *Journal of British Studies* 48:3 (2009), 564–86.

—. *Reformation England, 1480–1642*, 2nd edn, Reading history (London: Bloomsbury Academic, 2012).

Martin, Jan J. 'William Tyndale, John Foxe, and the "Boy That Driveth the Plough" ', *Religious Educator* 17:2 (2016), 86–105.

Miriello, Rosanna. 'La Bibbia portabile de origine italiana del xiii secolo: Brevi considerazioni e alcuni esempi', in *La Bibbia del xiii secolo. Storia del testo, storia dell'esegesi: Convegno della Società Internazionale per lo studio del Medioevo Latino (SISMEL) Firenze, 1–2 Giugno 2001*, ed. Giuseppe Cremascoli and Francesco Santi, Millennio medievale 49 (Florence: SISMEL, 2004), pp. 47–77.

Molekamp, Femke. 'Genevan legacies: the making of the English Geneva Bible', in *The Oxford handbook of the Bible in England, c. 1530–1700*, ed. Kevin Killeen, Helen Smith and Rachel Willie (Oxford: Oxford University Press, 2015), pp. 38–53.

——. 'Using a collection to discover reading practices: the British Library Geneva Bibles and a history of their early modern readers', *The Electronic British Library Journal* (2006): article 10.

Moorman, John R. H. *The Grey Friars in Cambridge, 1225–1538*, The Birkbeck lectures 1948–9 (Cambridge: Cambridge University Press, 1952).

Mozley, James Frederic. *Coverdale and his Bibles* (London: Lutterworth Press, 1953).

Murano, Giovanna. 'The Epistles of St. Paul of the Convent of San Domenico (Bologna, Biblioteca Universitaria, MS 1545)', in *Form and function in the Late Medieval Bible*, ed. Eyal Poleg and Laura Light (Leiden: Brill, 2013), pp. 127–46.

Narveson, Kate. '"Their Practice bringeth little profit": clerical anxieties about lay Scripture reading in early modern England', in *Private and domestic devotion in early modern Britain*, ed. Jessica Martin and Alec Ryrie (Farnham: Ashgate, 2012), pp. 165–87.

Needham, Paul. 'Book production on paper and vellum in the fourteenth and fifteenth centuries', in *Papier im mittelalterlichen Europa: Herstellung und Gebrauch*, ed. Carla Meyer, Sandra Schultz and Bernd Schneidmüller, Materiale Textkulturen 7 (Berlin: De Gruyter, 2015), pp. 247–74.

——. 'The changing shape of the Vulgate Bible in fifteenth-century printing shops', in *The Bible as book: the first printed editions*, ed. Paul Henry Saenger and Kimberly Van Kampen (London: British Library in association with The Scriptorium: Center for Christian Antiquities, 1999), pp. 53–70.

——. 'The customs rolls as documents for the printed-book trade in England', in *The Cambridge history of the book in Britain*, ed. Lotte Hellinga and J. B. Trapp (Cambridge: Cambridge University Press, 1999), pp. 148–63.

——. 'The text of the Gutenberg Bible', in *Trasmissione dei testi a stampa nel periodo moderno. Vol. 2, Il seminario internazionale Roma-Viterbo 27–29 giugno 1985*, ed. Giovanni Crapulli, Lessico intellettuale Europeo 44 (Rome: Edizioni dell'Ateneo, 1987), pp. 43–84.

Norton, David. 'English Bibles from c. 1520 to c. 1750', in *The new Cambridge history of the Bible. Vol. 3: From 1450 to 1750*, ed. Euan Cameron (Cambridge: Cambridge University Press, 2016), pp. 305–44.

Nyström, Eva. 'Codicological crossover: the merging of manuscript and print', *Studia Neophilologica* 86:sup1 (2014), 112–33.

O'Day, Rosemary. *The debate on the English Reformation*, 2nd edn, Issues in historiography (Manchester: Manchester University Press, 2014).

Orth, Myra Dickman. 'The English Great Bible of 1539 and the French connection', in *Tributes to Jonathan J.G. Alexander: the making and meaning of illuminated medieval & Renaissance manuscripts, art & architecture*, ed. J. J. G. Alexander, Susan L'Engle and Gerald B. Guest (London: Harvey Miller Publishers, 2006), pp. 171–84.

Owst, G. R. *Literature and pulpit in medieval England: a neglected chapter in the history of English letters & of the English people*, 2nd rev. edn (Oxford: Blackwell, 1961).

Pantzer, K. F. 'Berthelet , Thomas (d. 1555)', in *Oxford dictionary of national biography* (Oxford: Oxford University Press, 2008).

Parkes, Malcolm B. 'The compilation of the Dominican lectionary', in *Literarische Formen des Mittelalters: Florilegien, Kompilationen, Kollektionen*, ed. Kaspar Elm, Wolfenbütteler Mittelalter-Studien 15 (Wiesbaden: Harrassowitz, 2000; reprint, Malcolm B. Parkes, Pages from the past: medieval writing skills and manuscript books, ed. P. R. Robinson and Rivkah Zim (Farnham: Ashgate Variorum, 2012), §XIII), pp. 91–106.

Peikola, Matti. '"First is writen a clause of the bigynnynge therof": the table of lections in manuscripts of the Wycliffite Bible', in *Form and function in the Late Medieval Bible*, ed. Eyal Poleg and Laura Light (Leiden: Brill, 2013), pp. 351–78.

——. 'The Sanctorale, Thomas of Woodstock's English Bible, and the orthodox appropriation of Wycliffite tables of lessons', in *Wycliffite controversies*, ed. Mishtooni Bose and J. Patrick Hornbeck II, Medieval church studies 23 (Turnhout: Brepols, 2011), pp. 153–74.

Pettegree, Andrew. 'Printing and the Reformation: the English exception', in *The beginnings of English Protestantism*, ed. Peter Marshall and Alec Ryrie (Cambridge: Cambridge University Press, 2002), pp. 157–79.

——. 'Publishing in print: technology and trade', in *The new Cambridge history of the Bible. Vol. 3: From 1450 to 1750*, ed. Euan Cameron (Cambridge: Cambridge University Press, 2016), pp. 159–86.

Pfaff, Richard William. *The liturgy in medieval England: a history* (Cambridge: Cambridge University Press, 2009).

Plomer, Henry R. 'Anthony Marler and the Great Bible', *The Library, 3rd Series* 1:2 (1910), 200–6.

Poleg, Eyal. *Approaching the Bible in medieval England*, Manchester medieval studies (Manchester: Manchester University Press, 2013).

——. 'The earliest evidence for anti-Lollard polemics in medieval Scotland', *Innes Review* 64 (2013), 227–34.

——. 'The first Bible printed in England: a little known witness from late Henrician England', *Journal of Ecclesiastical History* 67:4 (2016), 760–80.

——. 'Inanimate conversion', *Material Religion* 14:4 (2019), 485–99.

——. 'The Interpretations of Hebrew Names in theory and practice', in *Form and function in the Late Medieval Bible*, ed. Eyal Poleg and Laura Light (Leiden: Brill, 2013), pp. 217–36.

——. '"A ladder set up on earth": the Bible in medieval sermons', in *The practice of the Bible in the Middle Ages: production, reception & performance in Western Christianity*, ed. Susan Boynton and Diane J. Reilly (New York: Columbia University Press, 2011), pp. 205–27.

——. 'Memory, performance and change: the Psalms' layout in late medieval and early modern Bibles', in *From scrolls to scrolling: sacred texts, materiality, and dynamic media cultures in Judaism, Christianity, and Islam*, ed. Bradford Anderson (Berlin: De Gruyter, 2020), pp. 119–51.

—. 'Wycliffite Bibles as orthodoxy', in *Instructing the soul, feeding the spirit and awakening the passion: cultures of religious reading in the late Middle Ages*, ed. Sabrina Corbellini, Utrecht studies in medieval literacy 25 (Turnhout: Brepols, 2013), pp. 71–91.

—. 'Introduction', in *Form and function in the Late Medieval Bible*, ed. Eyal Poleg and Laura Light, The written word: the manuscript world 27:4 (Leiden: Brill, 2013), pp. 1–7.

— and Laura Light, eds. *Form and function in the Late Medieval Bible*, The written word: the manuscript world 27:4 (Leiden: Brill, 2013).

Ramsay, Nigel, and James M. W. Willoughby. *Hospitals, towns, and the professions*, Corpus of British medieval library catalogues 14 (London: British Library in association with the British Academy, 2009).

Rankin, Mark. 'Reading the Wycliffite Bible in Reformation England', in *The Wycliffite Bible: origin, history and interpretation*, ed. Elizabeth Solopova, Medieval and Renaissance authors and texts 16 (Leiden: Brill, 2016), pp. 426–49.

—. 'The royal provenance and Tudor courtly reading of a Wycliffite Bible', *Journal of Medieval and Early Modern Studies* 47:3 (2017), 587–97.

Raschko, Mary. 'Taking apart the Wycliffite Bible: patterns of selective and integrative reading', *Journal of Medieval and Early Modern Studies* 47:3 (2017), 461–86.

Reudenbach, Bruno. 'Books for liturgical reading? Remarks on structure and function of early medieval Gospel Books', in *Clothing Sacred Scriptures: book art and book religion in Christian, Islamic, and Jewish cultures*, ed. David Ganz and Barbara Schellewald, Manuscripta Biblica 2 (Berlin: De Gruyter, 2019), pp. 261–72.

Rex, Richard. 'The crisis of obedience: God's Word and Henry's Reformation', *The Historical Journal* 39:4 (1996), 863–94.

—. *Henry VIII and the English Reformation*, 2nd edn, British history in perspective (Basingstoke: Palgrave Macmillan, 2006).

—. 'Thomas Vavasour M.D.', *Recusant History* 20 (1990–91), 436–54.

Robinson, Pamela R. 'A "prik of concience cheyned": the parish library of St Margaret's, New Fish Street, London, 1472', in *The medieval book and a modern collector: essays in honour of Toshiyuki Takamiya*, ed. Takami Matsuda, Richard A. Linenthal and John Scahill (Woodbridge: D.S. Brewer, 2004), pp. 209–21.

Rosier, Bart A. *The Bible in print: Netherlandish Bible illustration in the sixteenth century* (Leiden: Foleor, 1997).

Rouse, Mary A., and Richard H. Rouse. *Authentic witnesses: approaches to medieval texts and manuscripts* (Notre Dame, IN: University of Notre Dame Press, 1991).

Rouse, Richard H., and Mary A. Rouse. 'Statim invenire: schools, preachers, and new attitudes to the page', in *Renaissance and renewal in the twelfth century*, ed. Robert L. Benson, Giles Constable and Carol D. Lanham (Oxford: Oxford University Press, 1982; reprint, ch. 6 in *Authentic witnesses: approaches to medieval texts and manuscripts* (Notre Dame, IN: University of Notre Dame Press, 1991), pp. 191–219), pp. 201–25.

—. 'Verbal concordance of Scriptures', *Archivum Fratrum Prædicatorum* 44 (1974), 5–30.

Rudy, Kathryn. 'Kissing images, unfurling rolls, measuring wounds, sewing badges and carrying talismans: considering some Harley manuscripts through the physical rituals they reveal', *Electronic British Library Journal* (2011), 1–56 (Article 5).

—. *Piety in pieces: how medieval readers customized their manuscripts* (Cambridge: Open Book Publishers, 2016).

Ruzzier, Chiara. 'Entre Université et Ordres mendiants: la miniaturisation de la Bible au XIIIe siècle' (Ph.D., Université Paris 1 Panthéon-Sorbonne, 2010).

—. 'The miniaturisation of Bible manuscripts in the thirteenth century: a comparative study', in *Form and function in the Late Medieval Bible*, ed. Eyal Poleg and Laura Light (Leiden: Brill, 2013), pp. 105–25.

Ryrie, Alec. *Being Protestant in Reformation Britain* (Oxford: Oxford University Press, 2013).

—. *The Gospel and Henry VIII: evangelicals in the early English Reformation*, Cambridge studies in early modern British history (Cambridge: Cambridge University Press, 2003).

—. 'Whitchurch, Edward (d. 1562)', in *Oxford dictionary of national biography* (Oxford: Oxford University Press, 2004).

Saenger, Paul. 'The British Isles and the origin of the modern mode of biblical citation', *Syntagma* 1 (2005), 77–123.

—. *A catalogue of the pre-1500 Western manuscript books at the Newberry Library* (Chicago: University of Chicago Press, 1989).

—. 'The impact of the early printed page on the reading of the Bible', in *The Bible as book: the first printed editions*, ed. Paul Saenger and Kimberly Van Kampen (London: British Library in association with The Scriptorium: Center for Christian Antiquities, 1999), pp. 31–51.

—. 'Jewish liturgical divisions of the Torah and the English chapter division of the Vulgate attributed to Stephen Langton', in *Pesher Nahum: texts and studies in Jewish history and literature from Antiquity through the Middle Ages, presented to Norman (Nahum) Golb*, ed. J. L. Kraemer and M. G. Wechsler (Chicago: The Oriental Institute of the University of Chicago, 2012), pp. 187–202.

— and Laura Bruck. 'The Anglo-Hebraic origins of the modern chapter division of the Latin Bible', in *La fractura historiográfica: Las investigaciones de Edad Media y Renacimiento desde el tercer milenio*, ed. Javier San José Lera (Salamanca: Universidad de Salamanca, 2008), pp. 177–202.

Salter, Elisabeth. '"The dayes moralised": reconstructing devotional reading, c. 1450–1560', in *Pieties in transition*, ed. Robert Lutton and Elisabeth Salter (Aldershot: Ashgate, 2007), pp. 145–62.

Schmid, Otto. *Über verschiedene eintheilungen der Heiligen Schrift insbesondere über die Capitel-eintheilung Stephan Langtons im XIII Jahrhunderte* (Graz: Leuschner & Lubensky, 1892).

Schnurman, Josephine Case. 'Studies in the medieval book trade from the late twelfth to the middle of the fourteenth century with special reference to the copying of the Bible' (B.Litt., St Hilda's College, Oxford, 1960).

Sharpe, Richard. *English Benedictine libraries: the shorter catalogues*, Corpus of British medieval library catalogues 4 (London: British Library in association with the British Academy, 1996).

— and James Willoughby. 'MGLB3 (Medieval Libraries of Great Britain)', http://mlgb3.bodleian.ox.ac.uk.

Sheppard, Leslie A. 'A vellum copy of the Great Bible, 1539', *The National Library of Wales Journal* 1:1 (1939), 9–22.

Sherman, William H. *Used books: marking readers in Renaissance England*, Material texts (Philadelphia: University of Pennsylvania Press, 2008).

Slavin, A. J. 'The Rochepot Affair', *The Sixteenth Century Journal* 10:1 (1979), 3–19.

Slights, William W. E. ' "Marginal notes that spoile the text": scriptural annotation in the English Renaissance', *Huntington Library Quarterly* LV (1992), 255–78.

Smalley, Beryl. *The study of the Bible in the Middle Ages*, 3rd edn (Oxford: Blackwell, 1983).

Smith, Lesley. *The Glossa ordinaria: the making of a medieval Bible commentary*, Commentaria 3 (Leiden: Brill, 2009).

Solopova, Elizabeth. 'Introduction: new directions in research on the first English Bible', in *The Wycliffite Bible: origin, history and interpretation*, ed. Elizabeth Solopova, Medieval and Renaissance authors and texts 16 (Leiden: Brill, 2016), pp. 1–8.

—. *Latin liturgical psalters in the Bodleian Library: a select catalogue* (Oxford: Bodleian Library, 2013).

—. 'The manuscript tradition', in *The Wycliffite Bible: origin, history and interpretation*, ed. Elizabeth Solopova, Medieval and Renaissance authors and texts 16 (Leiden: Brill, 2016), pp. 223–45.

—. *Manuscripts of the Wycliffite Bible in the Bodleian and Oxford college libraries*, Exeter medieval texts and studies (Liverpool: Liverpool University Press, 2016).

—. 'Medieval ownership and use of the manuscripts of the Wycliffite Bible', in *Form and function in the Late Medieval Bible*, ed. Eyal Poleg and Laura Light (Leiden: Brill, 2013), pp. 333–49.

—. 'A Wycliffite Bible made for a nun of Barking', *Medium Aevum* 85:1 (2016), 77–96.

—. ed. *The Wycliffite Bible: origin, history and interpretation*, Medieval and Renaissance authors and texts 16 (Leiden: Brill, 2016).

Spencer, H. Leith. *English preaching in the late Middle Ages* (Oxford: Clarendon Press, 1993).

Spinks, Bryan. 'The Bible in liturgy and worship, c. 1500–1750', in *The new Cambridge history of the Bible*. Vol. 3: *From 1450 to 1750*, ed. Euan Cameron (Cambridge: Cambridge University Press, 2016), pp. 563–78.

Stern, David. *The Jewish Bible: a material history* (Seattle: University of Washington Press, 2017).

String, Tatiana C. *Art and communication in the reign of Henry VIII* (Aldershot: Ashgate, 2008).

Sutherland, Annie. *English Psalms in the Middle Ages, 1300–1450* (Oxford: Oxford University Press, 2015).

—. 'The Wycliffite Psalms', in *The Wycliffite Bible: origin, history and interpretation*, ed. Elizabeth Solopova, Medieval and Renaissance authors and texts 16 (Leiden: Brill, 2016), pp. 183–201.

Tadmor, Naomi. 'People of the covenant and the English Bible', *Transactions of the Royal Historical Society* 22 (2012), 95–110.

—. *The social universe of the English Bible: scripture, society and culture in early modern England* (Cambridge: Cambridge University Press, 2010).

Tribble, Evelyn B. *Margins and marginality: the printed page in early modern England* (Charlottesville: University Press of Virginia, 1993).

van Duijn, Mart. 'Printing, public, and power: shaping the first printed Bible in Dutch (1477)', *Church History & Religious Culture* 93:2 (2013), 275–99.

Verbraak, Gwendolyn. 'William Tyndale and the clandestine book trade: a bibliographical quest for the printers of Tyndale's New Testament', in *Infant milk or hardy nourishment? The Bible for lay people and theologians in the early modern period*, ed. W. François and A. A. den Hollander, Bibliotheca Ephemeridum Theologicarum Lovaniensium 221 (Leuven: Peeters, 2009), pp. 167–89.

Vulić, Kathryn, Susan Uselmann and C. Annette Grisé, eds. *Devotional literature and practice in medieval England: readers, reading, and reception* (Turnhout: Brepols, 2016).

Wabuda, Susan. 'Triple deckers and eagle lecterns: Church furniture for the book in late medieval and early modern England', in *The Church and the book: papers read at the 2000 summer meeting and the 2001 winter meeting of the Ecclesiastical History Society*, ed. R. N. Swanson, Studies in Church history 38 (Woodbridge: Boydell for the Ecclesiastical History Society, 2004), pp. 143–52.

Walden, Justine. 'Global Calvinism: the maps in the English Geneva Bible', in *Shaping the Bible in the Reformation: books, scholars, and their readers in the sixteenth century*, ed. Bruce Gordon and Matthew McLean (Leiden: Brill, 2012), pp. 187–215.

Warren, Nancy Bradley. *Spiritual economies: female monasticism in later medieval England* (Philadelphia: University of Pennsylvania Press, 2001).

Watson, Andrew G. *Catalogue of dated and datable manuscripts, c.700–1600 in the Department of Manuscripts, the British Library* (London: British Library, 1979).

Webber, Teresa. *Public reading and its books: monastic ideals and practice in England c.1000–c.1300* (forthcoming).

Werrell, Ralph S. 'Tyndale's disagreement with Luther in the prologue to the Epistle to the Romans', *Reformation & Renaissance Review* 7:1 (2005), 57–68.

Westcott, Brooke Foss. *A general view of the history of the English Bible* (London: Macmillan, 1868).

White, Eric Marshall. *Editio princeps: a history of the Gutenberg Bible*, Harvey Miller studies in the history of culture (Turnhout: Brepols, 2017).

Whiting, Robert. *The blind devotion of the people: popular religion and the English Reformation*, Cambridge studies in early modern British history (Cambridge: Cambridge University Press, 1989).

—. *The Reformation of the English parish church* (Cambridge: Cambridge University Press, 2010).

Willis, Jonathan P. *The Reformation of the Decalogue: religious identity and the Ten Commandments in England, c.1485–1625*, Cambridge studies in early modern British history (Cambridge: Cambridge University Press, 2017).

Wordsworth, Christopher, and Henry Littlehales. *The old service-books of the English Church* (London: Methuen, 1904).

Zutshi, P. N. R., Paul Binski and Stella Panayotova. *Western illuminated manuscripts: a catalogue of the collection in Cambridge University Library* (Cambridge: Cambridge University Press, 2011).

Manuscripts Index

Cross-references to figures and appendices are given in bold

General Index